W9-BLF-246

Please remember that this is a library book,
and that it belongs only temporarily to each
person who uses it. Be considerate. Do
not write in this, or any, library book.

Foundations of Education
for Prospective Teachers

Sandford W. Reitman
California State University
at Fresno

ALLYN AND BACON, INC.
Boston   London   Sydney   Toronto

For
Mitchell, Melanie, and Sharon

Library of Congress Cataloging in Publication Data

Reitman, Sandford W.
    Foundations of Education for prospective teachers.

    Includes bibliographical references and index.
    1. Education. I. Title.
LB17.R46   370   76–44382

ISBN 0-205-05677-6

Photo on page 193 courtesy of Suffolk Franklin Savings Bank. Photo on page 6 courtesy of Talbot Lovering. All other photos appearing in text courtesy of David Kelley.

Material on pages 230, 232, 233, 234, and 243–244 from *Adolescents and the Schools* by James S. Coleman, © 1965 by James S. Coleman, Basic Books, Inc., Publishers, New York.

Contents

Contents

Contents

Preface

This book stems from a long-term preoccupation with the educational ramifications of contemporary social change. Many have written and spoken on the subjects of change and the future in recent years, but comparatively little scholarship has concerned the meaning that social change holds for education. In particular, prospective teachers must be helped to come to grips with enormous implications of social change in their work with youngsters.

The central theme of this book is that we are a society in transition. The outlines of our new habitat are just now beginning to emerge, yet they are compellingly real. We have little choice but to accept them forthrightly as givens and to grapple with them as best we can. If we do not, future generations will accuse us of having been too myopic—too focused on the receding status quo to have adequately prepared them for their lives.

How we go about equipping the young people of today for meaningful lives in a society undergoing massive social change is an open question, a question with many alternative answers. This book considers these alternatives and attempts to assess them in light of historic and incipient human values and a wide array of organizational and behavioral trends.

It is a book in the tradition of the social foundations of education. The text attempts to synthesize data and concepts from a variety of disciplines and orientations in the social sciences and humanities (sociology, history, political science, anthropology, philosophy, and social psychology), rather than isolating one or two sources of specialized knowledge. In short, this text is an interdisciplinary effort, with a special focus on teachers about to begin their careers in a transforming period of history.

A number of people provided valuable help in organizing my ideas, testing them, and reproducing them on paper. In addition to expressing my appreciation for the encouragement of many of my foundations students and colleagues at the California State University at Fresno, I would like to personally acknowledge the continuing interest and support of Professors Maurice Hunt, Morris Bigge, and Jerome Leavitt and the editorial insights of Steve Mathews, Mary Johnson, and Cynthia Hartnett at Allyn and Bacon. Finally, no one was more understanding and constructive throughout the duration of this project than Faye, who at the time had her own preemptive problems to cope with.

Sandford W. Reitman

Underlying Ideas

I

1

Perspectives on Becoming a Teacher

A person who sincerely desires a career in the field of education, who wants to work with heart and mind with other people and to achieve self-determined goals, will find the prospects for completing a credential program and for finding rewarding employment excellent. The well-documented teacher oversupply ironically has created a situation in which intelligent and dedicated young men and women are favored for employment as teachers.[1] A relatively heavy influx of this "new breed" of teacher candidates is emerging, and they will probably dominate the field in a few years.[2] People with less motivation and qualification—who only a few years ago might have been welcomed into a then expanding field—will not make it, although they may find employment of an educational nature elsewhere. As word of the teacher oversupply spreads, the actual number of persons trying to enter teaching will begin to decline markedly, leaving room for those who genuinely want to work with the young in a learning environment.

The Challenge of Teaching Today

Teachers today face some unique and challenging problems that they will be forced to meet as they compete in a tight and changing job market. They will be working with a generation of children and youth even more different in background and general outlook from their own than you

3

are from your parents. The students will be products of a rapidly changing and highly pluralistic American society. Their educational needs and expectations cannot be met by repeating methods of a generation ago. Teachers will be called upon to respond positively to these varied and new needs and expectations, and to consider the often conflicting expectations of **significant reference figures** in education (parents, administrators, and fellow teachers).

Teachers will be working with over two million colleagues all over the country to upgrade their occupation by organizing in ways radically different from any attempted on a large scale by teachers in the past.[3] They will be strongly inflenced to become part of the new "teacher power" movement.[4] As teachers are drawn into this movement, they will discover that not everyone within the teaching ranks or outside of those ranks will approve of the movement's goals or methods. Coping with this important aspect of occupational life outside the classroom will be an immense challenge and require a large amount of "psychological strength."[5]

Many teachers are involved in programs and organizational experiments unheard of before in public school; for example, open spacing and the open classroom (which are different), team teaching, differentiated staffing, competency/performance-based teacher education, teacher–pupil contracting, educational parks, community schools, alternative schools, individually prescribed instruction, writing behavioral objectives, and variations of these and other educational innovations. Just learning the language of the "new" education is a major challenge, as is keeping abreast of new developments on the contemporary scene.

Most important, teachers will find themselves the center of an ongoing dialogue on the meaning and application of education and schooling in the modern world. This has become an increasingly important social concern in recent years. If teachers do not actively participate in this fundamental dialogue, vital decisions about learning and teaching will be made for them by persons with less knowledge about educational issues. By becoming actively involved in this dialogue, teachers can begin to take their rightful places in society as truly creative workers who share directly in the development of healthy human beings and indirectly in the construction of a viable society. To participate meaningfully in this social dialogue, teachers must develop and maintain occupational skills and be familiar with educational literature in general, as well as in their specialty. Teachers must involve themselves in after-school and summer consortia and university programs with other teachers and educational personnel, and keep abreast of political developments that affect education. Teaching cannot be a part-time job. Today a teacher must take full advantage of what this career can offer.

These are some of the major challenges that are likely to confront

4

teachers as they enter upon the new career of public school teaching. (The term *public school* as used throughout this text will ordinarily refer to universal compulsory schooling for children and adolescents, whether publicly or privately financed.)

Education majors who are not destined to seek or find employment in public education still may discover opportunities to work as teachers in interesting and challenging settings other than conventional elementary or secondary schools; e.g., in "free schools," vocational–technical training programs for adults, recreational programs for the aged, and other community programs. These kinds of settings offer relatively untapped opportunities to apply knowledge gained as a student of education to different teaching tasks.[6]

What Is Human Authenticity and Why Need It Concern a Prospective Teacher?

First and foremost, truly vital teachers should be highly authentic human beings. The humanistic psychologist Abraham Maslow conceives of authenticity, or "self-actualization," as the inner potential of all people:

> We may define it [self-actualization] as an episode, or a spirit in which the powers of the person come together in a particularly efficient and intensely enjoyable way, and in which he is more integrated and less split, more open for experience, fully functioning, more creative, more humorous, more ego-transcending, more independent of his lower needs, etc. He becomes in these episodes more truly himself, more perfectly actualizing his potentialities, closer to the core of his Being, more fully human.
>
> Such states or episodes can, in theory, come at any time in life to any person. What seems to distinguish those individuals I have called self-actualizing people, is that in them these episodes seem to come far more frequently, and intensely and perfectly than in average people. This makes self-actualization a matter of degree and of frequency rather than an all-or-none affair. . .[7]

Another humanist, social psychologist Carl Rogers, thinks of authenticity as fully accepting one's uniqueness; that is,

> . . . the experience of becoming a more autonomous, more confident person. It is the experience of learning to be one's self. . .
>
> From being persons driven by inner forces they do not understand, fearful and distrustful of these deeper feelings and of themselves, they move significantly. They move toward being persons who accept and even enjoy their own feelings, who value and trust the deeper layers of

their nature, *who find strength in being their own uniqueness, who live by values they experience. This learning, this movement, enables them to live as more individuated, more creative, more responsive, and more responsible persons. . .*[8]

In their path-breaking book on the family and the development of identity, Nelson Foote and Leonard Cottrell use the term "interpersonal competence" in referring to the idea of authenticity:

At the level of common sense observation, people are seen to differ markedly in their aptitude or ineptitude for dealing satisfactorily with others. At the level of theoretical speculation, interpersonal competence as a general phenomenon appears to be based on what certain existentialist philosophers call transcendence. This term summarizes the uniquely human processes of suspended action, memory, revery, foresight, reflec-

tion, and imagination, by means of which a person from birth onward escapes progressively from the control of his immediately given environment and begins to control it. It is by this freedom from the irresistible instincts and external stimuli, which chain the responses of lower animals, that the human being is enabled to modify his surroundings, to plan and create, to have a history and a future. His detachment from the present situation provides both the opportunity and the necessity for him to declare his own identity and values as an adult.

Instead of attempting . . . to further elaborate a general concept of the origins of interpersonal competence, our main strategy of definition will be analytical, to name its parts, as manifested in observable behavior. These we take to be: (1) health, (2) intelligence, (3) empathy, (4) autonomy, (5) judgement, and (6) creativity . . .[9] *(Emphasis added)*

Although they describe it differently, all these writers are essentially talking about the same phenomenon—the concept of authenticity. They are referring to a human quality that has been highly revered throughout our history. The authentic person—male or female, rich or poor, brilliant or average in ability—is one (1) who understands who he (or she) is in relation to other people and to his environment, and (2) who is capable of relating effectively to others, while retaining his unique identity.

Stated differently, the authentic human being is a distinctive person who is capable of participating as a part of a group and also as an individual. The authentic person can play many roles, according to the situations in which he finds himself; at the same time, he can sustain his special conception of self (his personality) in different situations.[10] The authentic person does not disavow role taking and role playing since they are basic facts of life, but he (or she) never takes on "unauthorized" roles (roles that do not fit one's unique personality); nor does he play necessary roles in a manner calculated to give a false impression of his true intent. Both kinds of "phoney" role taking and role playing jeopardize social relationships and social order and inhibit the flowering of a complete and meaningful identity.[11]

From an existential point of view, the authentic person makes choices freely, and takes full responsibility for those choices. But how can the concept of free will be reconciled with environmental determinism? We ask this time-worn question at the outset to set the tone of the book because it relates to the fundamental problem facing all teachers today: *how to achieve a reasonable degree of free choice within an established system in order to act in the best interests of the students.* According to the contemporary proponent of behavioralism, B. F. Skinner, free choice and environmental determinism cannot be reconciled. Maslow, Rogers, and Foote and Cottrell are simply wrong. As Skinner says:

Just as biographers and critics look for external influences to account for the traits and achievements of the men they study, so science ultimately explains behavior in terms of "causes" or conditions which lie beyond the individual himself...

Man, we once believed, was free to express himself in art, music, and literature, to inquire into nature, to seek salvation in his own way. He could initiate action and make spontaneous and capricious changes of course. Under the most extreme duress some sort of choice remained to him. He could resist any effort to control him, although it might cost him his life. But science insists that action is initiated by forces impinging upon the individual, and that caprice is only another name for behavior for which we have not yet found a cause.[12]

If, as Skinner maintains, human beings are solely conditioned by impinging environmental forces, authenticity appears to be merely another pleasant-sounding word without any real meaning—especially to those reared on the liberal-democratic conception of man's nature.

Fortunately, we are able to reconcile the existential notion of free choice, or free will, with determinism by drawing from social psychological theory. Herbert Blumer, a "symbolic interactionist,"[13] takes up from where the great forefather of modern social psychology George Herbert Mead left off, by telling us that:

Symbolic interactionism rests in the last analysis on three simple premises. The first premise is that human beings act toward things on the basis of the meanings that the things have for them . . . The second premise is that the meaning of such things is derived from, or arises out of, the social interaction that one has with one's fellows. The third premise is that these meanings are handled in, and modified through, an interpretative process used by the person in dealing with the things he encounters. . .[14]

Blumer is essentially saying that although environment does help to shape or determine personality, people interpret the meaning of environmental forces variously. It is this interpretive process that distinguishes the human being and frees him from the determinist mold. People are not, or need not be, the passive recipients of external forces that pure deterministic theory makes them out to be. Neither are they absolutely free from any form of social influence, as some extreme versions of existential doctrine maintain.

Is man free or determined? From an interactionist frame of reference, he is both. Man is both creature and creator, both acted upon and actor, both social and solitary. Man makes his world at the same time the world makes him. This ability to act upon as well as to be acted upon by others is most highly developed in what we are calling the "authentic" person, who is obviously an **ideal type.** The ability to interpret events, however, belongs to all human beings to a greater or lesser extent, and can be developed and refined under congenial conditions.

Modern Society, Massive Change, and Personal Identity

Since we live in a social system that is presently undergoing a phenomenal, and in some ways extremely painful, transformation of its structure and function, the traditional identities that people have sought are more difficult for most of us to locate. In more stable periods of history, personal identity was often ascribed to people by virtue of birth. In effect, one was born to be a cobbler or a king. Today it is rare to find an individual whose occupational identity has been handed down to him by his father at the time of his birth. Most children growing up today are forced to find identities on their own, although their parents may try, successfully or more often unsuccessfully, to help them.

Identity normally changes several times during the lives of most people. The anthropologist Margaret Mead eloquently stated the underlying reasons for this over two decades ago:

> ... the teacher of twenty years' experience may face her class less confidently than the teacher with only two.
>
> This is, of course, no more than the normal accompaniment of the fantastic rate of change of the world in which we live, where children of five have already incorporated into their everyday thinking ideas that most of the elders will never assimilate. ... The children whom we bear and rear and teach are not only unknown to us and unlike any children there have been in the world before, but also their degree of unlikeness itself alters from year to year.[15]

It is not an easy task to find one's identity in a rapidly changing milieu with few fixed posts to guide one. But with hard work, reflection, and the aid of sympathetic mentors and friends, it is possible to establish a stable and satisfying identity.

The Identity Problem of Modern Teachers

Prospective teachers may face an even greater problem of finding authentic identity than the average person, since teaching is at the epicenter of social and cultural concern. New teachers are entering the occupation at a time of extreme instability in society at large and in the school institution, which partly reflects society. Almost all social institutions and values seem to be in profound upheaval. The institution of education is strongly interrelated with other **subsystems** in American society. However education changes or whatever direction it ultimately takes, it is now in a state of extreme confusion and instability. There are unusual stresses, strains, and tensions for many of those who are closely involved with its operation.

Little can be taken for granted about education in the 1970s; curriculum, control of students, relations of teachers with the public, and the various tasks of teachers are all in flux. Therefore, the central problem facing any prospective teacher today is finding a "place," an "identity," an "authentic self" within an uncertain educational milieu. Otherwise, an individual may succumb to fashion and fancy, never knowing where he or she stands on important issues or how to deal responsibly with even minor, day-to-day problems. Whatever the nature of a position a teaching candidate eventually receives, or whatever type of community and school system he or she works in, he or she must first begin to build a semblance of selfhood as a person and as a teacher.

Why Should a Prospective Teacher Study the Foundations of Education?

Of course, simply reading a book cannot actually produce a highly developed sense of authentic identity, since this comes only after being deeply immersed in actual or simulated life situations in and out of schools and classrooms. However, in conjunction with other meaningful activities in a teacher's occupational preparation, a careful reading of the material presented here may provide an invaluable perspective on the educational world. Such a perspective in turn can help a prospective teacher envision his or her unique and important place and role. Without such a perspective, a teacher is no more than a functionary performing a series of pre-established tasks set by others who are external to the immediate context in which learning and teaching take place. And, in a society changing as rapidly and pervasively as modern America, educational priorities cannot be determined by those removed from the dynamics of teaching and learning.

The Meaning of Educational Foundations

What is commonly called the foundations of education is the study of the basic facts and principles underlying the search for worthwhile and effective educational policies and practices. These principles are the basis upon which the educational house is built. If the base is substantial, the rest of the structure will probably be strong, and vice versa.

An understanding of the foundations of education will help a prospective teacher to think more clearly about the essential meaning of the work in which he or she will be engaged as a teacher. It will help him or her to make tenable decisions about how to organize his or her energies to create optimal learning situations, to develop curriculum best suited to his or her students, and to work most effectively with parents, administrators, and other parties to educational endeavors, and much more. Such decisions are of the utmost importance to teachers today and require a command of the kind of data and concepts that are brought to light by study of the foundations of education.

For example, one cannot organize a classroom without some awareness of what peer groups are and how they operate at different ages and in different cultural contexts. Many teachers follow recipes bestowed by supervisors and professors who write manuals on such subjects. Unless a teacher's situation is identical to one conceptualized in these manuals, he or she will be frustrated by trying to follow the classroom organization recipes handed down from above.

However, many teachers recently wanted teaching recipes more than they wanted to use their own intelligence to plan and implement plans for their work with children. As Myron Brenton has cogently expressed it, "They have less need to analyze and reflect, less interest in solving problems, less willingness to gamble or take risks."[16] Until the recent influx of the "new breed" of teacher, this characterization of the average American teacher was probably accurate. Teaching solely by using the prescriptions of others is perhaps one reason why so many minority students are apathetic and rebellious and ultimately quit school. Teaching in this limited way also contributes to parents taking teachers for granted and, indirectly, to the common assumption that—unlike other service workers—teachers do not merit adequate remuneration.

It is impossible to do a competent job as a teacher, much less a highly creative one, by memorizing recipes, or by depending upon others to "analyze, reflect, solve problems, gamble and take risks."[17] The cry for recipes and other forms of dependency is in vain. Modern teachers must learn to work without someone else's blueprints if they are to be successful and happy in their careers. This can be achieved through study of the foundations of education as they apply to the specific conditions of teaching and learning environments. The study of the foundations of education will facilitate the following:

- Creation of educational policies
- Development of educational programs
- Implementation of educational policies and programs

Foundational Areas and
Their Importance

As conventionally understood, the foundations of education are actually several in number, although they may be more or less integrated in what are usually called the "social foundations of education." There are four major recognized foundational areas, which are normally conceived of as scholarly disciplines: the philosophy of education, the history of education, educational sociology, and comparative education.* Other foundational specialties currently being developed include educational anthropology, the politics of education, the economics of education, and educational aesthetics. Educational psychology is usually treated separately because it had an earlier start in this country than did most other foundational areas and from the beginning possessed a more distinct frame of reference.

The Philosophy of Education.   The philosophy of education is a branch of educational foundations that seeks to determine the normative purposes of education and to refine the language of education. Philosophers of education are concerned primarily with what "ought to be," rather than with what has been, is, or can be. In actual practice, however, the separation of **normative,** or value-related, concerns from considerations of fact is impossible and usually frowned upon by educational theorists.

According to the results of a 1972 national survey, most foundational scholars working with prospective teachers consider themselves to be first and foremost philosophers of education, at least in terms of having received the brunt of their specialized graduate school preparation in this area of foundations.[18]

Six major systems of philosophical thought, each with specific implications for teaching practice, are prevalent in the United States. They are commonly referred to as: Perennialism, Essentialism, Instrumentalism, Social Reconstructionism, Existentialism, and Linguistic Analysis. All except Linguistic Analysis are primarily systems of normative thought that are concerned mainly with the crucial problem of establishing the ultimate ends, or purposes, of education and schooling. Linguistic Analysis, or Analytic Theory, is concerned largely with the meanings of the language people use in conjunction with education. (See Chapter 11 for detailed discussion of these educational philosophies.)

All educational philosophies derive from Western philosophic thought that has developed over the centuries. Some of the greatest

---

* The orientation of the foundations of education to academic disciplines has been questioned in recent years by some scholars who prefer an inter-disciplinary approach and a change of the name of the field to "educational studies."

philosophers have been primarily concerned with educational problems, for example, Plato, Thomas Aquinas, John Dewey, and Martin Buber. (*See* Chapter 11 for discussion of some important philosophical ideas as they apply to a teacher's career.)

All teachers who purport to do more than mechanically follow instructions in their day-to-day work must philosophize about the meaning of their work, whether they consciously fit their thinking to some comprehensive scheme or not. As John Dewey, speaking generally about the meaning of philosophy, once said:

> The fact that philosophic problems arise because of widespread and widely felt difficulties in social practice is disguised because philosophers become a specialized class which uses a technical language, unlike the vocabulary in which the direct difficulties are stated ... But, when philosophic issues are approached from the side of the kind of mental disposition to which they correspond, or the differences in educational practice they make when acted upon, the life situations which they formulate can never be far from view. If a theory makes no difference in educational endeavor, it must be artificial. The educational point of view enables one to envisage the philosophic problems where they arise and thrive, where they are at home, and where acceptance or rejection makes a difference in practice.
>
> If we are willing to conceive of education as the process of forming fundamental dispositions, intellectual and emotional, toward nature and fellow men, philosophy may even be defined as the general theory of education. Unless a philosophy is to remain symbolic—verbal—or a sentimental indulgence for a few, or else mere arbitrary dogma, its auditing of past experience and its program of values must take effect in conduct.[19]

History of Education.   While philosophers study the ultimate values of the educational process, historians attempt to understand the temporal antecedents to its contemporary thinking and practice. American historians of education have looked primarily, although not exclusively, to the educational heritage of Western society, and particularly to that of American society from colonial days onward. The history of education involves the study of the sources of events and ideas that have shaped current institutional realities. It can also involve the study of educational thought and behavior, that is, the intellectual history of education.

In recent years, scholars have been making a significant impact upon educational thought by debunking much that has been taken for granted by most educators. Because of the work of **historical revisionists,** we now have strong reason to doubt that school reform in the United States and equalization of opportunity for all through educational means is as significant or complete as most of us have been led to believe.[20] The history of American education has been less glorious than some graduation day speakers have portrayed it, and we are now forced to realistically face our strengths and our weaknesses. In so doing, we must proceed with greater caution and care as we make and implement educational policies in the present and for the future.

Comparative Educational Systems.   The study of diverse educational systems throughout the world is almost as highly developed as is the study of comparative politics, although it is not as visible an area of study. Students of comparative education look chiefly at national systems of formal schooling and attempt to find similarities and contrasts between such systems. For instance, numerous studies have contrasted the educational system of the United States with the systems operating in other industrially developed nations, such as Great Britain, France, Germany, the U.S.S.R., and Israel. The developing nations of the Third World— Latin America, Africa, and Asia—have also come under scrutiny recently.

U.S. educators have studied intensely the British primary school (comparable to the U.S. elementary school) as a model of the open classroom ideal. And the notion of the U.S. comprehensive high school has been adopted by other nations, notably by England in 1944.

The comparative foundations of education, along with the history of education, are useful areas of study that help teachers to realize that educational policies and practices do not develop in isolated vacuums. Rather, they are the result of continuous cultural borrowing and of the diffusion of innovations made all over the globe. The United States system of formal education is not, as many have come to believe, a product wrought solely from the American experience. Much of what we now consider uniquely American is actually a modification of ideas borrowed from other cultures. Whenever a culture borrows an idea from another culture, it adapts the idea to fit its special circumstances. Thus, it is extremely doubtful that the open classroom idea now being carefully studied by visitors to England will retain much of its original shape once it becomes established firmly in American schools.[21]

Educational Sociology.   Educational sociology is the study of the institution of education in its broad social context and of various social groups and interpersonal relationships that affect or are affected by the functioning of educational institutions. In other words, it is the study of people associated officially and unofficially with education. It considers the various roles and values of teachers, students, parents, board of education members, special interest groups and their members, and government agencies and their personnel. In short, educational sociology is the study of the social and cultural conditions and consequences of formal and informal education in society, and particularly in modern societies such as the United States or Great Britain.

Some educators believe the knowledge produced by such study has enormous potential value for the development of educational policy and for the practice of teaching based upon the facts and principles of organized human living.

The Social Foundations of Education.   The term *social foundations of education* is defined as follows:

> ... that unique body of professional educational studies concerned with the underlying sociocultural, historical, comparative, and philosophical bases for understanding school policy and process. For example, while such studies as "social foundations of education," "educational sociology," the "politics of education," "educational anthropology," the "economics of education," etc., are fairly obviously social foundational in nature, for purposes of the present survey such disciplines as "philosophy of education," history of education, comparative education, and the like are also considered to be subsumable under the label "social foundations of education."[22]

The social foundations of education, then, is an umbrella construct covering several foundational areas already discussed, with the exception of educational psychology. Such a broad construction is the most satisfactory one to use in this book because an introductory text necessarily deals with basic educational concerns from a variety of perspectives— philosophical, historical, sociological, political, anthropological, etc. Such a text must be integrative rather than highly specialized, if it is to be significant and useful to beginning students of education.

The Approach of This Book

The emphasis here is on the dynamics of current interpersonal, organizational, and cultural factors that relate to education, and particularly to teaching in the United States. Much of the material is drawn from the burgeoning fields of sociology and social psychology and applied to educational concerns. Interwoven throughout the text are data and concepts derived from the educationally relevant work of political scientists, anthropologists, and other social scientists. Philosophical and historical areas of education are also considered.

This text is geared mainly to the interests of teachers, not to school administrators, supervisors, or parents. To be effective as a teacher in the formal educational system, it is necessary to understand the nature of American society's central institutions, particularly the family, social class, and peer group. Teachers should recognize that today many special-interest groups are trying to insert their own peculiar versions of "The

Truth" into school policies. Never before have such great demands and responsibilities been placed on teachers, who must realize that they are limited in what they are able to do, given the existing nature and structure of our society.

Today teachers are organizing to alter traditional conceptions of power and authority, and some teachers, along with some parents and their children, are even beginning to abandon the public schools to open and operate "alternative schools." Teachers must be aware of the potential of the alternative school movement to restructure the conventional public school. Moreover, they need to understand school culture and the micro social system of the classroom in order to cope with discipline problems.

Is the modern school a dehumanizing bureaucracy, as some of the rhetoric of the contemporary educational scene claims? In Chapter 15, we will carefully examine the meaning of bureaucracy and its place in American life and education. We will also address ourselves to some of the major issues confronting educators today. Is racism institutionalized in American schools? What about institutionalized sexism? Whatever one's gender, this issue is important to a teacher's approach to students.

These are a few of the central concerns treated in this introductory text. They are vitally important issues with which prospective teachers should be very familiar. As you study aspects of the foundations of education, bear in mind that there are three essential ingredients in any intelligent endeavor, including teaching:

• *Ends* to be achieved (values, goals, purposes, objectives, outputs, outcomes)
• *Conditions* to be taken into consideration that affect human endeavor, such as historical, social, and cultural elements. In the social foundations of education, social and cultural conditions are of paramount importance
• *Means,* or courses of action, by which desired ends can be achieved, given the facts and circumstances of an area of concern.[23]

Essentially, a teacher's job is to identify and apply worthwhile courses of action that are based upon a clear sense of what educational objectives are being sought in the classroom and without. Teachers must carefully consider the sociocultural conditions of the society and its educational organizations that promise to enhance or limit their chances of success with students.

There are three broad parts to this book:

Part I, Underlying Ideas.   The first part is designed to orient you to the field of education from a foundational point of view. It asks you to begin thinking seriously about why you have decided to become a teacher. This section also presents some conceptual models to give structure to past and present educational matters, and it describes the fundamental relationship between education and society.

Part II, The Fundamental Purposes of Education.   The second part of the book seeks to clarify and inform the search for desirable and possible goals for modern American schools. The nature of contemporary and emerging cultural patterns that influence and are influenced by the institutions of education are considered. These relate particularly to teachers and their significant others.

Part III, How Can the Purposes of Education Be Realized?   In this part of the book, we will be concerned with how to achieve educational priorities. We concentrate on two broad themes of paramount concern to modern teachers: the control of schooling and the internal organization and operation of schooling. The discussion in this part describes the educational structure of American society and provokes serious thought about ways in which this structure can be improved as we move into the future.

Major issues involving the purposes and process of contemporary education and schooling are treated forthrightly throughout the text. These issues deserve thoughtful consideration because we live in an era of controversy. Examples of crucial educational issues treated here are teacher and student rights, sexism in schools, how education applies to work and leisure, the separation of church and state; ways to finance public education; and alternatives to traditional schools.

Questions to the Reader.   At the end of each chapter there is a general question posed to the reader, such as "How can you participate in bringing about significant educational change?" The rest of the material in the chapter relates to these questions. They have been designed to ensure the application of the ideas introduced earlier in the chapter and may draw upon material from preceding chapters.

Related Concepts.   At the end of each chapter, several concepts that were used in the text are defined. Each is identified by boldface type in the text.

Summary

Jobs in teaching have become relatively scarce in the past several years and promise to become even scarcer in the next few. However, this situation should not deter one from entering a profession that today offers a number of challenges that should make life as a teacher highly interesting and worthwhile. The "new breed" of teacher candidates that are entering American schools of education promises to alter the face of education in this society.

The most important quality for a teacher to develop is human authenticity, a quality possessed in greater or lesser degree by everyone, but which can be enhanced. Today especially, it is important, and difficult, to strive for and maintain an authentic identity, which is so necessary to good teaching. A strong foundation in the social aspects of modern education will work toward cultivating the broad perspective that is an important part of an authentic identity.

The foundations that underlie education and teaching are several in number, four being pre-eminent: philosophy of education, history of education, comparative education, and educational sociology. Social foundations of education is the umbrella construct that integrates the several foundational areas and forms the basis for introducing the educational institution and the occupation of teaching to prospective teachers seeking a career in this challenging field.

Related Concepts

historical revisionists   Contemporary scholars who have revised many of the long-held assumptions about American educational history, especially the assumption that schools have played a significant role in social reform or that they have been key agencies for the equalization of opportunity.

ideal type   An intentionally exaggerated construction of a characteristic for the purpose of helping to explain the meaning of that characteristic. For example, since few people are actually as completely "authentic" as psychologists, social scientists, and humanists employing the concept might wish, it is useful to conceive of this characteristic as an "ideal type," one which only can be approximated by real people in real life. Another ideal type is "democracy."

normative   A term referring to universal standards or rules for behavior within a group, which are based upon values held by members of the group. For example, a norm applying to behavior at the beginning of many sports events is standing at attention in reverential deference to the American flag when the Star Spangled Banner is played. A norm for general behavior in most schools is orderliness.

significant reference figure   A person to whom one refers when contemplating behavior action related to a social role. For example, the school principal is a significant reference figure, or "significant other," to most American teachers.

subsystem   A system that is a component of a larger system. All human systems, from the social level down to the individual, can be viewed as subsystems of varying sizes and characteristics within larger systems. The educational institution, like other social institutions, is a subsystem of American society.

Suggested Activity

As a basis for class discussion, prepare a carefully thought-out essay on why you are planning to become a teacher when the educational field has an oversupply of teachers and is faced with other unusual challenges. Be honest with yourself, as you think of your motives and your potential contributions to the field.

References and Notes

1.   See, for example, Evelyn Zerfoss and Leo J. Shapiro, *The Supply and Demand of Teachers and Teaching* (Lincoln: University of Nebraska Printing and Duplicating Service, 1972).

2.   This assertion is supported by informal observation as well as by empirical data from a number of surveys made of college students in recent years. Student attitudes and values were analyzed by the Study Commission on Undergraduate Education and the Education of Teachers, using data gathered by the Carnegie Commission on Higher Education and the American Council of Education (Lincoln: University of Nebraska Press, 1975). A more recent study by Alexander Astin and the American Council on Education suggests that the number of students entering teacher-education programs has already begun to decline, leaving a more highly motivated teacher candidate in such programs. (Reported by Beverly T. Watkins in *The Chronicle of Higher Education* 12 [Jan. 12, 1976]: 3.)

3.   According to the U.S. Office of Education, there were 2,097,000 classroom teachers in the nation in the 1972 to 1973 school year; this was an increase of + 12.5 percent over the 1,863,967 figure of 1967 to 1968. (W. Vance Grant, *American Education* 9 (Aug.–Sept. 1973): 33.

4.   Although it is still in its infancy, the teacher power movement has begun to change the image of American teachers. For example, see "Teacher Power," in Emanuel Hruwitz, Jr. and Charles A. Tesconi, Jr., eds., *Challenges to Education: Readings for Analysis of Major Issues* (New York: Dodd, Mead, and Co., 1972).

5.   The term was borrowed from William Vernon Hicks and Frank H. Blackington, III, "The Profession as an Idea," in Frank H. Blackington and Robert S. Patterson,

eds., *School, Society, and the Professional Educator: A Book of Readings* (New York: Holt, Rinehart and Winston, 1968), p. 22.

6.   Zerfoss and Shapiro, *The Supply and Demand of Teachers and Teaching,* pp. 43, 44.

7.   Abraham Maslow, *Toward a Psychology of Being,* 2nd ed. (Princeton, N.J.: D. Van Nostrand, 1968), p. 97.

8.   Carl Rogers, "Learning to be Free," in Carl Rogers and Barry Stevens, eds., *Person to Person: The Problem of Being Human* (Lafayette, Calif.: Real People Press, 1967), pp. 47, 49.

9.   Nelson N. Foote and Leonard S. Cottrell, Jr., *Identity and Interpersonal Competence: A New Direction in Family Research* (Chicago: The University of Chicago Press, 1955), pp. 40, 41.

10.   A popularized discussion of the variability of role taking and role playing that demonstrates that a healthy human being can have many identities without being hypocritical, is presented by Kenneth J. Gergen, "Multiple Identity," *Psychology Today* 5 (May 1972): 31–35; 64; 66.

11.   For an excellent discussion of this problem of phoniness related to education, *see* Harold L. Hodgkinson, *Education, Interaction, and Social Change* (Englewood Cliffs, N.J.: Prentice-Hall, 1967), pp. 10–13.

12.   B. F. Skinner, "Freedom and the Control of Man," *The American Scholar* 25 (Winter 1955–56): 47, 53.

13.   *Symbolic interactionism* is a leading school of thought in contemporary social psychology, originating in the thought of such philosophers and sociologists as George Herbert Mead, John Dewey, W. I. Thomas, Robert E. Park, William James, Charles Horton Cooley, Florian Znanieki, James Mark Baldwin, Robert Redfield, and Louis Wirth. *See* Herbert Blumer, *Symbolic Interactionism: Perspective and Method* (Englewood Cliffs, N.J.: Prentice-Hall, 1969), p. 1.

14.   *Ibid.,* p. 2.

15.   Margaret Mead, "The School in American Culture," in A.H. Halsey, Jean Floud, and C. Arnold Anderson, eds., *Education, Economy, and Society: A Reader in the Sociology of Education* (New York and London: The Free Press, 1961), pp. 421–33.

16.   Myron Brenton, "Profile of the Average Teacher," in Glenn Smith and Charles R. Kniker, eds., *Myth and Reality: Readings in Education* (Boston: Allyn and Bacon, 1972) pp. 123, 124.

17.   *Ibid.,* pp. 123, 124.

18.   Sandford W. Reitman, "A Survey of Basic Social Foundations of Education Programs in the U.S.A. for Prospective Teachers," paper presented in Denver at the annual conference of the American Educational Studies Association, November 1973.

19.   John Dewey, *Democracy and Education: An Introduction to the Philosophy of Education* (New York: The Free Press, 1966).

20.   *See,* for instance, Michael Katz, *Class, Bureaucracy, and Schools: The Illusion of Educational Change in America* (New York: Praeger Publishers, 1971).

21.   For comparative portraits of open classrooms in Britain and in the United States, *see* Charles E. Silberman, ed., *The Open Classroom Reader* (New York: Vintage Books, Random House, 1973).

22.   Reitman, "A Survey of Basic Social Foundations of Education Programs."

23.   Adapted from a paradigm developed by Professor Richard Derr of Case Western Reserve University, and communicated privately to the author. The paradigm has been applied to reconceptualize the task of the social foundations of education in the following publications known to the author: Richard C. Derr, "Social Foundations as a Field of Study," *Educational Theory* 15 (April 1965): 154–60; *idem,* "The Capacity of School Policies and Techniques: An Educational Concept," *V.O.C. Journal of Education* 5 (August 1965): 13–18.

2

Different Ways of Thinking about Society and Social Change

With Auguste Comte, often called the father of modern social science, it is possible to agree that humankind has sought to give direction and meaning to individual and social life in what amounts to three fundamentally different ways of viewing the social order and its dynamics. Comte has constructed three models of these points of view, each of which is associated in his mind with a progressively advanced stage of history.

Models of Social Order and Change

The three types of models that Comte constructed and that we will consider briefly are the following:

1. Theological model, preeminent during Comte's stage of fiction
2. "Metaphysical" model, prevalent during the stage of abstraction
3. Scientific models, which Comte believed came to the forefront of intellectual endeavor during the most advanced stage of history, the era of "positivism"[1]

Another useful model (not associated with Comte) for conceptualizing reality can perhaps be termed an Existential, or no-model, model.

Of course, there are other ways of looking at the nature of human organization and change. One can refer to social, political, and intellectual postures, such as ideological versus utopian societies. Or one can envision the history of society in terms of cyclic responses to major social crises, as Arnold Toynbee would. One also could say that the interplay of primal drives and their repression by forces of civilization shape society, as Sigmund Freud would explain the course of history.[2]

This chapter will describe some major conceptual approaches prevalent in contemporary thought on society and education. An awareness of socioeducational thought will provide prospective teachers with insight into their usually commonsensical views of education and their relation to those of others involved in formal education.[3] This analysis will provide a sense of where contemporary educational thought is headed, and an idea of the effects in the classroom of the ways of thinking represented by the models.

The Theological Model
of Society and Social Change

People who operate largely according to a theological conception of society and social change tend to see most human affairs as having a religious intent and cause.[4] Whether their sectarian affiliation is Protestant, Catholic, or Jewish, their dominant conception of reality is founded mainly on some degree of faith in divine intervention and superior authority.

Nature of Society and Social Change

The Theological Model envisions society as the product of an overarching supernatural or cosmic force that cannot be understood fully and that determines the fate of the world. Those who subscribe to this model would reason that the social order we live in must be the best of all possible worlds because it is a world determined not by man, but by God. Society is headed wherever God wills it. As mere mortals, we have little to say about the direction of world events. Therefore, we should accept our places in the immutable scheme of things.

According to this view, superior minds and intuitive souls have been able to catch a glimpse of divinity and have constructed religious systems and laws based on sacred moral precepts. Individual members of society should not question the authoritative dogma of their leaders; they should devote themselves to carrying out their divinely inspired mission in life.

Society will change when its time for change has come according to the divine plan. The natural leaders of society will then emerge and determine when and how changes are to be made and will instruct the masses on their proper roles. If everyone accepts on faith his or her proper place in the cosmic scheme, society will evolve smoothly, and its members will be content with their lot.

Nature of Personhood and Authenticity

According to the theological construction of reality, the idea of individual authenticity (see Chapter 1) that encourages people to be masters of their own fate by independently interpreting the world is not valid.

However, one must judge the extent and quality of authenticity in an individual from the viewpoint of the individual's particular belief system—in this case, a theological one. Those who form a theological perspective may contend that their way of approaching life actually does allow for self-actualization. The issue becomes more muddied when untraditional conceptions of religious experience are brought into the picture, for example, contemporary versions of mysticism. Maslow claims that certain kinds of mystical experiences may produce episodes of intense self-actualization. He calls these episodes "peak experiences."[5]

Although all three major Western religions extol the idea of free will, it is usually understood to mean the will to follow God's commandments, it does not mean that an individual can assess the validity of those commandments. Dogma is the essence of the religious construction of life, and it presumes that behavior is primarily determined by forces beyond the control of the individual will. If one interprets the dogma handed down from on high as inappropriate and deviates from the dogma, one is usually judged evil or in error. Thus, conformity and obedience to some superior authority—rather than autonomous decision making by the individual—is considered proper behavior within a conventional theological interpretation of life.

Theologically Oriented Teachers

Whether they work in a church-related or public school, teachers who are strongly influenced by a religious conception of reality tend to be sternly bound to duty and to obey school authorities (usually men, as befits the religious conception of their "natural superiority") without question. These teachers believe their students have a long way to go before they can grapple with knowledge of the "higher truths."

Teachers with a theological orientation tend to work diligently in the service of the state or established church, which they conceive to exemplify order and coherency. They may demand the right to express their individual style by didactically implementing an orthodox curriculum. But they will rarely question the appropriateness of this curriculum. They are likely to be strict disciplinarians, as befits agents of an authoritarian view that applies sanctions to those who do not behave correctly. In short, teachers captured completely by a traditional Theological Model of reality are likely to be authoritarian in the school and classroom. They do not, however, always possess the guilt that studies of authoritarian personalities commonly attribute to such personalities.[6]

Evidence indicates that today few teachers are extremely doctrinaire about religious assumptions.[7] American society has moved relatively far away from being as strongly influenced by organized religion as it was in the eighteenth and early nineteenth centuries. In Cotton Mather's day, for example, authoritarianism prevailed in the classroom. "The whipping post became an important educational facility for Puritan New England. In educational practice, there can be little doubt that the doctrine of original sin was the religious justification for literally beating the devil out of children and also for the passage of the Massachusetts Act of 1641 and Connecticut's Act of 1672, which imposed the death penalty on unruly children."[8] While we have obviously changed a great deal in three hundred years, most American teachers, like most Americans, retain some vestiges[9] of a society dominated by the religious thought of the Reformation and earlier.[10]

"Metaphysical" Model of Society and Social Change

In his comprehensive scheme of thought modes that guide mankind, Comte placed "metaphysics" in the middle stage, between theology at the "lowest" level, and science at the "highest."[11] Comte's "Metaphysical" Model is primarily concerned with abstractions of the sort with which many philosophers have dealt, although refinements in the field of philosophy have led modern scholars to consider metaphysics as a separate branch of study concentrating on the nature of reality.

Philosophers are mainly interested in working with the logical implications of secular and religious ideas. The tools of logic, not acts of faith or experimentation, are used to substantiate or prove ideas. The primary tool of logic used by philosophers to derive conclusions about ideas is the syllogism. The *syllogism* is a paradigm used to reach a conclusion by deductive reasoning. There are three parts of a syllogism: two propositions, which are stated as assumptions and termed the *major premise* and the *minor premise,* and a conclusion, reached by logical inference from the two premises; for example, the classic syllogism below:

- Assumption 1 (major premise): All men are mortal;
- Assumption 2 (minor premise): Socrates was a man;
- Conclusion (inference): Socrates was mortal.

What aspects of social order and social change do "metaphysicians" speculate about? They speculate about whatever they choose to, casting social realities into philosophical models they have constructed or accepted. When their conceptual models become highly elaborate, they are termed "systems of thought." Just as in Western civilization the chief systems, or models, of religious thought and belief are Judaism, Catholicism, and Protestantism, so are there three or four major systems of "metaphysics" prevalent in contemporary Western culture. These are Idealism, Realism, and Pragmatism. (Existentialism will be treated separately from "metaphysics.")

Nature of Society and Social Change

Each of the primary philosophical models—Idealism, Realism, and Pragmatism—treats the nature of society and social change differently.

Idealism. Idealists, or more accurately, Ideaists, view society as a *mental construct,* sometimes indistinguishable from the kinds of constructions postulated by theologians. To Idealists, the mind is the controlling force. Social reality is the product either of a micro mind (Descartes' "I think, therefore, I am") or of a macro mind (God, or Hegel's Absolute Spirit, "whom I strive to emulate"). Thus, the mind—whether individual or universal—is responsible for the creation of social order and social change. To a greater or lesser extent—depending upon whether the mind is viewed as individual or universal—it can guide and control the character of social order and the direction of change, as change unfolds and develops in the universe of which society is a part.

Realism. Philosophical Realists depend upon a world *external* to the mind; that is, reality exists, whether one's mind apprehends it or not. If one closes one's eyes, the tree outside the window still exists, according to the Realist. "Not so," argues the pure Idealist: "If I don't see the tree, it is not necessarily there." For the Realist, society's structure and its ability to change are functions of natural laws, not of individual effort. It follows, then, that human beings cannot create social change; they can only facilitate its natural evolution by understanding the order and dynamics of society and perhaps by preparing for inevitable social change in the most mechanistic and efficient ways.

A perennial problem for philosophers is how to reconcile the Idealist notion of God with the Realist conception of nature and the mundane. This dilemma is usually explained by postulating a dualistic conception of the universe, one aspect of which can only be known by faith and intuition, and the other of which is comprehensible by sensory perception and reason.

Pragmatism.   Pragmatists believe they have resolved this problem of dualism by uniting the dichotomies of Idealism and Realism in a philosophy of operationalism, or instrumentalism. For the Pragmatist, *what works is "real"* and able to be coped with by the individual and by society. People can be instrumental in creating and modifying their reality through intelligent thought and effort. Pragmatic philosophy probably verges most closely upon the domain assumptions of modern science. Pragmatists believe in testing ideas by experimentation in order to determine their workability and utility and, hence, their validity.

For the Pragmatist, the social order is a large laboratory for trying out new modes of being and becoming more human, and social order and social change are part of that same process of being and becoming. Social order normally is dynamic, not static. The Pragmatist believes that once the myths of history are exposed—myths that extol stability, order, and closed societies—people will begin to participate democratically, and society will achieve a dynamic equilibrium. Society and its members will be improved if inductive and deductive scientific thought are used to test hypotheses and theories about the most viable ways to live together.

Nature of Personhood and
Authenticity

Idealism.   In its pure form, the Idealist model of thought is apt to produce passive acquiescence to a monolithic will or delusions of grandeur. It is not conducive to self-actualizing behavior as we have defined it. Idealists at times become so overwhelmed by their imagination at the expense of fact, and so frustrated by the failure of their ideas to become realized that they become cynical. However, Idealists usually bring conviction and commitment to an idea to bear strongly upon the goals they wish to achieve. These goals may be in the name of a worthy and just cause or a career demanding dedicated effort.

Realism.   In its extreme form, the Realist Model is also likely to result in a type of individual passivity. Instead of stoically accepting divine law, philosophical Realists subject themselves to the powerful determinism of natural law. (A good example of this sort of subjugation is the work of B.F. Skinner.) Realists accept being another cog in the machinery of the universe as it evolves naturally. They are thereby able to accept being conditioned to whatever forces happen to rule them. However, in striving to understand the laws of the universe, Realists can develop a perspective upon which to base their actions—if they have not become completely dominated by deterministic thinking.

Pragmatism.   What are the implications of pragmatism for development of authentic identity? This construction of reality offers the individual a great deal of promise to become self-actualized in the way we have defined it here. The Pragmatist's idea that "truth" is defined by what works, by reason and experience, corresponds to the American experience and the tradition of thought that experience has created. Pragmatic philosophy suggests that most people are capable of making value-oriented decisions. Both important and relatively mundane ideas can be tested, and assumptions verified or dethroned by experience. If verified, an idea provides a strong basis for control of further experience. This sense of control over events, a sense grounded in experience, is really what authenticity is all about.

The "Metaphysically" Oriented Teacher

Idealists.   Idealists are frequently found in the disciplines of the humanities where "hard" empirical data is not required to substantiate expression of ideas.[12] Such teachers often have a strong sense of right and wrong and of superiority and inferiority. They may be dogmatic about their standards of academic excellence and grading. The same is true of their approach to discipline; they believe that certain absolute norms for pupil behavior in the classroom should be maintained at all times.

Much reading, writing, and discussing are apt to characterize the classes of Idealist teachers. Both students and teachers are expected to upgrade themselves from an imperfect state to some higher level of academic excellence. Idealist teachers are usually demanding and exacting of themselves and of their students. They usually have some clear goals in mind as they work with students, and they are relatively inflexible about diverging from these goals.

Realists.   In contrast, Realist teachers tend to be uncomfortable with unconfirmed or unconfirmable ideas, unlike Idealist teachers. Accordingly, Realist teachers are more commonly found in the sciences and in mathematics. In these curricular areas they can work with and transmit to their students scientifically verified ideas. As opposed to Pragmatists, Realists may rely too much on external facts and concepts. They sometimes become highly dependent upon outside sources for guidance, both in choosing curriculum and methods of instruction and discipline. The exaggerated dependence of the Realist upon objectified reality often leads to acceptance of the "system" and all it demands of them and their students. Being mere cogs in a natural system, they rarely find reason to challenge this system. Thus, they become so dependent upon outside sources for guidance that they may have difficulty in teaching in a personal, exciting, and relevant way, unlike strong Idealists. Since the outside sources of guidance usually represent traditional educational thinking, Realist teachers do not experiment very much in the classroom. Their modus operandi tends to include the traditional lecture–recital–demonstration methods and little more. If not so extreme in their dependence upon forces outside of themselves, however, Realist teachers may help to temper unbridled student enthusiasm and prevent hasty conclusions.

Pragmatists.   The Pragmatists are actively engaged in remaking their world. They believe they can help to create the future, rather than, like Idealists or Realists, being manipulated by the course of events, whether **teleological** or evolutionary. They operate within their world to bring it under control. As teachers, Pragmatists see their role as helping their students to gain effective control of their lives through experiential learning. Pragmatist teachers are likely to be independent; they are not overly acquiescent toward authority, although they respect the proven ideas of others. They will not sit back and accept paternalistic commands; neither do they expect their students to rely on them as the final source of intellectual or moral authority.

Their classes are apt to be engaging, involving students in learning and demanding their wholehearted participation. Students are expected to actively explore the world they study, often through personal or collective projects, questions, reading, and whatever other methods they find successful in gaining personal control through careful investigation. In Pragmatists' classrooms, students do not receive information solely from class lectures and other teacher-centered instruction. Rather students use the library, build things, simulate reality, take field trips, and devise experiments of their own, while the teacher acts as a resource person. In brief, Pragmatic teachers are essentially "directors of student research."

The Scientific Model of
Society and Social Change

Comte had this to say about the Scientific Model of thought that he postulated:

> In the final, the positive state, the mind has given over the vain search after absolute notions ... and applies itself to the study of ... laws.... What is now understood when we speak of an explanation of facts is simply the establishment of a connection between single phenomena and some general facts the number of which continually diminishes with the progress of science.[13]

From the time of its rebirth in Western civilization during the Enlightenment, the scientific method has brought about great transformations in the way people view the world by disproving or seriously questioning the assumptions about society that are implied by the models we have previously discussed.[14] The Scientific Model differs from most of the other models of thought discussed here because it actively seeks to alter preconceptions; it does not rely on *a priori* reasoning, nor does it insist that its ideas are immutable. Its method, which is also the method advocated by the metaphysical Pragmatists, tests ideas by inductive reasoning. Continual development and refinement of its theories and laws is accomplished by means of deductive reasoning. The two processes ideally operate hand-in-hand, although in practice some scientists become specialists in one endeavor or the other.

There are two very broad and basically dichotomous Scientific Models of thought about the nature of society and social change: the older may be called the conservative, functional, or *Consensus Model;* and the more recent, the dialectical, conflict, or *Dissensus Model* of order and change.[15]

Consensus Model of Scientific Thought

Consensus means to be in agreement, to be in harmony with the prevailing scheme of things. The consensus view of reality places a premium on the harmonious integration of the components of the universe, including human beings. Those who accept this model tend to approve of such traits as cooperativeness and conformity to group norms. Conversely, they disapprove of nonconformity and idiosyncracy because these behavior traits may lead to disruption of group operation.

Nature of Social Order and Social Change.   The Consensus Model of social order and social change is the dominant model in the social sciences and in education, although it is rapidly beginning to decline. Its basic premise is that human existence is organized into social systems that are structured for integration and smooth running of all subsystems which include institutions and individuals. Ideally, society should function in a state of equilibrium, with all parts operating harmoniously for the welfare of the whole. Reciprocally, the whole contributes to the happy adjustment of all the parts, or people.

According to this model, social change is provoked initially by a force outside of the system that disturbs the members of the system. When such intrusive disturbances become powerful enough to affect the internal functioning of the system, the affected members respond to the tensions and stresses by seeking to return affairs to the prior state of equilibrium. This is usually attempted by innovating and borrowing ideas and technologies to "fix" the "damaged" parts. Thus, the emphasis in consensus models of social order and change is on stability and equilibrium. Change is considered an unwanted, although occasionally necessary, means for restoring systemic harmony.[16] This explication is of course highly oversimplified; rarely do systems undergoing change actually return to a state of equilibrium, particularly in this fast-paced world.

Nature of Personhood and Authenticity.   People who view human life from a consensus frame of reference tend to be interested primarily in retaining the status quo, not in seeking significant changes in the environment. In this respect, such people are similar to those who adopt theological and metaphysical models, which are dominated by convention and a great respect for cultural tradition.

Since most people are bound by the status quo, they rarely think beyond it, which causes many to accept the identity allocated to them by birth and growth in the "natural scheme of things." Unless the society in which he lives undergoes grave difficulties (war, famine, etc.), the average individual usually has little incentive to search actively for what we have called authentic identity. During relatively stable periods of history, people who are marginal to the dominant subcultural groups seem to possess the incentive essential to introspective searching for an authentic identity. These "marginal men" are frequently intellectuals or members of minority groups.[17] Only when a society is experiencing great instability, are large numbers of people stimulated to search deeply and creatively for new self-images.

In general, those who hold a consensus-oriented view of life seem to passively accept the status quo and reject individuals and influences believed to threaten the status quo. People who deviate from social norms or who offer ideals that threaten to alter the status quo are held suspect by those who wish to preserve their comfortable situation, those whom we call consensus oriented.

The Consensus-Oriented Teacher.   Consensus-oriented school teachers are likely to be conventional in the classroom and more interested in carrying out the will of those who make policy and administer it than in venturing out on their own. They are in tune with the broad conceptions of reality that give support to the maintenance of social order and favor stability over serious experimentation and change in educational affairs. They generally teach traditional subjects in traditional ways and demand that their students conform to the "Establishment's" expectations of appropriate pupil conduct. This behavior prevails unless consensus-oriented teachers are threatened by their students during periods of unusually turbulent and rapid social change. They are then forced to try newer teaching practices in order to survive in the classroom.

Dissensus Model of Scientific Thought

Dissensus means precisely the opposite of consensus: to be in disagreement or in conflict with the prevailing order. Those who view the world through the Dissensus Model of reality tend to emphasize the discordant elements of the universe. They devalue the very qualities of which the consensus-oriented approve (e.g., cooperativeness and conformity), particularly when these qualities are believed to unjustly benefit certain individuals and groups at the expense of others.

Nature of Social Order and Social Change.   In contrast to those who place a high value on consensus, proponents of the Dissensus Model of society and social change believe society is constantly in flux—normally changing or in need of change, unstable, chaotic, or simply functioning with a facade of order. Those whose views conform to the Dissensus Model have been a minority in history, but recently their numbers have increased, as evidenced by the activism of the 1960s that spawned organized movements for social change. Today, those whom society labels as radicals and malcontents—large numbers of which are members of the intellectual and academic communities—conceive of society as being run by an elite. They would prefer a society that defers to the many—to the masses or the proletariat, as Marxists would say.

To achieve the social change they desire, activists that fall under the Dissensus Model seek to take advantage of social tensions and to manipulate those tensions to create divisiveness great enough to cause a radical reconstruction of society or of its primary institutions, such as the economy, the family, and perhaps also education.

Nature of Personhood and Authenticity.   In its pure form, a Dissensus Model of reality does not generally promote development of genuine authenticity, as we have defined this quality (nor does adherence to a narrow version of the Consensus Model). Authentic identity requires a sense of self in relation to others that the often hostile and alienated dissensus position rarely fosters in a person. If the world is believed to be an essentially foreign and dangerous place in which the privileged few are favored, then the opportunities to grow as a person through healthy social interactions become limited. Although the alienated may gain a sense of self from those who are also disenfranchised, this situation is tempered with the unpleasant realization that one occupies an inferior and subordinate status in the society at large. Such negative feelings do not encourage the flowering of a secure personal identity.

The Dissensus-Oriented Teacher.   Teachers who accept a purely dissensus outlook on social reality are likely to go out of their way to challenge the status quo in education. Few people knowledgeable about contemporary education would deny that this institution is in a precarious state and would benefit from large doses of improvement. The holder of a pure Dissensus conception of society and education tends to see the situation in wholly negative terms, just as the holder of a strict Consensus outlook sees little virtue in anything that is not traditional and conventional.

Dissensus-oriented teachers are likely to be dissatisfied in the classroom, critical of the school administration and of their clients. Sometimes such teachers view their students as innocent victims who deserve more than they receive from the educational institution that "oppresses" them. However, continuous efforts by such teachers to demonstrate their alienation by rebelling usually lead to their termination or to a hostile reaction from their students or from parents.

A Variable Model of Scientific Thought

A third model has emerged from the thinking of social analysts in recent years. This model combines features of the Consensus and Dissensus models, and we shall call this synthesis a Variable Model of society and social change.

Nature of Social Order and Change.   As sociologist Piere L. van den Berghe has expressed it:

> *In a nutshell my argument is that, while societies do indeed show a tendency towards stability, equilibrium, and consensus, they simultane-*

ously generate within themselves the opposites of these. Let us begin with the assumption that values consensus constitutes the most important basis for integration, but it is also true that societies ... fall far short of complete consensus, and often exhibit considerable dissension about basic values...

Consensus, then, is a major dimension of social reality, but so are dissension and conflict.[18]

As more social scientists begin to develop theories that assume that both consensus and dissensus operate simultaneously within social systems, the either–or analysis (Consensus or Dissensus) becomes untenable.[19] The crucial question now is: *Under what conditions is there need to emphasize a consensus view of society and under what conditions a dissensus view?* A person may respect a consensus and a dissenus conception of society and social change, depending upon *variable* social conditions.

From this third frame of reference, then, social change is viewed not from a highly deterministic stance, but rather open-mindedly—at times as a result of relatively minor disturbances to society's equilibrium. At such times, only minimal adjustments are required, and they are agreed upon by the majority in the society—i.e., by a fairly broad consensus. At other times, social disturbance is seen as a function of severe, long-standing social dislocations that favor some groups at the expense of others. The responses to these more basic social problems range from major reform to revolution that restructures society. Revolution, the most extreme response to demands for social change, is usually provoked by intolerable political oppression and generalized poverty.

The Nature of Personhood and Anthenticity.   The person who can accept a Variable Model of society and social change obviously must be rational and capable of considering people and institutions as neither inherently "good" or "evil." Such a person is able to respond to a wide variety of attitudes openly and without paranoia. He or she perceives of himself or herself as worthwhile in relation to others, even when others disagree. In our terms, such a person can become an authentic human being.

The Variable-Oriented Teacher.   Teachers who interpret reality in this way also view students, parents, colleagues, and administrators as human beings—fallible perhaps, but human. Such teachers are usually experimental and nonjudgmental in the classroom and teach in a personal and constructive way. They can teach any area of the curriculum with an openness and respect for the truth that permits their students to think and feel with them. These teachers remain intellectually independent as they explore areas of concern with other teachers. Such teachers also will step forward and march on picket lines if confrontation is what they feel is necessary to bring about improved conditions for learning. They are not, however, contemptuous of the forces that prompt them to respond by striking—forces which, because of their own possible lack of awareness and authenticity, may be repressive. When conditions are such that students appear to be receiving the best that society and its schools can realistically offer, these teachers are willing to collaborate (in consensus with others) to accomplish mutually held goals.

In short, variable-oriented teachers are likely to uphold humanistic ideals for their behavior in the classroom and beyond. They are willing and able to try to attain these ideals through realistic means; that is, they behave pragmatically and with regard for others' feelings and viewpoints.

The Existential Model

The Existential Model of humankind is discussed separately from the other models because it is relatively new in the history of educational thought and has been associated at different times with theology, "metaphysics," and even science. In recent years, it has found increasing acceptance by serious educational scholars.

Nature of Society and Social Change.   Pure Existentialists tend to reject the very notion of social order and to extol the individual. Thus, only in a metaphorical sense does it seem possible that social scientists can use this model.

Existentialists maintain that the individual is the only tangible reality of any consequence. It is the individual who decides freely whether to become a member of a group or to remain aloof from what Existentialists believe to be an artificial and demanding social collectivity. It is the individual who chooses theologies, philosophies, or science to help him or her cope with his or her universe. Or the Existential individual may decide to remain detached from all such "crutches."

The individual, especially in the modern world, is born into a strange and lonely society, lives out his life, and dies. What happens after death is not important to most Existentialists. What counts is how the individual lives. The fundamental problem for every human being is making authentic choices about the way he will spend his life. He is responsible for his decisions because he possesses a free will. He cannot blame professors, spouse, the president, or the amorphous mass called "society." He is unqualifiedly alone. This solitary condition of modern life is terrifying, and, according to the Existentialists, it can be coped with only by the individual.

From such an **ontology** it follows that social change is the result of one's personal effort to construct a better world for oneself and one's fellow human beings. One may choose freely to dedicate one's life to improving social conditions, and, together with individuals who similarly choose, bring about worthwhile changes. This is not done primarily by the intellect, but rather by the force of one's free will. Intellect and strategic effort are merely functions or extensions of this fundamental life force.

Nature of Personhood and Authenticity.   To the Existentialist, the ability to choose freely is the essence of humanness. As Van Cleve Morris, an educator who is a proponent of existentialism, has remarked:

> *Existentialists would hardly be expected to concern themselves . . . with the problem of cultural change and social reconstruction. The way to the good life, according to the Existentialists, is not through social reform; that only tends to substitute one kind of social collectivity for another. In both, men are driven by tradition, custom, and public opinion. The way to the good life, or as the Existentialist would put it, the authentic life is instead for each individual human being to begin realizing himself by asserting his individuality and making his own choices instead of being stampeded into the choices of the collectivity.*[20]

Thus, authenticity for the Existentialist is the capacity to choose and to take responsibility for one's choices, without relying significantly upon others. In its pure sense, then, Existentialism is the opposite of environmental determinism in the way in which authentic identity develops. More so than do symbolic interactionists, Existentialists insist that each person can exert the will to choose freely and independently. As is the case with other models, it can be argued that it is not possible to judge the capacity of Existentialism to generate true authenticity.

The Existentially Oriented Teacher.   If one is truly free and responsible for one's choices, no system of education can influence the individual, according to Existentialists. The existentially oriented teacher accepts or rejects whatever elements of the system he decides do not help him to perform as a teacher. If the Existential teacher is forced to do what he has not willed himself to do, it then becomes his duty to change the system or leave it.

Many persons who associate themselves with this model of reality prefer to leave the system, rather than alter it. Free schools have many teachers who have taught in conventional public schools, found them wanting, and left to find work in the more open institution of the free school.

If an Existentialist elects to remain in the public schools, he or she is likely to teach, like many Idealists, subjects in the humanities. These teachers are apt to be highly independent in the classroom and to expect the same independence from their students. They act primarily as resource persons and friends who are available to help students learn more or less what they choose to learn. Existentialists disavow the use of lectures and assigned material.

Discipline is normally not a serious problem in the existentially oriented classroom, because students have no need to rebel against authoritative imposition of ideas and norms by adults. Being free to choose most of the time, students rarely cause trouble. If a problem does arise, they are allowed to work it out with the help of the friend who is their teacher.

In sum, the Existential teacher views his role as a teacher as giving the student the freedom to choose what and how he wants to study, and as always being available to act as personal friend and advisor to the student. This may entail what is sometimes called a "dialogic" relationship between teacher and student. In one writer's words, "relating to others dialogically, with its requirements of openness toward, acceptance of, and freedom for the others, are normative requirements for teachers."[21]

Which Model Should the Prospective Teacher Select?

All of us approach our studies with assumptions of one sort or another about the nature of the world we live in. These implicit assumptions largely determine what we select to attend to or not to attend to in our study, and they determine how we think about ideas. Much of our knowledge about education and schooling in society is dependent upon the scientific model of social behavior discussed in this chapter. The language used by educators, however, is not difficult to learn; you probably use many of the terms already or have become familiar with them in other courses.

Education and schooling are essentially *social* operations and experiences. Education always occurs in the context of human interaction in a society, or self-perpetuating system of social relationships. Each society possesses a unique culture, or learned social inheritance. Ideally, teachers should strive to behave authentically, acting on behalf of society

Table 2–1. Summary of Models of Society

	Society	The Individual	The Teacher
Theological Model	*Order:* Best of all possible worlds *Change:* Unfolding of divine plan	*Place:* Predetermined in divinely ordained scheme of things *Personality:* Duty-bound	*Position:* Agency of higher will, mediated through superiors *To Students:* Authority figure *Curriculum:* Unchanging revealed truth
Metaphysical Models			
I *Idealism*	*Order:* Based on laws created by micro or macro mind *Change:* Creative development of society	*Place:* Disciple or independent dreamer *Personality:* Idealistic, cynical, or disillusioned	*Position:* Conforming or highly independent *To Students:* Demanding, forceful model & leader *Curriculum:* Revered symbols and ideas; humanities
II *Realism*	*Order:* Based on laws of nature *Change:* Naturalistic evolution of society	*Place:* A cog in a mechanistic world *Personality:* Accepting of status quo	*Position:* Subject expert & organizational subordinate *To Students:* Demonstrator & information giver *Curriculum:* Usually physical sciences, math
III *Pragmatism*	*Order:* A laboratory for testing living arrangements empirically *Change:* Normal process of living actively	*Place:* A person among other people *Personality:* Active, experimental	*Position:* Self-determining *To Students:* Director of Research *Curriculum:* Flexible, democratic

Table 2–1. Continued

Scientific Models	Society	The Individual	The Teacher
I Consensus	Order: Institutional stability & structural equilibrium Change: Diffusion of tension-produced innovations	Place: A searcher for vested interest Personality: Usually conservative	Position: Usually an "employee" To Students: Usually a normatively prescribed relationship Curriculum: Cultural heritage, as prescribed
II Dissensus	Order: Disorder disguised as order Change: Social conflict	Place: Alienated Personality: The rebel	Position: Rebellious toward authority To Students: Hostile or protective
III Variable	Order: Blend of equilibrium & disequilibrium Change: Result of coping with problems	Place: A person among other people Personality: Active, experimental, flexible	Position: Self-determining, autonomous To Students: A fellow explorer Curriculum: Flexible & largely democratically determined
Existential Model	Order: Not relevant Change: Result of simultaneously willed individual efforts	Place: Alone Personality: Idiosyncratic; authenticity a mystic quality	Position: Independent To Students: Advisor & friendly resource Curriculum: Determined by students; the humanities usually

in guiding its younger members. A teacher is responsible for transmitting an understanding of the cultural life that society relies upon for its present and future welfare. Whether children should select the cultural items and lifeways that they are taught is a philosophical, as well as a sociological, question. In any case, most American children attend school from age five to age eighteen because adults believe they ought to be there. Adults want the younger generation to become familiar with the culture of their society and the ways of interpersonal and organizational behavior deemed appropriate for life in their society.

The job of a teacher, acting as an agent for society, is to interact with the students in his or her charge and to guide their interactions so that society's most important sociocultural patterns will be effectively and efficiently learned. Whether teachers succeed in facilitating genuine learning in their students is also largely dependent upon the quality of their social interactions with their students. Basically all educational endeavors, from establishing and financing schools to teaching in the classroom, involve social behavior and social values.

The instability and stress of our society and its educational institutions at this time in history is an even greater reason for prospective teachers to contemplate the social aspects of their work. Before making any firm commitment to one educational or teaching philosophy, you should find out as much as you can about the contemporary social context of education.

Summary

There are many ways of conceptualizing the nature of societies and how societies change. Theological, "metaphysical," scientific, and existential models of society and their implications for teachers and educational philosophy are presented in this chapter.

The language of the social foundations of education is largely, though not exclusively, derived from applied social science. It is not the language of the theological view of society, nor the language of abstract "metaphysics." This language expresses a conception of life that views education in all its ramifications as a preponderantly social affair that involves individuals and groups of people in more or less organized interactions with each other.

The authentic act of teaching is one of the most highly gregarious of all human endeavors. Whether one chooses to join in or to drop out of step with established convention, this book will attempt to help one to make a choice.

Related Concepts

ontology   In philosophy, the theory of being. The term is often used interchangeably with metaphysics, the study of theories of reality or existence.

teleological   Referring to the theological or philosophical notion that the universe has an ultimate purpose

Suggested Activity

To help to realize the determining influence of conceptual models of man, make several lists of people with whom you prefer being on various occasions and engaging in activities; for example, guests at a party; companions attending a musical event; professors of your elective classes; companions on a camping trip; partners in a business or professional venture; and fellow workers in an election campaign.

After you have completed your lists, analyze the names to determine (1) the extent to which the various names overlap, and (2) whether it is a pleasant personality that makes people attractive to you or something congenial about the way they normally think about life, in contrast to other people you omitted from your lists.

References and Notes

1. Rollin Chambliss, *Social Thought: From Hammurabi to Comte* (New York: Holt, Rinehart and Winston, 1954), p. 417. *See also* Auguste Comte, *A General View of Positivist Philosophy* (Dubuque, Iowa: Wm. C. Brown, 1972).

2. For a comprehensive discussion of models with relevance for educators, *see* Paul Nash, ed., *Models of Man: Explorations in the Western Educational Tradition* (New York: John Wiley & Sons, 1968).

3. Elsewhere I have discussed the matter of "common sense" logic and its influ-ence upon contemporary education. *See* Sandford W. Reitman, "An Alternative Field Work Model for Prospective Teachers," *Interchange* 4 (1973): 62.

4. For background material on this and the following models, *see* Chambliss, *Social Thought,* and Nash, *Models of Man. See also* James E. Crowfoot and Mark A. Chesler, "Contemporary Perspectives on Planned Social Change: A Comparison," *The Journal of Applied Behavioral Science* 10 (July–Aug.–Sept., 1974): 278–303; N.J. Demerath and Richard A. Peterson, eds., *System, Change, and Conflict: A Reader*

on *Contemporary Sociological Theory and the Debate over Functionalism* (New York: The Free Press, 1967); Jack L. Nelson and Frank P. Besag, *Sociological Perspectives in Education: Models for Analysis* (New York: Pitman Publishing Corp., 1970).

5.   Abraham Maslow, *Religions, Values, and Peak-Experiences* (Columbus: Ohio State University Press, 1964).

6.   *See* especially Theodor W. Adorno, et al., *The Authoritarian Personality* (New York: Harper & Row, 1950).

7.   H. Howard Lash and Thomas E. Spencer, "A Comparison of Value Commitments of Church School and Public School Teachers," summarized in *Phi Delta Kappan* 56 (October 1974): 147.

8.   Clarence J. Karier, *Man, Society, and Education: A History of Educational Ideas* (Glenview, Ill.: Scott, Foresman and Co., 1967), p. 14.

9.   Lash and Spencer, "A Comparison of Value Commitments," p. 147.

10.   Karier, *Man, Society, and Education,* pp. 2–10.

11.   Chambliss, *Social Thought,* p. 414.

12.   An informative and readable book on the dominant "metaphysical" models of contemporary educational thought is Van Cleve Morris and Young Pai, *Philosophy and the American School: An Introduction to the Philosophy of Education* 2d ed. rev. (Boston: Houghton Mifflin Co., 1976).

13.   Chambliss, *Social Thought,* p. 417.

14.   *See* Robert K. Merton, ed., *Social Theory and Social Structure* (New York: The Free Press, 1968), pp. 27–35.

15.   Within these two inclusive models of social organization, a number of submodels may be found, sometimes overlapping and variously named. For instance, the "symbolic interactionist" frame of reference can be viewed as one important way of thinking about individual and interpersonal behavior within more inclusive social organizations. Examples of other submodels are the role model, actually another name for symbolic interactionism; the Marxian model, one version of the Dissensus model to be discussed; and Erving Goffman's concept of "total institutions." *See* Nelson and Besag, *Sociological Perspectives in Education.*

16.   Robert Chin, "The Utility of System Models and Developmental Models for Practitioners," in Warren G. Bennis, Kenneth D. Benne, and Robert Chin, eds., *The Planning of Change,* 2d ed. (New York: Holt, Rinehart and Winston, 1969), pp. 297–312.

17.   Robert Park, a distinguished modern sociologist, is probably most responsible for refining the concept of "marginal man," originally coined by Everett Stonequist. *See* Park's *Race and Culture* (Glencoe, Ill.: The Free Press, 1950).

18.   Piere L. van den Berghe, "Dialetic and Functionalism: Toward a Synthesis," in Demerath and Peterson, *System, Change, and Conflict,* pp. 295, 296.

19.   *See* Alvin W. Gouldner, *The Coming Crisis of Western Sociology* (New York: Basic Books, 1970).

20.   Van Cleve Morris, "Existentialism and Education," in Van Cleve Morris, ed., *Modern Movements in Educational Philosophy* (Boston: Houghton Mifflin Co., 1969), p. 370.

21.   John R. Scudder, Jr., "Why Buber Would Not Endorse a Pseudo-Existentialist," *Educational Theory* 25 (Spring 1975): 198–99.

3

The Meaning
of Education in Society

Although we have become a highly "schooled" society, Americans receive the greater portion of their education in childhood and in adulthood from agencies other than the school. Some of these informal educational agencies will be discussed in this section.

Informal Education and Teaching

Social Institutions. Every society relies upon a number of **social institutions** for the performance of one or both of two basic social functions: (1) to help perpetuate the society's culture into the future and (2) to facilitate the process of social change.* Of these two basic functions performed by social institutions, preservation of the cultural inheritance has historically been the most crucial. Social institutions such as religion, warfare, and even art and literature have been enlisted in the service of continuing the sociocultural status quo. The idea of changing the status quo has traditionally been avoided by members of the elites that have controlled social institutions.

---

* To be more precise, social institutions actually serve one of four basic functions: (1) they maintain existing social structures; (2) they integrate diverse social elements; (3) they adapt structural elements to change; and (4) they attain goals of society.[1]

However, to perceive of social institutions as inherently conservative, as many people do, is incorrect. Throughout history and especially in the contemporary period, social institutions have also occasionally served the second basic function of helping society to change. This is clearly seen in the role art and literature play as social institutions in modern times. In direct contrast to the role of art and literature in the Medieval period of European history, most modern art and literature anticipates novel ways of thinking and behaving. By so doing, it helps people to adapt to change, or even to initiate change in their social and cultural milieux. Taking into consideration the peculiar conditions of modern life, one can say that these institutions perform primarily adaptive rather than "pattern-maintenance" functions for society, as they operate to help regulate human affairs.[2] The institutionalization of the scientific method during the Enlightenment, which was revolutionary in spirit and impact, performed an adaptive function in society. And, the institution of political democracy can be understood as a way in which many societies avoided armed revolution.

Human life, then, is grounded in organized cultural history and cultural transformation. Social institutions ensure that culture and the social behavior dependent upon cultural patterns are preserved through time, as well as modified and altered when that need arises.[3]

Educational Institutions

Certain institutions attempt to serve social pattern-maintenance or adaptive requirements by promoting teaching and learning behaviors of one sort or another. These institutions are termed *educational institutions*.

Societies and their subsystems always depend upon some institutionalization of educational practice in order to ensure that their individual members—particularly the youngest and the foreign born—will learn the group behavior and cultural patterns considered essential for satisfactory adjustment and self-fulfillment within the collective whole. Institutions of education thus reduce the necessity of relying upon political coercion to maintain social and civil order. Ideally, they help individuals to form their personal identities and to contribute to group life. They accomplish these things by means of **socialization, enculturation,** and **acculturation** processes.

It does not matter whether an institution was originally established solely for teaching and learning purposes; it may be considered educational in function if significant aspects of its operation depend upon teaching and learning behaviors. In fact, the great majority of educational institutions have no formalized curriculum, or program of instruction. In small, simple societies most teaching and learning is very informal and unorganized, usually occurring casually in a variety of contexts. The experiences of the members of simple societies can be termed educational if they involve gaining new ideas, skills, or values through the influence of a teacher, who may be a sibling, a parent, a friend, or a boss.

When an institution, although lacking a formalized curriculum, still carries on a substantial amount of teaching and learning as part of its operation, it is usually called an institution of *informal education.*

Even in highly complex societies of the world, such as that of the United States, most educational institutions are informal ones. The following *informal* educational institutions in contemporary American society serve primary functions *other* than that of education. But teaching and learning relationships have become so integral to the effective performance of these other purposes that we may properly call them educational institutions.

The Family.   The primary functions served by the family are species preservation and cultural adaptation. It would be impossible to raise children to eventual independence without teaching by the mother, the father, and often older siblings and relatives. Thus, the family has always been and still is the primary informal educational institution.

The Peer Group.   In modern society particularly, age cohorts are grouped to facilitate the development of their emerging identities, in a world which increasingly separates children and adolescents from adults. Cohorts, or peers, teach each other skills (e.g., how to fix a bicycle or an automobile), knowledge (e.g., the "facts of life"), and values (e.g., "appropriate" attitudes toward the opposite sex). Neither the family nor other institutions that socialize and enculturate young people today teach the type of skills and knowledge that peer groups do. For example, many contemporary parents have neither the desire nor the understanding and skill required to teach their adolescent sons the most current courtship practices; they rely upon their sons' peers to do the job for them.

The Mass Media.   The TV, radio, newspapers, popular magazines, and similar sources of entertainment and information are often extremely influential agencies of informal (and sometimes formal) education—not only for the young, but for all age groups in the United States. For instance, studies of radio and television soap operas strongly suggest that large numbers of women with small children, convalescents, and older people depend daily upon the "lessons" learned from these never-ending sequences of intimate problems, and apply these "lessons" to their own primary group difficulties—marital infidelity, in-law problems, demoralizing illnesses, parent-youth conflicts, and so on.[4]

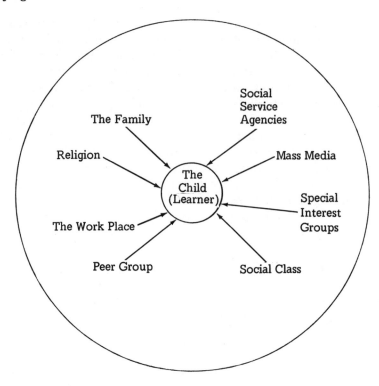

FIGURE 3–1.   *Society as Direct Teacher: Informal Education in Society*

The Work Place.   Almost fulfilling Emile Durkheim's prophesy that work in secondary industrial societies would become the center of life for most people, many modern adults are exposed to a variety of educational influences in their occupational lives. Many people receive their most meaningful education from their work place (during the coffee break, in interpersonal exchanges with coworkers throughout the day, and when engaged in after-hours sports and socializing).[5] During these times with work peers, they receive inside tips about the bosses' expectations and quirks, information on the limits of acceptable productivity in the eyes of coworkers, and advice about handling personal and family problems. If they are not unacceptable to their fellow workers for reasons of deviant behavior, stigmatized ethnicity, or unacceptable levels of personal ambition and aggressiveness, modern workers may gain a great deal of emotional satisfaction from their employment, even when they intensely dislike their jobs. Conversely, if a person does not fit into the primary work group, even satisfaction with one's job may not always be enough to prevent one from looking elsewhere for employment.

In a society that largely segregates economic life from family and from other affairs of day-to-day community living, the social environment of one's workplace becomes very important. Hence, it is critical that the complex educational environment of the workplace be understood by those who will someday enter the workforce.

The Church.   To the extent that a person is involved with organized religion today, he or she may receive an education from affiliation with his or her church or synagogue's Sunday School program and from sermons as well as from associating informally at picnics and other church social events with people in the community from all walks of life and all status ranks. (This statement is qualified to the extent that some religious denominations tend to attract individuals from similar walks of life and of comparable community status.) In the past, when organized religion was more influential in our lives than it is today, the church was a major source of doctrinal as well as secular education for great numbers of people in American society.[6]

The Street Gang.   This particular version of the peer group has been studied in depth for many years by sociologists and social workers.[7] Street gangs are a largely urban phenomenon and, for the inner-city youth, a tremendously important agency of survival, as well as a source of friendship, identity, and income for many lower-class boys and, increasingly, girls. The street gang offers its member a well-defined territory and protection from other street gangs. In order to belong to a gang, one must thoroughly learn the culture of the gang, especially its norms of sexual prowess and sex role behavior. The urban street gang is an informal educational institution with amazing power over the allegiances of large numbers of inner-city youth growing up in the United States.

Special Interest Groups.   Another example of informal education, which operates most often in the lives of middle-class adults, is the special-interest group. The special-interest group arises to meet the needs of individuals possessing common concerns, such as a hobby, occupation, sport, politics, or schooling. Since they are usually **secondary social institutions,** special-interest groups base their membership more on similarity of interest than on personal compatibility, although the two often converge. Teaching and learning occur in relation to developing skills or increasing knowledge in specific areas. As in other informal educational institutions, teaching and learning behaviors are not confined solely to the official "curriculum" of the interest group.

Social Service Agencies.   Our society has a growing number of organizations set up to educate people in a variety of ways. For example, social welfare agencies, while primarily responsible for helping the financial

situation of the poor, also offer psychiatric, career, and family counseling services to their clients. Other types of social service agencies that do
a great deal of educational work for their clients are drug counseling
centers, legal-aid services, income-tax services, veteran's organizations,
and youth organizations such as the Boy Scouts of America.

Social Class.   Another informal educational institution is the social class
or **social stratum.** To belong to a class in our society requires that the
member or would-be member learn the class culture and the expected
patterns of interpersonal behavior within the class and toward persons
belonging to other social strata. For instance, it is rarely enough to earn
even $50,000 a year to be accepted into the upper-middle class life of
American society. One must also know how to act "properly" with the
"right people," and how to converse easily with college-educated people.
   Similarly, perhaps the central problem in our society for those who
are downwardly mobile is not the stigma attached to a descent down the
social ladder but the fact that people are rarely educated to be "losers." If
people were more realistically prepared for life in a society in which
there are bound to be both "winners" and "losers," many of the latter
might find life in the lower social strata more bearable and less stigmatiz-
ing. The incidence of suicide, crime, mental illness, marital discord, and
other social pathologies might then decline significantly.[8]

A Sense of Belongingness as an
Incentive to Learn

Learning in informal educational institutions occurs by imitating established members' behavior, identifying with successful members, trial
and error, and testing of novitiates. (These are the same basic types of
educational experiences undergone in more formal settings.)
   Most informal educational institutions invariably have learners
who are motivated chiefly by their voluntary desire to participate in a
group, such as a sorority. A member of a family may be aware that success in belonging to such an unavoidable group depends strongly upon
acquiring and using at least some of its values, norms, and roles. The
basic human desire or imperative to *belong* provides the main incentive
to learn the group ways of informal educational agencies.[9] It is rarely
necessary to discipline recalcitrant "students" in an informal setting
because they conform by their own volition. The educational efficiency
of informal institutions is apt to be much greater than in formal schools,
where students are compelled to attend by state law and to participate
involuntarily in activities that may seem quite unnatural to some;
on this basis, sociologists label the formal school an "artificial
institution."[10]

After all the teaching recipes and formulas have been tried, it remains for the school and its teachers to somehow motivate students by producing environmental conditions that stimulate students to value belonging to the group—in this case, the class or other groups contingent upon successful achievement in the classroom. Students must be given incentives to put forth the same kind of effort they exert in other less artificial educational structures. It follows that extremist efforts to individualize learning are bound to fail, as are extremist efforts to continue with collectivized learning, the traditional pattern in mass schooling. The overwhelming majority of students want a secure identity in school; they do not want to be isolated with teaching machines, nor do they want to be herded around in large masses from one teacher-imposed task to the next, with little regard for their personal and affiliative needs.

Formal Education and Teaching

Although the powerful influence of informal educational institutions should not be ignored, most prospective teachers are planning careers in schools—institutions developed for the express purpose of specializing in certain types of learning.

The Rise of Formal Schools

In most small, simply organized societies, education may be almost entirely by informal means. Group ways are learned by imitating behavior of adults. In primitive societies, the major opportunities for the younger members of society to acquire insights into the cultural tradition by relatively formal means often occur during puberty or mating rites, or death rituals and other ceremonials.[11] But as a society becomes more complex and differentiated, informal educational institutions that once may have sufficed for inducing young people into the practices and cultural beliefs of the social system tend to become less effective. They fail to transmit the new ways of life necessary for effective socialization and enculturation, and for maintenance and adaptation of the society as a whole.

As the relatively easygoing practices of parents, uncles, and siblings, who once participated casually and spontaneously in the education of the young become obsolete, formalization and specialization of education increases. Eventually, some adults with the necessary skills take on the specialized role of teaching young members of society these skills. When a society becomes so highly complex that important cultural values, skills, or understandings are best taught by specialists who come

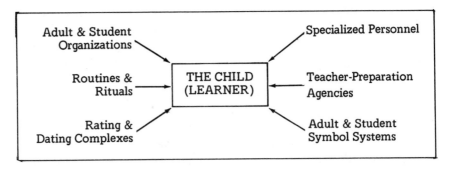

FIGURE 3–2. *The School as Direct Teacher: Formal Education in Society*

together in one place for convenience and cross-fertilization of ideas, the formal education institution known as the "school" is formed. Thus, schools are formed to assume the general function of transmitting residual cultural knowledge formerly handled by unorganized members of society.

The Systemization of Schooling

As time goes on, social complexity and the related need for educational specialization may become so great that schooling and teaching are more or less systematized. This is the case in the United States and in most of the rest of the modern world. Like most institutions, schools gradually develop the following components for efficient systemic operation:

• Buildings to house clients and materials in relatively accessible geographical locations
• Specialized personnel to increase the systemic efficiency of the schooling operation; especially teachers, principals, curriculum experts, central administrators
• A clearly patterned status-role structure to ensure that everyone in the complex system of schooling knows his or her role and the behavior expected of that role.[12] Figure 3–3 illustrates the hierarchical structure of status positions and associated status roles in a school.

Like most complex institutions, schooling systems develop customs, procedures, and agencies for their efficient and effective operation, maintenance, and modification.[13] They integrate and coordinate their components by holding regular staff meetings and student–faculty assemblies and by communicating within the system and with the community of which it is a part.

Formal educational institutions develop ancillary agencies to train

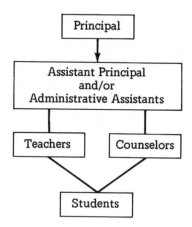

FIGURE 3–3.   *The Role Structure of the School*

specialized personnel. In the United States and many other societies, another institution, generally known as the "school of education," has emerged. Often with state, national, and international ties, these schools prepare teachers, administrators, and other educational specialists for their careers, and they retrain them as new knowledge and methods are developed. Schools of education also conduct and disseminate the results of empirical and theoretical research concerned with education and schooling. Similarly, local school districts, sometimes in conjunction with local universities, conduct workshops and similar programs after school or on weekends. This continuing formal education is designed to familiarize teachers and other school people with new practices and to assist them in solving unusually troublesome student problems.

As all institutionalized systems do, school systems manipulate special symbols to promote group loyalties of school system personnel and to prevent the public from becoming so familiar with system practices that it can threaten the ongoing operation of the system.[14] Symbols are also used to facilitate meaningful dialogue between teachers, educational researchers, and other educational specialists. Within the **school culture,** the code of teacher secrecy maintains that such "outsiders" as parents, new student teachers, and sometimes supervisors are to be excluded from entering the private congregating places of teachers in school buildings or from being privy to teacher discussions about students. This is a normative pattern with implications for informal socialization of prospective teachers to their career roles.

A second example of symbolic manipulation is the use of what some call "pedagoguese," the use in educational books, articles, and classes of specialized language that unnecessarily confuses the reader or listener.

Although there is some substance to this charge, most complex and specialized disciplines develop a language peculiar to the discipline in order to exchange ideas more readily. Education is no exception. The problem is not a specialized language that holds meaning only to educators; the real problem is determining whether teaching is actually professionalized—or, indeed, whether it should become so. (The question of the professionalization of teaching is discussed later in this chapter.)

The use of routines is an inevitable by-product of the institutionalization process, particularly when this process eventuates in the partial or complete bureaucratization of practice. In many aspects, the modern school has become a bureaucracy.[15] Or, to use Max Weber's classic definition of bureaucracy, a complex hierarchical system of organization pursuing its objectives largely through abstract rules determining allocation of positions and role-functions.[16]

Like most institutions, schools tend to develop mechanisms to encourage unity and loyalty of staff, students, and community. This helps to maintain stable relations between all concerned parties, especially during periods of extreme criticism and threat of withdrawal of support. Teachers are exposed to such integrative practices in school systems as the daily flag salute, faculty–student baseball games, trustee dinners, social get-togethers with staff, and other efforts to harmonize human relations and release group tensions.

Over time many formal institutions such as the school develop a variety of organizations to meet the individual and common needs felt by their members. Teachers have their own occupational organizations, as do administrators, board of education members, teachers of teachers, and parents. Organizations associated with formal education continuously develop, modify their structures, and disband in response to changes taking place in society and within their profession.

Development of "Anti-Systems" and Other Unintended Side Effects

Unintended side effects of school system operation eventually emerge and become more or less structured. Sometimes, such as when a new practice is introduced into schools, the resistance by vested interests is strong enough to produce what S.N. Eisenstadt has termed "anti-systems"—organized efforts to repeal systems or at least redirect them in ways more congenial to those affected.[17] An illustration of a major, unplanned anti-system in education is the recent development of the "teacher power" movement and the rapid increase of teacher unionization. The movement is a response to increasing pressures upon teachers since the end of World War II to conform to bureaucratic demands, cope with growing class sizes, inflation, and relatively low pay, and feelings of alienation and estrangement from many students and parents.

The side effects of institutionalized and bureaucratized formal schooling are felt not only by teachers and other personnel, but by the central clients in the enterprise—the students. Willard Waller, a pioneer in the field of the sociology of education, studied U.S. schools in 1932 and concluded that students almost invariably come into some conflict with the adults who control schools.[18] According to Waller, such conflict is inevitable because of the divergent interests of adults and children in an increasingly secondary society.

The conflict produced by sharp differences between adults and youth does not usually result in student anti-systems that are comparable to the teacher power movement. This is partly because students do not have as great an incentive to organize as teachers because they are not as permanently wedded to schools. Students, however, do influence school operation, especially through their own institutions. Client "institutions" help to make life at school more livable for students who otherwise would be completely under the domination of adults from age five to age eighteen. And, conversely, they prevent even the most well-intentioned efforts by teachers, principals, and other adults from being fully realized. Student organizations must be considered as part of the realm of education and of the educator.

Some of the client institutions discussed by Waller include:

Status-Role Structure of the Student Body. In almost every public elementary or secondary school, certain individuals tend to occupy positions as social leaders, scholars, class clowns, or power figures. This structuring of students into distinctive positions of higher or lower rank with characteristic role behaviors attached to each position serves to help students in the school detach themselves outside of classes (and, to some extent, inside as well) from their teachers and other authority figures. This frees them to live their own lives part of the time, in what would otherwise be an almost "total institution."[19] The student status-role system also deprives school authorities of the opportunity to overcontrol the daily lives of the students.

Student Associations and Movements. These are separate, formal status-role systems, formalized particularly during adolescence when students are struggling to exert their autonomy in seeking their identities. Middle- and upper-class youngsters belong to private and sometimes exclusive groups such as fraternities and sororities. Underground organizations and movements are more often composed of alienated student dissidents. And there are gangs of academically apathetic working- or lower-class boys and girls awaiting the legal age to drop out of school.

Some of these formalized groups and movements are closely watched by adults. If gang fights, excessive hazing of fraternity pledges, or advocacy of drug use by underground newspapers occur, for example, these groups are penalized in hopes of reducing their potentially great power and influence over school life.

"Rating and Dating" Complexes.   The average American public high school is not segregated by sex, as is often still the case in Great Britain and other nations. School is the place where many boys and girls learn to relate to the opposite sex. In high school, adolescents are preoccupied with establishing themselves in relation to the opposite sex. Patterns of competitive sex-role behavior emerge at this level. Students become known as more or less "eligible" as social partners for the other sex, qualifying for this status according to their social class, parents' income, physical attractiveness, or athletic prowess. Some students are rated as ineligible for dating and social intercourse with the opposite sex, often on the basis of some physical stigma such as acne or obesity. A student who fails to conform to conventional socioeconomic, ethnic, or ideological patterns in school (e.g., the lower-class student in a middle-class school, the black in a predominantly white school, or the "longhair" in a "straight" environment) may be relegated to the fringes of student social life. Whatever the configuration of rating and dating patterns in a school, such patterns occupy an important place in the lives of students in and out of school.

Special Symbol Systems.   Just as teachers and other school personnel develop their own ways of relating to members of their group, so do students communicate with each other in ways that are intended to exclude their teachers and other adults. This is done largely by means of highly original and stylistic patterns of language and dress.[20] The propensity of the adult world to imitate the speech and dress of youth causes younger people to abandon fashions and start new ones to prevent adults from gaining control over the few "territorial rights" possessed exclusively by them. Besides the formal language of the classroom that students use in conversing with all except trusted adults, young people also employ what Bernstein calls a "public language" code to converse with their peers.[21] Students regularly modify their public language to prevent most adults from becoming unduly familiar with the language.

The same kind of effort to preserve a separate identity is made in regard to dress and hairstyle. Often this is less successful because school rules and regulations insist on conventional style. In recent years, a number of cases have been heard in the courts concerning the rights of school officials to determine how students shall dress and wear their hair. As a rule, boards of education and school administrators have argued that students should dress "inoffensively." In matters of hair style, boys are usually expected to wear their hair no longer than the collar.

Although the courts until recently have viewed the schools as custodial agencies and, accordingly, generally sided with school officials on dress-code issues, this may change as more students and their parents seek legal redress for what they feel are infringements of their First Amendment rights.

In 1970, in a major case involving three high school students in Des Moines, Iowa, who wore black armbands to publicize their opposition to the Vietnam War, the United States Supreme Court ruled against the right of Des Moines school principals to institute an anti-armband regulation.[22] In Berkman's words: "The thesis of the Tinker opinion is that First Amendment rights in the classroom are actually essential to an effective educational process in a democracy rather than a source of disruption of that process."[23] And, in an important study of teachers' civil rights, Louis Fischer and David Schimmel have found that "schools are liberalizing their dress codes for teachers and students, and future courts may extend the same peripheral protection of the First Amendment to dress styles that beards receive today."[24]

Manifest and Latent Functions
of the School

As indicated before, educational institutions perform one or both of two elemental functions for the societies they serve: the maintenance of existing social patterns and the facilitation of changes in those patterns.

Sociologists view functions as consequences of organized human behavior and have divided the kinds of functions served by institutions into two types: manifest (or primary) and latent (or secondary).[25] A manifest function is any consequence of organized human behavior that was *intended* to occur. It is a social purpose.[26] One basic social purpose of schooling has been the transmission of traditional culture to the newer generations growing up in society.

A latent function of organized human behavior is a result of behavior that was *not* intended or anticipated. One of the latent functions of schooling in the United States has been the development of anti-systems such as the teacher power movement. No central control groups, in working to bureaucratize the school earlier in this century, intended that this process would someday produce teachers who strike for higher salaries or improved conditions for learning. This was an unintended, or latent, function of the bureaucratization of schooling in this society. An-

55

other latent function of the institutionalization of the secondary school has been the rise of what Waller calls "client institutions"—for example, the "rating and dating" system discussed earlier.

Sociologists often consider the latent functions of schooling to be as worthy of investigation as the manifest functions. What is intended, or manifest, may not always be achieved; but a latent, or unintended, function is an observable fact of life that can be described and analyzed, not simply speculated about.[27] For educators today, the crucial question of the school's ultimate social purposes—its manifest functions—is at least as important as descriptions of what the school has accomplished. As we study the school in its broad sociocultural context, the relationship between what schools and teachers attempt to do and the actual or potential results of these attempts will be shown. What the school's tasks in society have been, are, and what they ought to be in the modern world is the special concern of the study of the foundations of education.

Traditional Manifest Functions of the American School

Historically, the American school has been expected to accomplish a number of purposes for the society it has served, most of which continue to be demanded by various portions of the public.[28]

Selecting and Sorting People for Adult Roles.   The American school has almost always been a vehicle for separating the academically "more able" from the "less able." Those who succeed progress through higher levels of formal schooling and eventually into the preferred economic and social slots. Those who do not succeed generally are bound to occupy less privileged positions in society. The selecting and sorting task has undoubtedly been the most important of the schools' manifest functions throughout our history. However, the ethical legitimacy and actual results of this function have been seriously questioned in recent years by those who contend that this sorting function undermines the democratic ideal of equal opportunity, which the schools are supposed to provide. According to those who support this contention, schools cannot provide students equal opportunities to gain access to privileged economic and social positions if school systems determine student success and failure by criteria such as IQ tests.

Building and Maintaining Nationalism and Citizenship.   From Revolutionary days, American schools have been held accountable by the public for ensuring that children acquire strong loyalties to the national state, just as in colonial days the school was responsible for instilling strong loyalties to the established church of a community.

Transmission of Traditional Culture.   The enculturation or acculturation of the young to society's collective achievements has always been a central charge of schools. This is done through formal teaching of American history and American literature as well as by celebrating national holidays and dramatizing historic events.

The acculturation of immigrant children to American ways was emphasized as a school function from about 1880 to 1925, when the heaviest waves of immigration flowed to these shores. The children of immigrants received an education in American values and language at school during the day, and their parents often prepared for citizenship by taking courses in United States history and English at night. Now the acculturation of students from Mexico and Puerto Rico to American life and of lower-class minority youngsters to a dominating middle-class ethos is being attempted on a large scale with federal support, under the rubric of "educating the disadvantaged."

Socialization.   Another important function of our schools has been socialization. This process of learning differs from enculturation and acculturation in that it refers to acquiring the actual behavior patterns that a society considers as skills. Enculturation and acculturation, in contrast, refer more to acquiring knowledge of the past that is handed down as culture.

In school the child is socialized by such practices as waiting patiently and courteously for his or her turn to speak with others—usually by learning such established school norms as raising a hand in class—and by competing for desired positions and honors—primarily by working for grades. On the other hand he or she is enculturated or accultured to knowledge about the transition from horses to automobiles through formal study of history.

Propagation of Religious Faith.   This function was a major reason for the development of schools during the colonial period of our history. At that time, schools were little more than extensions of the theocratic state.

Acquisition of Basic Skills.   This is another central purpose of American schooling, particularly at lower grade levels. Instruction in the "3 Rs" has traditionally been the primary focus of childhood education in our society, although changes in our lifestyles and cultural patterns have brought the stress on acquiring these fundamental skills into serious question.

Vocational Training.   Some attention at the secondary level of schooling has been given to occupational education, attention which is periodically renewed in the United States. At present, more vocational training in high school (commonly called career education) is being urged particularly for students who are not qualified for college. Vocational education is also seen as helping to lower the numbers of chronically unemployed workers.

Character Education.   Since early colonial days, many people have considered this function to be even more important than establishing basic literacy or selecting and sorting individuals for adult roles. For this reason, teachers, like the clergy, have always been viewed as ideal role models for children. They are consequently often held to restrictive standards of behavior, including dress and speech, standards not expected of other members of the community. Because the definition of what constitutes "good character" is undergoing widespread debate and dramatic change in contemporary society, the traditional obligation of schools and teachers to conform to one set of moral and ethical norms is being questioned and altered. This situation illustrates a central principle of education and schooling in its environmental context: *The school normally reflects the society it purports to serve;* it does not lead society in society's efforts to adapt and change. Schools tend to change *after* the rest of society changes, not before. (The matter of whether schools *should* lead or follow social change will be discussed more fully in Chapters 10 and 11, when we again focus on the purposes of education.)

Emerging Manifest Functions of the School

The manifest functions of schooling in the past can be stated as established facts, whether or not they have been satisfactorily achieved. The newer functions, however, are often controversial and not yet implemented universally, such as sex and family life education. Controversial manifest functions can be considered educational *issues*. Some of the newer and often controversial conceptions of school purpose are presented in the following paragraphs. They are discussed here to provoke thought about the fundamental assumptions of education that are held by many people in this society. They are not established purposes of all schools today.

Personal and Social Problem Solving.   In a complex, transitional society, individuals and organized groups need to be able to think in ways that were not essential during more simple periods. They must solve difficult problems relating to their personal lives (e.g., mating and family problems, mental health, drugs, and vocation) and problems of the larger society of which they are members (e.g., control of crime and delinquency, effective government, the rights of minorities, reduction of poverty, eradication of war, and social planning). Since the turn of the twentieth century, major educational thinkers, such as John Dewey and George Counts, have urged that the central function of American education be to teach individual and social problem solving. To date, the social studies curriculum has been the primary area of education that has embodied this ideal.

Social Competence in a Secondary Society.   As society was radically altered in the wake of twentieth-century depressions and recessions, world wars, and recently the Vietnam War, the interpersonal competencies of a rural America have become largely outmoded and obsolete. Most of us now live in a heterogeneous, urbanized milieu in which, as anthropologist George Spindler puts it, "people are rubbing shoulders in polyglot masses."[29]

The Appalachian farmer migrating to industrial Cleveland, for example, is often lost in the big city and mired in poverty and disillusionment. How will his children fare in such a milieu? Problem-solving skills are needed to help the uprooted American, to help not only the poor, but also the occupationally mobile middle **SES** groups. Besides problem-solving skills, people need behavioral competencies that they can readily enact without elaborate intellectual rehearsal. Many sociologists, social psychologists, anthropologists, and educators today urge that schools teach children behavioral competencies needed for adequate social intercourse in an essentially new society. These competencies can be developed through work in integrated classrooms, through small-group projects, through community study to develop community-action skills of students, and through simulation of "real life" interpersonal situations.*

Diffusion of New Knowledge.   Even scholars cannot keep abreast of the "knowledge explosion"—the new findings of scientists, technologists, and other investigators. However, some of this new knowledge must be acquired by youngsters if they are to successfully cope with a society as different from that of their parents' childhood as their parents' society was different from the frontier period.

Many people believe that the school has little choice but to transmit some of the new cultural items continually being developed by scholars

---

* The possibilities for employing role play, creative dramatics, and other forms of simulation in teaching and in teacher education are beginning to be recognized. Commercial aids are available for teachers interested in exploring useful strategies such as role playing to develop social competencies.

and technicians. However, to date, schools have concentrated on technological feats, such as space pilots flying to the moon, and avoided the diffusion of new ideas in the arts and in the social sciences. (Of course, much that is novel is gained as incidental knowledge by students attending schools influenced generally by new technologies. New math and science programs and organizational innovations stress importance of expertise in human affairs.) Most of the new knowledge suggests to the child that such knowledge is synonymous with technological wizardry and gadgetry. This preoccupation with technology tends to be at the expense of the study of human values.

Providing Equality of Opportunity for a Social Position.   This key functional area of schooling is undergoing critical assessment today. Efforts are being made on a national scale to ensure that *every* child—rich or poor, black or white, male or female—receives an equal chance to succeed as an adult through the provision of educational opportunities that allow him or her to compete in the economic market place that most Americans believe is the primary source of access to the "good life." Despite severe criticism by such respected agencies as the Westinghouse-Ohio University research group and the Stanford Research Institute, among others, compensatory education programs, such as Headstart for preschool children, continue to be encouraged by many state and federal officials.

The recently created National Institute of Education, a division of the Department of Health, Education, and Welfare, has been advised that grants for research on cultural pluralism will receive less priority than grants to reduce poverty through compensatory education efforts.[30] HEW argues that efforts to reduce poverty do not necessarily entail significant alterations in the human arrangements involved in learning; that is, they do not depend upon radical social change. However, there is a growing acknowledgment by social scientists and educators that social inequalities are created and perpetuated by institutionalized discrimination based not only upon economic disparities, but upon cultural and racial discrimination.

Sex and Family Life Education.   The family, the church, and the local neighborhood may no longer realistically hope to educate youngsters informally about relations with the opposite sex and raising children. The social functions of the family, church, and community have decreased markedly. The public and its representatives in government are extremely concerned, particularly about adolescent sex relations and their ramifications for society and the individual. The incidence of venereal disease and of divorce are apparently at all time highs. A number of states have already instituted sex and family life programs into official school practice in order to help youngsters cope with these very crucial areas of their present and future lives. Many people and organizations, however, are opposed to the transfer of these functions from the social institutions of the family and church to the school. The schools, they contend, should confine their responsibilities to teaching academic subjects, and not encroach upon the traditional roles of the family and the church. This emerging manifest function of American schooling is still distinctly controversial and unresolved.

Increased Functional Literacy.   The same kind of argument against change is often applied to the teaching of newer forms of communication capabilities. Despite the phenomenal growth of television and other electronic media, believed by McLuhan[31] to symbolize the emergence of a new age in which the printed word has lost its relevance, lay people and educators still assume that reading, spelling, English grammar, and mathematics are the most important skills for individual survival. However, the inculcation of skills, values, and knowledge relating to the literate utilization of visual media affects almost everyone's life intimately with its news, entertainment, and educational potentialities, and the mathematical computer eliminates much of the necessity of memorizing "times" tables and methods of borrowing.

Still, some relatively modest attention is being given to the problem of redesigning the "basic skills" component of the curriculum to incorporate study of how to interpret visual media. This attempt usually takes the form of using the newer technological media as adjuncts to traditional school media such as blackboards and textbooks.[32] **Literacy** has taken on a broader meaning.

Development of Cosmopolitan Attitudes.   In a secondary society like ours in which we "rub shoulders in polyglot masses," intolerance toward ethnic, class, and ideological minorities can no longer be countenanced. The idea of cosmopolitanism is not confined to improving attitudes toward minorities. It also extends to developing an ability to intelligently critique the marketplace, the place of work in modern life, expertise, and authority figures, including the president, who is viewed by many young children as a powerful father figure.[33] In short, modern urban life requires sophisticated cosmopolitanism not needed when 91 percent of the people of George Washington's day lived in isolated small towns without the benefit of television or the supersonic jet to make them feel a part of an increasingly international community.

Schools today need to educate youngsters to live in such an urbanized, secular, global community—or to create a sense of community out of secondary relations that now produce anomie and alienation. Such an emerging function is required of schools unless and until other institutions are created to take the place of the school, the only institution outside of the family that intimately affects children daily, for at least ten of the most formative years of their lives.

Existential Creativity.   Although not yet widely diffused, recognized, or understood, the rather sudden development in the late 1960s of the "free school" movement and the "open classroom" anticipates the idea that public schools should facilitate personal authenticity.

In "pursuit of loneliness," vast numbers of Americans have lost their sense of community and their sense of an interrelated self.[34] Although the study of individual and social problems is vitally important to relocating the individual within a community context, this may not be enough. Many people now have the leisure to brood introspectively and often neurotically—or to begin to realize themselves as worthwhile by doing something creative with their personal time. They can learn to write essays, paint pictures, sculpt, ponder oriental philosophy, or, if they prefer, study political science or join community groups. *What* people do in their personal time is probably far less important than whether they are engaged in what seems important to them; that is, that they become involved in life.

Devoting a minimum of one hour every day, or one day each week, to an activity freely chosen by every individual student might counterbalance the now overwhelming emphasis on socializing and enculturating children for the purposes of others. Adults who may have no comprehension of what a child will live through no longer have the right to completely confine a child's every emotion and thought in school to what is acceptable to the state.

Children need to be educated for personal identity in an anomic, confused, and changing social order. They need an arena for the expression of personal choice in their daily lives if they are to grow into self-actualizing people and not merely self-adjusting cogs in the expanding social machinery. Teaching students to develop their creativity can help to integrate all other purposes of the school.

Some Examples of Latent Functions of the School

In addition to the intended purposes discussed above, schools perform the following unintended functions for American society:

• *Marriage broker.*   Schools act as marriage or mating bureaus, particularly at the secondary and college levels.

• *Babysitting.*   Schools serve as a babysitting service at the elementary levels, especially for women who work outside the home.

• *Entertainment.*   They are a distinctive source of entertainment for adults as well as children; e.g., by sponsoring varsity sports, weekly dances, etc.

• *Regulation of labor force.*   Schools are a means of temporarily keeping young people out of an overcrowded labor market and for keeping potentially disruptive unemployed youth off the streets.

• *Social life.*   Schools are centers for student social life in a mobile mass society with relatively few major centers in which youth can participate in a peer culture.

The manifest and latent social functions performed by schools illustrate how important it is for prospective teachers to begin thinking about why schools are so highly valued by society and about some of the tasks to be eliminated or added to the repertoire of formal educational endeavors in a changing social order.

Curriculum of the School

The functions of education require implementation in programs if they are to be realized. The school serves public purposes by converting the desired outcomes of educational endeavors into an educational process. The primary means for ensuring that social purposes are realized as educational programs is the curriculum.

The Official Curriculum.   The formal curriculum of a school consists of the subjects, or learnings to be undergone by students in interaction with their teachers. If the school reflects a traditional concept of social purpose, its curriculum accordingly will tend to be one that emphasizes such subjects as reading, writing, arithmetic, American history, geography, grammar, science, American literature, physical education, and music and art.

On the other hand, if the school attempts to reflect a changing conception of educational purpose, its curriculum may include the following: language arts; an integration of social and physical science, a "core curriculum"; applied and pure mathematics; and freely chosen activities to encourage creative expression, such as dramatics, creative writing, music composition, and painting and sculpting.

In addition to formal curriculum, schools may also engage students in voluntary extra-curricular activities. In more progressive schools,

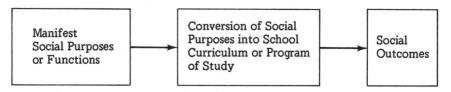

FIGURE 3–4.   *A Highly Generalized Paradigm of the Curriculum Conversion Process*

activities termed extra-curricular by traditional schools, are part of the regular curriculum.

The Invisible Curriculum.   Schools have "invisible" or hidden curricular activities, as do informal educational institutions such as the family and the workplace.[35] The invisible curriculum of the school may be understood as school activity that commonly goes on as part of the implementation of the official program, but which is not officially programmed. For instance, when teachers in a suburban school make casual references to the magnificent record of the school in getting its graduates into ivy league universities, they are engaging in the implementation of an invisible curriculum. Their references are intended to produce learning outcomes that reinforce their students' sense of superior station in society. Such statements also have the effect of sustaining student motivations to study well and obtain the grades necessary for admission to such colleges. Many educators believe that the invisible curriculum of the school, like that of informal educational agencies external to the school, may have as much or more influence on what schools actually accomplish educationally than does the formal curriculum.[36]

The Misunderstood Concept of the Teaching Role

One of the best definitions of the concept role is: People (1) in social positions (2) behave (3) with reference to [normative] expectations (4) that are affectively charged.[37] (The numbers here refer to key elements in the overall concept.)

Human existence tends to be largely, if not entirely, organized by various kinds of social institutions, the school being one important social institution of modern times. Every individual associated with the schools is allocated a more or less specific position in that institution—for ex-

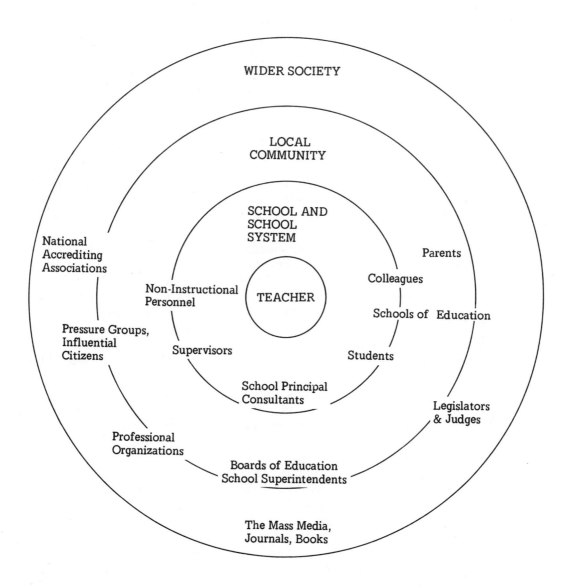

WIDER SOCIETY

LOCAL
COMMUNITY

SCHOOL AND
SCHOOL
SYSTEM

Parents

Colleagues

National
Accrediting
Associations

Non-Instructional
Personnel

TEACHER

Schools of Education

Pressure Groups,
Influential
Citizens

Supervisors

Students

School Principal
Consultants

Legislators
& Judges

Professional
Organizations

Boards of Education
School Superintendents

The Mass Media,
Journals, Books

FIGURE 3–5.   *The Teacher's Role System and Reference Groups*

ample, the positions of teacher, student, school superintendent, or school board member. Each position associated with the school has specific behavioral privileges and duties attached to it. For instance, a duty of most teachers, which students do not have, is to be at school before students arrive and to remain until they have left. A privilege exclusive to teachers in most schools is allocating tasks for students to perform. These rights and duties related to position, or role, are not arbitrarily undertaken by the individual occupying the role. They are *assigned* as behavioral *expectations* to all persons occupying a certain position, regardless of his or her personal wishes. The people who possess the authority to assign expected behaviors to people in institutional positions are called "significant others," or "generalized others," depending upon the immediacy of their influence. They constitute parts of the **reference group** to whom position incumbents refer as they go about their institutional business. Figure 3–5 illustrates the kinds of reference-group influences operating on the modern teacher's behavior. Note that such influence is normally reciprocal.

The behavior of role incumbents in schools is affective, or emotionally charged; it is not accepted with neutral feelings. Sometimes individuals are unable or unwilling to behave in conformity with role expectations because they find such expectations to be morally untenable, excessively demanding, conflicting with other expectations, or overly ambiguous. When this happens—most commonly in periods of substantial social upheaval and change—position incumbents may encounter psychological stress and tension in the performance of their roles. They may develop "role strain."

In short, roles are emotionally charged behaviors expected of persons occupying specific institutional positions. According to anthropologist Ralph Linton, an early formulator of the role concept, they are the dynamic aspects of a status, although in common parlance both concepts are tied together in one word, "role."[38]

Insofar as most of human life takes place in institutional contexts, it follows that most individual behavior is role-related. But even such role-dominated behavior as that associated with the occupational position of school teacher allows for some greater or lesser degree of idiosyncracy at times. This is illustrated in Figure 3–6.

As the Figure 3–6 indicates, a teacher or student is usually given greater freedom (or assumes that it is granted) to behave in his or her own way during activities that are considered relatively unimportant. He or she is under greater compulsion to put the more unique aspects of his or her personality aside during activities commonly deemed more important. Some degree of personal style, however, always accompanies role-related behavior in schools. Even during formal study, such as when children are learning to read, a teacher usually injects an element of levity and personal character into the lesson.

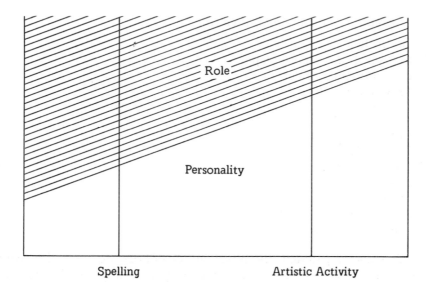

Role

Personality

Spelling   Artistic Activity

FIGURE 3–6.   *Teacher Behavior in the Classroom during Two Different Types of Activities: Behavior is a Function of Role and Personality (Adapted from Jacob W. Getzels and Herbert A. Thelen, "The Classroom as a Unique Social System," The Dynamics of Instructional Groups, Fifty-ninth Yearbook of the National Society for the Study of Education, Part II [Chicago: University of Chicago Press, 1960], p. 70. Reprinted by permission of the National Society for the Study of Education.*

Most descriptions of the roles of teachers exclusively emphasize the instructional aspects of this position. Important as the teacher's role in instruction is, there are other dimensions to his or her role that directly and indirectly affect instruction.* The following paradigm of role functions shows that teachers are assigned at least three broad and interrelated types of roles: "extra-class roles," "executive and administrative roles," and "instructional roles."[39]

Role-Function Paradigm

Extra-Class Roles

1. Faculty member and member of an occupational group
2. Community agent
3. Learner

---

* A common criticism of contemporary education is that teachers are expected to perform too many roles in addition to their primary one of instructing. Although there is some credibility to this criticism, certain non-instructional roles, such as pupil control, are directly related to instruction. They should not be ignored as responsibilities of a teacher; if they are, the quality of instruction will suffer.

Executive and Administrative Roles

4. Controller
5. Measurer and recordkeeper
6. Learning-aids officer
7. Program director

Instructional Roles

8. Skills instructor
9. Knowledge instructor
10. Values instructor
11. Evaluator
12. Motivator
13. Counselor
14. Agent of change

The above paradigm is useful in considering actual and possible differences in teacher roles based on ideal types of schools. For instance, if we consider the traditional American school, which is still fairly typical, we may describe the roles of its teachers according to the paradigm as follows:

Extra-Class Roles

1. Faculty member and member of an occupational group=Follower in an organization and occupational subordinate
2. Community agent=Follower of the community
3. Learner=Graduated learner

Executive and Administrative Roles

4. Controller=Disciplinarian
5. Measurer and recordkeeper=Measurer and recordkeeper
6. Learning-aids officer=Textbook translation source
7. Program director=Program implementor

Instructional Roles

8. Skills instructor=Drill sergeant
9. Knowledge instructor=Information dispensor
10. Values instructor=Indoctrinator of tradition
11. Evaluator=Judge
12. Motivator=High pressure salesperson or entertainer
13. Counselor=Healer of subject matter wounds
14. Change agent=Resistor of innovations

On the other hand, if we are describing the roles of teachers in a free school, the same dimensions would lend themselves to dramatically different interpretations:

Extra-Class Roles

1. Faculty member and member of an occupational group=Independent artist

2. Community agent=Ignorer of community

3. Learner=Continuous informal learner

Executive and Administrative Roles

4. Controller=No "control," individual advisor

5. Measurer and recordkeeper=Very casual and informal "measurer" and "recordkeeper"

6. Learning-aids officer=Tutor

7. Program director=Program rejector

Instructional Roles

8. Skills instructor=Humanistic guide to student self-determined skills

9. Knowledge instructor=Guide to student self-determined knowledge; resource person

10. Values instructor=Guide to student in determining own values

11. Evaluator=Guide to self-evaluation, and responder–adapter

12. Motivator=Stoker of a burning engine

13. Counselor=Friend

14. Change agent=Continuous innovator

This same paradigm can be used for inferring the basic roles of teachers in almost any kind of school. In general, the role dimensions do not change, but the specific roles vary according to the type of school milieu. And, it should by now be evident that it is probably futile for a teacher to hunt for teaching skills without first determining what kind of school he or she expects to work in and what specific roles he or she will be assuming.

The Controversial Notion of Professionalism in Teaching

What Is a Profession?

According to the average layperson, anyone engaged in work activities that involve a high degree of skill is a professional. From this perspective, good carpenters are professionals, as are surgeons. A fast-talking advertising man selling gas-wasting cars on TV can be considered a professional on the same grounds because he certainly is skillful in manipulating the consumer. Professionalism is obviously a word that means different things to different people. What do scholars mean when they refer to the concept?

William Hicks and Frank Blackington say that profession is a concept:

> The word "profession" clearly implies that members profess something. What do they profess? They profess ... that they are different from the larger society in at least two basic ways: 1. That social function is the primary reference point for guiding their activity (work). 2. They possess ... a specialized knowledge and means of verifying claims to knowledge that enables them to perform this function with an economy unique to that individual or group.[40]

Thus, to Hicks and Blackington, the irreducible characteristics of any profession are (1) that the professional's primary motive is service to the public, not money or power and (2) this service is based upon the professional's specialized knowledge and means of verifying that knowledge for other members of society.

The following is a detailed list of criteria that, according to Everett Hughes, apply to professions and to professionals:

• Professionals profess to know better than others the nature of certain matters and to know better than their clients what ails them or their affairs. This is the essence of the professional idea and the professional claim.

• On the basis of their specialized knowledge, professionals ask that they be trusted by their clients in the performance of their practice.

• The professional also asks for protection from unfortunate consequences of his sincere efforts.

• Professionals strive to define some aspects of their interests, such as the nature of disease and health, the capacity of the school, and the optimum conditions for learning.

• Professionalism is dependent upon strong solidarity of members of a profession, thus creating a group apart with a separate ethos.

• This in turn implies deep and fairly long-term (ideally, lifelong) commitment to one's occupation.

• New professions arise from developments in society requiring complex new skills; e.g., social work is the secular replacement for services formerly performed by the church and the family in close-knit primary communities.

• The main themes of professionalization are balanced detachment toward a client (or student), with simultaneous interest and concern for all cases of the kind. Related to this is the pursuit and systematization of pertinent knowledge that concerns a client.

• The professional seeks a *balance* between the *theoretical* and the *practical.* A long period of formal study and *apprenticeship* are required to prepare for the professional life. Often, because of the need for both formal coursework and apprenticeship, a strain ensues between professionals and their representatives in academia, who are accused of being in an "ivory tower."

• Professionals seek independence, recognition, and autonomy in their work. For the teacher, this is what academic freedom is all about.

• Professions are increasingly being practiced in large organizations (as in the cases of engineering and social work) rather than privately (as in medicine or law).[41]

"The professions will, in any case, be a large and influential element in our future, and in that of all societies which go the road of industrialization and urbanization."[42]

Hicks–Blackington

In light of the Hicks–Blackington and the Hughes criteria presented above, which outline the essence of the professional idea, where does school teaching presently stand on a continuum ranging from "a job" to "a profession"?

Service Function.   Is teaching an important social service, despite a lack of consensus about what all the elements of this service should be? Definitely yes, it may be argued. Teaching is unquestionably a distinctive and important social service, even if this ideal has not been fully achieved yet. Its primary intent is to benefit the public, not its practitioners.

Specialized Knowledge Claim.   Do teachers possess a specialized body of knowledge and means of easily verifying their claim to specialized knowledge? This is a debatable question. Teaching is dependent on several bodies of knowledge, just as medicine is dependent upon anatomy and physiology. But, do teachers typically rely strongly upon an available body of knowledge underlying professional practice when considering curricular and instructional matters? In the past, teachers often took required foundational coursework grudgingly, added some methods and curriculum coursework—largely for the recipes rather than the principles they could collect—and then picked up much of what they practiced through trial and error on the job. This practice has often led lay people to question whether teachers do in fact possess verification skills superior to their own. However, a body of solid knowledge of relevance to teachers is in the process of being developed. This knowledge is being made more readily available to practitioners for their use, and more teachers appear to be taking advantage of it.

Hughes

Specialized Knowledge. Do teachers in fact know better than their
"clients" (students primarily) what their educational problems are, and
how they can best be resolved? Teachers are generally knowledgeable
about the needs of their students as a class and about how to best fulfill
these educational needs. But in relation to practitioners in many other
fields, their professional knowledge is quite limited.

Furthermore, the extreme complexity of the organizational structure
in which teaching takes place in this society prevents the full utilization
of the professional knowledge possessed by increasing numbers of highly
educated and trained teachers. Perhaps teachers have more occupational
knowledge than many critics have realized, but the maximum expression
of what they know has been precluded to date by factors in their working
environments that limit the use of their knowledge; for example, role
constriction by superordinates and community reference figures, and the
inadequate relationship between teacher preparation agencies and school
systems. Overall, it seems fair to say that more and more teachers meet
this criterion, although still only moderately.

Trust. Are teachers trusted by the people they serve and by their professional superordinates? Again, the answer must be qualified and cast in
relative terms. If teachers are subject matter specialists, usually at the
secondary level and increasingly at the elementary level, or have
specialized credentials, they tend to receive a greater degree of trust from
both parents and administrators than do teachers who are "generalists."
Parents, board members, legislators, and administrators, however, still
behave as if teachers are not worthy of unqualified professional trust.
Laws that are not designed by teachers have been passed to ensure accountability by teachers to others (e.g., the Stull Bill in California). Most
professions have standards established by the professional group itself.
The occupational autonomy of teachers has been greatly limited by
administrative evaluations of their work; many teachers would prefer to
be evaluated by their colleagues.

Protection. Do teachers receive protection when students fail to learn or
claim to have been abused? The courts have usually decided the second
question in favor of teachers accused of severe disciplinary practices and
the like.* Furthermore, after three or four years of not receiving much
protection, teachers may obtain tenure. From that point on, it is relatively

---

* These decisions are usually rendered using the principle of *in loco parentis*
("in place of the parents"). Of course, when a student can show that a teacher
has abused him or her unnecessarily, the courts take a different view. The
principle of *in loco parentis,* then, has its boundaries.

difficult to terminate a teacher except for "moral turpitude" or very gross incompetence, which is often difficult to prove in court.

However, tenure laws are presently undergoing critical review by legislators representing a public that is increasingly demanding of its teachers. Some people would do away with this vestige of protection altogether, on the grounds that it facilitates the continued employment of incompetent teachers. In response, teacher organizations are seeking greater protection, not only for experienced teachers but for anyone possessing a license to teach, however long he or she has practiced. They argue that a teacher's competence cannot be judged as readily as can that of practitioners in fields where the results of a professional's work are immediately visible. Further, teachers are still occasionally intimidated for reasons not related to the performance of their work—for example, their civil rights to dress and speak with the same impunity as other citizens are sometimes denied by portions of the public. Therefore, professional protection for teachers is incomplete at present.

Definition of Their Interests.   Do teachers now have significant opportunities to determine important aspects of what their work shall entail? Unlike physicians, who insist on being closely and constantly consulted when medical policy is being established by the public, teachers have relatively little to say about who shall be admitted to practice and under what conditions. Neither can they determine what shall be taught in schools or, in many cases, how subjects shall be taught.

The general public in the United States—much more than in other countries such as England—believes it has the right to rigorously control almost every aspect of the work of teachers—from creating school policy to the implementation of this policy through curricular and role-related decisions. Teachers have traditionally accepted close public scrutiny and control, thereby appearing to confirm the public's belief that teachers have little right or interest in participating actively as leaders in the educational decision-making process. However, this is beginning to change with the rise of the teacher power movement in our society. If this movement is relatively successful, among its several gains for teachers will be a substantial increase in their willingness and capacity to define their own occupational interests. One can say, then, that the profession of teaching is striving with increasing success to define its own interests.

Close Solidarity.   Are teachers a close-knit and identifiable occupational group? The occupational socialization of teachers in college and upon entering schools of education has tended to make the kind of solidarity found among prospective physicians, social workers, attorneys, or engineers difficult to achieve. The great numbers involved in the profession of teaching prevent the kind of close-knit camaraderie that is common among members of those other professional groups with relatively fewer members.* Also, the coursework in most schools of education in the past often was not rigorous enough to stimulate intellectual interaction of peers, which can help to develop group pride, as is often the case with doctoral candidates in graduate school.[44] Once on the job in the field, however, this may change, particularly if teachers, many of whom are still relative **sociological strangers** in their communities, become more integrated and involved members of their profession. More teachers are concluding that they have only themselves to rely upon in a society that does not adequately appreciate the remarkably unique challenges of their work.

For these and related reasons, teachers are coming together as never before and striving to identify their common interests in serving the public by joining structured occupational organizations. The American Federation of Teachers is expanding in numbers and influence rapidly, complementing the already large National Education Association. Strong occupational organization is one of the essential features of a profession and of the professional struggle. Professionalism is a group—more than an individual—affair.

Is professionalism an ideal worth striving for? Many thoughtful people today contend that professionalism may actually impede quality education by lowering the standards of a group. However, standards established by professional groups are always minimal in order "to insure that no incompetent is allowed to practice."[45] This still allows for exceptionally creative teachers to go beyond the minimum standards; it actually allows individual practitioners greater freedom, rather than restriction. Admittedly, the service of "eminently qualified people who are making significant contributions elsewhere"[46] may at times be thereby lost. "This is the high price of standard setting."[47] By banding together, professionals can ensure better services to the public. Teachers are becoming a distinctly identifiable occupational group today.

Deep and Life-long Commitment.   This criterion is difficult to assess because in the past many people entered the teaching field rather casually or simply because it offered employment. As we mentioned earlier, a new breed of teacher is beginning to enter schools of education—a type of person who really wants to teach. More and more people are becoming teachers because of a deeply felt commitment to the goals of the profession.

The Rise of a New Profession.   Our discussion thus far seems to point to the revitalization of the teaching field. Teaching is in fact an essentially

---

* Schools of education generally have the largest enrollments in universities. Until recent years, as much as one-third of all students attending institutions of higher education in the United States were planning to become teachers.[43]

new career. Whether this new career will be considered a profession is a question that cannot be answered at this time.

Balanced Detachment and Concern Based on Systematic Knowledge. This requirement of a profession has yet to be demonstrated by teachers. Teachers first must understand what this characteristic really means. To be "detached" is to be objective toward students, although still capable of helping them. Some teachers, however, still think that it is better to become deeply involved with students. They believe an objective person is cold and unfeeling. They try to personalize their work without necessarily relying upon systematic knowledge and without always considering the general welfare of their students. In short, there are teachers who enter the field not so much to perform an interesting, enjoyable, and vital social service based upon application of relevant knowledge, but primarily because they hope to receive intense emotional gratification from the students with whom they work. By rejecting objectivity and application of systematized knowledge, this type of teacher hopes to be perceived by students as "human," and more acceptable than other teachers. However, objectivity does not necessarily entail unfriendliness or impersonality, both of which will of course inhibit learning and the social service function of teaching.

The problem is one of perspective. To work compassionately with fellow human beings in the interest of teaching them to cope with their world requires that teachers relate to children realistically. They must learn to accept their strong and their weak points. This acceptance is aided by an understanding of young people, of the social purposes and conditions surrounding learning, of what is to be learned, and of how to interact to bring about learning. The highly successful teacher, usually an experienced and well-educated one, can put these diverse ingredients together in such a way as to be "real" or "authentic" in the classroom.

But until this difficult set of interrelated ideas is widely grasped, there will probably be teachers who overemphasize objectivity, causing them to appear impersonal, or who misplace their need for affection. This important criterion of professionalism is not completely met.

Balance Between the Theoretical and Practical.   Gaining the sense of perspective, the understanding, and the practice needed to integrate the many diverse elements involved in successful teaching demands more than an either–or attitude toward theory and practice. Theory and practice are both essential, and they should ideally be correlated, not isolated as is common practice. Today theory courses are usually taught prior to student teaching instead of integrating academic study and field work.

In the last few years, many students of education have understandably reacted negatively to the traditional separation of theory from practical work. Unless this tradition is overcome and the application of theory more adequately explained, everyone concerned with teaching will suffer. Already some have proposed that teacher preparation be transferred from institutions of higher learning and placed in the hands of practitioners. To a point, this idea appears to make sense; teachers-to-be benefit greatly from the field work experience, if it is a well-considered experience. On the other hand, this idea could be disastrous if overdone. If the professionalization of teaching is valued as a goal, the fundamental principles upon which professional practice are founded cannot realistically be acquired except in academic settings. An institution of higher learning brings the prospective practitioner into contact with new scholarship and with professors who have a coherent understanding of the overall educational picture.

Although there is growing danger of a damaging split between academics and practitioners, it may be averted, or at least minimized, if the occupation wants professionalization enough to produce a profound internal dialogue on the meaning of the concept as it relates to career preparation. At present, however, this is not certain, so we must infer that there is not yet an adequate balance between study and apprenticeship, or between theory and practice.

Independence, Recognition, and Autonomy. Do teachers have autonomy? This ingredient of professional work is highly dependent upon the organizational power of teachers and upon the belief in the possession of a firm body of theoretical and practical knowledge. Although organizational unity is increasing in the teaching profession, there is some question about the kind of knowledge needed to be a teacher and how to acquire it. Until the question of an appropriate knowledge base is firmly settled, teachers may have to accept a relative dependence upon others for control of much of their work. These others may be school managers, such as the building principal or a representative of the local teacher organization. A third possibility is that a relatively small cadre—perhaps 10 to 15 percent of all teachers—[48]of highly educated, trained, and sophisticated people will become more or less autonomous leaders in teaching, and that schools will be organized by what is commonly called a "differentiated staffing" pattern. If this happens, the word "professional" will probably be reserved for these relatively few leaders and the remainder will be expected to carry out the plans initiated by them.

The Organized Professions. Sociologist Wilbert Moore believes that the newer professions emerging are characteristically different from the traditional "business professions" (dentistry, law, medicine, etc.) because they are practiced in relatively large-scale organizations.[49] In the past, many people defined a field as professional in part on the basis of whether or not its workers received fees directly from their clients. Such a conception is clearly inadequate today. The prototype of the organized profession today is perhaps engineering, an occupation that possesses many of the attributes we have assigned to a profession.

At one time, many teachers worked for themselves, but today this is rare, since even private schools normally are operated by staffs with several teachers and other personnel. Teaching, then, is not excluded from the class of occupations entitled to be called professions, even if its workers practice primarily in highly organized settings and receive salaries instead of direct fees.

Americans are living in a society that has moved even beyond the stage of Industrialism. Schooling and teaching become focal interests of any advanced urban, Post-Industrial society because the educational needs of its members are far too great and specialized to be handled by informal educational institutions such as the family. (Contemporary writers, such as Ivan Illich and Everett Reimer, in apparent refutation of this social fact, have urged the *deschooling* of modern society.[50]) The social services to be performed by the educational institution in such complex societies require a high degree of intellectual and clinical preparation by teachers. If teaching cannot yet be considered completely professionalized, it has every expectation of becoming so by the end of the twentieth century if broad trends in modern society continue along their present lines.

Is Teaching a Profession Today?

Teachers profess to know better than their clients what their profession and its clients need, but not everyone agrees with them. Teachers want to be trusted as they practice, but public trust is often lacking. Their traditional demands for minimal protection through tenure laws and court protection from claims of abuse are being questioned in a society that demands a great deal of its schools, but does not always realize that changing times and conditions require new and increased forms of support. Teachers have not been strongly encouraged to take substantial interest in defining the parameters of their work. The public and its elected and appointed school officials and administrators often feel threatened by close and powerful solidarity of teachers. The new breed of teacher promises to offer a deep and in many cases lifelong commitment to the occupation, as the occupation itself prepares for the serious task of general reconstruction. Many teachers continue to be confused about the necessity for reasonable objectivity and application of available knowledge as it becomes synthesized. They also continue to heavily emphasize the value of practical work while ignoring theoretical study. Although moving gradually toward greater autonomy based upon organizational solidarity, teachers will be limited in their efforts to achieve significant independence in their work until they fully overcome their resistance to the intellectual elements of professional practice, as have engineers and, increasingly, social workers and even nurses.

In complex, urban, and organizationally dominated societies such as ours, the pressure is clearly in favor of occupations such as teaching, which seems to have essential, distinctive, and irreplaceable social service functions to perform for the public, to become ever more and more professionalized, as such a mode of work structure becomes the predominant wave of the future.

In weighing the evidence presented, one must conclude that teaching is not a mature profession at present. The occupation of teaching, however, is in the process of becoming a profession. If this professionalization appears to progress more haltingly than some other occupations, it is because teaching is more limited by historical and cultural traditions of dependence upon other social institutions. The issue of teacher professionalism may be one of the most important issues that contemporary students of education will face in this century.

Summary

In light of the conceptual overview of education and schooling presented in this chapter, we will now present some tentative ideas about what it means to be a school teacher in modern society.

A school teacher is not simply anyone who teaches, for we all "teach" each other informally as we interact with our peers, our parents, our children, our neighbors, our coworkers, and our friends. Much of this "teaching" is done casually and without self-consciousness. Our "students" are people who come to us voluntarily to learn.

A *school teacher* is not an informal educator. School teachers are institutional position holders who are expected to perform certain duties and are given certain privileges in the performance of these duties. They are also granted greater or lesser opportunities for self-expression in the performance of their roles.

A *professional school teacher* is one who performs his or her roles with a self-conscious eye toward the social service nature of his or her work. He or she has a great deal of personal autonomy and the knowledge and ability to apply, directly or indirectly, systematic principles of interpersonal behavior. A professional teacher has a close attachment and commitment to a reference group of fellow service workers. Most teachers today value this professional ideal.

Thus, school teaching may be defined as a highly ethical occupation, based on knowledge of institutional behavior that will facilitate learning. The school teacher is a moral individual—i.e., moral in the broadest social sense—a learned individual, and an organizationally attached individual. He or she enjoys working with young people to help them grow intellectually and emotionally. To be a school teacher, then, seems to involve a very important responsibility.

To teach school responsibly in a fast-paced, complex society requires that a teacher keep abreast of events and forces in the social environment outside the school which affect the school's operation, and of intrinsic changes in the school milieu and system. Only by so doing can modern teachers maintain their roles and role-related skills and teach dynamically and authentically, in tune with the times and the changing educational needs of their students.

Related Concepts

acculturation   The process of learning the basic cultural elements of a host society. Immigrants to a new country undergo the process of acculturation.

enculturation   The process of learning the cultural elements of one's native society

literacy   In its broadest sense, the ability to interpret communicated symbols of any type and from any source

reference group   A group to which one refers for guidance when contemplating behavior. Its members may be "significant others" or "generalized others," depending upon the closeness of their relationship to those who use them as references.

school culture   The unique social heredity of a particular school or school system

secondary social institution   An institution that is larger and more formal, specialized, and indirect in its relationships than are primary institutions such as the family. The modern public school is usually considered a secondary institution.

SES   A commonly used abbreviation for "socio-economic-status," or "social class"

social institutions   Standardized solutions to the problems of collective life in society. Also, the basic structures for normal social functioning, including language, the family, education, schooling, politics, the economy, etc.

socialization   The process of acquiring modes of interacting effectively in a society or group

social stratum   A layer in the horizontal division of society into identifiable social classes and ranks

sociological stranger   A person residing in a community who does not belong to a group in that community. Because of their unusual geographical mobility, teachers have often been sociological strangers.

Suggested Activity

Interview several professional people (physicians, attorneys, scientists, engineers, social workers, journalists, etc.). Using the criteria for professions discussed in this chapter, try to discover what, if anything, the occupations of the people you interview have in common.

Follow this up by talking with some teachers at the elementary, secondary, and college levels to assess their occupational self-conceptions in comparison with the first group interviewed.

References and Notes

1.   See Alvin Boskoff, "Functional Analysis as a Source of a Theoretical Repertory and Research Tasks in the Study of Social Change," in George K. Zollschan and Walter Hirsch, eds., *Explorations in Social Change* (Boston: Houghton Mifflin, 1964), pp. 213–44.

2.   *Ibid.*

3.   A major work on the nature of social institutions is J.O. Hertzler, *Social Institutions* (Lincoln: University of Nebraska Press, 1946).

4.   For example, *see* Anne F. Kilguss, "Using Soap Operas as a Therapeutic Tool," *Social Casework* 66 (October 1974): 623–43.

5.   *See* Studs Terkel, *Working: People Talk about What They Do All Day and How They Feel about What They Do* (New York: Pantheon Books, 1974).

6.   Will Herberg, "Religion and Culture in Present-Day America," in Amatai Etzioni, ed., *Anatomies of America: Sociological Perspectives* (New York: The Macmillan Co., 1969) pp. 255–65.

7.   Frederic M. Thrasher, *The Gang* (Chicago: University of Chicago Press, 1927).

8.   Dominick La Capra, *Emile Durkheim: Sociologist and Philosopher* (Ithaca: Cornell University Press, 1974), pp. 144–86.

9.   For further elaboration of this idea in the context of student teaching, *see* Sand-

ford W. Reitman, "An Alternative Field Work Model for Prospective Teachers," *Interchange* 4 (1973): 61–79.

10. For an excellent and still relevant treatment of the somewhat artificial institution of the formal school, *see* Willard Waller, *The Sociology of Teaching* (New York: John Wiley & Sons, 1932).

11. Anthony Wallace, "The Kinds of Learning," in Jonathan C. McLendon, ed., *Social Foundations of Education: Current Readings from the Behavioral Sciences* (New York: The Macmillan Co., 1966), pp. 272, 273.

12. *See* Hertzler, *Social Institutions,* pp. 50–67.

13. *Ibid.*

14. *See* Howard S. Becker, "The Teacher in the Authority System of the Public School," *Journal of Educational Sociology* 27 (November 1953): 128–41.

15. There is some disagreement over the extent to which public schooling has become bureaucratized. For instance, one recent study of the professionalization of teachers is based on the belief that modern society and its schools have become dominated by bureaucratic forms of organization. The movement toward professionalization of teachers is essentially an effort to counter this dominant trend. *See* Ronald G. Corwin, *Militant Professionalism: A Study of Organizational Conflict in High Schools* (New York: Appleton-Century-Crofts, 1970). But another noted sociologist of education disputes this thesis, arguing that although bureaucratic rules and red tape are common in schools, teachers and students are often forced to disregard them in the classroom in order to interact well. Thus, although school administrators might desire bureaucratic organization for efficient management, school teachers and their students limit the extent to which management values control the institution. *See* Robert Dreeban, *The Nature of Teaching: Schools and the Work of Teachers* (Glenview, Ill.: Scott, Foresman and Co., 1970), pp. 47, 48.

16. Peter M. Blau, *The Dynamics of Bureaucracy: A Study of Interpersonal Relations in Two Government Agencies,* 2nd ed. (Chicago: The University of Chicago Press, 1963), pp. 1, 2.

17. While the concept is derived largely from writings on the political process, it may have significant implications for modern educational thought as well. S.N. Eisenstadt, "Processes of Change and Institutionalization of the Political Systems of Centralized Empires," in Zollschan and Hirsch, *Social Change,* p. 449.

18. Waller, *Sociology of Teaching,* p. 9.

19. This concept emerges from some of the numerous writings of a major contemporary social psychologist of the so-called "dramaturgical" school. *See* Erving Goffman, *Asylums* (Garden City, N.Y.: Doubleday, 1961).

20. Waller, *Sociology of Teaching,* pp. 176–87.

21. Basil Bernstein, "Social Class and Linguistic Development: A Theory of Social Learning," in A.H. Halsey, J. Floud, and C.A. Anderson, eds., *Education, Economy and Society* (New York: The Free Press, 1961), pp. 288–314.

22. Richard L. Berkman, "Students in Court: Free Speech and the Functions of Schooling in America," *Harvard Educational Review* 40 (September 1970): 567–95.

23. Berkman, "Students in Court," p. 581.

24.   Louis Fischer and David Schimmel, *The Civil Rights of Teachers* (New York: Harper & Row, 1973), p. 73.

25.   The first person to formulate these ideas systematically was Robert Merton. See "Manifest and Latent Functions: Toward the Codification of Functional Analysis in Sociology," in Robert Merton, ed., *Social Theory and Social Structure,* 2nd ed. (Glencoe, Ill.: The Free Press, 1957), pp. 19–84.

26.   Richard L. Derr, *A Taxonomy of Social Purposes of Public Schools* (New York: David McKay Co., 1973).

27.   For example, see Goslin's discussion of primary and secondary functions. David A. Goslin, *The School in Contemporary Society* (Glenview, Ill.: Scott, Foresman and Co., 1965), pp. 1–18.

28.   This discussion of traditional and to some extent the following discussion of emerging functions have been developed through borrowing and adapting from a variety of sources, notably Gordon Lee, "The Changing Role of the Teacher," in *The Changing American School,* The Sixty-fifth Yearbook of the National Society for the Study of Education, Part II, Herman G. Richey, ed. (Chicago: The University of Chicago Press, 1966), pp. 9–31, and Goslin, *The School in Contemporary Society.*

29.   George Spindler, "Education in a Transforming American Culture," *Harvard Educational Review* 25 (Summer 1955): 156.

30.   United States Office of Education, *Report on Education Research* 6 (Jan. 30, 1974): 1.

31.   Marshal McLuhan and Quentin Fiore, *The Medium is the Message* (New York: Random House, 1967).

32.   A fine discussion of the changing role of the media in the lives of young people and its implications for teachers is found in John B. Haney and Eldon J. Ullmer, *Educational Communications and Technology: An Introduction for Teachers* 2nd ed. (Dubuque, Iowa: Wm. C. Brown Co., 1975).

33.   John J. Patrick, *Political Socialization of American Youth: Implications for Secondary School Social Studies* (Washington, D.C.: National Council for the Social Studies, 1967), pp. 6, 7.

34.   For an excellent discussion of the problem of loss of community, see Philip E. Slater, *The Pursuit of Loneliness: American Culture at the Breaking Point* (Boston: Beacon Press, 1970).

35.   For an extended discussion of the "invisible curriculum," see Mario D. Fantini and Gerald Weinstein, *The Disadvantaged: Challenge to Education* (New York: Harper & Row, 1968), pp. 41–93.

36.   *Ibid.*

37.   Leila Calhoun Deasy, *Persons and Positions: Individuals and Their Social Locations* (Washington, D.C.: The Catholic University Press, 1969), p. 227.

38.   Ralph Linton, *The Study of Man* (New York: Appleton-Century-Crofts, 1936), p. 114.

39.   The following list is adapted from William Clark Trow, "Role Functions of the Teacher in the Instructional Group," in *The Dynamics of Instructional Groups,* the Fifty-Ninth Yearbook of the National Society for the Study of Education, Part II, pp. 30–50.

40.   William Vernon Hicks and Frank H. Blackington, "The Profession as an Idea," in Frank H. Blackington and Robert S. Patterson, eds., *School, Society, and the*

Professional Educator: A Book of Readings (New York: Holt, Rinehart and Winston, 1968), pp. 21, 22.

41.   This list was adapted from Everett C. Hughes, "Professions," *Daedalus* 92 (Fall 1963): 655–68.

42.   *Ibid.,* pp. 666–67.

43.   Paul A. Olson, Report of Study Commission on Undergraduate Education and the Education of Teachers (Lincoln: University of Nebraska, 1973), p. 1.

44.   Don Lortie, "Shared Ordeal and Induction to Work," Howard Becker, *et al.* eds., in *Institutions and the Person* (Chicago: Aldine Publishing Co., 1968), pp. 252–64.

45.   Hicks and Blackington, "Profession as Idea," p. 21.

46.   *Ibid.*

47.   *Ibid.*

48.   Harry Broudy, *The Real World of the Public Schools* (New York: Harcourt Brace Jovanovich, 1972), p. 60.

49.   Wilbert E. Moore, *The Professions: Roles and Rules* (New York: Russell Sage Foundation, 1970).

50.   Ivan Illich, *Deschooling Society* (New York: Harper & Row, 1971), and Everett Reimer, *School Is Dead: Alternatives in Education* (Garden City, N.Y.: Doubleday and Co., 1972).

4

The Historic Development
of Schools

Both formal and informal agencies of learning and teaching have played important roles in the education of people throughout history. In this chapter we will be concerned with the growth of such agencies in the past and with some of the important leaders who have been associated with their development.

Education and Teaching
in Preliterate Society

Informal Aspects

During the thousands of years of history preceding the development of writing, human societies strove to educate their young to the prevailing cultural patterns and lifeways of the group primarily through informal processes of education. Institutions that performed educational functions for preliterate peoples were rarely separated from other social activities. Children learned the folkways and mores of their society through direct involvement in day-to-day affairs of the tribe. In a sense, they anticipated John Dewey and the progressive educators by several millennia as they "learned by doing," by participating fully in community life. The chief incentive to learn in primitive societies was the desire to belong, which is always a primary source of motivation to learn. And education in preliterate societies encouraged strict conformity to the status quo, not creative independence.

Formal Aspects

The school as we conceive of it today did not play a role in preliterate society, but some types of formal education did take place. Anthropologists sometimes refer to the institutions that carried on such activities as "mystery schools." Wallace lists three kinds:

> ... the bush schools, which indoctrinated pubescent males and females with the secret lore of adults; the religious schools which induct novitiates into religious cults and secret societies; and the professional schools which instruct young shamans in the arts of their profession. These schools have developed out of rites of passage, particularly initiation rituals, and hence are sometimes called initiation schools.[1]

The "bush schools" have been most widely observed by anthropologists. When a boy was about to be inducted into the mysteries of adulthood in the tribe, he was often sent out to live in the bush for a period during which sacred tribal myths and rituals were inculcated. The novitiates were isolated from the outside world and sworn to secrecy by the religious leaders (teachers) of the tribe, as they made the symbolic passage from childhood to adulthood. Failure to be a "good student" brought severe punishment, and attempts to escape occasionally brought the penalty of death.[2] Girls received a somewhat comparable schooling, usually closer to the village.

The Development of Schools as Separate Institutions

Wallace defines a school as "an institution that deliberately and systematically, by the presentation of symbols in reading matter, lecture, or ritual, attempts to transform from a condition of ignorance to one of enlightenment the intellect, the morality, and the technical knowledge and skills of an attentive group of persons assembled in a definite place at a definite time."[3]

The true forerunner of the modern school did not begin to appear until the advent of written languages, sometime around 3000 BC. At this time, nomadic tribes began to settle down and develop more complex civilizations in the "Fertile Crescent"—the region around the Tigris–Euphrates Valley in the Middle East—and along the Indus and Ganges rivers in India and the Yellow River in China.[4]

The school evolved chiefly as a means to perpetuate the language and literature of these early oriental societies and to teach some of its members to write in order to engage in commerce or to copy sacred literature. Later the development of centralized monarchies brought about a need for written government documents to communicate from the king's offices in the capital to the provinces. This further encouraged the development and refinement of rudimentary schools for segments of the population.

At first, formal schooling was intended primarily for the privileged upper-classes, who dominated religious, economic, and political affairs. The majority of people—as was true until fairly recently—continued to receive most or all their education from informal sources in their families, workplaces, or temples.

In general, these first schools performed the latent, if not manifest, function of preserving existing cultural patterns of their societies. They did this by venerating the written literature of their past through teaching practices that stressed copying passages of this literature and rote memorization almost devoid of concern for meaning. A partial exception to this are the Hebrew primary and secondary schools, which existed on a fairly widespread basis.[5] Although they emphasized the authority of religious leaders, the Jewish people have always considered it important that boys (most schools excluded girls) learn to discuss and interpret the laws and the traditions of the group. The Hebraic stress on ethical monotheism and individual morality influenced Christianity as it developed in the Roman Empire. Since the fall of Rome, Western history has been profoundly influenced by Christian values and customs, even when formally secularized, as in the United States. Scholars accurately refer to the Judeo-Christian heritage of modern civilization and of education.

Some Examples of Schooling in Societies of the Past

Education and schooling always reflect some aspects of a society's culture and dominating ethos. They either seek to preserve sociocultural values and behavior or to adapt society's members to sociocultural change (a much rarer function). Schools normally operate to maintain the existing social order; they are usually mechanisms for safeguarding society through the acquisition of knowledge, values, and skills. With these ideas in mind, let us examine briefly some of the diverse forms of schooling that prevailed during the formative periods of Western society.

The Ancient Period

Among the early civilizations in the Western world whose educational systems have been studied in depth by scholars are those of the ancient Greeks and the Romans. Both societies developed highly advanced cultures that have profoundly influenced modern life and education.

Education in Ancient Greece.   The ancient Greeks have customarily been considered our chief progenitors in the intellectual realm. However, the honor accorded ancient Greece is reserved primarily for the Athenians. In actuality, Greece had numerous city-states, each with its own conditions and educational forms.

Sparta was the most powerful city-state in lower Greece, having been first settled around the eighth century BC. It was under constant attack from its hostile neighbors, and developed an educational system that reflected a predominantly warlike ethos of social and cultural life. The educational system was almost entirely under state control.

The central function of formal education for boys was to become brave, skilled warriors for the state and for girls to become mothers of warriors. All boys from the citizen class were taken from their parents after the age of seven and schooled in reading, writing, and how to be cunning and hardy future soldiers. At age eighteen they received intensive military training for two years, and from age twenty served actively in the army for ten years. If they survived their military experience, they were made full citizens and required to marry at age thirty.

Girls stayed at home for their education, but were also organized for regular physical training sessions in order to strengthen their bodies for their future roles as bearers of strong and healthy sons for the army.

Sparta is an example of an early educational system designed intentionally to reflect the drive for self-preservation of a totalitarian society.

Sparta's major rival, Athens, developed a very different type of educational pattern. This city-state did not have the continual problems with foreign invaders that Sparta did. Athens developed into a world trade and cultural center that at first respected enlightened social participation and political democracy and later extolled extreme individualism.

Three of the most profoundly influential thinkers were Athenians. After the Golden Age of Athens in the fifth century BC and prior to its subjugation by Macedonia in the third and second centuries BC, each of these thinkers left a deep imprint upon Western educational theory and practice. They were: Socrates (469–399 BC) who left no writings, Plato (427–346 BC), a student of Socrates who put his teacher's words onto paper, and Aristotle (386–322 BC), the leading pupil of Plato and probably the most influential of the three until recent years.

Socrates was a pragmatist who employed a method of instruction whereby his students, mostly young men of wealth who followed him around on the streets of Athens, asked their teacher questions about life and justice and were led to reason out their own answers. The *Socratic method* of dialogics is admired and sometimes employed even today.

Plato is usually viewed as the prototype of the idealist. Instead of teaching from the streets, like his mentor Socrates, he opened a philosophical academy where he taught that truth was ultimately determined by reason alone. To Plato, ideas, and not the mundane "real" world, were the substance of all truth. Education, then, must be highly abstract and nonempirical. Plato set down much of his educational theory in the *Republic*. This text developed the utopian ideal of a state run by philosopher-kings selected from the best minds in society, after having undergone a very extensive educational experience that at first was universal for all citizens. Plato influenced the thinking of early Christian scholars, such as Saint Augustine, who, in turn, influenced the medieval Church and its educational values.

Aristotle was a realist, an early "scientist." Through his influence on his student King Philip of Macedon and his writings on the value of leisure, temperance, and contemplative rationality, Aristotle had a profound effect upon the late Middle Ages. Thomas Aquinas, the great philosopher of that period, rationalized the Catholic Church's dominance over human affairs by synthesizing the notions of Christian faith with Aristotelian reason. Renaissance and Enlightenment thinkers were also heavily indebted to Aristotle.

Athenian education was a family responsibility up to about age seven. Beyond that age, male children of the citizen class, especially the sons of the aristocracy, were often tutored by slaves (*paidagogos,* or pedagogues). They were given instruction in music, poetry, reading, writing, and some arithmetic, and then sent to a private *palaestra* for physical training. At age fifteen, the wealthy would attend public *gymnasia* for more physical exercises or for more academic work.

Later in the Grecian era, private teaching sophists instructed older adolescents in grammar, rhetoric, and oratory for fees. Finally, the young men might attend a school of philosophy, such as Plato's, or a lyceum to learn natural science.

The schools of Athens never had a prescribed curriculum, diplomas, or degrees. In general, they were much more informal than our schools today.[6] Teachers in Athens held either an extremely high status—particularly those who, like Socrates, Plato, and Aristotle, worked with older, upper-class youth for no pay, or a very low status—usually elementary level teachers other than slaves who needed to accept fees in order to support themselves.

As in Sparta, girls were educated at home primarily by informal methods, as were poorer boys who apprenticed as carpenters or other craftsmen.

Athenian education, at least in its idealized form, reflected a flourishing society and the concern of the leisure class for public service and for a healthy balance of mind, body, and emotions.

Education in Ancient Rome.   When Rome was a republic (fifth century to the first century BC), education was largely an informal responsibility of the home. Gradually, private schools began to appear and by about 200 BC were common as Rome expanded its colonization of the Mediterranean world, and Greece came under its domination.

As Rome grew to be a world empire, the influence of Greece upon its educational institutions also increased. The Romans adopted Greek ideas of schooling and teaching, and incorporated them in secular schools (for the wealthy primarily), although they modified these ideas to suit their own conceptions of life, which were essentially utilitarian.

The Roman elementary school (the *Ludus*) and secondary school (the *Grammaticus*) were often staffed by Greek teachers who, at least initially, instructed in the Greek language. The elementary schools concentrated on teaching reading, while the secondary schools taught Latin or Greek grammar. Eventually rhetorical schools arose for advanced education. These schools concentrated on the preparation of future statesmen as orators primarily through instruction in rhetoric, as well as the other liberal arts of grammar, classical literature, logic, geometry, astronomy, music, physics, civil law, and philosophy. As a practical people, the Romans used their schools and subject matter for much more utilitarian ends than did the comparatively esoteric Hellenes from whom they borrowed their basic notions of education and many of their most highly regarded teachers.

One of the world's great educators was a Roman who lived during the early empire period, Quintilian (c. AD 35–97). In contrast to most of his harsher contemporaries, Quintilian considered good teaching to be a matter of individualizing instruction within small groups and avoiding corporal punishment.

As the Roman Empire began to deteriorate and decline, its schools concentrated increasingly upon sterile form and rote memorization instead of upon preparation for service to the community and current realities. By the fifth century AD, Rome was sufficiently demoralized as a society for invasion from outside to be successful.

The Middle Ages (AD 500 to AD 1300)

As the Roman Empire declined, Christianity became the dominant cultural force in Western Europe. It eventually was institutionalized in the Roman Catholic Church, which controlled most of life—including education—during the Dark Ages, the first part of the Middle Ages. Monasteries and monks, knights and crusades, feudalism and serfs characterized society in this era. Craft and merchant guilds were established by skilled artisans of the rising bourgeoisie who had begun to concentrate in towns and cities to escape feudal ties and to gain material prosperity.

As in all historical periods, the educational institutions of the Middle Ages reflected the sociocultural order that preceded and gave rise to those institutions. In addition to the informal educational agencies of the home, the Church, and the feudal system that taught the majority of people in the Middle Ages, there also arose a number of patterns of formal education and schooling to serve religious functionaries, the landed aristocracy, craftsmen, and burghers, among others.

The most common formal education, particularly in the early Middle Ages, was religious in character. Catechumenal, catechetical, monastery, and cathedral schools arose to inculcate Christian ideology, ritual, and Latin literacy in those who wanted to become members of the Church or to become priests and monks.

A parallel system of chivalric education developed to enable children of the nobility to become warrior knights or ladies-in-waiting. "School" was the court of the overlord, where boys from fourteen to twenty-one studied the arts of gentlemanly grace and courtesy and learned the art and science of warfare. Some rudimentary training in reading, writing, and religion was also sometimes given. At the completion of his service as an attendant to the nobility, the young man of wealth was usually knighted and expected to assume the military and romantic roles for which he had been educated. Girls of the noble class were taught the arts and crafts of home management, how to read, write, and keep books, and proper religious faith to prepare them to become ladies-in-waiting or for marriage.

Like Spartan education, chivalric education for both sexes during the Middle Ages was not scholarly, or practical, as contrasted with most other formal education before and since.

For the working class, the craft guild, which became highly organized toward the end of the Middle Ages, furnished an education based on apprenticeship. A young boy would be bound over to a master craftsman for several years in order to learn the skills of his trade, as well as perhaps some reading and writing helpful in carrying on the trade. After this period—which lasted from three to twelve years—the young man became a journeyman, traveling about and gaining more experience by working for a variety of masters for a fee set by the guild. Finally, after creating his "masterpiece," he was fully admitted (licensed, in effect) as a member of the guild, permitting him to open his own shop and take on his own apprentices.

Besides Church-controlled schools, the chivalric tradition, and the apprenticeship system, some private secular schools emerged in towns during the later Middle Ages. These schools were conducted by public school teachers who offered grammar, classical literature, law or medicine at a relatively low level.[7] Such town schools represented the beginnings of formal education for members of the emerging middle class who saw practical advantages in acquiring skills useful in retail trade and the professions.

Finally, we should note the beginnings of higher education in terms somewhat similar to the university system of today. The medieval university at first was established and controlled primarily by the Church for the preparation of priests. Later many universities became cosmopolitan centers of liberal education and prepared professionals in theology, medicine, and law. Their students, who often came from many countries, organized themselves into student guilds for protection from townspeople and from their teachers, as well as for purposes of national identification and pride. Aside from the minute, analytic study of the Greek classics (scholasticism) and of their prospective professions, the young men attending medieval universities often enjoyed a drinking and socializing life somewhat akin to that in which many contemporary college students engage.

Some of the teachers and professors at the medieval universities became important intellectual influences upon the development of the culture of that period and the historical periods that followed. Thomas Aquinas (1225–1274) was a scholar at the University of Paris who attempted a major reconciliation of the secular Aristotelian logic or reasoning with the Christian faith. In *Summa Theologiae,* he held that we live in a world of universal truth ordered by the perfect God; this world is revealed to men primarily through faith in God's laws, with the secondary aid of reason. Through his writing, St. Thomas altered the official doctrine of the Catholic Church and allowed for the resurgence of theoretical studies of the classics in an academic world that had been dominated almost exclusively by religious thought. He thus paved the way for the secular Renaissance and Enlightenment thought which in turn set the course for much of the advanced scholarship and collective action in the modern age of Western civilization.

Although formal learning was at a relatively low level during the Dark Ages, it was never completely abandoned. The university was a highly respected form of formal education, as were the learned university scholastics who helped revive learning as the Middle Ages came to an end in the twelfth century. Religious thought predominated in schooling and teaching throughout most of the period. With the reconciliation of classicism with Christianity, the influence of medieval education continues to the present day.

The Renaissance and the
Rise of Humanism

With no sudden break from the overriding spirit of the Middle Ages, changes began to occur in the thinking and interests of some, particularly upper-status people from about the fourteenth century on. As religious restrictions began to diminish with the gradual decline of the medieval Church and the development of national states throughout much of Europe, an interest was revitalized in the classical and secular literature of ancient Greece and Rome by the humanists, "radical" scholars of the Renaissance who sought to understand more about human nature by studying the original works of men such as Plato and Aristotle and Virgil and Cicero.

As the revival in classical literature by the humanists was occurring, there was an even more dynamic and creative flowering of expression in painting, sculpture, and architecture. The great Renaissance works, which today occupy places in metropolitan museums, began to depict the human body and other natural forms, a practice that the spiritualism and Gothic formalism of the Christian Church had arrested. Original literature was produced by authors writing in their vernacular language; for example, Dante's *Divine Comedy,* written in Italian, and Chaucer's *Canterbury Tales,* written in Middle English. The beginnings of modern science are seen by the invention of gunpowder and the printing press. The end of the long period of medievalism and the beginnings of the modern period were signalled by the Renaissance and the revival of learning in the period from about 1300 to 1500.

One of the most exemplary figures of the later part of the Renaissance is the humanist scholar Erasmus of Rotterdam (1466–1536). He was caught between the Catholic Church and Luther's effort to repudiate the authority of the Church. Erasmus criticized both and stood alone in his efforts "to unify faith and reason by a feat of piety and scholarship that would synthesize Christianity and antiquity ... to cleanse, purify, and strengthen Christianity through the study of its classical sources."[8]

As an educator Erasmus urged careful attention from the earliest years of a child's life to the study of the classics in home and school, and mild and gentle treatment of students by refined and knowledgeable teachers:

Much of Erasmus' character and thought is reflected in his educational theory. We find in it the religious and moral reformer, the advocate of peace, the satirical critic of the follies of mankind, the man who hopes for the reconciliation of faith and reason, the liberal and tolerant personality endowed with a fine understanding for human nature, the admirer of classical letters, the scholar of the literary, not the experimental type, and the wanderer without a vernacular or a nation.[9]

Erasmus embodied the humanist ideal of the time, and formal education sought to impart this ideal to the sons of the wealthy nobility and the emerging well-to-do middle classes, particularly through secondary education by tutors or in private schools. According to Pounds:

Renaissance education, which had a very great effect on Europe and later on America, was largely for the elite and stressed classical literary humanism and the consequent development of the gentlemanly graces.[10]

Although the humanists were chiefly interested in the education of the upper classes in Greek and Latin, the masses began to feel some of the period's effects. Elementary schools began to teach reading and writing of the vernacular language to some of the common people. This education was generally inadequate compared to what was offered in secondary schools; as some still believe even today, the Renaissance man thought that anyone can teach younger children. The prejudice of the age also was against vernacular literature and languages; Greek and Latin languages were considered superior to contemporary studies.

During the Renaissance, the universities did not change much from the scholastic tradition within which they had developed during the late Middle Ages. As is often the case today, older institutions of foremost prestige and renown, such as the University of Paris, steadfastly held onto pre-humanist patterns of curriculum and instruction. The education at these universities continued to be Church-related, while newer, less prestigious universities led the way in curricular and instructional reform along humanist lines.

Thus, the Renaissance acted as a sort of wedge between the past and the future, helping to further open up the door to the secular, as well as to dissident religious trends of succeeding periods of Western culture and education.

The Reformation and the Scientific Revolution (1500–1700)

Patterns of education in Europe, and subsequently in America, were significantly affected and substantially altered by the events of the Reformation. During this period of great unrest and conflict, the Catholic Church, which had dominated Western religious and civil affairs since

the Middle Ages, came under severe attack by Martin Luther (1483–1546) in Germany, John Calvin (1509–1564) in Switzerland, and other Protestant reformers. The first stirrings of an inductive science, based on empiricism, began to be felt in intellectual circles formerly ruled by Aristotelian deductive logic.

As the Protestant Reformation and the Catholic Counter-Reformation were altering the religious basis of European culture, and the Scientific Revolution was transforming the foundations of serious scholarship, important events were taking place on the political and economic fronts of Western civilization. A long-term trend toward nationalism and loyalty to the nation-state, first embodied by a central monarchy, developed during the Reformation. The increased power of the "third estate"—the commercial middle class of the cities and towns —seriously challenged the institution of feudalism. These and related movements and events altered European conceptions of education and planted the seeds from which contemporary systems of schooling ultimately grew.

However, the single major influence of the period upon education continued to be the religious institution. The Protestant reformers wanted all children—rich and poor, boys and girls—to be literate in order to read the Bible in the vernacular tongues of their nations. Efforts were made, especially in the countries of northern Europe, to establish universal, publicly supported elementary schools and to ensure that school teaching became a respectable and carefully supervised occupation.

As a result of Protestant pressures, the Catholic Church began to make some efforts along these lines as well. The consequences are not especially noteworthy. The two-class educational system that had operated since the days of the Greeks and before still dominated the thought of traditionalists and reformers alike. Most of the reformers, with the possible exception of a few such as the great pansophist John Comenius (1592–1670), still believed that the well-to-do (which now included in part the commercial middle classes, as well as the nobility) should receive the benefits of a classical secondary education in the Latin grammar schools, which had become entrenched during the Renaissance. The masses were to be satisfied with a limited education in the vernacular languages and under repressive disciplinary arrangements, and with learning a trade. As crude and narrowly conceived as they were, the elementary schools that began to emerge during this period represented a previously unconsidered source of enlightenment for great multitudes of people.

The qualifications required to teach in the public schools of this period were improved. As Luther said in a letter to German community leaders, after urging that provisions for elementary education be made by each town for the enhancement of Christian principles:

> But each one, you say, may educate and discipline his own sons and daughters. To which I reply: we see indeed how it goes with this teaching and training. And where it is carried to the highest point, and is attended with success, it results in nothing more than that the learners, in some measure, acquire a forced external propriety of manners; in other respects they remain dunces, knowing nothing, and incapable of giving aid or advice. But were they instructed in schools or elsewhere, by thoroughly qualified male or female teachers, who taught the languages, other arts, and history, then . . . they could regulate their views, and order their course of life in the fear of God, having become wise in judging what is to be sought and what is to be avoided in this outward life, and capable of advising and directing others.[11]

Along with the religious impact of the Reformation and Counter-Reformation on European society and culture, came a trend toward nationalism. One of the educational consequences of this trend was a transfer of school control from private and religious sources to civil authorities, primarily at the elementary level. The elementary school has been more or less under public control since its inception during the Reformation. The classical secondary school—the school for the well to do—until the nineteenth century, and later in England, generally was considered the domain of private interests. Of course, more was said about public and universal education than was ever actually done to bring it about at this time. The idea, however, was planted for later proponents of nationalism to tend more carefully. It is of interest to note, however, that as early as 1531 a law was passed in the Netherlands requiring that all children either go to school or be apprenticed.[12] And, about one hundred years later in the New England colonies, Massachusetts passed the first American laws requiring elementary level instruction and providing for public elementary school teachers and Latin grammar schools.[13]

As regards the influence of the newly powerful middle classes and commercialism upon education, the dramatic rise to importance of the "third estate" brought in its wake a desire by prosperous merchants to send their children to already established humanistic private schools or to help found new schools to teach the utilitarian interests in trade, navigation, geography, and communication. The middle class also participated to some extent in providing philanthropic schools for the education of the increasing numbers of poor children who thronged the cities as the rural feudal system was broken down by the commercial revolution.

Another major impact upon the thought of this time, and eventually upon formal education at advanced levels, was the introduction of *inductive logic,* as explicated by Francis Bacon (1561–1626) and other scientists of the time. Aristotelian versions of realism which depend upon deductive logic, and Platonic idealism, which relies upon *a priori* reasoning, were strongly challenged by Bacon's work. Bacon's *Novum Organum* ("New Method") argued that truth, as opposed to dogma, is discovered by accumulating experiences (or data) of a common type in order to induce or draw a generalization.

The early version of empirical knowledge, or knowledge dependent upon the senses, is now considered obsolete. Contemporary scientists construct an *hypothesis,* or implication deduced from a *theory* (itself a result of synthesized experience) to test ideas through experience. The early conception of inductive science, crude as it may be by modern standards, was a radical step forward in the history of ideas. It helped ease the way for future generations of secular intellectuals by forcing some sectarian thinkers of the period, both Catholic and Protestant, to the conclusion that the older ways of rationalizing religious and intellectual schemes were unduly dogmatic and the conclusions not necessarily valid.

For most of the leaders of the established orthodoxies of the time, however, the introduction of inductive science was a potentially dangerous threat to their vested interests in the status quo. Science and scientific ways of teaching were discouraged in the expanding school systems of the Reformation period. And, in fact, science has not yet come fully into its own on the educational scene of Western Europe and America, except perhaps in the universities. The religious and idealistic influences of the Reformation still are very powerful.

Although never a widespread intellectual development during the Reformation—when new versions of old dogmas were the main cultural innovations—the scientific revolution did stir some of the more open minds of the day, including those of a few educators. A Moravian bishop, John Amos Comenius (1592–1670) was one of the most brilliant educational thinkers of his era. Because his ideas were far ahead of his time, he was not particularly instrumental in effectuating educational change while he lived. His contributions to education, like those of the new scientists who inspired him, influenced the great educators of the succeeding Enlightenment, not those of his own generation.

Comenius wrote a number of books on universal education and on teaching, the most famous being the *Didactica Magna* ("Great Didactic"). He also wrote what was probably the first children's picture book *Orbis Sensualim Pictus* ("The Visible World Illustrated"). Comenius was a "sense–realist", an educator who, like the new scientists, believed that learning occurs primarily through one's sensory perceptions of the world. He proposed that all children be formally educated from birth on and that those who show academic promise be permitted to continue to adulthood, regardless of the social rank ascribed to them by the accident of birth.

Comenius believed that children should learn initially through direct experiences in which their five senses are confronted. Words should be used to convey meaning, not employed for memorizing passages by rote. Comenius also urged that children work together in classes so that they could gain ideas from each other; today, we call this "peer teaching." And, finally, we might consider his early interest in what are now called "simulation games," a teaching strategy used when actual experience cannot be readily or safely used in class.

Comenius, who was influenced by modern scientific method, was a radical educational thinker for his time. If the Reformation began with an effort to reform organized Christianity, it could be said to have moved toward its conclusion with an effort to revise all thought, including that of education. We know today that the scientific revolution ultimately had an even greater impact upon the subsequent history of the world than did the religious Reformation. However, the public still debates whether or not to teach the Biblical story of creation along with the Darwinian theory of evolution in science classes.

The Enlightenment, or the
Age of Reason (1700–1830)

The Enlightenment was essentially a reaction by intellectuals of the eighteenth and early nineteenth centuries to the parochialism and authoritarianism of the Reformation. It was a major intellectual movement encompassing a variety of spheres of thought, including inductive science, secular rationalism, and a growing belief in the dignity of the common man, particularly the middle class man. The Enlightenment symbolized the rise of faith in laissez faire economics and social liberalism. These new faiths were accompanied by significant political efforts to reduce the power of centralized monarchies, who based their claim to rule upon divine right, and to replace them with democratic forms of government based upon the natural rights of all citizens.

The Age of Reason was reflected in educational developments. These were not always embodied in specific school reforms, but the thoughts of educators of this period later influenced European and American schooling patterns of the nineteenth and twentieth centuries.

John Locke (1632–1704), an Englishman, contributed greatly to the formation of American ideas about republican government, organized around a balance of power between the legislative, judicial, and executive branches. Locke argued that governments become legitimate and rational by obtaining the consent of the propertied citizenry through exercise of the franchise.

Locke also wrote on the need for a system of schools for the poor, a less bookish gentlemanly education for the sons of the upper-middle and upper classes, and most importantly on the **epistemological** roots of human learning.

According to Locke, whose general ideas on this subject are now taken for granted by most social scientists, human beings are not born with innately held ideas as most scholars since Plato had believed. Instead, at birth the mind is a *tabula rasa*—a blank tablet upon which environment makes its imprint. The person receives sensory impressions, or perceptions from his experience with the environment, and reflects upon these perceptions. A good education is one that helps a child to develop his sensory apparatus and his ability to think in a disciplined fashion about what he has experienced. The advocates of formal discipline of the various faculties that at that time were believed to determine human effort took Locke's views on the need for training the ability to reason as a justification for the continued domination of the curriculum by the classics.[14] Locke, however, was concerned far more with developing the capacity of individuals of the "better classes" to think independently in order to become worthy leaders of society.

The major intellectual counterpart of Locke was the Frenchman Jean Jacques Rousseau (1712–1778) who championed social liberalism and the natural rights of all men, not just those with property. In his great educational work, *Emile*, Rousseau proposed an individualized teaching (tutorial) program from birth to adulthood for boys. (His view on the place of girls was as unenlightened as most other thinkers of the period.) Rousseau's educational theories were designed to preserve man's natural virtue from the "corrupting" influence of civilization. By means of careful psychological guidance through several maturational stages, a child would eventually grow up to survive in a society that was essentially degenerative. This educational theory of romantic individualism unblemished by the corruptive influence of culture has had some influence in the twentieth century; notions of child-centeredness and "progressive education" are related to it.

Another renowned Enlightenment educator from whom innovations were borrowed by U.S. educators was Johann Heinrich Pestalozzi (1746–1827). Unlike Locke and Rousseau, Pestalozzi was a Swiss school teacher of the poor. He wrote about what he was trying to do with war orphans in Switzerland and attracted thousands of educators from around the world to observe his efforts. Like Comenius, he was essentially a sense-realist, although his ideas were infused with a strong religious idealism. Pestalozzi believed that children should be allowed to learn from nature, and that language must be connected with sensory impressions at all times in order to build concepts. Like Rousseau, he believed that teachers should patiently follow the child's natural and individual development and avoid harsh disciplinary practices. Another teacher and writer of this period was the innovator of the kindergarten ("child's garden"), a German mystical idealist named Friedrich Froebel (1782–1852). Froebel worked with Pestalozzi for a time and was partly influenced by the latter's sense-realism. In Froebel's kindergarten, many kinds of objects were designed and made available for young children to play with and learn from as they played, and numerous activities were developed using his conception of the child's spiritual nature as a guide to educational process. To Froebel, play was the essence of childhood, and the precursor of creative adulthood:

> Play is the highest phase of child development—of human development at this period; for it is self-active representation of the inner—representation of the inner necessity and impulse. Play is the purest, most spiritual activity of man at this stage, and, at the same time, typical of human life as a whole—of the inner hidden natural life in man and all things. It gives, therefore, joy, freedom, contentment, inner and outer rest, peace with the world. It holds the sources of all that is good. A child that plays thoroughly, with self-active determination, perseveringly until physical fatigue forbids, will surely be a thorough, determined man, capable of self-sacrifice for the promotion of the welfare of himself and others—Is not the most beautiful expression of child-life at this time a playing child?—a child wholly absorbed in his play?—a child that has fallen asleep while so absorbed?[15]

Unlike Pestalozzi or Froebel, Johann Friedrich Herbart (1776–1841) was a college professor of philosophy and psychology in Germany who was interested in formal education. His ideas about the ethical development of the individual, especially during adolescence, through the correlation of historical and literary studies, influenced later efforts to introduce social studies into American schools.

Herbart also introduced the concept of "apperception," which involves bringing new learnings into integral association with ideas previously held. He is perhaps most familiar for his application of the notion of apperception to the systematic ("scientific") planning of lessons—i.e., for the "lesson plan" which was to help or hinder teachers from his day until the present. The Herbartian lesson plan as adopted in the United States had five fundamental steps: (1) preparation; (2) presentation; (3) association; (4) generalization; (5) application. When rigorously followed, as many efficiency minded supervisors of teachers during the latter part of the nineteenth century and early twentieth century believed it should be, the lesson plan was often excessively routine and ritualistic—devoid of real value for the teacher. Undue reliance upon formal lesson planning in this country has given rise in recent years to counter claims by the naive or inexperienced that planning for teaching is unnecessary—that a good teacher is always spontaneous and flexible in his work with students.

The great Enlightenment thinkers had some, but not a very great impact, upon the actual operation of schools during that period. In Europe, institutional rigidities precluded significant reform until the 20th century. As Pounds expresses it:

> The forces which were unleashed by Enlightenment had greater effects upon the political climate of the times than on the schools. They were very slow to make themselves felt in educational ideas and practices. . . Even here . . . [U.S.A.] the methods and general climate of much of the teaching was not affected until late in the nineteenth century.[16]

Classical studies continued to prevail in most secondary schools and universities, although representatives of the rising middle classes, such as Benjamin Franklin, did make efforts to develop private academies for the study of navigation, accounting, and other subjects believed to be of practical value for individuals interested in commerce or industry. In elementary schools, the emphasis was still, as it is today, on teaching children how to read, although writing, arithmetic, and music were also often taught.

In general, the influence of older, more conservative forms of thought in the religious and secular realms continued to dominate formal schooling during the eighteenth and nineteenth centuries. More scientific and generally liberal reforms in education emerged in the twentieth century. However, inroads were being made where thinking educators and teachers of teachers were able to make an impact on schools and on schools for the preparation of teachers in more open and receptive environments, such as the United States.

American Education

The Puritans and other early settlers in the New World were Europeans who brought with them the social and cultural patterns of England, the Netherlands, Scandinavia, Germany, France, and other Western European nations. Only gradually did a uniquely American society and culture begin to evolve.

The Colonial Period (1600–1800)

Coming to these shores for a variety of reasons—religious, political, economic, and personal—the early colonists brought with them a mixture of unsettled medieval, Renaissance, and Reformation values. These values were blended and partly replaced in the eighteenth century by Enlightenment conceptions of the good and the true.

Puritan New England had the greatest influence upon what eventually became the United States educational system. The Puritans, a dissident group of English men and women, emigrated to escape religious intolerance, but when they arrived here, they imposed an even more intolerant theocratic culture upon others. They established an **oligarchy,** a ruling class comprised of church members, freemen, and people with property, and tied the church tightly to the new state. The Puritans' main interest in life here, as in Europe, was religious. As Clarence Karier has phrased it:

> The Puritan was a man with a sense of purpose and mission directed by God. That mission was to live in the world, engage it, destroy the anti-Christ, and build a city of God in the wilderness. He saw himself not so much pioneering a new world as establishing a base of operation from which he and his fellows could lead the chosen children of God to attack Old World corruptions. In this way he usually viewed his own migration from the Old World as only a tactical retreat from Old World forces.[17]

The great sociologist Max Weber's analysis of Protestantism and the rise of capitalism demonstrates that Calvinistic beliefs in original sin and predestination were made to fit the human drives of the Puritans for material advancement. The Calvinist ethic held that hard work, thrift, and material prosperity were favorable signs that a person was spiritually redeemed:

> ... This prosperity, though not an absolute guarantee of salvation, could be taken as a favorable clue that the force of the universe was on one's side. In Puritan New England, neither prosperity nor salvation was ever

a certainty. But when the doctrine of the elect was combined with the doctrine of work, the economic life of the entrepreneur was religiously justified.[18]

Thus the way was laid for the preponderance of the capitalist ethos of hard work, thrift, and reverence for money. It continues to the present day in America, long after Puritanism has retreated from the scene as a major religious force in the culture.

These and similar values of Puritanism came together to order the development and character of American schools to the present day. The original mission of formal education in the colonies was largely religious, although it was also to ensure economic well being and community involvement.

Although most of the educating of children then, as always, was informal—taking place in the family, the church, and community agencies—formal schools were established early. By 1642 Massachusetts had passed the first law in the colonies requiring that parents take steps to ensure that their children read and understand the principles of religion and the major laws of the colony. Failure to educate one's children resulted in a fine or the apprenticing of the child. And, in order to prevent the "old deluder, Satan," from keeping people from knowledge of the Scriptures, a 1647 Massachusetts law required that all townships of fifty or more households hire a reading and writing teacher and all townships of one hundred or more households establish a Latin grammar school to prepare youth for the university.

There was no well-organized system of schooling then, but rather a variety of types of schools, reflecting local community demands and locally controlled. The schooling at the time was borrowed from England and other European countries: dame schools were established in a woman's home where reading and writing were taught to young children; some children were apprenticed to learn a trade; and middle-class adolescents interested in commercial and related careers attended academies. For the affluent, there were traditional European-type Latin grammar schools that led to Harvard or, in the South, to William and Mary College. Both colleges were modelled after European medieval universities.

Early New England schools in general were run with an even harsher philosophy than schools in Reformation Europe. The witch hunts, after all, occurred in New England. The Puritans believed in literally beating the devil out of children, if necessary. Young children, in reading the *New England Primer,* learned that "In Adam's fall we sinned all." This tone prepared children for authoritarian treatment by their teachers, who were fully supported by the theocratic state.

In the late colonial period, the strength of the Puritan ethos diminished, although many of its values—hard work, moralism, belief in public involvement with education—remained.[19] Religious rivalry between a growing number of diverse sects forced the end of the Puritan theocracy.

At the same time, Enlightenment ideas from Europe began to influence the more highly educated and intelligent members of the upper and middle classes. There was an increased secularization of life toward the end of the seventeenth century, a growing commercial class, and more strife between the colonies and England. These developments contributed to weakening the original religious function of schooling and to strengthening nationalistic and economic motives. The separation of church and state became a dominant American belief as colony after colony repealed old laws supportive of a theocracy. With victory by the colonies in the War for Independence and the adoption of the First Amendment of the Bill of Rights, the separation of church and state was codified into law. The First Amendment had profound implications for American education, although it was many years after its adoption that American schools were completely freed from their religious roots. Historically, American schools have been dominated by local community interests, often representing religious predilections. With the inclusion of the "reserved clause" in the Tenth Amendment of the Bill of Rights, schools became the legal responsibilities of the individual states, further supporting local control.

By the end of the eighteenth century, the road had been paved for the development of the secular public school system that we have today, although the full actualization of the American common school was not realized for more than a hundred years. At the time of the Revolution, there was a hodgepodge of types and levels of schooling in this country, representing a wide diversity of values of a localistic and unsettled frontier society with diverse religious and secular interests.

The American experience favored the eventual institutionalization of Enlightenment ideas of progress, science, and humanitarianism in education, along with more traditional conceptions of Puritan morality and industry, and an emphasis on the 3 Rs. The extent to which these opposing conceptions of educational purpose and process have been harmonized is a topic to which we will turn shortly.

Contributions to Educational Thought by Enlightenment Thinkers. Benjamin Franklin (1701–1790) symbolizes the bridge between the Puritan-dominated society of the seventeenth century and the competitive capitalist society of the nineteenth century.[20] He was essentially middle class and the prototype of the rags to riches entrepreneurial ideal. Franklin was interested in commerce, science, and philosophy, was a **deist** and a political statesman. In 1749 he proposed a publicly supported academy for Pennsylvania with a secular, practical program of commercial studies, agriculture, accounting, and English, along with some classical studies including religion. Although his proposal was not accepted, he established his own private academy, which became a leader among the numerous academies that were subsequently established for the middle-class city people of the era.

Thomas Jefferson (1743–1826), the writer of the Declaration of Independence and the third president of the United States, epitomized the gentlemanly ideal of John Locke, as well as the humanitarian values of the French Enlightenment thinkers. One might say he was a well-rounded scholar, gentleman, and humanist. Jefferson proposed a system of education for the colony of Virginia whereby after three years of public school, poor boys would be selected on the basis of academic ability to go on to private Latin grammar school with full board and tuition paid. The top student of limited means in the graduating class would then be given a three-year scholarship to William and Mary College. As was Franklin's, Jefferson's proposal was also turned down, modest though his idea seems today. He did, however, help to found the University of Virginia.

Neither Franklin nor Jefferson lived to see his major educational ideas implemented. But in the next century, in part as a result of Enlightenment ideas and in part because of altered social conditions, the United States established one of the world's first secular, public, free, and universal systems of elementary and secondary schooling.

The Public School Movement of the Nineteenth Century

The following passages were written over one hundred years ago by Horace Mann, who is often acknowledged as the leading spirit of the comprehensive public school system with which we are familiar today in the United States. Have his ideals of political, economic, and moral education, and nonsectarian public schools been completely achieved? Are those ideals liberal and humanitarian?

On the natural right to an education, Mann says

I believe in the existence of a great, immutable principle of natural law, or natural ethics, a principle antecedent to all human institutions and incapable of being abrogated by any ordinances of man, a principle of divine origin, clearly legible in the ways of Providence as those ways are manifested in the order of nature and in the history of the race, which proves the absolute right of every human being that comes into the world to an education; and which, of course, proves the correlative duty of every government to see that the means of that education are provided for all.

On the functions of schooling:

> ... under a republican government, it seems clear that the minimum of this education can never be less than such as is sufficient to qualify each citizen for the civil and social duties he will be called to discharge; such an education as teaches the individual the great laws of bodily health; as qualifies for the fulfilment of parental duties; as is indispensable for the civil functions of a witness or a juror; as is necessary for the voter in municipal affairs; and finally, for the faithful and conscientious discharge of all those duties which devolve upon the inheritor of a portion of the sovereignty of this great republic.
> Without undervaluing any other human agency, it may be safely affirmed that the Common School, improved and energized, as it can easily be, may become the most effective and benignant of all the forces of civilization.[21]

On equality of opportunity:

> According to the European theory, men are divided into classes—some to toil and earn, others to seize and enjoy. According to the Massachusetts theory, all are to have an equal chance for earning and equal security in the enjoyment of what they earn. The latter tends to equality of condition; the former to the grossest inequalities.
> Education..., beyond all other devices of human origin, is the great equalizer of the conditions of men—the balance-wheel of the social machinery... it gives each man the independence and the means, by which he can resist the selfishness of other men ...

On controversy in the school program:

> ... it will come to be understood, that political proselytism is no function of the school; but that all indoctrination into matters of controversy between hostile parties is to be elsewhere sought for, and elsewhere imparted ... thus ... will that pernicious race of intolerant zealots, whose whole faith may be summed up in two articles, that they, themselves, are always infallibly right, and that all dissenters are certainly wrong, be extinguished—extinguished, not by violence, nor by proscription, but by the more copious inflowing of the light of truth.

On the novelty of the common school:

> But this experiment has never yet been tried. Education has never yet been brought to bear with one hundredth part of its potential force, upon the nature of children, and, through them, upon the character of men, and of the race... Here, then, is a new agency, whose powers are just beginning to be understood, and whose mighty energies, hitherto, have been but feebly invoked ...

On the separation of church and state in relation to public education:

> If, then, a government would recognize and protect the rights of religious freedom, it must abstain from subjugating the capabilities of its children

to any legal standard of religious faith, with as great fidelity as it abstains from controlling the opinions of men. It must meet the unquestionable fact, that the old spirit of religious domination is adopting new measures to accomplish its work—measures which, if successful, will be as fatal to the liberties of mankind, as those which were practiced in by-gone days of violence and terror. These new measures are aimed at children instead of men ... The sovereign antidote against these machinations is Free Schools for all, and the right of every parent to determine the religious education of his children.[22]

This selection of major ideas of the reformist superintendent of public instruction of Massachusetts, Horace Mann, illustrates the thinking of leading proponents of public education during the nineteenth century. During this period, the elementary and secondary school system of today was constructed in the United States. By about 1880 education had become free, tax-supported, compulsory, and universal. According to revisionist historian Michael Katz, it had also become "bureaucratically arranged, class-biased, and racist" by that date.[23] Others also believe that we have been the victims of a great myth. Richard Pratte argues that:

The school legend claims too much by contending that the PSM [public school movement] of the first half of the nineteenth century arose from a largely humanitarian effort combined with the need for an enlightened citizenry. It is closer to the truth to claim that the movement for the establishment of public schools was and still is deeply enmeshed with the rest of society, and the reform of this period reflects more clearly a conservative response to massive social change.[24]

Whether the historical revisionists are correct or not is not an issue here. We do, however, continue to have severe problems of bureaucracy, socioeconomic inequalities, and institutionalized racism and sexism in our society over one hundred and twenty-five years after Mann wrote his optimistic reports to the Massachusetts Board of Education. What we must realize is that the school establishment arose out of and largely reflected the tensions and struggles of a society undergoing deep and pervasive social change. The transformation of American society and American education has not been completed, nor are there reliable indications that it is nearing completion. We are an extremely dynamic society, and our schools tend to reflect this dynamism. The nineteenth century was no exception.

It was a century in which values and norms were secularized; a period when nationalistic propensities were gathered together to form a relatively unified society, out of what had earlier been a group of ethnically mixed colonies; an era when democratic and equalitarian notions of political and social behavior were wrought from the experience of men and women with an expanding geographical frontier; the period when Jacksonian democracy emerged; and, in the late nineteenth century, the transformation of American society from a predominantly rural and agrarian one to a heavily industrialized and urban society. This latter and perhaps most crucial aspect of the nineteenth century was spurred by the development and diffusion of new machine technologies and waves of European immigrants who supplied the labor for the fast-growing factory system controlled by a new economic elite. The social, political, economic, and moral climate of the nineteenth century was right for the rise of the public school movement. Times had changed and the institution of education could not help but change also.

What specifically happened to education and schooling from 1800 to 1920? A massive public elementary and secondary school system was constructed under the reformist leadership of men like Horace Mann. It was institutionalized as a system for the protection and evolution of what came to be known as "the American way of life," a way especially devoted to entrepreneurial industrial capitalism. One of the major rationalizers of this essentially conservative purpose was William T. Harris, a Christian absolute idealist, superintendent of schools, and an early commissioner of the Bureau of Education after it was formed in 1867 (now the United States Office of Education).

Each state and its local communities were encouraged to develop and control, largely by means of lay representation, their own public school systems. Cross-fertilization of ideas and practices was common, however, and the eventual result was that a child could travel almost anywhere in the United States and find a school much like the school he or she had previously attended. In this sense, the beginnings of a national system of formal education had evolved by the end of the nineteenth century, and the trend toward an official national system continues to the present day.

The ladder system was developed, whereby a student could attend free public schools from kindergarten (and now, in some cases, pre-school) through high school, and in many cases through college and graduate school. This system contrasted sharply with general European practice (up to about the end of World War II) of the two-class system of schooling, which tended to provide children from families of modest means only an elementary level education.

Public schools became nonsectarian, free, and tax supported first at the elementary level, and later at the secondary. This was often after severe struggles with conservative power groups who were opposed to such "socialistic" notions. Schools in the burgeoning urban areas often had a difficult time attracting children whose immigrant or formerly rural parents failed to understand or feared the consequences of a formal education. Hence, compulsory school attendance laws came into being in order to force children to go to school, despite their parents' wishes. The first law was passed by Massachusetts in 1852:

> Every person who shall have any child under his control, between the ages of eight and fourteen years, shall send such child to some public school within the town or city in which he resides, during at least twelve weeks, if the public schools within such town or city shall be so long kept, in each and every year during which such child shall be under his control, six weeks of which shall be consecutive.[25]

In general, the functions of the public schools during this period were modifications of older functions. The major functions of the schools included molding character, imparting morality, enculturating native-born citizens, acculturating immigrants, ensuring literacy, and, most importantly, selecting and sorting children for future adult vocational and social roles—still the predominant manifest function of our schools. Other subordinate functions of the schools included the enhancement of physical health and fitness, general knowledge, and social facility—all related to an urbanizing society in which informal institutions no longer were able to ensure the acquisition of such learnings.

The public elementary schools tended to emphasize such subject matter as the 3 Rs, English, spelling, American history, and geography. Later, some of them also included nature study (science), drawing (art), music (especially singing), and physical education.

The public secondary schools developed slowly from private, classical Latin grammar origins and from the commercial and practical academies. Despite their slow beginnings, secondary schools proliferated rapidly and by the end of the Civil War there were several hundred of them in the United States. The Kalamazoo case in the Michigan Supreme Court session of 1874 set a precedent by upholding tax-supported local public high schools. By 1900 there were some 6,000 of them enrolling over 80 percent of all secondary students.[26]

The early high schools had several **tracks:** the traditional college preparatory track, science, business, technical, home economics, etc. All except the college preparatory track were intended to be practical. The system of several tracks within a single large school came to be known as the "comprehensive high school." It evolved into a coed institution offering required and elective courses for both middle-class students bound for college and for lower-class students who generally did not go to college. Tracking is criticized today by educators and others who believe that a disproportionate number of poor and minority students are conditioned from the earliest years in school to remain on the non-academic, non-college preparatory track. This defeats the purpose of equal educational opportunity, which the selecting and sorting function of public high schools was originally supposed to have served.

In conjunction with the problem of equal opportunity, it should be noted that public schools, particularly throughout the South, were often segregated by race on a *de jure,* or legal, basis until 1954 and the Brown decision of the United States Supreme Court. Before the Brown decision, the Court ruled in 1896 in *Plessy v. Ferguson* that schools may be separate and yet equal:

> ... *we cannot say that a law which authorizes or even requires the separation of the two races in public conveyances is unreasonable or more obnoxious to the 14th Amendment than the acts of Congress requiring separate schools for colored children in the District of Columbia, the constitutionality of which does not seem to have been questioned, or the corresponding acts of state legislatures.*[27]

In order to assure a large supply of competent teachers for the expanding public school system, normal schools were established in many states to prepare elementary teachers (who were largely women from this time on). These teacher-training institutions were often controlled by a local school district. They usually offered a basic secondary education to prospective teachers; they taught specific methods, such as how to teach cursive writing, but without the underlying principles. High school teachers received a more or less classical education at colleges or universities.

In 1862, the Morrill Act was passed, granting public lands to states and territories for the development of colleges designed "to promote the liberal and practical education of the industrial classes in the several pursuits and professions in life."[28] Eventually, many normal schools and teacher colleges became liberal arts colleges and universities with graduate schools, with facilities for advanced research in education as well as other studies. With the growth of teacher-education institutions also came the systematization of laws requiring teacher credentials, which were to ensure minimal competence. These laws are still being modified, and requirements for eligibility to teach are being upgraded. As normal schools and teacher colleges increased in number and function, along with general interest in upgrading the competencies of school teachers, some of the ideas of Europeans such as Pestalozzi, Froebel, and Herbart were borrowed and applied here, the most notable being Froebel's kindergarten.

As in colonial days, teaching was for many a stultifying career, especially in rural areas where the often rigid control of education by lay-dominated boards of education required that teachers be exemplars of moral perfection. Although teachers in the nineteenth century were not as personally and occupationally circumscribed as in colonial days, they were not as free from restrictions on their lives as are most present-day teachers. During the religious colonial period, for example, one teacher in New York had the following extracurricular tasks imposed on him:

> He shall be chorister of the church, keep the church clean, ring the bell three times before the people assemble, and read a chapter of the Bible in the church between the second and third ringing, he shall read the Ten Commandments and the twelve articles of our faith, and then set the psalm. In the afternoon, after the third ringing of the bell, he shall read a short chapter on one of the psalms of David, as the congregation are assembling; afterwards he shall again sing a psalm or hymn.
> He shall give the funeral invitations, dig the graves, and toll the bell.[29]

By the time of the public school movement over one-hundred-fifty years later, women had become the chief mainstays of the occupation. The following rules were in force in one of the new state normal schools in Massachusetts:

> It is expected, as a matter of course, that the young ladies will conform to the general order and usage of the families in which they reside. . . .
> The hours for rising, studying,&c., will vary somewhat the season of the year. For the winter and autumn terms, the pupils will rise at six o'clock, and study one hour, either before or after breakfast, as may suit the custom of the family. In the summer term, they will rise at five o'clock and study two hours. In the afternoon, they will study from four till five and a half o'clock. Evening study hours for the winter and autumn terms commence at seven o'clock and continue two hours, with a short recess; for the summer term, evening study hours commence at eight o'clock, and continue one hour. . . . All study hours are to be spent in perfect quietness.
> It is expected that the pupils will attend public worship on the Sabbath, health, and weather, and walking permitted; preserve order and quiet in their rooms, and throughout the house; and refrain from everything like a desecration of the day.
> ORDER, PUNCTUALITY and NEATNESS in their persons and in their rooms, and a kind and respectful demeanor, are expected of all.[30]

With such a stringent tradition, it is easy to understand how a teaching contract in a southern community, as late as 1927, could expect as idealistic behavior as the following:

> I promise to take a vital interest in all phases of Sunday-school work, donating of my time, service, and money without stint for the uplift and benefit of the community.
> I promise to abstain from all dancing, immodest dressing, and any other conduct unbecoming to a teacher and a lady.
> I promise not to go out with any young men except in so far as it may be necessary to stimulate Sunday-school work.
> I promise not to fall in love, to become engaged or secretly married.
> I promise not to encourage or tolerate the least familiarity on the part of any of my boy pupils.

I promise to sleep at least eight hours a night, to eat carefully, and to take every precaution to keep in the best of health and spirits, in order that I may be better able to render efficient service to my pupils.

I promise to remember that I owe a duty to the townspeople who are paying me my wages, that I owe respect to the school board and the superintendent that hired me, and that I shall consider myself at all times the willing servant of the school board and the townspeople.[31]

With recent serious efforts to professionalize the field of teaching, many of the traditional images of school men and school marms are being revised.

Besides being constrained by community forces that have separated them from other members of society, American teachers are subordinate to non-teaching school workers such as administrators. In the late nineteenth century, a line–staff relationship developed between superordinates who ran schools and subordinates who taught in them. It was a by-product of a society becoming rapidly industrialized and urbanized.[32] School leaders sought to emulate the successes of businessmen and industrialists in efficiently accomplishing economic ends. In other words, the school was perceived as a sort of factory into which came raw products (children) to be processed (educated) and in a few years packaged and distributed to their appropriate slots in the factories and families of industrial civilization. Speaking of the rise of what he calls "incipient bureaucracy" in American schools, Katz says:

> *The values to be instilled by the schools were precisely those required for the conduct of a complex urban society...*
>
> *Schoolmen over and over again raised the example of industry as an idealized standard ... They often described their school system as factories and used metaphors based on the corporation and the machine...*
>
> *Schoolmen pointed out that a professionally supervised school system based on the division of labor should have certain structural features and that its participants should have certain attitudes. An elaborate hierarchical structure and an explicit chain of command were necessary to keep each member working at his particular task in a responsible and coordinated fashion. At the head of the hierarchy should be one "vested with sufficient authority" to "devise plans in general and in detail" and to "keep all subordinates in their proper places and at their assigned tasks." Within the hierarchy, moreover, roles and duties should be defined clearly to avoid the possibility of conflict, and all members should give unquestioning obedience to the orders of their superiors. The great danger in a complex organization ... was "disintegration," caused chiefly by "nonconformity," something not to be tolerated in either pupils or teachers.*[33]

The development of a hierarchical semi-bureaucracy, modelled largely upon the industrial system in the United States, was the chief legacy of nineteenth century to twentieth century schooling. The public school movement was the structural embodiment of this form of educa-

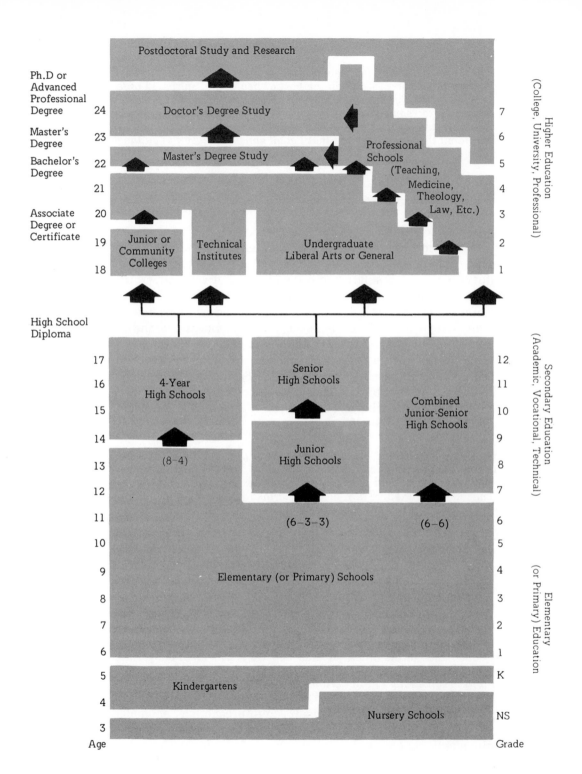

Postdoctoral Study and Research

Ph.D or Advanced Professional Degree — 24 — Doctor's Degree Study — 7

Master's Degree — 23 — 6

Bachelor's Degree — 22 — Master's Degree Study — 5

Professional Schools (Teaching, Medicine, Theology, Law, Etc.)

21 — 4

Associate Degree or Certificate — 20 — 3

19 — Junior or Community Colleges — Technical Institutes — Undergraduate Liberal Arts or General — 2

18 — 1

High School Diploma

Higher Education (College, University, Professional)

17 — 12
16 — 4-Year High Schools — Senior High Schools — 11
15 — Combined Junior-Senior High Schools — 10
14 — 9
13 — (8–4) — Junior High Schools — 8
12 — 7
11 — (6–3–3) — (6–6) — 6
10 — 5
9 — Elementary (or Primary) Schools — 4
8 — 3
7 — 2
6 — 1

Secondary Education (Academic, Vocational, Technical)

5 — Kindergartens — K
4
Nursery Schools — NS
3

Age — Grade

Elementary (or Primary) Education

112

tional organization. The chief results of the bureaucraticization of education are not yet completely understood.

The Modern Period (1920 onward)

In the last seventy-five years or so, the structure of schools in American society has changed comparatively little from what it was during the nineteenth century. This is not to imply that schools have not changed at all—they have; however, most of the changes that have occurred since about 1920 have been related to improving technologies within the extant school system ("in-system" changes), rather than basic changes of that system (known as valuational changes).

After long and hard struggle, the U.S. school system was constructed and institutionalized as a free, universal, tax-supported, and compulsory system of elementary-, intermediate-, and secondary-level enterprises for the efficient transmission of sociocultural patterns to almost "all the children of all the people." It became widely viewed by most lay people, educators, and public officials as having found its proper place as a service agency in the overall framework of American society. From this point on, the kinds of changes perceived as needed in schools have been largely modifications, or additions to—not reconstructions of—the existing structure, in response to demands from a variety of interest groups that the school more effectively meet their particular needs.

In the 1970s, most elementary and secondary schools in the United States are establishments performing traditional functions of selecting and sorting individuals for future positions; inculcating nationalistic patriotism; molding traditional conceptions of character; developing literacy and arithmetic ability; preparing youngsters for public responsibility, or citizenship; providing opportunities for physical health; and offering vocational guidance and preparation. To these historic functions have been added, over the past fifty to seventy-five years, the responsibility of facilitating interpersonal and intergroup social behavior; aiding individuals to grow and develop in personally fulfilling ways, in accordance with modern psychological theory; providing greater equality of economic and social opportunity for individuals from subgroups in the society, previously excluded from the mainstream; and teaching individuals how to think and solve problems of living.

Since the turn of the century, serious movements to significantly

FIGURE 4–1. *The Structure of Education in the United States Today (Education Division, Department of Health, Education, and Welfare,* Digest of Education Statistics: 1975 [Washington, D.C.: U.S. Government Printing Office, 1976], p. 4.)

alter the overriding structure of public education in the schools have been urged, along with other efforts to keep schools responsive to changing times and human needs. However, most of them have not been highly successful. One major effort to overhaul the American school along the lines of industrial modernism was the "progressive education" movement of the 1920s and 1930s. While it often strayed from its original intellectual moorings in John Dewey's philosophy of instrumentalism (see Chapter 11), this reform movement was aimed at educating individuals and groups to intelligently cope with a complex and changing social environment. This was to be done largely by applying the methods of science to human affairs and to the learning process. In school, this meant a strong emphasis on contemporary social studies and great involvement of students and teachers in determining the curriculum and in "learning by doing."

The progressive education movement died out by about the end of the Second World War because of confusion in the ranks of its leading proponents; conservative reactions from a public frightened by Cold War events and the launching of Russia's Sputnik I; the effort by some of its more radical advocates to make schools leading agencies of social reform during the depression years of the 1930s; and a general desire by Americans to settle down to more conventional ways of living and learning following the agonizing years of World War II.[34] The progressive education movement has since been revived in somewhat different form due to increasing criticism of public schools in recent years. Progressive education was most influential in American schools during the 1920s and 1930s. Progressive teachers guided students in discovering their world. Many schools, particularly in the urban areas, became centers of dynamic and experimental thinking and behaving.

Reactions to this movement set in strongly after 1950, during the Cold War years when Senator Joseph McCarthy came to power as the leading anti-Communist, anti-intellectual force in the nation. A number of books harshly critical of the modern trend in formal education were written and widely read by the general public. Despite efforts by some educational scholars to sustain the progressive movement, the American school returned to older, more conventional tasks of teaching the "basics."

However, some of the ideas of the progressive education movement were transferred to a new concern that brought the federal government into the public education arena, formerly dominated by the states and their municipalities. The civil rights movement of the 1950s began in the South and later spread to northern states. The U.S. Supreme Court in 1954 ruled in *Brown* v. *Topeka* that schools cannot be separate for different races and still be equal. Most southern states had relied upon the "separate but equal" principle enunciated in *Plessy v. Ferguson* in 1896.

Since 1954, attempts to desegregate American schools by busing students and by other measures have been fought by liberals and conservatives. The Department of Health, Education, and Welfare is vested with the responsibility of ensuring that every state and local school district complies with the law by meaningfully desegregating its schools.

The role of the federal government in education has increased with the passage of several laws since the late 1950s, granting funds to states and their educational subdivisions for the purpose of equalizing educational opportunity. These federal funds are to be spent to develop special "compensatory education" programs for the poor to upgrade academic competency through innovative means of teaching. Most of these means correspond directly or indirectly to Dewey's comprehensive system of ideas about learning, and also to his notions about what students should learn. Under the several National Defense Education Acts and Elementary and Secondary Education Acts, the United States Office of Education and recently the National Institute of Education have funded a variety of projects to understand how "disadvantaged" youngsters learn best and how schools and their teachers can best serve the educational needs of the "disadvantaged." Project Headstart is an example of the effort to equalize educational opportunity through compensatory education of the poor, in this case preschool children.

By the 1960s frustration had grown to such an extent among blacks in urban areas that riots broke out in major cities, including Los Angeles, Cleveland, and Detroit. The resulting pressures upon school systems to reform to better meet the needs of minority groups intensified. Efforts to respond to the urban crisis by passing legislation providing federal funds to build new schools and **educational parks** and to revitalize existing facilities and programs mounted. Following the lead of the **freedom schools,** which had begun to crop up throughout the South during the 1950s, storefront schools were established in cities. Demands were made to decentralize metropolitan districts so more community control could be assumed. In 1968 in New York City, an attempt was made to take the control of schools out of the hands of the school board and the central administration. Parents also registered demands to fire certain white teachers believed to be racist and to replace them with teachers selected by the black community. A bitter battle ensued between black parents and the New York City United Federation of Teachers. The local union affiliate of the American Federation of Teachers was accused of having racist and bureaucratic interests in defending centralization and its member teachers against the local community's demands. The result was a stalemate in which decentralization eventually occurred, but the union continued to control allocation of teaching personnel. The community control movement is still an open question for the future, but the teacher power movement is definitely becoming one of the major developments in public education since the public school movement of the nineteenth century.

Many proponents of teacher power argue that the movement is a significant step toward true professionalization of the occupation. It aims at freeing teachers from domination by managerial personnel so that they can work more creatively on behalf of the educational interests of school children. Its detractors claim that teacher militancy is a radical and immoral effort by arrogant and often incompetent teachers to get more pay for less and less professional effort. The battle goes on bitterly between rival teacher organizations and between teachers and administrators claiming to represent the general public.

Free Schools. As this struggle is waged, there is another potentially significant outcropping of the decade of the 1960s. It primarily involves middle-class, educated, dominant group Americans, not minority group members and the very poor. When college students rebelled in defiance of established institutional assumptions and patterns during the late 1960s, some of them decided to enter education on their own terms. They decided that the only way to overhaul what they considered a monolithic and unresponsive school establishment was to capitalize on the private school tradition in America. Private schools operated by respecting the wishes of parents, religious and other special-interest groups to form and run their own schools without substantial benefit of public funds. These young educational reformers decided to bring some like-minded anti-Establishment parents together and start their own "free schools." Many of the free schools were organized along some of the lines of the earlier Dewey progressive schools; A.S. Neill's Summerhill experiment also figured prominently in determining a free school philosophy.

The free school movement in this society has some intellectual grounding in philosophical instrumentalism and existentialism. In the late 1960s, free schools were formed in small and large towns throughout the United States. Their founders insisted upon the student's right to decide what he or she wants to study. Sympathetic teachers helped students to learn only when students asked for help. The movement was associated with radical social and political beliefs, and many free schools went out of business or were forced out by local officials. The movement has grown and changed, however; original organizers have resigned and been replaced, and more sophisticated methods of operating and educating have been instituted. At present, the free school seems to be developing as an alternative to public schooling for children and adolescents who have severe difficulties in public school or whose parents no longer have faith in the public school system. As will be demonstrated later, the free school movement may have a very significant long-term impact upon the future of public education.

Whether the free school movement has already affected public schooling or is simply an aspect of certain new features of the public school movement is uncertain at present. The open classroom, discussed in earlier chapters, is in many respects similar to the free school; that is, in its concern for children's freedom of expression, their right to be consulted in determining what they shall study and how, and the emphasis on the teacher's role as a resource person. The open-classroom concept, which is being used in some public schools today, has a great deal in common with the free school. The origins of both can be traced to the earlier work of educational intellectuals such as Dewey and Rousseau and to educational experimenters such as Neill and Froebel.

Other Twentieth-Century Educational Reforms.   There are other developments of this period that have emerged from traditional educational concerns and from the strong reform efforts of early twentieth-century Instrumentalists and Progressivists. For example, the junior high school is now an almost universal institution in the U.S., although in many areas, it is presently being replaced by the "middle school," which contains grades five through eight.

We now have an impressive number of teaching machines and other electronic instructional machinery and "soft" gadgetry in our schools, besides the conventional blackboard and textbook. New architectural forms are being used for school buildings. There is great emphasis today upon teacher preparation based on a minimum four-year college program. Paraprofessionals, or instructional assistants, are available to help teachers. Secondary schools offer more and more extra-curricular activities. Elementary school education is being organized into "open space" learning situations with "team teaching," as opposed to the older "self-contained" classroom with a single teacher. Individually prescribed instruction (IPI) and "performance contracting" are being used in some schools. Teachers are often asked to demonstrate accomplishment of behavioral objectives—to be accountable. Special education programs for the physically handicapped and other atypical youngsters are being refined, as are vocational education programs for students not intending to go to college. For those intending to seek further formal education after graduating from high school, the opportunities for free or inexpensive higher education are being dramatically broadened by the two-year community (or junior) colleges that offer both terminal degrees as well as transfer to four-year colleges and universities. Also of importance are: "individualized instruction," "programmed learning," "computer-assisted instruction," the "voucher system," "flexible scheduling" and the "module," "differentiated staffing," "interaction analysis," "microteaching," "simulation" and "gaming," and "sensitivity training."

Almost all of these innovations and refinements are essentially ex-

Table 4–1.   Some Important Dates and Names in the History of Education

c. 3,000 BC	Beginnings of written languages and schooling in the Middle East and Asia
479–338 BC	Golden Age of Greece: Socrates, Plato, and Aristotle lay foundations of Western thought
303 BC	Greek teachers in Roman Schools
167 BC	First Greek Library in Rome
35–97 AD	Quintilian, Roman educator, disavowed harsh treatment of students
c. 500–1300	Middle Ages and predominance of Christian and chivalric education and apprenticeship system
c. 1100–1300	Rise of the medieval university and scholasticism
1225–1274	Thomas Aquinas, whose *Summa Theologica* synthesized Greek and Christian thought
c. 1423	Invention of movable type
1456	First book printed
1466–1536	Erasmus, humanist and educational theorist, who stressed reliance on the classics for education
1483–1546	Martin Luther, Protestant religious reformer, promoted reading the Bible in the vernacular
1531	Compulsory school law in the Netherlands
1561–1626	Francis Bacon, author of *Novum Organum*, in which he emphasized inductive reasoning
1592–1670	John Amos Comenius, sense–realist and advocate of universal education; author of *Great Didactic* and first children's picture book
1636	Harvard College founded
1642	Massachusetts law requiring parents to ensure a basic formal education for their children
1647	Massachusetts law requiring the hiring of teachers to instruct children in writing and reading; establishment of Latin grammar schools for older youth
1685	First normal (teacher-training) school established at Rheims, France
1632–1704	John Locke, who justified independent thinking and related education to democracy
1712–1778	Jean Jacques Rousseau, champion of romantic naturalism and author of *Emile,* in which he stated his theories on the education of man
1701–1790	Benjamin Franklin established first academy in American colonies
1743–1826	Thomas Jefferson founded the University of Virginia
1746–1827	Johann Pestalozzi, Swiss sense–realist, advocated education for the poor
1782–1852	Friedrich Froebel, German innovator of the kindergarten and author of *The Education of Man*
1776–1841	Johann Friedrich Herbart, scholar and proponent of apperception and its application to systematic lesson planning
1821	First American high school
1823	First teacher-training school established in the U.S. at Concord, Vermont
1827	Massachusetts law requiring towns to establish public high schools
1796–1859	Horace Mann, leader of the public school movement and author of influential reports to Mass. Board of Education
1839	First public, state-supported teacher-training school established at Lexington, Mass.
1852	First compulsory school attendance law in U.S. passed by Mass. legislature
1855	First kindergarten established in U.S. at Watertown, Wisconsin
1862	Morrill Land-Grant Act setting aside acreage in states and territories for

Table 4–1. *Continued*

	the express purpose of founding public colleges and universities
1867	United States Office of Education established
1874	In Kalamazoo case, Supreme Court said tax-supported schools were legal
1896	*Plessy v. Ferguson* "separate but equal" decision of Supreme Court
1909–1910	First junior high schools established at Berkeley, Calif., and Columbus, Ohio
1910–1911	First junior colleges established at Fresno, Calif., and Joliet, Ill.
1917	Smith–Hughes Act passed, which encouraged high school and vocational education in agriculture, industry, and home economics by federal funding
1859–1952	John Dewey, philosopher and major intellectual influence on Progressive education movement in the U.S. and abroad
1945	First GI bill of Rights provided veterans funds for higher education
1945	The United Nations Educational, Scientific, and Cultural Organization (UNESCO) initiated efforts to improve educational standards throughout the world
1954	*Brown v. Board of Education of Topeka, Kansas,* decision required racial integration of U.S. public schools
1958	National Defense Education Act provided funds to strengthen and improve educational programs to meet critical national needs
c. 1960	The teacher power movement begins
1965	Elementary and Secondary Education Act provided funds to strengthen and improve educational quality and opportunity—especially for poor children—and stimulated much innovation in American education
1968	Community control movement led by minority parents in Oceanhill–Brownsville, New York
c. 1968	Free school separatist movement begins, anticipating later alternative education movement in public schools
1972	Formation of the National Institute of Education to facilitate educational research
Present	Rapid decline in growth of school-aged population; other pressures upon schools stimulating serious consideration of local, state, national, and international educational priorities for the future

Portions of this list are from James A. Johnson, Harold W. Collins, Victor L. Dupuis, and John H. Johansen, *Introduction to the Foundations of Education,* 3rd ed. (Boston: Allyn and Bacon, 1976), pp. 345–47.

tensions of prior innovations and developments that have come down to us through the long ages of Western history. They have been modified and expanded to meet the needs of a frontier people during the seventeenth, eighteenth, and especially nineteenth centuries. Most of the changes in education that have brought us to the present period have been changes in the technology of schooling and school teaching, technological changes designed to more efficiently accomplish goals of lay people and educators. Fundamental values of education have not changed as much; it is in this area that many social analysts believe educational change is most crucial at the present stage of American history.

To What Extent Are Prospective Teachers Bound by Historical Traditions?

There are basically two ways to answer this question: The teacher is an agent carrying out the cultural expectations of forebears, as mediated through certain authority figures in the community and in the school system or: The teacher must interpret for himself or herself what aspects of history are worth conserving. Perhaps contemporary students will be best served if they are offered a solid grounding in their cultural heritage through a program of American history and geography, with a heavy emphasis on reading and writing and some math and science and a foreign language to develop their deductive capabilities. On the other hand, perhaps this society is so out of joint with historic trends that existed prior to World War II that emphasis in the curriculum upon tradition and convention will not be useful to them. What then? Is it necessary to start from scratch and develop a totally new program, without connection with history?

In the final analysis, each teacher must decide in which direction he or she will head as an instructor of the young. The teacher's values, supported by knowledge of modern society and the place of the public school in society—the expectations held for it, its capacity, and its limitations as an institution—will determine his or her attitude toward the past. This chapter has presented a general picture of the forces that have constructed the educational institution of today. Your decisions and behavior as a teacher within the educational institution of today will determine the nature of formal education in the future.

Summary

As an integral social institution, education reflects the historical experiences of the society in which it exists.

In preliterate societies, education of the young takes place informally within the daily routines of group life. Significant events, such as the onset of puberty, involve formalized teaching and learning of cultural values and norms. The main task of education in preliterate societies is transmission of traditional culture.

Schools were established in early civilizations. The school arose with the emergence of relatively complex civilizations and the development of written languages, in order to educate people to conduct official business and pass on elements of the cultural heritage preserved in writing.

The first major civilization to arise in the West was Greece. One of its city-states, Sparta, developed a formal educational system designed almost exclusively to prepare warriors for combat in numerous wars. Ancient Athens developed a more complex educational pattern, which reflected the values of contemplative individualism and social participation in the polis.

The educational system of Rome was partly adopted from Athenian Greece, but modified to suit the political, administrative, and professional needs of an expanding empire and the personal needs of a self-indulgent aristocracy.

After the fall of Rome and the rise of medieval Christianity, formal education took on a decidedly religious cast for several hundred years. Subsidiary educational institutions prepared feudal lords and ladies, skilled workers of the towns and cities, and the intellectual and professional classes.

The medieval pattern was generally maintained throughout the Renaissance period, although increasing secularism brought a renewed interest, known as humanism, in the classical writers of ancient Greece and Rome. Secondary schools that taught the classics were established for the elite. Nationalism and the use of vernacular languages marked the period, and elementary schools for the masses, with instruction in the vernacular, appeared.

Interest of Protestant reformers in reading the Bible in the vernacular led to rapid expansion of formal elementary education during the Reformation. Continued growth of secular humanism and revision of scientific methodology promoted the refinement of classical Latin grammar schools.

These trends were solidified during the Enlightenment. Academies for the practical education of the burgeoning commercial middle classes were added. A number of major educational thinkers in Europe exerted an influence upon American ideas about education during this period.

The social and political environment in Europe during the Reformation and Enlightenment had a significant influence upon the educational views and practices of the early colonists, who borrowed and bent European ideas for implementation in their own schools. Colonial education was mainly religious in character, although it became more secular after the Revolution.

In the late eighteenth century, the new nation began to construct a free, tax-supported, universal, and compulsory system of elementary and secondary schools for all the people. The Constitution delegates responsibility for education to the states and indirectly to local communities. The post–World War II period has witnessed increased federal involvement in education, however.

The U.S. school system has become institutionalized, refined, and differentiated in the twentieth century. At the present time, it is receiving strong criticism and demands for reform, which have prompted efforts to make formal education more responsive to contemporary problems and needs.

Related Concepts

deism   A religious belief that maintains that after God created the universe, natural laws took over. Several of the "founding fathers" of the United States were deists.

educational park   One of several responses to the problem of desegregating schools. An educational park is a large-scale complex of one or more elementary, secondary, and, perhaps, higher-level schools at a single geographical location with superior and readily available facilities for instruction.

epistemology   In philosophy, the theory of knowledge and its acquisition

freedom schools   Temporary schools established in Mississippi and other states of the Deep South during the 1960s. College students from the North taught black children what their civil rights were and how to attain them in these schools.

oligarchy   A society ruled by the few, as contrasted with a democracy, in which power ideally is vested in many people

track   One of several types of curricula available in American comprehensive high schools for students with different goals and abilities

Suggested Activity

One of the best ways to gain a sense of educational history is to read the writings of leading educators in the original. Borrow one or more of the anthologies cited in the present chapter from your college library, and spend some time reading selections from the writings of noted educational thinkers. You may be surprised at how modern or relevant the ideas of many of the great educators are to contemporary life.

References and Notes

1. Anthony Wallace, "The Kinds of Learning," in Jonathan C. McLendon, ed., *Social Foundations of Education: Current Readings from the Behavioral Sciences* (New York: Macmillian, 1968), p. 273.

2. Donald S. Seckinger, "Education in Primitive and Modern Societies," in Hugh C. Black, Kenneth V. Lottich, and Donald S. Seckinger, eds., *The Great Educators: Readings for Leaders in Education* (Chicago: Nelson-Hall Co., 1972), p. 46.

3. Wallace, "Kinds of Learning," p. 273.

4. Ralph L. Pounds, *The Development of Education in Western Culture* (New York: Appleton-Century-Crofts, 1968), p. 18.

5. *Ibid.*, pp. 26, 27.

6. *Ibid.*, p. 48.

7. *Ibid.*, p. 99.

8. Paul Nash, ed., *Models of Man: Explorations in the Western Educational Tradition* (New York: John Wiley & Sons, 1968), p. 169.

9. Robert H. Ulich, *History of Educational Thought*, 2nd ed. (New York: Van Nostrand Reinhold, 1968), p. 138.

10. Pounds, *Development of Education*, p. 117.

11. Martin Luther, Selections from Luther's "Letter to the Mayors and Aldermen of All the Cities of Germany in Behalf of Christian Schools (1524), Black et al., eds., *The Great Educators*, p. 387.

12. Pounds, *Development of Education*, p. 153.

13. *Ibid.*, pp. 141, 142.

14. Nash, *Models of Man*, p. 251.

15. Friedrich Wilhelm Froebel, selection from *The Education of Man* (1826) in Black, et al., eds., *The Great Educators*, p. 499.

16. Pounds, *Development of Education*, p. 186.

17. Clarence J. Karier, *Man, Society, and Education: A History of Educational Ideas* (Glenview, Ill.: Scott, Foresman, and Co., 1967), p. 1.

18. Karier, *Man, Society, and Education*, p. 13.

19. According to one revisionist historian, "It was largely from this Puritan background that the U.S. quite early developed a sense of mission, a commitment to demonstrate to the world how a nation should provide liberty and justice for all." Robert A. Carlson, *The Quest for Conformity: Americanization through Education* (New York: John Wiley & Sons, 1975), p. 4.

20. Karier, *Man, Society, and Education*, pp. 33–35.

21. Horace Mann, selections from *Tenth Annual Report to the [Massachusetts] Board of Education* (Boston: Dutton and Wentworth, State Printers, 1847), p. 112.

22. Mann, selections from *Twelfth Annual Report to the Board of Education* (1848), pp. 55, 59, 60, 89, 90, 94, 138.

23. Michael B. Katz, *Class, Bureaucracy, and Schools: The Illusion of Educational Change in America* (New York: Praeger Publishers, 1971), p. 106.

24. Richard Pratte, *The Public School Movement: A Critical Study* (New York: David McKay Company, 1973), p. 45.

25. Selection from *An Act Concerning the Attendance of Children at School* (1852), in James William Noll and Sam P. Kelly, eds., *Foundations of Education: An Anthology of Significant Thoughts and Actions* (New York: Harper & Row, 1970), p. 251.

26. Pounds, *Development of Education*, pp. 203, 204.

27. Selections from *Homer Adolph Plessy v. John H. Ferguson* (May 18, 1896), in Noll and Kelly, eds., *Foundations of Education*, p. 270.

28. Selections from *An Act donating Public Lands to the several States and Territories which may provide Colleges for the Benefit of Agriculture and the Mechanic Arts* (1862), *ibid.*, p. 254.

29. Quoted in Raymond E. Callahan, *An Introduction to Education in American Society: A Text with Readings*, 2nd ed. (New York: Alfred A. Knopf, 1963), p. 384.

30. Quoted in Henry Barnard, *Normal Schools and other Institutions, Agencies, and Means designed for the Professional Education of Teachers*, V. 1 (Hartford, Conn.: Case, Tiffany and Company, 1851), p. 73.

31. Quoted by Willard Waller, in his *The Sociology of Teaching* (New York: John Wiley & Sons, 1932), p. 43.

32. Katz, *Class, Bureaucracy, and Schools;* Raymond E. Callahan, *Education and the Cult of Efficiency: A Study of the Social Forces that Have Shaped the Administration of the Public Schools* (Chicago: University of Chicago Press, 1962).

33. Katz, *Class, Bureaucracy, and Schools*, pp. 32, 68, 69.

34. Lawrency Cremin, *The Transformation of the School: Progressivism in American Education, 1876–1957* (New York: Alfred A. Knopf, 1961), pp. 338–53.

The Fundamental Purposes of Education

5

Models of
Modern American Society

The conceptions teachers have about the society in which they live are vitally important. They act as cultural determinants, orienting teachers generally and specifically toward their work in the classroom and outside of it. The conceptions of society that are presented in this chapter consciously or unconsciously serve as models that guide the thinking, feeling, and behaving of educators.

In this chapter, five important models, or images, of contemporary society and culture will be reviewed on a macro plane. Each image has significant implications for schooling and teaching. Because several images can be extracted from recent social thought, it is apparent that there is no common view of America to which all lay people and social analysts subscribe. Current fads and fashions, however, do play a role in determining which view is most popular at one time.

Five Images of Contemporary America

America as a Businessman's Civilization

Contemporary America is often characterized as a businessman's civilization. Using this image of America, it is possible to relate the activities of modern schools to the fulfillment of the basic creed of American business.[1] This creed includes the following beliefs and assumptions:

- the centrality of free enterprise capitalism as the dominant institutional configuration in this society
- the evils of ever-encroaching big government
- scorn for welfare programs and all versions of socialism
- the assumption that unregulated, or laissez faire, capitalism provides for the common good
- the claim that prices are kept low through competition in an oligopoly, i.e., a market shared by a few sellers, such as major oil companies
- the tenet that human nature is basically competitive rather than cooperative; hence, a Spencerian version of survival of the fittest controls human society
- according to all of the above, the premise that the fundamental job of schools is to teach people how to compete in a free market, so that, like the mythical Horatio Alger, some of the "fittest" may rise from "rags to riches"
- an economic determinism, that alleges that all our liberties are dependent upon free-market competition; businessmen are to be regarded as the most beneficent humanists of the modern era
- the boast that a materially wealthy society is a great society[2]

There are those who believe that the businessman's civilization is an accurate description of America, whether they advocate such a civilization or not. Many critics of society use this model as the reality they are seeking to change.

Those who believe that this general image of society prevails argue that laissez-faire capitalism controls the economic institution which, in turn, dominates all the other major social institutions in this interdependent society, including the schools. This is similar to the argument that racism is institutionalized throughout American society and dominates the operations of American institutions at all times.

The dominance of business over most sociocultural affairs is asserted by economic determinists to be evidenced in ways such as the following:

- Leadership of most cities and towns in the United States is held by powerful elites consisting largely of successful businessmen. This allegation is often supported by Floyd Hunter's important 1953 study of community power structure.[3] Sociologists and political scientists have debated for years whether leadership in communities is in fact in the hands of a few behind-the-scenes businessmen or diffused "pluralistically" among a variety of institutional elites, such as spokespersons for organized religion, school superintendents, mayors, and other local governmental officials.[4]
- The social structure of American society has an upper-class com-

posed predominantly of wealthy businessmen and industrialists. Most of the rest of us wish we could reach "the top" and join this group.

• Our values and customs have become overly materialistic, as seen by our indulgence of the mass media, particularly TV, with its extensive brainwashing by commercials. Holidays such as Thanksgiving and Christmas have become little more than opportunities for businessmen to make large profits and consumers to increase their material possessions. And according to members of less privileged groups, liberals, radicals, and the counter culture, businessmen exploit woman and ethnic minority workers in order to save money on wages, and they exploit consumers by offering them shoddy goods whenever they can get away with such practices.

Whether one is a privileged and satisfied adherent of the business creed or an alienated opponent, an individual who accepts its premises as principal operating facts of modern American life tends to see the primacy of competitive business and economics in almost all aspects of society, from the market place to the altar.

According to the businessman's image of America, schools are perceived as agencies by means of which the business image is preserved as the central cultural ethos of society, and children are socialized to behave in accordance with this image. The following illustrates the conception of business preeminence in the United States as reflected in school philosophy and practice:

• Most of what is taught in the majority of United States schools is intended to create in children an acceptance of the economic status quo and to fit them into the business system as acquiescent workers or managers and as uncritical consumers. The main reason for teaching children reading and arithmetic, for example, is to develop a competent and skilled workforce that can make more money for industrialists and commercial people. This intention may not always be consciously recognized as a manifest function of schooling.

• The materials used in schools to instruct are favorable to the business-industry point of view and ignore organized labor's positive role in our society's historic development. Textbooks avoid any statements that even faintly resemble criticism of free-enterprise capitalism. The textbook–media industry itself is a big business in this country. A number of studies indicate that the points of view presented by these materials often vary according to the region in which the materials are to be sold and used. In the Deep South, for instance, the important role of blacks in the construction of an agrarian economy has largely been distorted or underplayed.[5] Furthermore, teachers are frequently given free posters and classroom demonstration materials by large industries, often with their corporate names clearly imprinted. Tours, or field trips, are often made to industrial plants and guided by management representatives.

•   Teachers are perceived as subordinate workers in a hierarchical system composed of management (administration), labor (teachers), and goods (children). Many teaching practices are believed to be primarily reflective of business-industrial standards, intended to socialize children to take their "proper" place in the environment upon leaving school, having been selected and sorted at an early age for their socially ascribed or achieved slots. Thus, report cards are viewed as a teacher's way of representing to students the supervisorial aspects of life in the business world, where judgments about a worker's efficiency and competitiveness on the job or in the market place are made continually. The same is true of daily grading practices[6] and of organized sports. Work—not play—is extolled by teachers acting as agents on behalf of a business- and work-oriented society. The clock and bell still dominate schools, teaching children that time and efficiency are desirable qualities for those who are to work hard in a world ruled by businessmen. Pupil conformity and docility, rather than creative independence, are demanded by many teachers. Truly independent thinkers might make waves in the organizations in which they are expected to spend their future working lives. However, for boys of the middle classes who are to obtain managerial positions in industry, this emphasis on conformity is mitigated somewhat by an acceptance of greater independence than is typically allowed of girls.[7] Girls are not even considered as prospective businesswomen. Girls and boys in schools with predominantly lower socioeconomic status students are commonly believed to require much more discipline in order to learn to obey orders from their foremen and supervisors when they grow up.[8]

These and a number of similar attitudes and practices are alleged by those who see America as a businessman's civilization to control the contemporary American school. The public school and its teachers, according to this view, serve a business-dominated social order. This social order has its origins in the Reformation and Enlightenment notions of predestination. American society has further stressed the ethics of hard work and rugged, competitive individualism. A rising entrepreneurial class validated this image on the American frontier and in the urban factories of the nineteenth century. Children are prepared to compete at all costs, to work hard, and to conform to ideas of success or failure, and to play their proper class and sex roles as future workers, managers or owners, and faithful but nonaggressive wives.

In sum, the image of modern U.S. society as a basically businessman's civilization is one reflected in the belief that the overarching structure of the American school has been designed and maintained to reflect and to serve the interests of the commercial and middle and upper classes. This design is an unconscious one, perpetuated by the public, school managers, school workers, and students who tend to take this system for granted as the natural way of life in this society.

American Society as a
Pyramidal Oligarchy

This increasingly influential image of modern United States society is held primarily by alienated segments of society, rather than by both critics of the Establishment and its members. The vision of contemporary America as a pyramidal oligarchy is largely the possession of the extreme "New Left," which wants to revolutionize American society along radical political and economic lines. This view is also held by some members of the emergent counter culture, who prefer to leave the mainstream of society and its politics to find a simpler life in urban or rural communes.

The major articulator of the **power elite** theory of modern America was C. Wright Mills, a self-admitted Marxist.[9] The extent to which New Left thinkers feel indebted to Mills for his vision of modern society is expressed in the following quote from a recent compilation of articles on the theme of an emerging "radical sociology":

> With a few exceptions, chiefly among the pre-war [World War II] eminences, today's prominent sociologists are the direct financial creatures, functionally the house-servants, of the civil, military, and economic sovereignty.
>
> A postwar exception like the late C. Wright Mills only proves the rule. Though the most widely read sociologist outside the academic world, Mills was barred by his university from training graduate students, for fear that he would raise up others in his image ... the chance of another Mills arising in sociology is about equal to the chance of a Fidel Castro emerging in the State Department.[10]

C. Wright Mills' basic image of America (see Table 5–1) is distilled in the words "civil, military, and economic sovereignty." He believed that since about the end of World War II, the United States, partly as a result of wartime developments, had come to be dominated by a triple alliance of businessmen/industrialists, political leaders in Washington, and important military men ("warlords") in the Pentagon. No longer did business alone control society. Now an oligarchy of educated, affluent, leaders with similar beliefs are said to constitute a powerful "military-industrial-governmental complex."

According to Mills and his disciples, since about 1945 the majority of American people have lost almost all of whatever influence they may

Table 5–1.   The Main Ideas of Mills

LEVELS	a. Unified power elite b. Diversified and balanced plurality of interest groups c. Mass of unorganized people who have practically no power over elite
CHANGES	a. Increasing concentration of power
OPERATION	a. One group determines all major policies b. Manipulation of people at the bottom by group at the top
BASES	a. Coincidence of interests among major institutions (economic, military, governmental)
CONSEQUENCES	a. Enhancement of interests of corporations, armed forces, and executive branch of government b. Decline of politics as public debate c. Decline of responsible and accountable power—loss of democracy

Seymour Martin Lipset and Leo Lowenthal, *Culture and Social Character: The Work of David Riesman Reviewed* (New York: Macmillan, 1961), p. 261. Copyright © 1961 by the Free Press of Glencoe, Inc.

once have had on the society in which they live. Americans now exist in relative isolation, as an unorganized mass to be manipulated by the new power elite.

In the middle, between the top elite and the hapless masses, are the middle levels of power. These are relatively unimportant, representing a myriad of special interests on national and regional levels. Its spokespersons are congressmen, religious and labor leaders, and some regional public officials. Leading educators are not likely to be represented at either the top or middle levels, according to this view. The three groups together comprise a pyramid of three levels.

From the oligarchical frame of reference, formal education is little more than that of several willing lackeys working for the power elite. Its basic job is to keep the large mass of people passive, confused, and docile so that the rulers at the top can wage their wars to keep prices up in a bankrupt economic system and, in other ways, go about their selfish business unimpeded:

> ... *the mass is more or less firmly controlled, depending on the needs of the power elite, by various institutions such as education, religion, unions, the press, the movies, radio, and TV...*
> *The institutions of society have lost or abdicated whatever position they once had as centers of rational thought, freedom, and initiative. The*

schools long ago abandoned any opposition to the Establishment.[11] *(Emphasis added)*

The argument for what American schools do as willing tools of the oligarchy clearly runs along lines similar to—although more extended than—that offered by the image of a businessman's civilization. Schools, being agencies of a nationalistic, industrial, big-government state, are to prepare the masses for acquiescence to the power figures who really run the state. At the same time, schools maintain a posture of preparing students for a democracy that no longer exists, except in the minds of the naive. The variety of **technological innovations** created in the past few years prove that schools and teachers are willing automatons of a social elite that manipulates students by using complex electronic and social gadgetry. Those who view American society from this perspective believe that compensatory education programs are designed to keep the otherwise dangerous poor from believing that the state has totally abandoned them.

Underneath the superficial modifications currently being made in schools, older patterns of belief and behavior are permitted to continue as long as they are useful in keeping people in line. A pretense of preparing boys and girls for active roles in a democratic society offering "equal opportunity" is maintained by "misguided" teachers who accept the myth of American greatness and opportunity. These teachers encourage this myth as a result of their own socialization and enculturation by institutions that are dominated by the ruling elite.

America as a Technological Monstrosity

Some people believe that a technology that is beyond the control of humankind is the dominant image of contemporary America. Herbert Muller feels this way:

> Technology is the "science or study of the practical or industrial arts." In modern usage emphasis has been on industrial techniques, based on the machine. I am using the term in a broader sense to cover as well the definitive practices that have been generated by the rise of industrialism. These include large-scale organization throughout our society, professionalism in all activities, and the ways of thinking and doing indicated by such typically modern terms as "system," "systematic" methods, and "methodology." Modern technology may be broadly defined as the elaborate development of standardized, efficient means to practical ends. A comparable definition is John Kenneth Galbraith's "the systematic application of scientific or other organized knowledge to practical ends."
> My primary concern is the systematic neglect or abuse of what

> I consider essential human values. *The matrix of our problems, especially in America, is the common assumption that it [advanced technology] is an end in itself . . . I am committed to the simple, old-fashioned assumption that the proper end for man is the good life.*[12]

Technology, an outgrowth of the Industrial Revolution, has applied rational and scientific *means* to the improvement of human ends. However, we now rely so much on technology that it has virtually become *the end* purpose of life in our society. Unlike the oligarchical vision that is held by the most socially and politically alienated, the image of American society as a technological monstrosity is adhered to by many liberals, as well as by most members of the New Left and the counter culture. It has become fashionable in recent years to blame most, if not all, of society's ills on the ubiquitous growth of technology, which has penetrated all aspects of institutional life. Of course, there are moderates who acknowledge that modern technology has benefitted society but must be brought more under intelligent human control.

The image of a technology that is beyond the control of society visualizes society as confused about its basic values and headed toward an Orwellian future. This future will witness individual behavior that is controlled by an efficiency oriented bureaucratic leadership of professionals and **technocrats.**

According to those who fear the overemphasis on technology, technocrats have already taken over the formal educational system. They are the top- and middle-level managerial functionaries who administer schools and school systems—i.e., school superintendents, curriculum directors, and school principals. And, it will not be long before most teachers—having succeeded in winning power and full professional status through united organizational effort—either replace the present technocrats or join with them in wresting all control of the schools from the lay public. The new "professional education establishment" will condition future generations of Americans to full acceptance of life devoid of feeling, that is, to acceptance of the technocratic civilization. As one writer puts it, "The subservient schoolhouse is increasingly being co-opted by the influence of the megamachine."[13] One merely has to look at the way schools are presently operating to realize this, say the fearful. Schools are being perfected as bureaucratic organizations with increasingly clearcut line–staff–client relations—formally differentiating the roles of adults and children. In the curriculum, one sees the ascendency in status of such subject areas as the "new math" and the "new science" and the concern of teachers of English, history, and other traditional subjects that their time-honored prerogatives are being usurped by these new fields and approaches to instruction.

One cannot help but be aware that the federal government for several years now has strongly encouraged projects that depend upon gadgetry, such as teaching machines and computers. Projects concentrating on the use and development of human values and interpersonal and group relations are neglected.[14]

In short, according to holders of this view, the school is being mechanized by a society that is losing its human identity to technology. We have forgotten that science and machines are supposed to be used for the benefit of people.

The outlook seems bleak or at least highly uncertain to some:

The surrender of society to the free play of market forces is now on the wane, but its subservience to the impetus of the scientific ethos is on the rise. The prospect before us is assuredly that of an undiminished and very likely accelerated pace of technical change.[15]

Aldous Huxley, another critic of technology says:

Man has always thrown his weight around and upset the natural order. Now, with the enormous resources of modern technology he can tilt the balance disastrously. Even when his powers were small he was remarkably successful. It is astonishing how rapidly human beings can destroy their surroundings even in primitive countries. What mankind has made of its environment is a depressing spectacle.[16]

For the technologically fearful, the central question for modern men and women is how to cope with the materialistic civilization that technology has produced. We must reevaluate our basic social priorities and commit ourselves to reconstructing these priorities along more human lines. There is also a sense of urgency within this view of society, a sense of impending doom wrought by technology itself.

America as a Pluralistic Sociocultural System

The notion of sociocultural pluralism is the most widely held of all organizing conceptions of American society. In recent years, however, views of society as primarily oligarchical and technological have been adopted by more social scientists.[17] The "businessman's civilization," the "pyramidal oligarchy," and "technological monstrosity" images each postulate a single factor as the root cause of social and cultural reality; that is, each image represents some version of economic, organizational, or political determinism.

The pluralists, however, reject deterministic thinking based on a single cause. They argue that all life in every society is more or less dependent upon the complex interplay of a number of interdependent variables that each contributes to the functioning (or disfunctioning) and integrity of the social system. This is a gross simplification of the pluralist position, but because it is the most complex of all under discussion, there is no way of avoiding this.

According to the pluralist view, life is vastly more complex than determinists—in their zeal to find quick and easy answers to difficult problems—believe it is. It follows then that American society must be a highly complex one, regardless of what specific characteristics it may take on at various periods in time.

Perhaps businessmen have had a rather important role to play in our frontier society. Since we were isolated from Europe, we had little recourse but to industrialize much more quickly and effectively in order to settle the continent. After World War II and Soviet efforts to colonize the world, the United States depended rather heavily for important decisions upon its major military, government, and industrial leaders who were in the best positions then to make such decisions. But this phase was only temporary, as reactions of people to the Watergate scandal, which involved members of the political elite, testify. If the masses are merely unthinking automatons of a national power elite, then why have recent congressional and other elections been running heavily against this "elite"?

The pluralists say that America is a society dominated not by one or a few interest groups and cultural patterns, but by numerous and varied ones, including a large number of diverse social institutions, such as religion, politics, the economy, the family, and education; a large number of ethnic subgroups, such as blacks, Chicanos, Japanese, Jewish, Polish, and Italian; a variety of value systems that agree on certain elements of faith, such as faith in the individual, belief in progress, toleration of human differences, and willingness to help the underdog; and by a great number and kinds of serious social problems, such as the dehumanization of society caused by technology.

But it is important to bear in mind that a pluralistic sociocultural complex, such as America has been in the past and remains in the present, is capable of meeting the needs of people with diverse concerns and interests. It is also capable of resolving major social problems as they arise. This is because such a society is not frozen by a centralized command characteristic of totalitarian systems. Being relatively loosely organized, even today, it may sometimes take longer for an open society to respond to specific needs, but in the long run more needs will be met by an open, flexible structure, and more freedom and creative expression will be engendered in more people.

The schools reflect this pluralistic order, even if they have been somewhat slow to respond to new social imperatives. Modern elementary and secondary schools are accommodating problems of poverty, for example, by providing **compensatory education** programs for children of the ghetto. Schools are gradually becoming racially desegregated in the North and the South, as a result of minority demands and enlightened judicial decisions. Teachers are receiving higher salaries and increased status as professionals. Their preparation for teaching improves with the recognition that their jobs are crucial to society and involve more challenge than was previously thought. Technological innovations for education currently are being made at a rapid rate because more sophisticated mechanisms are available for obtaining feedback about how well the institution is performing its social functions. Schools are able to respond by developing advanced technologies to serve people. Even textbooks are beginning to acknowledge more of the accomplishments and the contributions of minorities.

In these ways, both school and society have become more, not less, humane. In the classroom, teachers no longer take children for granted. In matters of discipline, both psychology and the law have combined to reduce propensities to treat children as second-class citizens. For instance, a "bill of rights" for children is part of a wide-ranging special study report presented to the California legislature. This report asserts "that persons who occupy the status of children are people within the meaning of the Bill of Rights of our federal Constitution."[18] One of the several proposals to be considered by the state legislature is that urging total abolition of corporal punishment, such as spanking. (Although subsequent legislation in California did abolish spanking by school people without advanced written permission from the parents of the children, in 1975 a conservative U.S. Supreme Court ruled in favor of a teacher's right to spank students as a disciplinary measure in "extreme" cases.)

None of these changes in the educational milieu mitigates the overriding structural conservatism of schools and teaching in a society whose educational institution has been slower than most other institutions to change significantly. But recent developments do offer hope that schools are not totally unresponsive to change.

Parsonian functionalism, or sociocultural pluralism, is a constructive image of modern civilization, because it views prevailing structures as basically worthwhile, although occasionally in need of repair.

America as an Emerging
Post-Industrial Civilization

The most recent image of modern life to emerge in the scholarly literature holds that today we live in a world best characterized as one of massive social change. We are progressing from a state of industrialism to what is now variously termed "post-industrialism," "super-industrialism," "post-modern society," the "service state," or "post-civilization." According to Daniel Bell, the United States is the world's first post-industrial civilization. In Bell's words:

> We are now in the first stages of a post-industrial society. We have become the first nation in the history of the world in which more than half of the employed population is not involved in the production of food, clothing, houses, automobiles, and other tangible goods.
>
> The period since the end of World War II has produced a new consciousness about time and social change. One might well say that 1945 to 1950 were the "birth-years," symbolically, of the post-industrial society.[19]

The basic ingredients of emerging post-industrial civilization include: an increased emphasis upon the theoretical aspects of science; the development of new intellectual schemes that derive from a technological age, such as systems analysis and gaming; the emergence of a service economy that replaces one based on material goods, and of service as the major feature of social and economic institutions; a fundamental transformation in values from traditional to emergent ones; a higher degree of individual and social self-consciousness; the rise of urbanism as the prevalent mode of human existence and the concurrent disappearance of agrarian patterns of living; more active involvement in community and social affairs by people, replacing the earlier twentieth century development of excessive spectatorship and its related anomie; the movement in politics and government toward international controls at the long-term expense of traditional nationalistic systems of control; and the trend, despite glaring exceptions such as China and South Africa, toward more open societies, countering the notion of society as a closed corporation.[20]

According to its proponents, many aspects of this overall trend toward Post-Industrialism are disconnected, and change is continually being manifested in many subtle, small-scale "in-system" modifications, as well as in major alterations of entire societies. Such discontinuities and micro-level dynamics in no way detract from the overall characterization of this historical period as one of massive social change. Social change is massive today because it is occurring everywhere all the time, in every institution to a greater or lesser extent. It takes the form of responses to challenges by neglected minority groups, to problems caused by evolutionary trends (e.g., the growing problem of air and water pollution), and to conditions of living and working in a mass, secondary society that demands great flexibility and adaptation by the individual.

Just as the Reformation symbolized vast changes in Western civilization's mode of conceptualizing and behaving—changes from an essentially medieval ethos to one of pre-modernism—and the Industrial Revolution symbolized vast changes from pre-modern modes of thinking and behaving to what we call modern ones, so the emergence of the Post-Industrial age is believed to represent a fundamental transformation in the history of industrially mature societies. According to Alvin Toffler, "I believe we are at the edge of the most revolutionary changes in American history, that we are faced with the need to create a new future for this country."[21]

The designation of this new age as an emerging one indicates that we have already entered this age, although most of us have been unaware of the fact, so caught up are we in our day-to-day lives that tend to connect us mentally and emotionally to the past. Whether we reside in small towns, farms, or metropolitan cities, we are touched by aspects of Post-Industrialism, such as an automobile or a means of public transportation, a television set, electricity, a telephone, access to public social welfare centers, access to modern medical facilities, and access to modern institutions of higher learning. Unless one lives on a mythical commune *totally* out of connection with the rest of the world and its problems, then one is, to a greater or lesser extent, part of a society that has for some time been moving more pointedly into the future than any previous society in history.

The usual objection to this idea seems to come from small-town dwellers who wonder how their lives have been touched by emerging post-modernism, even if they can grant that the lives of big-city inhabitants might be. Proponents of Post-Industrialism would reply that the confusion arises largely from the mistaken but fairly common assumption that life goes on somewhere else than at home and that significant social change must be highly visible and dramatic—the type that receives attention on national television. It is true that not everyone rides supersonic jets to work or drinks desalinated ocean water or works in a "think tank" or pushes buttons on a computer or has flown to the moon and back or is receiving a guaranteed annual income. But it is not necessarily true that not everyone is affected in some way by these and related phenomena. Post-Industrial thinkers would claim that they fail to recognize that we are a pluralistic society with institutions that tie us to each other, including our most intimate ones, such as the family. When a woman goes to work outside the house in order to help support her family's affluent life style, and, as a result of the subtle influences she receives as a member of a new work force in American society, objects to unequal pay for equal work, she is leaving the past and entering the future. Not only are her conceptions of a woman's place challenged on the job, but when she returns home at night, her life as a wife and mother is often altered by seemingly minor modifications in what she expects of her husband and children (and, reciprocally, what they come to expect of her and themselves). Now she no longer has the time to run a home in the way her own mother did.[22] The same ideas apply to minority group members, who are aided by **affirmative action** laws of the state. The interconnections between inter- and intra-institutional roles expected of and performed by people is tremendous, and the changes wrought by new group and interpersonal involvements are irreversible.

In short, according to adherents of this image of society, life in America is changing at a pace and to an extent unheard of even ten years ago, much less a generation ago. The average child growing up today is apt to be as different from present-day adults in what he or she knows and feels as are young adults from their grandparents, even if, superficially, he or she appears to be just like children have always been, a common, if inaccurate observation. Is a child of ten walking home to his condominium from school with a piece of computer tape with mathematical formulas on it the same child a young adult of today was at ten? Is a teenager hanging around a drug store after school "rapping" with his friends about graduating and traveling around the world on student fare the same teenager today's adult was? Are the young interracial couples walking down the street hand-in-hand the same as the couples with whom today's young adult grew up? The average child today tends to think in many ways as did the so-called "hippies" of the late 1960s—for example, in relation to more relaxed sex norms which his parents would never condone. All these new social mores clearly have important implications for schools and teachers.

Evaluation of the Models of Modern America

The Businessman's Civilization Model

Much of what adherents to the businessman's civilization position say is unquestionably true—particularly about practices occurring in schools today. However, this position, taken as a whole, seems somewhat unsatisfactory as a reliable guide to the actual character of contemporary life and education. It assigns one factor as the basis for an entire civilization's operation. This image does not adequately take into consideration that civilization will undoubtedly continue to change. At crucial points, it relies upon erroneous or at least highly conjectural empirical data (e.g., the Hunter power elite model of community leadership that has recently been reevaluated).[23]

There is no question, however, that American society, for a variety of historical reasons, was heavily undergirded with a business–industrial ethos in the past and that the Industrial Revolution of the eighteenth and nineteenth centuries had a great impact upon the public school movement, which has not yet been significantly modified.[24] The public school in this society perpetuates historically relevant sociocultural elements, despite innovations and modifications in the technology of education (e.g., teaching machines, team teaching, and performance contracting). To a large extent, the American public school as we know it today, born largely of the Industrial Revolution, continues after 1970 to reflect these origins in its philosophy, its curriculum, its organization, and the teacher's roles in the classroom and outside it. It does extol such industrial virtues as competitiveness, hard work, efficiency, obedience to authority, and struggle for **open-class vertical mobility.** Whether it does more than this and whether these virtues are still desirable for members of a society moving toward the twenty-first century are questions to ponder as we move forward in our analysis.

The Pyramidal Oligarchy Model

This model of U.S. society and its schools is highly objectionable to a great number of people, particularly teachers who are viewed as naive dupes by the proponents of this view. Some claim that this image is simplistic, extreme, inaccurate, biased, and based upon faulty data. One of the basic arguments against this image has come from sociocultural pluralist Talcott Parsons, who says:

> Mills gives us the impression that "eliteness" in any society, including our own, is overwhelmingly a question of the power that an individual or a group can command. By this, he means . . . influence on the "big" decisions directly affecting what happens in the society in the short run. But there are many elements in the society which are relatively powerless in this sense, but nevertheless of the greatest functional importance.[25] [Emphasis added]

If Parsons is correct, then schools and teachers, although not highly visible as sources of influence on the lives of the American people, are nonetheless actually or potentially powerful agencies of human development. They are not manipulable pawns of an elite group in society. They reflect a complex and differentiated society, not one whose influences upon schools are highly centralized in one oligarchical group as Mills believed.

To which the New Left elitists, like their counterparts on the far right, have a ready-made answer that can never be refuted logically, even if completely false: "Anyone who doesn't agree with us proves thereby that he has been 'bought' by the Establishment; he demonstrates just how successful their conspiracy has been." No matter how carefully one points out facts, in attempting to refute such a charge, one must fail because facts are capable of a variety of congenial interpretations.

Those of us who really want to understand schooling and teaching in contemporary American society have a moral obligation to look objectively at the available evidence and to strive to interpret this evidence in a way that is fair to the children growing up in this social order. The evidence on schools and teachers as reflections of this society's structure does not support the theses of Mills, the radical New Left, or the apologists for the status quo.

The Model of Society as a Technological Monstrosity

As with the business image and to some extent the pryamidal image of society, there is more than a grain of truth to the assertion that technology has overstepped its bounds in the United States today. We have serious water and air pollution and pervasive feelings of being controlled by a technology that estranges us from our work and from each other. But these social problems appear to be symptoms of a larger set of phenomena that are radically influencing our lives. They do not derive from a single cause. A misused technology is misused by *people*, who possess values that may be productive of individual and social harmony or of social fragmentation. Thus, we may hope that Kranzberg and Davenport are correct in saying that:

> Blaming technology for all the troubles of Western civilization in the mid-twentieth century is, of course, a "cop out"—it is an answer, but not an explanation. By placing the blame for all the ills of the human predicament in the last decades of the twentieth century on some impersonal force—"technology"—men can hope to avoid responsibility for their own actions.[26]

The Pluralist Model of Society

The major problem with pluralism as a description of American society is that it describes society in highly abstract terms. It tells us that life in general is complex and many faceted, but appears to stop at this point. It is useful primarily as a theoretical construct to set the descriptive stage, not to grace it.

We need a view of America that goes a bit further, by showing how life in this complex society at the present time can be characterized in reasonably broad configurations. It must show how the educationally relevant facets of society are specifically related to the larger society, so that those aspects of social life can be analyzed and dealt with.

The Post-Industrial Model of Society

The requirements lacking in the pluralist image are met in the model of Post-Industrialism. This model is not deterministic, and it does not argue that a single factor defines the nature of society. It says that certain features of society are more determining of society's direction than others.

The Post-Industrial model helps us see where we are coming from— a businessman's civilization or, more precisely, a civilization ruled by the ethos of industrial growth. This model does not deny that elites in the military, the government, and large corporations have powerful and at times inordinate influence upon the lives of every member of the society, including teachers. Nor does this image ignore the problems of a technology that has been permitted to run rampant because of its own success. And, this image acknowledges that the United States is a complex, many-faceted society with numerous subcultural groups and ideologies.

This image of modern life is useful as a guide to analysis also because it points to the reality that the American economy is becoming a service economy of white-collar workers. Scientific theory is replacing a former dependence upon the collection of data in the more advanced fields of scientific endeavor. And our basic social values are undergoing dramatic alteration. Most significantly, the analysis of society by the Post-Industrial model stresses that American civilization is in the process of experiencing phenomenal change. This characteristic of the Post-Industrial model is the one which offers a central theme to this book. If anything defines the nature of society today, and, by implication, the needs that our schools and teachers should be serving, it is the theme of massive change affecting all our lives. Thus, without abandoning the other images, the model of Post-Industrialism shall serve as a framework to organize the discussion for this study of education and society.

The Cultural Lag of the American School

What are some of the fundamental educational needs of children growing up in the emerging Post-Industrial society? To what extent are society's schools and teachers responding to these needs? Are educators making a serious effort to respond with up-to-date programs and practices of high quality?

Emergent Educational Needs

Contemporary American society demands that certain educational needs be met if we are to live together successfully. These emergent educational priorities are important to the Post-Industrial society as it strives to become a more humanistic society. Some social analysts fear that this society may become a garrison state (a military dictatorship) unless present problems of living related to growing individual and social alienation are not resolved soon.[27]

New Human Relations.   One major educational need is to teach children how to relate in a caring, non-hostile manner with people from diverse cultural backgrounds with different values. In our society, people must learn to establish good relationships easily and quickly and also learn to end these relationships rapidly.[28] This is true not only on the job but in social life as well. For example, many people in American society are geographically mobile. As soon as they settle in a community and begin to make friends, either they or their friends move to a new city or state to begin a new job. Through such experiences, many people become fearful of investing too much emotional energy in relationships that could eventually entail a sense of loss.

One is forced to learn to quickly forget or reconcile the past. The alternative is to permanently remain where one's job is, but employment is not easily controlled by the individual. It is difficult, for example, for people in the business world to decline opportunities to advance occupationally, which often require moving to another community. This "temporary society" is part of organizational life; the emotional stability offered by defined relationships is often lacking in space agencies, universities, and businesses. New capabilities for satisfying human relationships are educational priorities of the emerging Post-Industrial age.

New Ideas, Values, and Problems.   A second educational need for people today centers around the ability to tolerate and perhaps to integrate novel ideas and different values that are a part of a pluralistic culture. Society must cope with the great diversity of new and increased personal and interpersonal problems in an age of instability and new opportunities. The kinds of problems amenable to educational treatment today are how to cope with divorce, with racial violence, and with personal alienation from the political–governmental process and those who represent the individual in government.

Schools can do far more in raising the consciousness of children and adolescents in regard to changing patterns of thinking and valuing. Schools are ideally situated to confront young people with the significant problems of living in a new age. They can help children to analyze such problems and to test hypotheses for resolving them, perhaps through community-action projects or in settings that simulate social behavior. The phenomenon of what Alvin Toffler calls "future shock" is upon many of us now, and it will probably increase.[29] We must learn how to deal with the dramatically increased personal and social stresses and strains that, in one form or another, affect all of us in a dynamic Post-Industrial age.

Human Uses of Technology.   A third major area of educational need for this emerging period is learning to use an advanced technology for humane purposes. To use inexpensive pocket computers when we go shopping, to tally grocery items instead of relying upon deductive skills, is not inherently dehumanizing.

   We can learn to help each other by applying the techniques of simulation, or role playing, to the resolution of complex interpersonal relations problems that require insight into the feelings of our role partners. Instead of trying to get into the shoes of our friends and lovers when we are in trouble, most of us still blame the other and rationalize our own negative contributions to the problem.

This is an age of new intellectual technologies, and we need to learn to employ them wisely for humanistic ends, not permit them to become our masters.

Original Personal Lifestyles.   A fourth major educational need for people growing up in Post-Industrial society is the ability to find personal fulfillment in a constantly changing environment that no longer possesses institutional structures that define the individual's role or place in the community. We must accept the inevitability of a certain degree of existential loneliness and ambiguity because of the loss of a primary community of friends and relations.[30] And it is becoming more and more certain that a career alone will not suffice to furnish meaning to a life, as it may once have for some. Most people cannot realistically expect to have an all-encompassing career to occupy their time and energy. The increased amount of leisure time has strong implications for personal life style and must be reckoned with as we move into the future.[31] How do we live our personal lives? What do we do with our "free" time? For most people, watching television in isolated suburban houses or searching for empty pleasures are only temporary palliatives to an essentially lonely and disconnected existence. Americans need to learn how to live life on a personally rewarding basis. They need to learn to become involved with other people, to develop artistic outlets for creative expression and ideas that engage the mind and heart. This matter of finding new and fulfilling lifestyles may be the most crucial one of modern times for educators.

In sum, there are at least six major areas with which educators must concern themselves: human relations, new ideas, values, and social problems, the human uses of technology, and developing personal life-styles.

To What Extent Are American Schools Meeting the Emergent Needs of Students?

To what extent are the teachers who occupy the central positions as educators in schools dealing with these imperative needs? Toffler offers a critical assessment of current education:

> What passes for education today, even in our "best" schools and colleges, is a hopeless anachronism. Parents look to education to fit their children for life in the future. Teachers warn that lack of an education will cripple a child's chances in the world of tomorrow. Government ministries, churches, the mass media—all exhort young people to stay in school, insisting that now, as never before, one's future is almost wholly dependent upon education.

Yet for all this rhetoric about the future, our schools face backward toward a dying system, rather than forward to the emerging new society. Their vast energies are applied to cranking out Industrial Men [and Women]—people tooled for survival in a system that will be dead before they are.[32]

Nor is Toffler convinced that the flood of innovations purportedly revolutionizing American education is preparing children for successful human relations, for changing ideas and values, for improved personal life styles, or for proper use of new technology. Since most of the innovations of contemporary education are technological, not **valuational,** they may only help to familiarize and condition people to living in a tech- nologically sophisticated system. They do not necessarily help people to use technology for worthy human ends. Certainly, technological innovation alone will not make education serviceable as a means for learning how to live in a transitional society. Education must become more concerned with innovation in the realm of human values.

In terms of responding to the new needs of a massively changing society, schools are operating in a vacuum. They are attempting to fulfill outdated needs of an industrial society by supplying new technological gadgetry and forms of organization. They are concentrating almost exclusively on teaching the written word in an age of electronic media; on arithmetic in an age of computers; on chauvinistic national history in an international age; on physical science in an age of social science and new humanistic studies; on production of material products in an age of human services; on acceptance of one's ascribed slot in an age requiring creative and flexible decision making and problem solving. The educational needs of emerging Post-Industrial society are basically for open and creative adaptation to social change—not for acceptance of a closed and rigid social system or for maintenance of cultural patterns that no longer exist. The American school is performing pattern-maintenance functions in a period calling for adaptive ones. In many respects, our schools seem to be lagging severely behind much of the rest of American society, in regard to their educational purposes, and also in the processes by means of which these purposes are effectuated.

What Can a Prospective Teacher Do About Cultural Lag?

Many teachers view their work as separate from their "real" lives. In their alienation from their students, they eventually become alienated from themselves; they learn to function more or less routinely, without much feeling and without much positive impact upon the students.

Pressures to reduce the existing lag between the school and society are becoming more intensified. As we move further into the post-modern age, escapism will not work as a mechanism for coping with one's problems.

To be an effective teacher, one must make an authentic effort to determine where to head with students, parents, administrators, and everyone else concerned with education. You should proceed intelligently and gradually, using all the alternative means learned throughout your pre- and post-service preparation. This is not to disdain collaborative involvement with other educators, citizens, and students, but rather to suggest that on the basis of your educational values and understanding of educational process and strategy, you should decide just how, when, and to what extent to work collaboratively with others.

A professional is a public service worker who makes autonomous and complex decisions based upon theoretical knowledge and experience that is shared to some extent with colleagues. A professional assumes existential responsibility for his or her work.

We live in an essentially new and extremely dynamic period in human history. The school is a creature of this social order, and school teachers educate for human life in the present and future, not for life in the past. The challenges you face as a school teacher will be tremendous, but they can be ennobling and enriching for those who can respond and who enjoy living a vital life with young people.

Summary

Since society and education are inextricably interrelated, the way in which a teacher perceives of society tends to shape his or her ideas about the purposes of education and, correspondingly, how he or she behaves as a teacher.

Most views of contemporary American society and education can be found somewhere within one or more of five broad images, or models, of modern civilization:

- America as a businessman's civilization
- America as a pyramidal oligarchy
- America as a technological monstrosity
- America as a pluralistic sociocultural complex
- America as an emergent Post-Industrial society

Although each image has some degree of accuracy, the first four are considered either too simplistic or lacking in descriptive power. Hence, they are rejected as tenable models of *modern* society and education for prospective teachers. The fifth image of contemporary America as a Post-Industrial civilization subsumes the other models within the conception of massive social change. It is offered as a particularly useful model for teachers.

In the emerging Post-Industrial society, people need to be educated for adaptability, for what Alvin Toffler calls "cope-ability." As he says:

> For education the lesson is clear: its prime objective must be to increase the individual's "cope-ability"—the speed and economy with which he can adapt to continual change.[33]

Four general areas of learning for which teachers must be responsible in Post-Industrial America appear to be:

- Learning to deal effectively with complex human relations
- Learning to handle new ideas and values and to solve difficult personal and social problems
- Learning to employ an advanced technology for humane ends
- Learning to develop personal lifestyles

To date, most American schools have not responded substantially to these new educational needs. Schools continue to function predominantly as pattern-maintenance institutions, rather than as adaptive ones. They lag behind the rest of the transforming social order.

Prospective teachers must authentically confront the real educational needs of students in a fast-changing world. They must accomplish this within a frame of reference that frankly acknowledges and intelligently provides for the limitations of the organizational tradition in which teachers work as existential decision makers.

Related Concepts

affirmative action   A term commonly used nowadays to refer to preferential treatment of minorities formerly denied equal treatment in job hiring and promotion, admission to colleges, etc. Such action has been urged for women, blacks, Chicanos, native Americans, and Puerto Ricans, in particular.

compensatory education   Special education intended to compensate for alleged deficiencies or disadvantages of minority members of society who historically have failed to achieve in school according to standardized expectations. This type of educational program is often federally funded and directed.

feedback   Used by system analysts to connote information that comes into a system from the external environment and tells how well the system is performing its functions

open-class vertical mobility   Referring to a relatively fluid hierarchical system of social class that offers opportunities for up and down movement (especially through competition). Social position is not exclusively dependent upon one's position and rank at birth in a society with open-class vertical mobility.

power elite   An oligarchy, or government by a few. For reasons of wealth, birth, education, or any other exclusively held characteristics, members of an oligarchy become an aristocracy in a society. In contemporary America, some refer to the power elite of the "military-industrial-governmental complex."

technological innovation   A creation, material or nonmaterial, aimed primarily at improving people's ability to accomplish their purposes or ends. Technological innovations are innovations in means (e.g., an electric typewriter, a teaching team).

technocrat   A technician, or specialized expert, involved in ruling society; for example, engineers, nuclear physicists, and physicians are sometimes said to be the leaders of society.

valuational (innovation)   A nonmaterial creation aimed primarily at improving people's lives by establishing essentially new purposes or ends (e.g., a constitutional revision, a new curriculum).

Suggested Activity

In order to obtain a firsthand impression of where contemporary schools stand in relation to changes in the rest of society, sample school activities in your own community. Pick an elementary and a secondary school at random. Visit each school one or more times. (This may be part of a broader class project involving participant-observation in the field to augment your foundational studies.) Observe several classes during various parts of the day to determine the extent to which students are being exposed to subject matter pertinent to their lives in the present and future.

Make notes on your findings and, along with your peers in class, report on and discuss their meaning and significance.

References and Notes

1. Grace Graham, *The Public School in the New Society: The Social Foundations of Education* (New York: Harper & Row, 1969), pp. 17–41.

2. *Ibid.*, pp. 22–24.

3. Floyd Hunter, *Community Power Structure: A Study of Decision Makers* (Chapel Hill: University of North Carolina Press, 1953).

4. The modern pluralistic theory of power is often credited to Edward Banfield and Robert Dahl. *See* Banfield, *Political Influence* (New York: Free Press, 1961), and Dahl, *Who Governs? Democracy and Power in an American City* (New Haven: Yale University Press, 1961).

5. *See,* for example, Michael B. Kane, *Minorities in Textbooks: A Study of Their Treatment in Social Studies Texts* (Chicago: Quadrangle Books, in cooperation with the Anti-Defamation League of B'nai B'rith, 1970), pp. 77–111.

6. And recent studies suggest that grading practices—at least in high schools—have changed little since the turn of the century: "... data from the National Longitudinal Study would indicate little recent experimentation with alternatives to traditional grading systems." (Barbara Moretti Pinchak and Hunter M. Boreland, "Grading Practices in American High Schools," *The Education Digest* 39 [March 1974]: 23).

7. *See* Matina Horner, "Fail: Bright Women," *Psychology Today* 3 (November 1969): 36.

8. Graham, *New Society,* p. 29.

9. Ralph Miliband, "C. Wright Mills," in G. William Domhoff and Hoyt B. Ballard, eds., *C. Wright Mills and the Power Elite* (Boston: Beacon Press, 1968), p. 10. *See also* C. Wright Mills, *The Power Elite* (New York: Oxford University Press, 1956).

10. Martin Nicolaus, "The Professional Organization of Sociology: A View from Below," in J. David Colfax and Jack L. Roach, eds., *Radical Sociology* (New York: Basic Books, 1971), p. 51.

11. Eugene V. Schneider, "The Sociology of C. Wright Mills," in *C. Wright Mills,* pp. 19–21.

12. Herbert J. Muller, *The Children of Frankenstein: A Primer on Modern Technology and Human Values* (Bloomington: Indiana University Press, 1970), pp. 3–5.

13. Tom Sine, "The Megamachine and the Schoolhouse," *Phi Delta Kappan* 60 (March 1974): 473.

14. According to a recent report, research projects to be funded in the near future by the National Institute of Education, which in turn, is supported by the U.S. Office of Education and the president, are to concentrate on compensatory education and basic skills, not on human relations education. These research priorities are the same as those suggested in recent months by former NIE Director Thomas K. Glennan and approved by the National Council on Educational Research. A fifth priority suggested by Glennan and approved by the Council was dropped from the list: "increasing diversity, pluralism and opportunity in American education." (*Report on Education*

Research 6 [Jan. 30, 1974]: 1).

15. Robert Heilboner, "Do Machines Make History?" in Melvin Kanzberg and William H. Davenport, eds., *Technology and Culture: An Anthology* (New York: Schocken Books, 1972), p. 39.

16. Aldous Huxley, "Achieving a Perspective on the Technological Order," in *Technology and Culture*, p. 125.

17. For an interesting discussion of the erosion of pluralism in social thought, see Alvin W. Gouldner, *The Coming Crisis of Western Sociology* (New York: Basic Books, 1970).

18. *Fresno Bee*, April 8, 1974, p. 1.

19. Daniel Bell, *The Coming of Post-Industrial Society: A Venture in Social Forecasting* (New York: Basic Books, 1973), pp. 343, 346.

20. For more detailed analyses of these trends, see the following works: Bell, *Post-Industrial Society*; Kenneth Boulding, *The Meaning of the 20th Century* (New York: Harper & Row, 1964); Amatai Etzioni, *The Active Society: A Theory of Societal and Political Processes* (New York: The Free Press, 1968); Wilbert E. Moore, *Social Change* (Englewood Cliffs, N.J.: Prentice-Hall, 1963); Muller, *Children of Frankenstein*; George D. Spindler, "Education in a Transforming American Culture," *Harvard Educational Review* 25 (Summer 1955): 145–56.

21. Alvin Toffler, "The American Future Is Being Bumbled Away," *The Futurist* 10 (April 1976): 101.

22. The matter of time and its cost in a Post-Industrial society is one with which teachers as well as others will have to grapple in the future. See, for example,

Daniel Bell, "The End of Scarcity," *Saturday Review of the Society* (April 21, 1973): 52.

23. For an in-depth discussion of this model, see Michael Aiken and Paul E. Mott, eds., *The Structure of Community Power* (New York: Random House, 1970).

24. Michael Katz, *Class, Bureaucracy, and Schools: The Illusion of Educational Change in America* (New York: Praeger Publishers, 1971).

25. Talcott Parsons, "The Distribution of Power in American Society," in *C. Wright Mills*, p. 74.

26. Kanzberg and Davenport, *Technology and Culture*, p. 23.

27. See Willis Harmon, "Nature of Our Changing Society: Implications for Schools," in Philip K. Piele, Terry L. Eidell, with Stuart C. Smith *Social and Technological Change: Implications for Education* (Eugene: The Center for the Advanced Study of Educational Administration, University of Oregon, 1970), pp. 1–67.

28. Warren G. Bennis and Philip E. Slater, *The Temporary Society* (New York: Harper & Row, 1968).

29. Alvin Toffler, *Future Shock* (New York: Bantam Books, 1970).

30. See Philip E. Slater, *The Pursuit of Loneliness: American Culture at the Breaking Point* (Boston: Beacon Press, 1970).

31. Vance Packard, *A Nation of Strangers* (New York: David McKay, 1972).

32. Toffler, *Future Shock*, pp. 398, 399.

33. *Ibid.*, p. 403.

6

Institutional Changes Affecting Education

Societies are large-scale arrangements of culturally patterned human behavior, and social institutions are the major vehicles in society for ordering and patterning human behavior. Thus, social institutions form the basis for collective life in society. One can even say that society amounts to an integration of its several institutions. Most daily life occurs within institutions, and social change eventually becomes institutionalized. In short, social institutions are the major working components of societies.

Although formal education itself has become a highly specialized social institution, the school feels the impact of other institutions and, in turn, it affects other institutions directly or indirectly. Therefore, the study of school and society is in part the study of the interworkings of major social institutions.

In this chapter, we will examine important social institutions in American society and their implications for schooling and teaching, as well as major trends that crosscut institutional life.

Social Institutions in Modern Society

Americans have always admired the pragmatic spirit, but in the past this admiration was limited largely to the material realms of life. Before the influence of Charles Peirce, John Dewey, and William James, the successfull implementation of pragmatism was based on common sense, rather

153

than on formalized systems for solving problems. The pragmatic spirit was exemplified by the rugged individualist of the western frontier, building a "paradise" out of the "chaos" of nature. However, with the gradual diffusion of Enlightenment ideas of rationalism and with the impetus of the Industrial Revolution and Reformation theology, America underwent a profound change in its conceptualization and utilization of pragmatic ideology.

Science and Technology

The last hundred years of our history have wrought a revolution in social and economic organization based upon the self-conscious employment of science as a system of intelligent thought and upon technology as a system of problem solving born of science.

Although science and technology have become highly institutionalized primarily in material realms of life (we are a materialistic society), it is a serious mistake to assume that these two revolutionary offspring of the pragmatic spirit have limited their influence to material realms, such as designing and producing durable goods and developing mechanistic theories for such production. Actually, the spirit of science and technology has pervaded American life and thought, especially since the end of World War II. Today we are accustomed to such terms as "social science," "human engineering," "scientific management," "systems analysis," the "science" of politics—even the "science" of education.

It is now probably more appropriate to call America a "scientific—technological" society rather than a materialistic society. The former designation more accurately describes the dominant cultural ethos of modern America, and forms the basis upon which most of society's focal organizations are structured and operated. Science and technology now extend to almost all fields of endeavor in America.[1] Increasingly, all areas of life are being permeated by the ethos of rationality, which is manifested by our emphasis on organizational and social planning, based upon empirical research and logical, well-constructed theories. The scientific—technological society has become very much dependent upon highly trained experts for guidance in affairs ranging from physical and mental health and marriage and family counseling to educational management and program development, city and regional planning, and high level government decisions, labor management, and economics.

This new age of experts signifies the preeminence of the professional–managerial classes in modern American society, and provokes fundamental questions about the average person's place in the system or "Establishment." Bigness, or large-scale bureaucratic organizational life controlled largely by experts and scientifically oriented managers of ex-

perts, has become the dominant social style in America.[2] Despite the stresses such a life entails, most people do not want it any other way. In recent years, however, a different impression may have been conveyed by the mass media, by its extensive coverage of a comparative handful of malcontents, who demand a return to allegedly more innocent times.

Schooling in this society has been strongly influenced by the scientific–technological impulse. American schools are large-scale enterprises; hundreds or thousands of students attend one elementary or high school. Schools are often highly organized and administered according to norms of rationality and efficiency. They are increasingly run by technocrats— experts in administration and instruction. Education is currently preoccupied with advanced technological "hardware" for instructional purposes. Although efforts are being made by some minority groups and some liberal parents and teachers to offset this technocratic impulse, most schools today remain large-scale technocratic enterprises. They cost a great deal of money to run and require a plethora of technical skills on the parts of their personnel.

Modern technologies can be employed in the interest of humane learning for humane living, rather than in the interest of accomplishing increasingly obsolete ends more efficiently. Perhaps by speeding up the learning of basic skills with technological aids, youngsters can spend more time discovering how to solve complex human problems or how to develop new lifestyles.

The Economic Institution

Nowhere can the spirit of technocracy be seen more clearly than in the economic realm of modern American society. The scientific–technological revolution began with the efforts of eighteenth-, nineteenth-, and early twentieth-century industrialists to build their fortunes upon such time- and manpower-saving mechanical and managerial innovations as the Watts steam engine, the internal combustion engine, and the scientific management concepts of Frederick Taylor. America idealized the business–industrial ethos as the key to its phenomenal growth from a wilderness to a highly developed nation.

Whether or not we agree with the broad assertions of writers who continue to uphold the claim of economic determinism,[3] it is difficult not to be aware of the importance of the business–industrial influence on this society's development in the past. If we are not simply a businessman's civilization, we have, nonetheless, been heavily influenced by the spirit of business, or more properly, by the spirit of pragmatism and progressivism as manifested by science and technology in the economic realm.*

Although the American economy was once dominated by the individual farmer and small businessman, today's economy is controlled by large corporate enterprises. Even farming has become a big business, and small retail establishments have become franchises, or chains. In America today, one-half of 1 percent of business controls two-thirds of the national sales.[4] With big business has come the evolution of a highly organized workforce. Today's blue-collar worker is usually a member of a nationally or internationally controlled union. The unions themselves are controlled by efficiency experts from universities, private consulting firms, or government agencies, employed to effectively bargain with management.

To a large extent, the average worker has become a kind of "nonperson" on the job, despite the efforts of management and labor leaders to make him or her content and productive through such nostrums as the regular coffee break, factory bowling teams, and other endeavors geared to improving human relations. Most people today, whether they are employed by private enterprise or public agencies, work in large, bureaucratic organizations where efficiency and standardization of interchangeable parts—material and human—are important goals. A job is perceived by more and more people solely as a means to other ends outside of the forty- or thirty-hour work week. For most white-collar and blue-collar employees, their job does not involve meaningful labor. Jobs are tolerated primarily in order to obtain paychecks for the purpose of consuming desirable products or services in one's free time.[5]

---

* This statement in no way denies the Weberian thesis that the Protestant ethic provides the underpinning for the American business ethos.

For the comparatively small, but growing percentage of professional, technical, and service workers in the emerging Post-Industrial economy, work has a different meaning than it does for the majority of semi-skilled or unskilled blue-collar and clerical workers in giant corporations and government agencies. A society that is unmistakably becoming organized around service to the consumer and to the public requires that some people be highly qualified technically and professionally. The professional, technical, service people in modern America are finding their work more challenging on intellectual grounds and in terms of time required. So, while the majority of modern workers increasingly perceive their jobs as primarily means to other ends outside of their workplace, a growing but smaller segment of the working population is being called upon to live for their careers.

Different occupational opportunities and challenges correspond to different life styles, leisure-time activities, access to privilege, residence, and social and personal problems.* The leaders of the emerging civilization are often the experts—the technocrats who are charged with the management of society because of their highly specialized occupational skills. Overseeing the technocrats are members of the new managerial classes. Although officially called "generalists," they are often recruited from the ranks of the technocrats; many industrial firms promote highly specialized engineers and scientists to top managerial positions.

With the great changes in modern business and industry made possible by technological advances, including **automation** and cybernetics, the initial job training of the average worker quickly becomes obsolete. Younger and younger mandatory retirement ages are partly due to this situation. It is now suggested that the average worker will need to retrain several times during his working life, possibly by returning to school in order to maintain his usefulness to his employers.[6] The rate of technological change affecting work today is so great that continuing vocational education will become a fundamental requirement for most employees in the future.

At the same time as job skills are being made obsolete by advances in technology, automation and cybernation have brought a decrease in jobs for the unskilled and the young, a trend toward jobs demanding skilled control of machines, and a problem of increased leisure time for most workers. Although these occupational trends have altered the concepts of work and leisure in our society, the outputs of the industrial market's **black box** have rapidly increased, ensuring the theoretical capability of general material prosperity for all people.

Although increased productive capability has benefited male, white, and middle-aged workers and their families by providing increased in-

---

* As we will point out later, these differences are being offset by a growing homogenization of American cultural life.

comes and greater ability to consume, it has not significantly affected the prosperity of women, racial minorities, and older workers. Recent civil-rights legislation and movements to reduce economic and educational disparities, however, do give hope that earning and consuming capabilities will become more nearly equal soon.

The American economy is no longer a free enterprise economy, although the free enterprise ethic is invoked by some vested interests. The economy is increasingly influenced and controlled by the federal government, which has become involved in regulating the once autonomous affairs of business and labor. The interests of the comparatively unorganized consumer recently have been given a voice in government.* Examples of government controlling the economy are the partial nationalization of passenger railroad services, the 1971 freeze on wages and prices, and the 1973 refreeze. Change in the economy has been vast, if relatively slow in comparison with many other nations in the world. These changes are in line with the phenomenal growth of complexity in society and the problems associated with this growth.

At present schools are geared largely to what we have called the "businessman's civilization." Essentially, education is devoted to developing skills and values related to a life of hard work in small business establishments, professions, or large factories. Life in a Post-Industrial society, however, involves new conceptions of work, and hence a new kind of preparation for work. Rather than being exclusively preoccupied with fitting people into the existing industrial order, schools may now need to prepare people to choose their own style of life. They may need to prepare them to make choices of all sorts, work being only one among many decisions to make in a service-oriented society. In this sense, perhaps schools ought to become more responsive to individual desires. Some contemporary students may want to study the work world in depth, while others may prefer to learn about philosophy or politics or poetry. If schools do concern themselves with work, perhaps their concern should be for changing, not static, job requirements and for the benefit of affluent as well as poor youngsters.[7]

Intelligent consumption of services and goods may need to become a part of the curriculum of the modern school. Children and youth of today need to know how to intelligently select what they will consume, instead of relying uncritically upon the commercial propaganda continuously spewed forth on television.

While the changing economy deserves attention in modern schools,

---

* The failure of private enterprise and of the government to take a responsible interest in the consumer has resulted in the rise of consumer protection efforts by private individuals and groups in recent years. Witness the rise to national prominence of Ralph Nader, for example.

the kind of attention that may best serve children may be helping them to freely and critically choose their occupation, lifestyle, and what they will consume. Learning to make such choices is perhaps best done by objective study in the social studies of work and consumption.

Welfare

As American society becomes increasingly complex, differentiated, and mass-oriented, and as traditional forms of social control in such primary groups as the family, neighborhood, and church lose their influence, the average person becomes more and more dependent upon public, professional, and legally sanctioned forms of counsel, training, and material aid in his or her struggle to remain human and to possess some of the fruits of an advanced technological civilization.

The concept of the human community in socialistic societies, such as the USSR, or in social systems still committed to some degree of economic individualism, such as the United States, has expanded so that even in non-socialistic societies, human welfare is gradually being recognized and accepted as a responsibility not only of the individual and his primary group affiliations, but of the entire secondary society. More public education, massive financial assistance, the eradication of poverty, recreational development, physical and mental health services, road building, public housing, city planning designed for human needs, and civil rights are symbolic of this expanded sense of community. They also show an expanded conception of the individual's social needs. The federal government is increasingly responsible for social welfare, as illustrated by growing federal involvement in education and by promises of income-assistance guarantees to individual members of society.

These trends toward the **welfare state** have also caused various reactions to the unequal distribution of funds for support of expanded public services. The inability of the "haves" to provide for the "have-nots" under antiquated tax laws and the cultural lag between the American value of rugged individualism and the requirements of a mass secondary society have caused conflict. The scientific–technological society has largely destroyed the myth of rugged individualism and replaced it with the concept of opportunity as the basis for success or failure in life.

At present, the future of human services in American society appears to be at the crossroads. We will either move ahead in the direction of a more or less complete welfare state that guarantees opportunity for health and happiness to everyone, or we will attempt to stall the human evolutionary process as long as possible by depending upon outdated ideological arguments. The latter alternative is more typical of the

American experience, and the stance it represents continues to be assumed by the majority of people and their political representatives today.

How long can a cultural lag between archaic ideology and the demands of Post-Industrial evolution be maintained? Will some kind of fundamental social disequilibrium occur? Will it cause more incurable social fragmentation and other systemic dysfunctions? The present criticism of the welfare institution suggests that we are perhaps reaching a turning point.

The average person's notions about human welfare and the human community are clearly lagging behind the realities of life in a secondary society where voluntary private services no longer ensure life, liberty, and the pursuit of happiness for all. The school, in aiding and abetting such privatistic notions by stressing rugged and competitive individualism, may be performing a disservice for society. Students need to learn that a new conception of human community is in order and that it is dependent upon cooperative, corporate involvement, rather than solely upon individual responsibility for self and success. In curricula and general operations, schools need to facilitate sharing and mutual growth.

Such a change in emphasis need not destroy individual initiative, independence, and creativity. Quite the contrary, by deemphasizing the rugged individual mythology, students should be enabled to contribute their diverse, unique talents and interests to the classroom group without anxiety. Self-actualization will be vastly increased and become possible even for individuals once believed to possess little potential.

Symbolic Institutions

America has always had a tradition of openness to entrepreneurial enterprise and expansion. Basic democratic ideals have placed a preeminent value upon the individual and, to a lesser extent, upon the notion of equality of opportunity. America has a number of separate ethnic subcultures, racial and religious subcultures, and subcultures based upon social stratification systems that have developed as society has matured and selected and sorted some people into elite groups and others into the lower and middle classes.

Such a cultural patterning continues to operate today and is perpetuated by those who have social advantages and by those who are socially disadvantaged. Minorities now have pride in their racial or ethnic identities and have succeeded in many schools in implementing minority studies.

Cultural pluralism notwithstanding, American society may be characterized as in the process of becoming a mass, or homogeneous, culture. The social institutions contributing most to this trend since post–Civil War acceleration of the scientific–technological revolution have included the economic institution which, until recently, produced consumer goods cheaply enough to allow a large portion of the American people to become members of the middle class. Although many experts believe functional illiteracy is still excessively high,[8] the rapid development of universal public education has greatly reduced illiteracy in the United States. It also has aided in the widespread diffusion of an elaborated language code, so useful in working and living in a complex society with a middle-class culture.[9] Increased years of schooling have allowed great numbers of young people to learn what at one time only the wealthy could afford to learn. More significantly, perhaps, increased opportunities for higher education have permitted people from different cultural backgrounds to associate informally in the peer groups of formal educational structures. Many believe that peer groups do most of the actual educating of people in schools, or at least strongly influence the formal education process.[10] The knowledge explosion is coupled with a general explosion of popular culture, offering more and more people access to books formerly available to only a very few, as well as to creative thought and feeling through public displays and performances of gifted artists and musicians.

Mass culture has other institutional ramifications, such as television advertising and public relations experts who have the power to create and diffuse new mass images and felt needs related to consuming and to political decision making. The potential of the symbol makers who control the influential electronic media to arouse the best and the worst in all of us has been well documented. Whether they operate for selfish or public ends, these symbol makers have influenced our awareness, if not our values.

Image making and the rise of mass culture are phenomena that can be viewed as incomplete. They may be harbingers of the kind of deadly uniform society disturbingly portrayed by Orwell in *1984*. Or they may help to reintegrate a confused and disparate society. By employing science and technology, society can be redirected and renewed.

Two major implications for schools can be inferred from the discussion presented above:

• To discourage the trend toward uniformity, it may be vital that schools encourage the study of diverse cultures, including but not limited to the traditional linguistic, artistic, and musical forms of the groups whose children attend a particular school. In this way, appreciation for the uniqueness of other groups in American society as well as of one's own may be fostered.

• To facilitate development of a sophisticated and viable mass society to which a variety of distinctive subgroups may yet adhere, the

161

schools might incorporate instruction in formal language into the study of important and real problems affecting students' lives. This might mean teaching language arts and social studies as one subject, rather than as separate subjects.

Mass society and culture are realities of our time. Our schools can help to ensure that such a society be made better, while promoting the appreciation of cultural pluralism as an antidote to the uniformity of modern life.

Politics and Government

In discussing the changing institutions of the economy, welfare, science, and technology, we must inevitably discuss the changing role of government and politics. The political and governmental institutions of America seem to have changed gradually in response to continuous change in the rest of society. In recent years, these institutions have taken the initiative in leading in the process of change in certain areas— notably in coping with poverty through educational and economic legislation and dispersal of monies and services. (To some extent, such efforts are determined by what groups are in power at a given time.) The institutions of politics and government are closely interrelated with almost all aspects of social life, due to their critical social control, integrative, and goal-attainment functions.[11] Because of their assigned responsibility to all the people in this society, it is easy to understand that basic change in society is both reflected in and reflective of politics and government.

Essentially, the trend has been away from a primarily local and regional scope for political and government affairs to one operating on at least three levels: local, state, and national. The national level is emerging as the most significant in shaping our destiny in a social order that has become in fact, if not in the mind of every citizen, highly nationalistic. Although there is continuous discussion of international control of human activity, to date this has really meant little more than an increased role for the autonomous nation-state in world affairs.

The greatly magnified scope of government affairs in the United States has resulted in a vastly increased and bureaucratized civil service at all levels to handle the immeasurable tasks presently assigned to the institution. These tasks now include military endeavors, internal security and policing, public education, welfare, taxation, research, labor–management arbitration, and economic and community planning. Government no longer functions solely to raise taxes, wage wars, and secure citizen safety. Government today is ponderous in size, scope, and complexity of operation.

Not all Americans are happy with this transformation of government. A deep mistrust of big government resides in the American tradition as the symbolic antithesis of the rugged individualist ethos. Fear of bureaucracy and corruption in high places (reinforced by scandals such as Watergate) is basic to many citizens who hark back to puritanical, frontier roots. These same people frequently ignore the bureaucratic components of modern private enterprises and the corrupt elements of local government. Despite continued resistance, government of an unprecedented size and scope appears to be a permanent part of the emergent Post–Industrial civilization.

While large-scale government enterprise accompanies profound change in society generally, the political system, viewed separately as the institutionalized means for acquiring legitimate leadership in governing the society, seems to have remained relatively unchanged. Government scope and function have expanded greatly in America while politics lag somewhat behind the times. However, many politicians have become proficient in using the mass media to present a trustworthy image to the public.[12] And, especially at the federal level, some younger political aspirants have attempted to comprehend the changed nature of modern life to more effectively represent their constituents.

American politics as a system, however, continues to be operated much as it was one hundred years or more ago. Politicians still seek patronage from the wealthy in order to pay for expensive campaigns. They still make promises to people to get a vote, rather than in the genuine interest of the good of the majority. Politicians still try to appear publicly as "men of the people." The two-party system reigns supreme for good or ill, although third-party movements have arisen in recent years to challenge the major parties. As a product of a civilization undergoing fundamental transformation, the relative stability of the political system, with all its inadequacies, may provide an important source of cultural continuity necessary for harmonious progression from one historic era into the next. It suggests that the social system is internally viable, although it is experiencing dramatic alterations in its structure and in the ability of its substructures to function properly.

There is evidence that the school has been inadequate in preparing youngsters for the realities of citizenship in a transforming society.[13] The average person is confused, misguided, and filled with a sense of impotence over the trend toward big government. Youngsters growing up in an increasingly interdependent world order need to understand how they are controlled and what they can realistically do as citizens, individually and collectively, to ensure that the leaders they elect to control them are adequate to the demands of the times.

An education to develop political sophistication is evidently in order at this time, an education dwelling more upon the present and future and less upon the historic tradition which has been superceded by new and more complex structures and ways of behaving.

Religion

The religious institution has not been unaffected by the major trends of the pragmatic-progressive social order. Although we are often called a Christian society, Judaism, Mohammedanism, and other non-Christian religions also exist in this society. Modern religion has long ceased to be oriented toward Christianity in the sense of a deeply devout people organizing their lives and basic values around Biblical injunctions and the church. For a while after the Second World War, there was a revival of church building and attendance, but this has tapered off in recent years. Even those who are still closely affiliated with organized religions are often motivated primarily by the social opportunities available through church attendance. By and large, many aspects of religion have become secularized to meet the limited demands of a public more interested in work or play than in spiritual redemption.[14] This seems to hold true with the exception of some of the most fundamentalist of sects, those orthodox religious groups which still take their religion seriously enough to be intolerant of nonbelievers.[15] Along with the decreased emphasis on organized religion is an increasing fraternization between members of different religious groups and a growing incidence of intermarriage.[16]

There have been numerous movements within various churches to revitalize the goals of religion and to renew its human meaning. They include change of liturgies, support of social reform movements in the wider society, advocacy of birth control by many Catholic priests, efforts to loosen traditional restrictions over the private lives of nuns and priests, and **ecumenicalism.** In addition, religious cults have sprung up in recent years. These cults reflect the striving of a transitional society's members to find new sources of spiritual communion within a confusing and often atomizing reality. Some of these cults are closely associated with use of mind-expanding drugs, others with mysticism, with variations of the human potential movement, including psychoanalysis and group sensitivity training.

It is an open question whether America's future will be one that includes a fundamental reorganization of traditional religious forms, the institutionalization of major new forms, or a general increase in agnosticism and atheism related to widespread diffusion of scientific or existential principles. At present it seems clear that in general the religious institution is undergoing profound structural and functional alterations caused by pressures from other parts of a changing social order.

Despite the gradual decline of organized religion, Americans continue to be a highly religious people; that is, they continue, perhaps more urgently than ever, to seek integration with the larger order of things in the cosmos.

Therefore, despite our tradition of separation of church and state, which never is perfectly observed anyway, perhaps schools should teach children about religion as a fundamental experience of all people, past and present. At the same time as they study religion as a universal institution, students could study art as a serious endeavor also designed to integrate human life with the essential order of things.

The study of human spirituality, especially through religion and art, would seem to contribute to the growth of personal identity in a disruptive period. Of course this study would be intellectual only; it would have to avoid any indoctrination of students in a particular religion. Students would be allowed to objectively examine a variety of major world theologies, as well as new religious responses to the confusions and problems of contemporary living. If students wish to choose a particular religion as their own after studying a number objectively, that is a matter of personal choice—just as, after studying politics and government, a person's political behavior is viewed as his or her independent choice. A democratic education ought to be the means by which individuals become capable of making meaningful choices in many important areas of living.

Leisure and Recreation

America was once a work-oriented society, in harmony with the religious and economic demands stressing labor as the main source of personal salvation, self-improvement, and social perfection. Today, mainstream U.S.A. is rapidly becoming what some consider a leisure-oriented society.* The work ethic is declining along with the decline of organized religion, the "taming of the frontier," a lack of felt rewards in the job for many, and the normally greater ease of earning a livelihood for most. Coupled with these trends is a shortened work week, related to automation in industry. Increased leisure time produces pressures and oppor-

---

* One author considers America's basic social problem to be a crisis in identity that is related to rising expectations and lowered incentives to work, which produces boredom in many. Klapp says that "Safe (square) identity search modes include fun, fad and fashion, drama and fiction, recreation, crowd enthusiasms, hero worship, and therapy. Nonsquare (identity) search includes style rebellion, extreme faddism, violent sensation, cultic devotion to extremist play, and deviant kicks, rebellion, and minority crusades."[17]

tunities to spend some of one's earnings on what were formally considered luxuries. Collectively, changes in attitudes and relationships to work can be correlated with a fundamental alteration in society's cultural values from "traditional" to "emergent" values of hedonism and a preoccupation with the present.[18]

Increased leisure time offers more choices of activities to people no longer bound to the home and extended kin group as in the past when community was centered in the small town or neighborhood and relatives worked and lived close to each other. It also poses potential problems for those who cannot afford or have not learned to utilize this free time.[19] Given additional leisure time, many people prefer to engage in spectator activities, such as watching organized sports, rather than pursuing activities requiring direct involvement.[20]

The leisure time pattern that is emerging as a by-product of the affluence and decreased work requirements of a scientific-technological civilization has enormous implications. It can be a tremendous boon to the construction of a creative and less guilt-ridden society, if opportunities are made easily and inexpensively available to people. Or this emerging pattern instead could contribute to the continuing dehumanization of American life.

A society in transition from a work ethic to one of leisure and recreation needs to prepare its young for effective use of increased leisure time. Because there is much evidence that many Americans do not feel comfortable with their increasing leisure time, learning how to occupy oneself meaningfully during one's free time should be an educational concern. The schools, especially through their efforts to help people learn about new lifestyles and how to cope with personal problems, may have much to offer in teaching youngsters effective use of leisure time. Schools can perhaps do even more by ridding themselves of the pressurized work ethic that dominates them. If schools were generally more relaxed, low-keyed institutions where learning was equated with pleasure, students might sense what it means to be leisurely in a world rapidly moving toward that style.

Some Major Trends and Social Problems

In addition to describing some of the basic changes occurring in America's institutional patterns, it might be useful at this time to briefly enumerate some of the broader trends and social problems crosscutting these patterns.

Population

The U.S. population has been steadily increasing. It presently stands at more than 210 million, and is expected to reach 240 million by 1985.[21] Much of this growth can be attributed to a decreased death rate due to improved medical techniques. Except for a brief period following the World War II "baby boom," the birthrate has declined among the dominant middle classes, although relatively high birthrates continue to prevail among the disadvantaged, despite the availability of birth control pills and other birth-control devices. Such a growing population poses long-term problems related to housing, employment, education, and other institutional concerns.

Urbanization

The United States is highly urbanized. The latest census figures show that California, for example, is over 91 percent urbanized.[22] Along with the basic trend toward urbanization has come a movement to the suburbs of large cities. With their romanticized image of better schools, cleaner air, and newer houses, suburbs are growing very rapidly at the expense of the central city to which many suburban residents commute without paying taxes. We now have a society of urban dwellers, where the term "urban" includes both the inner-city poor and the more affluent suburban middle classes.

Homogenization

America is becoming a national community. In the eyes of most Americans the center of gravity in the past was the local community or sometimes the state. We are still a pluralistic society, becoming increasingly conscious of our differences. At the same time, Americans are becoming one people in many of their beliefs, institutions, core values, and general lifestyles. One can travel the entire nation and stay in modern chain motels, eat in modern coffee houses, buy food in modern supermarkets, and send one's children to similarly organized and operated schools. Interchangeability of system parts—including people—has become a reality in this society. Much of this homogenization is related to reduction of immigration as well as to the development of transportation and media technology. Both elitists and universalists despair of this trend, but a mass, homogenized culture at the national level is apparently a reality.

Bigness

There is increasing scale and bureaucratization of life in a complex, interdependent world. Bigness is the rule in almost every area of life, including the economy, education, and government. It has stimulated bureaucracy, with its orientation to efficiency. Some writers are beginning to suggest, however, that bureaucracy is no longer capable of meeting human and productive needs. As a response to the growing impotency of bureaucratic operations, "bureautechnocracy"[23] has been proposed by some as the eventual organizational trend in this society. Bureautechnocracy is the marriage of the formal structure of bureaucracy with the processes of technology in a society in which bureaucratic structures and operations are becoming unsuccessful. If this organizational marriage takes place within most of the nation's large-scale bureaucratic structures, as some believe it will in the near future,* small, temporary teams of experts will develop quickly to tackle particular problems as they arise. These experts will be quickly disbanded when their projects are completed, as is already the case in certain industries, such as the aerospace industry. Bigness, rational planning and organization, and flexibility, combined with advanced technological skills are expected to be placed in the service of human and productive needs in the emerging mass society.

Compartmentalization

With bigness, technology, bureaucracy, and the development of a mass homogeneous society comes the problem of more rigid compartmentalization of individuals with regard to social class, jobs and the prospects of future jobs, housing, and education. Labeling and stereotyping take on new forms; for instance, today one is almost always viewed as either "straight" or "hip," "radical" or "conservative," a "worker" or a "manager," a "plebian" or an "aristocrat." It becomes increasingly difficult for most people to escape their ascribed or achieved compartments in the social system, once slotting—especially through the selecting and sorting function of schooling—has taken place. But within these compartments, mobility and interchangeability of human parts occur; that is, the factory worker may have several different jobs in one factory or around the country in several factories during his occupational life. **Other-directedness** and quick and intense relationships suited to a compartmentalized society are more common, requiring flexibility and new kinds

---

* Either the marriage has already taken place or bureaucracy is not as dysfunctional as some believe. One sociologist studied 3,101 employed civilians in 1964 and concluded that those who worked in bureaucratic organizations, especially government agencies, tended to be more intellectually flexible, more open to new experiences, and more self-directed in their values than those who work in nonbureaucratic organizations.

of values. Furthermore, increased intellectual requirements for effective participation in almost every social compartment are demanded as the technological-scientific impulse gains momentum.

Growing Openness to Change

More people are more open to change. Although change tends to create resistance in many people affected by it, resistance usually occurs in initial stages of the process and lessens later on. Once the boundaries of a social system or subsystem are intruded upon by powerful external forces, the ensuing systemic tensions and strains are apt to lead to further loosening of the system's structures—its institutions, values, and roles.[25]

People are at the root of all social system reality. Their mental and emotional sets are loosened by prolonged exposure to social changes which, though initially intrusive, eventually become part of reality. Thus, despite the prevalence of what Toffler calls "future shock," the American people, now long exposed to massive social change, are beginning to grow habituated to such change, more open to it, and even desirous of further changes in the social system. In effect, change breeds more change.

Outside of the material and productive realms of human affairs, Americans until recently have been a comparatively conservative people.[26] A case can be made for the proposition that the last major socio-intellectual revolution prior to World War II can be summed up as the rise of the **Protestant ethic.** Within this ethic, acceptable social changes were largely material or technological and efforts to break through socio-intellectual boundaries were strongly resisted until recently. Although conservative forces continue to resist change, the parameters of basic social change have abruptly expanded to include non-material as well as material concerns. The American social system has begun to open up to the forces for change which are presently operating to restructure its basic values and institutions. The American people are now becoming more restive and open to change in general. This is a basic pattern of the emerging Post-Industrial society.

Confused and disturbed Americans everywhere are reassessing their values and lifestyles. The young are not only dressing, but thinking and feeling in new ways. New forms of social intercourse are being experimented with, the most prominent being communal living. New religious forms are being developed, some closely connected with the use of mind-expanding drugs, others related to encounter groups and mysticism. Americans of all ages are beginning to question the fundamental assumptions of their educational, medical, religious, and political leaders. The fairly recent SST affair reflected popular feeling against building a supersonic airplane at the expense of other domestic priorities, including health and welfare. Until the "energy crisis," the ecology movement was beginning to have legislative success in controlling air and water pollution. Consumer movements are finally beginning to affect the production standards of automobile and other manufacturers.

All these trends point to the fact that American society has reached a point in its overall development at which it is more receptive to the kinds of fundamental restructuring of society required for life in a new age. In this sense, America is undergoing a very real cultural revolution that promises to reshape its society.

Social Planning

Social planning is on the increase. Until recently, most Americans rejected the idea of planning in nonmaterial areas. By and large, laissez faire ruled the American world. This has greatly changed with the advent of atomic weapons competition and the recent awareness of many people that our cities have deteriorated dangerously. Water and air are severely polluted, schools and universities are not functioning viably as agencies of socialization and enculturation, medical facilities are providing inadequately for the health needs not only of the poor but also of middle-class people, and economic institutions are not preventing large numbers of children from starving or growing up malnourished due to lack of adequate family incomes.

Prodded by worried futurists, such as Alvin Toffler who urges that we quickly develop comprehensive planning strategies that are democratic ("anticipatory democracy"), growing numbers of institutional leaders are beginning to take more seriously the concept of social planning at all levels and in more areas of social life.

One of the important questions about planning the future is whether or not our plans should be long-term or short-term. Some authorities are cautious about long-term planning since, they argue, we are living in a "temporary" society.[27] In order to accommodate the many subtle aspects of temporary society's evolutionary process, some authorities suggest we plan bravely, but not for an unforeseeable future. Others are in favor of longer range planning (ahead twenty-five to one hundred years or more), believing that without some serious efforts to chart our movements into the future, we may have no viable future to look forward to.[28] In any event, we are becoming increasingly aware of the consequences of a lack of foresight and are giving serious attention to the need for some long- or short-term planning strategies.

The unanticipated and unwanted consequences of uncoordinated growth and development have been implicit throughout this discussion. Our social problems have become staggering. They extend to problems of mental health and human security; of identity and alienation; of marriage and family; of rising crime and delinquency; of sex roles (e.g., the feminist movement); of the very young and the very old; of intergroup relations and social deviation; of depressed rural and urban areas in an affluent society; of population and ecology; of citizenship and representative government in a mass society; of war and peace in an atomic world no longer able to tolerate war; of work, human dignity, and meaning in a technological social order; of drugs and alcoholism; and of entropy and an unauthentic system geared to fear, survival and passive spectatorship.[29]

If America is to survive intact and become what Amatai Etzioni has called the "active society"—a Post-Industrial order that is person-centered, nonmanipulative, and democratic[30]—then sophisticated social planning may be the most important commitment facing the present generation.

This commitment necessarily extends to all who now work or hope to work in formal educational settings. If schools are to help children and youth growing up under the conditions we have discussed above, then teachers must be dedicated to planning programs of study that reflect these trends and problems. The school must become an agency concerned with life in all its aspects and complexities—not life as it may once have been, but rather as it is becoming, and as youngsters will be required to live it.

If new problems of living in large-scale, temporary organizations are to be faced by most young people in the future, then schools have an obligation to educate their students for effective participation in such organizational life. If modern life is to be lived in urban areas instead of in small towns and on farms, then schools are obliged to prepare students accordingly. If the population is increasing to the point of dangerous overcrowding, then schools need to work with students to help them learn to cope with these new challenges. To truly educate in a period of massive social change, school people must continually conceptualize and plan concretely for the present and the future, because the past can no longer serve as a complete guide to educational policy and practice.

How Are Teachers Affected by Social Institutions and How Can They Affect These Institutions?

The contemporary school is part of an elaborate, interdependent network of social institutions operating in American life. The manner in which this framework is structured is far from simple (see Figure 6–1). Schools and school teachers are affected more or less directly by the operations of some institutions (e.g., the family, social welfare, politics, and government) and more or less indirectly by others (e.g., religion). The influence upon the schools of various institutions is shifting as modern society becomes transformed. Institutions that at one time were relatively peripheral to the schools have now become central and vice versa (e.g., science–technology has become more immediate, while religion has become more peripheral). The totality of all institutional (and extra-institutional) influences upon schools amounts to the impact of society upon formal education.

In their turn, schools are believed to have an effect upon other social institutions—as well as being influenced by them. Schools affect a number of different social institutions more or less directly. In turn, these institutions affect each other. The extent to which each institution is affected and the quality of this influence are not well understood as yet.

A school teacher is the primary adult member of the school institution. The teacher's role is to interact with other adults and with students. He or she deals with people as a primary part of his or her work. Directly or indirectly, teachers are also representatives of a variety of

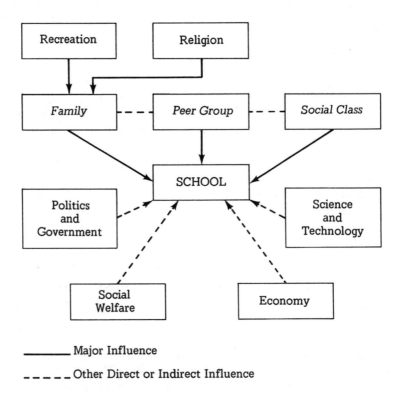

_____ Major Influence

_ _ _ _ _ Other Direct or Indirect Influence

FIGURE 6–1.   *Examples of Social Institutions That Influence the School*

other social institutions. When teachers talk to a mother or a father of a student, they are interacting with a representative of the changing family in America. When teachers converse with a school principal, they are interacting with a "middleman broker" between the school and several other institutions—particularly the family, the polity, the economy, and perhaps religion.

Ultimately, the job of school teaching is one upon which the rest of society comes to focus, because the teacher is held accountable for directly carrying out the educational ends of a variety of institutional interests. When we speak of the school as an interdependent social institution, we are really thinking about teachers, students, administrators, curriculum specialists, and other people connected with schools as they interrelate with people in other influential institutions—parents, public officials, religious leaders, businessmen, labor representatives, social workers, youth group directors, and so on.

It is hoped that through skillful performance of his or her several roles, the teacher will have an impact upon the lives of his or her students that will induce them to enter the larger society as active citizens, knowledgeable parents, and emotionally and physically healthy individuals. These and other desired characteristics are demonstrated in all of life's activities—that is to say, in all the social institutional activities in which a person engages.

Teachers today may be caught between performing roles that no longer have much utility and becoming independent of conventional stereotypes. If teachers give in wholly to convention—as supported by their adult colleagues, by the parents of their students, and by other influential members of their **role set**—they may fail their students. On the other hand, if they ignore the role expectations of influential adults and independently respond to their sense of what students need to learn in a new age, then they risk conflict with the institutional power figures who pay their salaries.

The question then is: How can an enlightened teacher, who wants to meaningfully affect his or her students, do so without encountering the psychological phenomenon known as "role strain"? How can a teacher avoid this anxious feeling of being caught in a conflict between more than one set of mutually incompatible social expectations, some of which are believed to be more legitimate than others?[31]

In our transforming social order, teachers cannot completely escape role conflicts and ambiguities. By trying to accommodate every influence upon them, teachers may avoid displeasing most of their **significant others,** but they will find it difficult to fulfill every role demand made upon them and as a consequence may lose their sense of personal integrity. Other teachers may cling rigidly to one set of expectations— either their students' or their principal's or their educational psychology

173

textbook's. If they do this, they will in effect be meeting the role demands of one reference group at the expense of others. Such a teacher cannot really avoid a degree of role strain.

One author suggests that modern teachers neither vacillate nor overcompensate in one rigid fashion or another, but rather accept themselves essentially as they are—as individuals with preferred styles of living and working.[32] If one is essentially a progressive teacher, who works with those who are traditionalists, one should not try to become a traditionalist. This would be unnatural and self-defeating. On the other hand, if one is essentially conservative in personal and professional outlook, one should accept that orientation.

Our schools, as part of a pluralistic society in transition, have room for more than one style of teaching. As long as you maintain a personal style without undue rigidity, you are likely to be accepted by a variety of reference groups, both adult and student alike. Your flexibility will help you to cope intelligently with most role conflicts you encounter.

Teachers who possess a definite sense of personal and professional identity and direction and at the same time are open enough to acknowledge other perspectives on life and education, are likely to have minimal role conflicts. They can therefore concentrate on what they want to accomplish with their students and move forward, on the basis of their deliberate decisions, to action in their students' best interests.

Summary

A number of changing, interdependent institutions affect the American school directly or indirectly. Included among them are science and technology, the economy, social welfare, politics and government, symbolic institutions, religion, and recreation. A number of broad trends and related social problems that crosscut these institutions have implications for modern education. Examples of such trends are: a growing population, growing urbanization, homogenization of the population, increasing scale and bureaucratization of organizations, compartmentalization of people, increasing openness to social change, and decreasing resistance to social planning.

Whether by intention or by default, the school has an impact upon other institutions and trends. The school has a great deal of untapped potential for educating people to cope with a shifting institutional order. The school must be open to the influences of newer or dramatically altered institutional and extra-institutional developments if it is to realize this potential in the crucial years ahead.

Teachers are the school's central agents for effectuating its institutional objectives in relation to other institutions. In a period of major sociocultural transformation such as the present, many stereotyped role expectations held for teachers are no longer realistic, but may still be maintained by school control groups. In order to effectively work within often conflicting expectations, teachers must first accept themselves as authentic individuals; they must have stable identities that are flexible enough to interact successfully and without extreme strain with significant others who possess different institutional expectations for their role behavior.

Related Concepts

automation   Operation of productive processes automatically rather than directly by people

black box   A concept used by systems analysts to symbolize the internal conversion, or transformation, of inputs to a system into different outputs of the system

ecumenicalism   A movement to bring together and harmonize disparate religious sects

other-directedness   Referring to people who tend to be more highly attuned to the expectations of other people than they are to a small group of highly significant others, such as parents

Protestant ethic   In social science, the idea popularized by German sociologist Max Weber that the Protestant emphasis on hard work as a means of attaining spiritual salvation formed the basis for a capitalistic and materialistic society

role set   Positions and roles most directly associated with one's position in an organization. For instance, the role set of a school teacher includes students, supervisors, the principal, fellow teachers, and possibly parents

significant other   An individual member of some reference group whose imagined or real opinions are of great significance to another person

welfare state   A society whose government is heavily involved in promoting the common welfare of the people in many areas of life through special legislation and programs

Suggested Activity

Sit down with a close friend or relation and have an in-depth conversation about your long-range life plans. Talk about your career aspirations, your feelings about marriage and family, about religion, about your concepts of leisure and recreation, and so on. Are these institutions undergoing such rapid change that they are untrustworthy as lifetime planning guides?

Then talk to your parents or some other older people. Ask them if they had any difficulty in planning their future lives when they were your age, and whether or not many of their early expectations were realized.

References and Notes

1.   For an elaboration of these ideas, *see* Johannes Ponsioen, *The Analysis of Social Change Reconsidered* (The Hague: Mouton and Company, 1962), p. 49, and Bertram Morris, *Institutions of Intelligence* (Columbus: Ohio State University Press, 1969), pp. 41; 80–106.

2.   However, some writers wonder whether bureaucracy will atrophy because of its increasing inability to cope with the very changes in sociotechnical processes that it was originally developed to control. *See* Warren G. Bennis and Philip E. Slater, *The Temporary Society* (New York: Harper & Row, 1964), pp. 55, 56.

3.   Grace Graham, *The Public School in the New Society: The Social Foundations of Education* (New York: Harper & Row, 1969), pp. 17–41; C. Wright Mills, "The Power Elite: Military, Economic, and Political," in *Problems of Power in American Democracy,* ed. Arthur Kornhauser (Detroit: Wayne State University Press, 1957), pp. 154–67; Floyd Hunter, *Community Power Structure: A Study of De-* *cision Makers* (Chapel Hill: University of North Carolina Press, 1953).

4.   W. Lloyd Warner, ed., *Large Scale Organizations;* "The Emergent American Society," vol. I (New Haven: Yale University Press, 1967), p. 1021.

5.   Studs Terkel, *Working: People Talk About What They Do All Day and How They Feel About What They Do* (New York: Pantheon Books, 1974).

6.   For a well-documented discussion of the educational implications of this and related needs, *see* K. Patricia Cross and John R. Valley, *Planning Non-Traditional Programs* (San Francisco: Jossey-Bass, 1974).

7.   *See,* for example, Sidney P. Marland, H old Lichtenwald, and Ralph Burke, "Career Education Texas Style: The Skyline Center in Dallas," *Phi Delta Kappan* 56 (May 1975): 616–20.

8.   For example, one author says that "some estimates of 'functional literacy' find nearly 50 percent of this country illiterate." (James Duggins, "The Right to

Read," *Phi Delta Kappan* 52 [April 1971]: 457.)

9. *See* especially Basil Bernstein, "Some Sociological Determinants of Perception," *British Journal of Sociology* 9 (June 1958): 159–74.

10. *See* James Coleman, et al., *Summary Report, Equality of Educational Opportunity* (Washington, D.C.: United States Government Printing Office, 1966).

11. Alvin Boskoff, "Functional Analysis as a Source of a Theoretical Repertory and Research Tasks in the Study of Social Change," in George K. Zollschan and Walter Hirsch eds., *Explorations in Social Change* (Boston: Houghton Mifflin Co., 1964), pp. 213–43.

12. *See,* among his several other books, Erving Goffman's *The Presentation of Self in Everyday Life* (Garden City, N.Y.: Doubleday and Co., 1959).

13. A number of studies documenting this assertion are cited in John J. Patrick, *Political Socialization of American Youth: Implications for Secondary School Social Studies* (Washington, D.C.: National Council for the Social Studies, Research Bulletin No. 3, 1967). More recent findings confirm the NCSS report.

14. Will Herberg, "Religion and Culture in Present-Day America," in *Anatomies of America: Sociological Perspectives,* ed. Amatai Etzioni (Toronto: The Macmillan Company, 1969), pp. 255–65.

15. *See* Charles Y. Glock and Rodney Stark, *Christian Beliefs and Anti-Semitism* (New York: Harper & Row, 1966).

16. Irving R. Stuart and Lawrence E. Abt, eds., *Interracial Marriage: Expectations and Realities* (New York: Grossman Publishers, 1973).

17. *See* Orrin E. Klapp, *Collective Search for Identity* (New York: Holt, Rinehart and Winston, 1969), p. 203.

18. *See* George D. Spindler, "Education in a Transforming American Culture," *Harvard Educational Review* 25 (Summer 1955): 145–56.

19. Recent studies suggest that many people who are offered a shorter work week take on an extra job instead of relaxing or using their free time for non-occupational pursuits. *See* David Riesman, "Leisure and Work in Post-Industrial Society," in W. Warren Kallenbach and Harold M. Hodges, Jr., eds., *Education and Society* (Columbus, Ohio: Charles E. Merrill Books, 1963), p. 362. *See also* Rolf Meyerson, "Is There Life After Work?" *Saturday Review/World* (May 4, 1974): 14–16.

20. *Ibid.*

21. "1971 World Population Data Sheet: Population Reference Bureau, Inc." Reprinted in *Social Education* 36 (April 1972).

22. *Statistical Abstracts of the United States,* 93rd ed. (Washington, D.C.: United States Department of Commerce, Bureau of the Census, 1972), p. 18.

23. *See* Bennis and Slater, *Temporary Society,* pp. 55, 56. *See also* Charles Tesconi, Jr., "Bureautechnocracy: A New Perspective in Schools and Society," in *Proceedings of the Second Annual Meeting of the American Educational Studies Association* Thomas D. Moore, ed. (Chicago: The American Educational Studies Society, 1970), pp. 58–74. (Mimeographed)

24. Melvin L. Kohn, "Bureaucratic Man: A Portrait and an Interpretation," *American Sociological Review* 36 (June 1971): 471–74.

25. Parsons puts the matter in the fol-

lowing terms: "A boundary is thus conceived as a kind of watershed. The control resources of the system are adequate for its maintenance up to a well-defined set of points in one direction; beyond that set of points, there is a tendency for a cumulative process of change to begin, producing states progressively farther from the institutionalized patterns." Talcott Parsons, "A Paradigm for the Analysis of Social Systems and Change," in N.J. Demerath and Richard A. Peterson, eds., *System, Change, and Conflict: A Reader on Contemporary Sociological Theory and the Debate over Functionalism* (New York: The Free Press, 1967), p. 195.

26.   Anthony F.C. Wallace, "Schools in Revolutionary and Conservative Societies," in Frederick Gruber, ed. *Anthropology and Education* (Philadelphia: University of Pennsylvania Press, 1961), pp. 25–55.

27.   *See,* for example, Bennis and Slater, *Temporary Society.*

28.   For a competent defense of this position, *see* Donald N. Michael, *The Unprepared Society: Planning for a Precarious Future* (New York: Basic Books, 1968). *See also* Alvin Toffler, *The Eco-Spasm Report* (New York: Bantam Books, 1975), a brief, informative, and highly readable explication of some of the problems of change and unpreparedness, with a section outlining "anticipatory democracy."

29.   Jules Henry, *Culture Against Man* (New York: Vantage Books, Random House, 1963).

30.   Amatai Etzioni, *The Active Society: A Theory of Societal and Political Processes* (New York: The Free Press, 1968).

31.   *See* Carl Backman and Paul F. Secord, *A Social Psychological View of Education* (New York: Harcourt, Brace, and World, 1968), pp. 116–45, which presents other causes of role strain.

32.   Spindler, "Education in Transforming Culture."

7

Social Stratification and Its Implications for Teachers

The concept of social class has long been considered of prime importance to an understanding of economic and political affairs. Until fairly re-recently, however, it has not received the attention it deserves from students of educational affairs. Renewed interest in the meaning of the words "equal opportunity" has prompted American social scientists and educators to give a new priority to the concept.

The American Belief in Social Mobility

For generations, native and foreign-born Americans alike have been taught that any boy with brains and common sense who studied in school could expect later to obtain a good job in business or the professions and advance to the top. If he failed to achieve a modicum of success in life, it was his own fault and no one else's.

Growing numbers of social scientists, educators, and lay people, however, believe that complete personal responsibility for success in life is largely a myth that acts, intentionally or unintentionally, to justify a never-ending striving of most Americans. Only a comparative few can ever hope to achieve success, regardless of their inherent abilities or keen efforts, because the social system is structured to keep all except a hand-ful of people in the places to which they were born. To those who make such a claim, public elementary and secondary schools (and colleges and universities) are regarded as important sources of the myth of equal opportunity.

Whether the claim is true or not, one thing is fairly certain: Schools and teachers do have an increasingly important part to play in determining who will become the doctors, lawyers, and garbage collectors in a society that, rightly or wrongly, continues to value some people more than others. Put simply, "Education in the United States is still widely regarded as the royal road to success in life."[1]

The Concept of Social Stratification

The organizing concept employed by scholars to connote social position and rank in a society with positions of unequal value and rank is social stratification. Every society, including the preliterate "protodemocracies" that minimize social stratification, the totalitarian dictatorships like Nazi Germany or Communist China that deny it, and the partly open societies like the United States that evade it, has some type of system whereby people are stratified in more or less distinct layers, or strata, called social classes.*

Social class is "a stratum in society composed of groups of families of equal standing." Further, "all persons of the same social level of prestige and esteem who consider themselves to be social equals, form a distinct social class."[2] The family, then, is at the center of the system of social stratification, or social-class standing. Individual members of society initially have an **ascribed status,** derived from the family; later, they may pass on their **achieved status** to their own children. Such achievement is possible only if society has a relatively open class system in which achievement of a different rank is at least theoretically possible, such as in the U.S. In a closed, or caste, system of stratification one's rank at birth cannot be altered (as under the system of slavery in southern U.S. society prior to the Civil War). The social rank held by a child by virtue of his family's position in the community is immensely important to his academic career. Boocock says:

---

* Most students of social class are careful to point out that the boundaries that separate one class from another are not hard and fast, but rather overlap and are imprecise. Members of a social class, however, do tend to share characteristic values and life styles, which are not shared by most members of other classes.

The family characteristic that is the most powerful predictor of school performance is socioeconomic status (SES): the higher the SES of the student's family, the higher his academic achievement. This relationship has been documented in countless studies and seems to hold no matter what measure of status is used (occupation of principal breadwinner, family income, parents' education, or some combination of these). It holds with a variety of achievement-aspiration variables, including grades, achievement test scores, retention at grade level, course failures, truancy, suspensions from school, dropout rates, college plans, and total amount of formal schooling. It also predicts academic honors and awards, elective school offices, extent of participation in extracurricular activities, and other indicators of "success" in the informal structure of the student society. It holds, moreover, even when the powerful variables of ability and past achievement are controlled.[3]

Social class, then, is heavily bound up with the institution of the family and is commonly measured by a person's own or parental level of income, type of occupation, and, increasingly, by amount of formal schooling. It is also associated with the kind of neighborhood one resides in, the kind of house one lives in, the car one drives, the way in which one speaks, the types of books or art forms one enjoys, and other indicators of income, education, or occupation.

Since the three variables of income, education, and occupation tend to be manifested by certain behavior patterns, certain attitudes and values often suggest a basic lifestyle common to persons of the same social class. We may cautiously view a social class as a more or less distinct subculture, which partly transcends racial, ethnic, and religious lines.[4] People belonging to identifiable **social class subcultures** tend to mingle with members of their own subculture in their leisure time and during work, since most of us are most comfortable with the familiar.

American sociologists of education have made major studies of the phenomenon.[5] If, as they believe, a fluid class structure is essential to the viable functioning of an open and democratic society, then school teachers—the key agents of socialization and enculturation—clearly should understand the nature of this structure. They may uniquely affect this structure by their attitudes toward themselves and their behavior toward their students who come from a variety of social class backgrounds. In the words of one student of social stratification:

> ... *social classes are not simply forces, such as death and taxation, that one must live with; they are decisive elements which help shape and color virtually every facet of our lives. As such, they must be comprehended with clarity and insight. Helpful as it is for the person who would know the behavior, motives, and values of others to understand the "typical" American, it is infinitely more critical that he understand, say, the "middle-class," and better, the "lower-middle-class" American.*[6]

Characteristics of Different
Social Class Cultures

Sociologists who study the phenomenon of social class in the United States usually find differences between class structures in small communities and those in larger metropolitan ones.

Havighurst and Neugarten conclude that small rural communities have in the past tended to exhibit a three-tiered class structure consisting of an "upper crust" of elites, who in large cities would be considered upper-middle class (physicians, successful businessmen, and farmers); a large majority class of working people, who in larger communities would comprise the lower-middle class and working class; and at the bottom of the stratification hierarchy, the lower-lower class, or the lower working class of most metropolitan areas.[7]

Havighurst and Neugarten have found that small cities with populations ranging from about 5,000 to 15,000 people tend to exhibit a five-tiered class structure; that is, the class structure becomes differentiated from the three basic levels found in villages and small towns. In such communities, there seems to be an upper class consisting of about 3 percent of the population, some of whom were original descendants of pioneer settlers who had become wealthy, others of whom were factory executives, owners of local banks and the most profitable businesses, and large landowners. Professionals, most other business executives, small business owners, and successful independent farmers constitute

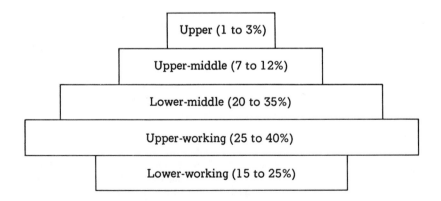

FIGURE 7–1.   *The National Social Class Structure (From Robert J. Havighurst and Bernice L. Neugarten,* Society and Education, *4th ed. (Boston: Allyn and Bacon, Inc., 1975), p. 25. Reprinted with permission.*

an upper-middle class in small cities (about 10 percent, according to Havighurst and Neugarten). There is a "lower-middle class," whose members are mainly white-collar workers (bookkeepers, store clerks, owners of small retail businesses, a few foremen and skilled manual workers, and most of the prosperous farmers in the area). "These people [about 30 percent] were said by those in the classes above them to be 'nice people,' but social 'nobodies.' "[8]

Below the lower-middle class is the working class, "people who worked as skilled and unskilled laborers and as tenant farmers."[9] These are the majority of the small city's population—about 35 to 40 percent. On the lowest rung of the stratification ladder are the members of the lower class, about 15 percent of the population; they are those who labor to hold onto a "respectable kind of poverty" and those perceived by the rest of the community as essentially "immoral, lazy, and defiant of the law."[10]

Studies of larger communities of 100,000 people or less in the Midwest seem to confirm this type of five-tiered class structure found in small cities (as well as in large cities, such as Kansas City). One important study of a New England town of 17,000 made just before World War II found a six-class structure, however. The chief difference between this arrangement and the five-tiered one was in regard to the top status group. In Warner and Lunt's "Yankee City," the upper crust consisted of both an "upper-upper" group of old lineage families with wealth and "breeding" and a "lower-upper" group of *nouveau riche* industrialists who had newly acquired money but lacked solid tradition in the community.[11] While most of the *nouveau riche* were unlikely to make it into the top elite during their own lifetimes, some of their children had a good chance.

The small-town studies, which were made mostly before 1950, emphasized income and occupation as major criteria used to measure socioeconomic status, or social-class rank. Educational level, however, tends to be linked with income and occupation, whether emphasized by a researcher or not. Although there are exceptions, those with high incomes and highly ranked occupations also tend to possess the most years of schooling at the more prestigious schools and universities. Conversely, most people with an advanced formal education tend also to possess relatively high incomes and prestigious jobs. A recent study by the U.S. Census Bureau fixed an approximate *lifetime* income on a twenty-two-year-old male with the following educational attainments:

- less than 8 years of schooling: $159,000
- grade school graduate: $192,000
- 1 to 3 years of high school: $216,000
- high school diploma: $264,000
- 1 to 3 years of college: $301,000

- college degree: $388,000
- 5 or more years of college: $443,000[12]

More importantly, as we have changed from a Frontier to an Industrial to a Post-Industrial civilization, formal education has become more central as a determinant of what sort of chances one has in obtaining an occupation and an income. Some sociologists even believe that today education is the most important determinant of social position in the United States. In comparing the social stratification structure of a large metropolitan city (Kansas City) with those of other communities in 1971, Coleman and Neugarten hypothesized that "education itself as a dimension of status may be taking on more significance than occupation."[13]

When land was free or relatively inexpensive and when little capital was required to start a business, opportunities to advance up the social ladder depended far less upon formal educational credentials from accredited institutions than they do in a society whose land frontier has closed, whose businesses and industries require huge outlays of capital, and whose professions have become vastly more difficult to learn because of rapidly expanding knowledge and standards of public service. In contemporary Post-Industrial society, the son of the father who once opened a small weekly newspaper and expanded it into a major regional daily must now go to college to study journalism before being permitted to write simple copy. Or he must find another occupation that also requires advanced schooling if he is to retain the position in society that his father had carved out for himself and his family. Education, not income, appears to be the determinant of social rank. Jobs that once required only a high school diploma or a year or two of college now require a bachelor's degree, and this trend will probably continue. School teaching, once a position that often required no more than a high school diploma or a normal school diploma, now requires at least a bachelor's degree and will eventually demand a minimum of a master's degree or its equivalent for initial entrance into the profession and for advancement on the job.[14]

The Disadvantaged and Education

Much has been written about the problem of educational opportunity for the very poor. The lowest socioeconomic group, the often-called "disadvantaged," today includes members from both majority and minority groups, although minorities are disproportionately represented.

A Hypothetical Example. Bill and Genine, who are black, live in the inner-city near the downtown area. This area has been steadily expanding outward in recent years as more and more blacks and Chicanos move into the city from rural areas. Middle- and working-class people are moving out to the suburbs, often to avoid living with the poor and with racial and ethnic minorities.[15]

Bill and Genine live in an apartment building with their mother who is on welfare. Their father comes to visit, but he does not live with them, since they fear that if the welfare department found out, their mother's regular AFDC check would be cancelled. Therefore, their mother is the head of the household. She tries to be a good mother but is generally tired from trying to make enough money to supplement her meager welfare check. She has little energy left at the end of a day for her children. Their apartment is old and decrepit and the landlord will not fix anything. It's not very pleasant inside the apartment, so Bill and Genine spend much of their time on the streets. Here they have learned the "facts of life" at an early age, as well as how to cope with these facts.

The facts they are supposed to learn in school are somewhat different, and despite vast amounts of money spent on stimulating new educational technology and on training teachers to better deal with youngsters such as Bill and Genine, they still find school tedious.

Genine's high school has four fulltime security guards on duty to prevent fights and to break them up when they start. Genine is in the 10th grade, but reads only on an 8th grade level. A new program for teaching English as a second language (ESL), is trying to bring all students' reading levels to their grade level by the time they graduate.

Most of Genine's teachers are white. Despite the special in-service workshops they have attended to enable them to better understand and help "disadvantaged" minority youngsters, many of them still dislike their present assignments. They talk about how much nicer it would be to teach in an area with a "better class of people." In the inner-city, some teachers feel they act primarily as babysitters or police officials.

A few students at Genine's school take a college prep course, and will probably go on to a junior college or even to a four-year college. Genine, like most of her peers, will not; her achievement test scores are too low for counselors to encourage her along those lines. She is in a career education program that offers her concrete work experiences as a secretary in nearby firms, which cooperate with the school in return for free student help. When she graduates from high school, she plans to become a secretary. A black woman with a skill such as she is learning in school has opportunities today that her mother never had.

Her brother Bill is only 10 years old, but he has already been in trouble with the law for shoplifting at a department store. Bill's teacher does not like him; she considers him one of her worst discipline problems, since he rarely does his assigned seatwork and is continually fomenting trouble among his friends when she is talking. Now that all the teachers are using rotating learning centers, he is even more of a nuisance. Part of the theory behind the learning center idea was that

young children working in small groups would learn better than by traditional class methods, because they would be free to move around and help each other. But Bill fools around more now that he is not forced to stay in his seat all the time. Bill's teacher has called in one of the school system's psychologists because she thinks he may be "hyperactive," a common explanation for non-conforming behavior in school boys living in the ghetto. She has no grounds for having Bill transferred to a "special" class, since he tested out at 94 on the state-mandated group IQ tests this year. (The class average was 83.) She remembers her student teaching in a suburban school in which the school average was 119, and some students had IQs over 150. Since teaching jobs are difficult to obtain lately, she cannot complain about her teaching situation. She and some other teachers once spent a morning at a demonstration school that was integrated. The children at this school seemed so much more alive and interested in learning that she went away wondering if there was hope after all.

Since leadership is poor at Bill's school, the morale of both faculty and students is very low. This in turn creates more student apathy, anger, and alienation from the school, which, in its turn, causes most teachers to dislike themselves and to project their own low professional self-concepts onto their convenient scapegoats, the minority students and their parents.

Therefore, despite the availability of heavy federal and state outlays for Bill's school, he still does not achieve as the test makers think he ought to. His record card will probably lead future teachers and counselors in secondary schools to think he is a permanent troublemaker and poor student who will eventually drop out. In defensive reaction to such a negative self-fulfilling prophesy, he is likely to do so.

Completely equal opportunity to rise out of the ghetto is probably largely a myth in this society, despite a heavy emphasis in recent years on compensating through education for the alleged cultural deficits of poor people. Confirming other data, an important study by Robert Crain indicates that only when "disadvantaged" black people are placed in classes with "advantaged" whites do they have a realistic chance to succeed in school.[16] In an integrated class, they may begin to feel psychologically acceptable to the larger society. A raised self-concept appears to induce the "disadvantaged" to strive academically—not elaborate, technological teaching methods of which many are so fond.

Unless teachers believe in their students and refuse to pocket them into reading or math groups based on ability, for example, students realistically cannot be expected to think much of themselves.[17] Confidence in students seems to be rare in segregated ghetto schools. As long as low pupil and teacher self-concepts are maintained, few students born into the lower class have a strong chance of changing their social status through education. (This is particularly true for males.[18]) And, since schooling is central to upward mobility in contemporary society, only a comparative few from the inner-city are likely to move up in the stratification system. (This situation is beginning to change as growing numbers of minority students go on to college and to middle-class lifestyles. Affirmative Action policies, coupled with lower enrollments of dominant-group students are causing college admissions officers to actively seek out new populations and to offer a variety of novel programs.)

Although the ghetto school may have begun to sort and select a few poor children for higher status positions in society, real equal opportunity for the majority of lower-class people does not exist in the present structure of schools. To a lesser extent, this is also true for children of the working class and the lower-middle class. Equal opportunity to succeed continues to be most applicable to discussions of upper-middle-class students whose parents have already achieved higher social station. Schools appear to offer children of the elite a fairly equal opportunity to stay where they are on the social ladder, and to avoid downward mobility.

Social Class and Education:
Actualities and Potentialities

The concept of social class has a number of important implications for immediate practice by individual teachers (actualities) and for long-term policy determinations (potentialities).

Actualities

Teachers need to be aware that different people want different things from the schools, although these differing expectations are less certain during periods of major social change than during more stable periods.

From the data available, we may generally infer the following about social class and education in the United States.

Importance of Social Class for Educational Success. Social class patterns in this society, as in others past and present, profoundly affect the kind of informal and formal education youngsters receive and, accordingly, their life chances. A child's family and his or her parents' aspirations for him or her are vitally significant in determining how and to what extent he or she will benefit from school.[19]

Upper-class children are not usually concerned with schooling and academic achievement to the extent that children of other social strata are (notably the upper-middle class), because they have already "reached the top." Their schooling is public or private (or both), and largely for the purpose of acquiring a basic upper-class culture (upper-class "refinement") and meeting useful contacts for later life. Education primarily helps to confirm their present position, not improve it. The teacher's job in preparing upper-class youngsters for adulthood is basically to ensure that attitudes of exclusivity and noblesse oblige are built into their personalities by example and through peer-group interaction. These students enroll in a college preparatory curriculum designed to enable them to meet the requirements of the "better" colleges, at which the process of social class preservation will be continued.

Middle-class children are normally expected by their parents to achieve for the future. Motivation to achieve in the future is ordinarily reinforced by peers as well as by school personnel. For upper-middle-class, as well as for lower-middle-class youngsters, success in school greatly helps to ensure success in adult life, either by confirming their present social status or by offering opportunities to become upwardly mobile.

188

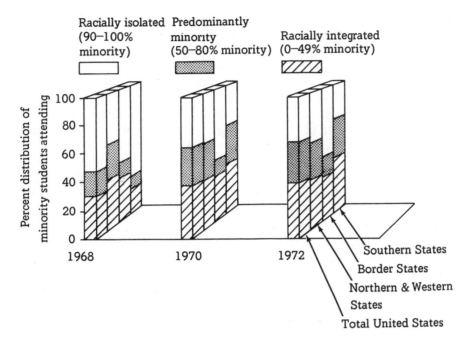

FIGURE 7–2.   *The Racial Composition of Schools by Region (Education Division, Department of Health, Education, and Welfare, The Condition of Education (Washington, D.C.: U.S. Government Printing Office, 1976), p. 67.*

The school programs of upper-middle-class elementary and secondary schools tend to be heavily committed to preparing youngsters for entrance into and subsequent success in college and the professions, although they may also offer alternative tracks for those not destined for higher education.

Many teachers like to work in schools with predominantly lower-middle-class students. In these schools, parents are usually cooperative without being aggressive, as is sometimes true of upper-middle-class parents. The students tend to be well-behaved and earnest, if not always as brilliant as their upper-middle-class models who are, on the whole, the greatest strivers after academic and occupational success in society. But, because many lower-middle-class children have ambitions of becoming members of the upper-middle class, the teacher of lower-middle-class students will usually encounter a good number of hard working students. Increasing resistance to the achievement orientation is being offered by middle-class, and especially upper-middle-class students caught up in the developing counterculture.[20]

Working-class children (often the offspring of foreign-born parents even today) are the single largest group in the schools. They may or may not have the achievement drive of the middle classes, depending mainly upon their parents' and peers' aspirations. Some working-class parents want their offspring to get ahead, while others hope they will remain in the same class subculture to which they were born; some parents are indifferent.[21] Thus, the school encounters some students from the working class who are socially, and hence academically, mobile and others who are relatively disinterested in what the school has to offer them. Lacking powerful parental or school pressure to rise out of their socioeconomic stratum, many working-class youngsters tend to strive to achieve in school only to a limited extent. Unless reference-group influences upon them change significantly at some point in their school careers, they often make an effort to rise modestly from their parents' status, but not to advance dramatically in the social pecking order.

Lower-class children, particularly members of racial minorities, are not necessarily urged to achieve for the future through the school, but rather to literally survive in the bleak present. As in most human affairs, there are exceptions to this rule; these exceptions are becoming more common as attempts to correct the situation are being made by those who want to see socioeconomic inequality eradicated in a society that has professed its belief in equality of opportunity through equality of education.

Two contradictory lines of attack on the problem of educational inequality are currently being experimented with. The most widely supported is the *compensatory education* movement, heavily funded by the federal government. According to sociologists who have studied it, this movement has in effect often served to effectively keep blacks and other "disadvantaged" minorities in segregated schools, while attempting to upgrade the qualities of such schools.[22] The other line of attack is the still controversial effort to *integrate* public schools in accordance with the 1954 Supreme Court decision [*Brown* v. *Topeka*] which held that schools which are separate are inherently unequal, no matter how apparently high their internal quality.

The School's Selecting and Sorting Function.   Opportunities to rise in the stratification system today depend largely upon the number of years spent in formal education and upon the degrees and credentials attained. The "self-made" man of the frontier has disappeared.

The school only "selects" a minority of lower-class youngsters to rise in the stratification system; this was the case when Jefferson tried to pass a law giving "poor boys" scholarship aid over one hundred fifty years ago. The great majority of lower-class adults remain in the same class into which they were born, despite massive compensatory education efforts ostensibly designed to increase opportunities for upward social mobility. Even if the school were to become more successful in reducing inequality, it could only prepare children and youth for adult-hood: it cannot—as an educational and not a political organ—guarantee acceptance into the sociocultural mainstream, because it cannot assure jobs, adequate incomes, or worthwhile opportunities to interact socially in a way which facilitates social mobility once students leave school. In this last respect Christopher Jencks was correct in asserting recently that schools cannot ensure equality of opportunity.[23] However, improved schooling can probably greatly help to increase the competencies, atti-tudes, and knowledge which may in turn, produce a cultural climate more amenable to such opportunity.

Those who do rise socially in the stratification hierarchy in the pro-cess may lose touch with their class-based cultural roots and become encumbered with severe status anxieties. This has happened, for ex-ample, to a number of black men and women who have left the inner-city ghetto to become members of the middle class.[24]

Such a painful experience for the successfully mobile is far more likely to be psychologically traumatic for individuals who are over-ambitious; that is, for those who strive to attain a status position that they are unable to fully achieve. Unless they can return to their class of

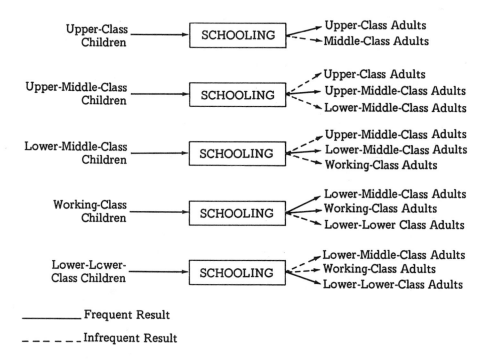

FIGURE 7–3. *Selecting and Sorting Functions of Schools for Children from Different Social Classes*

origin, which is a difficult and unlikely prospect, they remain more or less permanently marginal. Social marginality has negative consequences (neurosis or psychosis, drug addiction, crime, etc.), as well as positive ones (unusual creativeness and worthwhile contributions to the social order).[25] These consequences must be seriously weighed by modern teachers and other educators who in general accept the American ethos of vertical mobility, which was somewhat more readily achieved in the past than at present.

The growing ratio of *horizontal mobility*—that is, movement from one job to another on the same status level, from one geographical location to another, or from one house to another—seems to be becoming far more prevalent in the United States than vertical mobility. Allowing for periods of recession, most Americans are on the move today, and the shortness of stay in one place or job or house or marriage may be temporarily unsettling.[26] Because horizontal moves can be controlled more certainly by the persons involved than vertical moves, they are less likely to result in long-term psychological damage than are unsuccessful moves up the social class ladder or moves down that ladder. To say this in no way implies that teachers should cease to urge vertical social mobility on the grounds that the risks involved are too great. Even if the risks are greater than in the past, teachers probably have no right to stand in the way of students who wish to take such risks, provided the students know what the consequences may be. Teachers may have an obligation to help youngsters understand how to cope with real human problems, by teaching problem-solving methodology and by furnishing the facts pertinent to resolving specific problems. The days when teachers could afford to remain ethically aloof from the difficult areas of personal and social problem solving are over. Even the most highly specialized teacher of reading or history or English must become a teacher of human problem solving. And, the teacher of social studies may have a uniquely important role to play in this regard.

Potentialities

Although some implications of the close relationship between socioeconomic status and education have already been suggested, there are others to consider:

The Need for a Multicultural Perspective in Education.   Acceptance of the reality of cultural differences between social classes in achievement orientations and expectations of formal education is necessary if school people are to have any real success with the majority of American chil-

dren. It is becoming clear that we need a multicultural frame of reference if we are to meet the educational needs of youngsters growing up in a pluralistic society. Such a frame of reference has been resisted in the past because, in idealizing an open-class system, Americans find it difficult to admit that such a system can still be highly stratified. In an open-class society such as ours, **contest mobility** means that desirable positions on the stratification ladder are theoretically available to anyone who competes in the socioeconomic race; it does not mean that the society is classless. No society is!

Some accommodation to subcultural differences related to learning styles, speech habits, and knowledge possessed prior to coming to school may be essential for success with a heterogeneous population. For example, it is now believed that many lower-class ("disadvantaged") students are less articulate (in the school's terms) than most middle-class children. Bernstein has demonstrated that while middle-class youngsters tend to possess both a "public" language code useful for informal primary group relations, as well as an "elaborated" code useful for academic work, the majority of lower-class youngsters possess only a public code when they first come to school.[27] They are then educationally disadvantaged *unless* their teachers recognize and accept this fact. Teachers can respond positively by permitting the use of slang in class discussions, by utilizing comic books as *educationally* relevant materials during the initial stages of teaching youngsters to read or in motivating them for substantive learning.

To the extent that schools become desegregated under the pressure of law, the problem of accommodating subcultural class differences of learning patterns will become enormous unless teachers are thoroughly prepared by professional schools to work in genuinely multicultural settings. At present, only a few schools of education appear to be doing a great deal in this area, although many have instituted more limited bicultural and bilingual programs.[28]

Levels of Well-Informed Teaching.   If the school *over*-accommodates subcultural uniqueness, it may contribute to a breakdown of society by further fractionating an already divided population. It seems evident that a balance must be struck that fits the needs of subgroups and social classes within the social system; for example, instruction in ethnic studies *and* compensatory education programs could be provided within integrated schools.

There are three basic levels of well-informed teaching:

- Teaching to meet the needs of the society as a whole
- Teaching to meet the needs of subgroups within the larger society
- Teaching to meet the needs of unique individuals in the society and its subgroups

There seem to be two kinds of naivete prevalent among practicing teachers: (1) Many teachers naively try to gear all work toward the individual child, when individuals and the groups to which they belong are intimately related, each influencing the other. (2) Other teachers are naive about trying to completely accommodate the demands of the larger society—that is, they try to gear all work to the group and ignore individual needs.

McMahon recently attempted to reconcile the two dichotomies by asking:

> What is to be gained by emphasizing either sameness or uniqueness over the other? On the one hand, affirming the student's individuality, we can urge him to a life of autonomy and personal integrity; on the other, offering the solidarity of man, urge that he identify with the community. Either way alone leads to error. The human images must be balanced: Man is grand enough to accomodate the two.[29]

In order for American teachers to help all their students, rather than only middle-class ones who are predisposed to succeed in school, they must become students of anthropology as well as of psychology and the other disciplines that have dominated teacher education. In the preparation of teachers, the amount and quality of field work experience in a variety of community educational settings needs to be vastly increased over what it typically entails at present. The theoretical and empirical study of people in action must continue after obtaining a teaching position.

The Need for Heterogeneous Grouping in Schools.   In order for schools to help all children obtain equal educational opportunity, schools must be organized so that youngsters of different social class backgrounds rub shoulders in the corridors, on the playground, and in the classroom. Although individual teachers cannot control the way in which schools as a whole are organized, they can control the way in which their own classrooms are structured. Segregation of children based on their social class standing is common in American classrooms; this segregation is not intentional and is due to a lack of correct information about how people learn. There is much evidence that children are grouped homogeneously for reading and other valued subjects from the first days of school. Such groupings, while ostensibly based on the results of formal or informal testing, are actually closely correlated with social class status.[30] Whether techniques for allowing children to mix with each other in the classroom are highly formalized or kept very informal, mixing of people of different backgrounds, values, and skills in the classroom will probably do the most in furthering open-class equality of opportunity by educational means.

Can Teachers Avoid Being a "One-Class" Role Model for Students?

A role model is a person whose behavior is imitated by others. A "one-class" role model, is a person who presents for emulation by others a single social class in his or her attitudes and behavior. Prior to entering the occupation or shortly thereafter, most teachers are (or become) more or less middle class in their thinking, values, and behavior. Teaching has traditionally been a means by which some lower-class individuals have become vertically mobile, and the American public until recently expected all its school teachers to be paragons of middle-class virtue.

This means that, by and large, the lives of teachers outside of school are probably going to continue to be lived in much the same way as the lives of most other middle-class people. They will undoubtedly continue to buy homes in the suburbs and to commute to work, to bring their own children up according to Dr. Spock or one of his disciples, to want their children to go to college, to visit art museums with the family, and occasionally to attend a ballet. Even the growing union movement among teachers is likely to change little about their out-of-school lives; it merely indicates that unions can appeal to white-collar workers as well as blue-collar workers.

Insofar as students see a great deal of their teachers in their personal lives, many will be seeing a "one-class" (i.e., middle-class) role model. However, this prospect is increasingly unlikely in urban America. Can teachers deemphasize their class-boundedness enough to permit their students to feel free to express their own class-related lifestyle preferences? If not, only students who are already middle-class or distinctly middle-class mobile are likely to receive much help from the school. Students clearly learn best when they are at ease—when they like themselves, regardless of what their socioeconomic status. Unfortunately, American schools are not structured to develop high self-regard in every student:

> American education tends to be reflective of middle-class values, attitudes, and symbols. The schools should, according to this ethic, prepare good, solid citizens; armed with speaking and calculating proficiency; clean of mind, thought, and deed; and concerned with getting a good job. Students are expected to be pleasantly docile, to speak when spoken to and to give specific answers, to do neat work, not to cause trouble, to be respectful, not to ask embarrassing questions, to be stylish in appearance, to have money, to participate in school affairs; in short, to conform.[31]

The traditional middle-class bias of schools and many teachers keeps students from other strata from selecting their own models to emulate. And the bias has not been substantially reduced in recent years. Although a sample of teachers studied not long ago said they believed that ideal children are humanistic, honest, creative, and independent—characteristics that transcend social strata—these teachers also believed that the best students are cooperative, competitive, obedient, and conforming—essentially middle-class characteristics.[32] Like other highly enculturated agents of a rank-ordered society, many teachers apparently take for granted the dubious cultural claim that to be a member of the lower class is to be inferior and to have inferior parents.

As long as such internalized feelings of superiority and inferiority remain unavailable to teachers' conscious minds, they can never be completely free to relax and enjoy working with each and everyone of their students, because they never know when they might forget and automatically say the "wrong thing," raise their brows the wrong way, or in some other subtle way imply by word or gesture that all of their students are not indeed equal in their eyes. And, once a child is slighted by a teacher his or her self-image declines. When this happens, the child usually reacts by rejecting the source of his pain. Unless trained to be objective, as psychiatrists are, teachers tend to respond to children's responses to rejection by returning them in kind. This sets the ball rolling for a vicious circle of rejection and negative response to rejection, which frequently results in basically well-intentioned teachers feeling alienated from some or all of their students, and vice versa.

So, in addition to acquiring knowledge of social class-based differences in children's orientations to learning in school and learning to appreciate children from every walk of life, it is important that middle-class teachers and prospective teachers become skillful in bringing to the surface and analyzing their own deeply internalized social class prejudices. Then perhaps they can cope with situations in which misunderstandings related to social class occur.

One inexpensive and often excellent way to do this is to engage in simulation work with fellow teachers and teachers-to-be, possibly in conjunction with student teaching.[33]

If your school of education presently has little to offer in the way of opportunities for intensive and personalized explorations into the cultural aspects of the dynamics of teaching, you and your fellow students may want to request special help from your professors and college supervisors in setting up role analysis and simulation situations within pre-existing foundations, methods, or other educational classes. Or you may want to do some simulation work on your own, with the help of an interested and qualified group leader.

Only by actually experiencing the feelings of other people in the teaching milieu—in this case, of students from different social strata and perhaps their parents—can you develop the self-confidence and skill needed to work successfully with all kinds of youngsters. Simulation work in small, ongoing groups may be an excellent training strategy for future teachers because it is safer for novices than being in the actual classroom where, once a "mistake" is made, it may be difficult to overcome. Also, most student teaching at present is not comprehensive enough in scope to permit the novice teacher to participate in the variety of activities required to elicit the range of behavioral responses actually encountered by teachers on the job.

By participating actively in simulated micro teaching and analytic experiences, you can move from theory to practice in a laboratory setting demonstrated to be highly productive in reducing cultural and other misunderstandings between teachers and their students—misunderstandings that may inhibit optimum learning by every student, in spite of your best intentions.

Simulation is one way teachers may avoid being one-class role models to their diverse students. Can you think of some other ways?

Summary

Although traditionally underplayed by commentators of the American social scene, we now recognize that almost everyone in American society is profoundly influenced by cultural patterns of their social class that largely determine individual lifestyle and motives. Because schools in this society have been assigned the role of preserving these patterns by equitable methods of selecting and sorting, prospective teachers need to be knowledgeable about the stratification system and about their own location within it. Most studies of community social stratification have found a class structure ranging from a minimum of three classes in small communities to five or more in medium- and large-sized cities. Members of each of these strata tend to react to the experience of schooling differently and to be affected differently by that experience as a result of acquired dispositions toward formal education and cognitive styles developed in family life. As traditional representatives of middle-class values and norms, teachers have come into growing conflict with youngsters of different classes, particularly from the lower class.

Opportunity to become upwardly mobile has become more dependent upon acquiring academic credentials. If teachers are to adequately serve *all* youngsters, they will need to modify their middle-class role model status by allowing youngsters to select their own models and by helping them to make intelligent choices based upon skill in solving complex problems and upon factual information pertinent to life in the contemporary world. One way teachers may develop the self-confidence and competence needed to enable them to do these things is through simulation work in small groups.

Related Concepts

achieved status   An earned class position. This type of status is personified by Horatio Alger's fabled "rags to riches" characters of American life.

ascribed status   An unearned class position; for example, the children of British royal families are ascribed upper-class status at birth, and normally retain it throughout their lives.

contest mobility   Upward vertical mobility achieved as a result of success in long term, continuing, open educational competition for desired, but scarce class positions in the stratification system. (This is the idealized form for middle-class people in the United States.)[34]

social class subculture   Patterns of collective life learned and upheld by persons ranked similarly in the social stratification system of a society.

Suggested Activity

Ask one of your professors of education to invite a high school guidance counselor and a college admissions officer to class to discuss changing patterns of occupational counseling and college student recruitment in your community.

In particular, focus your questions on the advising and recruitment of lower SES students in recent years.

References and Notes

1.   George Gallup, "The First Five Years: Trends and Observations," in Stanley Elam, ed. *The Gallup Polls of Attitudes toward Education 1969–1973* (Bloomington, Ind.: Phi Delta Kappan, 1973), p. 2.

2.   Henry P. Fairchild, ed., *Dictionary of Sociology and Related Sciences* (Totowa, N.J.: Littlefield, Adams and Company, 1970), p. 278.

3.   Sarane S. Boocock, *An Introduction to the Sociology of Learning* (Boston: Houghton Mifflin Company, 1972), p. 36.

4.   See Robert J. Havighurst and Bernice L. Neugarten, *Society and Education,* 4th ed. (Boston: Allyn and Bacon, 1975), p. 26.

5.   R. S. Lynd and H. M. Lynd, *Middletown: A Study in American Culture* (New York: Harcourt, Brace and World, 1929); W. L. Warner, R. J. Havighurst, and M. B. Loeb, *Who Shall be Educated?* (New York: Harper & Row, 1944); A. Hollingshead, *Elmtown's Youth* (New York: John Wiley & Sons, 1949); Harold M. Hodges, Jr., "Penninsula People: Social Stratification in a Metropolitan Complex," in W. Warren Kallenbach and Harold M. Hodges, eds., *Education and Society* (Columbus, Ohio: Charles E. Merrill Books, 1963), pp. 389–420.

6.   Hodges, "Penninsula People," p. 390.

7.   Havighurst and Neugarten, *Society and Education,* pp. 22–31.

8.   *Ibid.,* p. 23.

9.   *Ibid.*

10.   *Ibid.*

11.   W. L. Warner and P. S. Lunt, *The Social Life of a Modern Community* (New Haven: Yale University Press, 1941).

12.   *Phi Delta Kappan* 55 (May 1974): 644.

13.   Richard P. Coleman and Bernice L. Neugarten, *Social Status in the City* (San Francisco: Jossey-Bass, 1971), p. 280.

14. For a critical analysis of the trend toward increased years of schooling, *see* Ivar Berg, *Education and Jobs: The Great Training Robbery* (New York: Praeger Publishers, 1970).

15. Along these lines, George Gallup claims that "a successful resolution of the problem of discipline would almost certainly bring a change in the attitudes of those parents who are moving to the suburbs chiefly to remove their children from inner-city problems." (Gallup, "The First Five Years," p. 5.)

16. Robert L. Crain, "School Integration and the Academic Achievement of Negroes," *Sociology of Education* 44 (Winter 1971): 1–26. *See also* James S. Coleman, et al., *Equality of Educational Opportunity* (Washington, D. C.: United States Department of Health, Education and Welfare, U.S. Government Printing Office, 1966).

17. Ray C. Rist, "Student Social Class and Teacher Expectations: The Self-Fulfilling Prophecy in Ghetto Education," *Harvard Educational Review* 40 (August 1970): 411–51.

18. John P. Hewitt, *Social Stratification and Deviant Behavior* (New York: Random House, 1970).

19. Boocock, *Sociology of Learning.*

20. Gouldner calls this subculture the "psychedelic culture." (Alvin Gouldner, *The Coming Crisis of Western Sociology* [New York: Basic Books, 1970].)

21. *See* Brian Jackson and Dennis Marsden, *Education and The Working Classes* (London: Routledge & Kegan Paul, 1962).

22. Jane R. Mercer, with Marrietta Coleman and Jack Henloe, *Racial/Ethnic Segregation and Desegregation in American Public Education*, U. S. Office of Education, OEC-9-72-0137 (Riverside: University of California, 1974), pp. 28, 29.

23. Christopher Jencks, et al., *Inequality: A Reassessment of the Effect of Family and Schooling in America* (New York: Basic Books, 1972).

24. Abram Kardiner and Lionel Ovesey, "The Social Environment of the Negro," in *The Disadvantaged Learner: Knowing, Understanding, Educating* (San Francisco: Chandler Publishing Company, 1966), p. 158.

25. An excellent listing of these consequences is given by Richard LePiere in his book, *Social Change* (New York: McGraw-Hill, 1965), p. 138.

26. Vance Packard, *A Nation of Strangers* (New York: David McKay Company, 1972).

27. Basil Bernstein, "Social Class and Linguistic Development: A Theory of Social Learning," in Halsey, Floud, and Anderson, *Education, Economy, and Society*, pp. 228–314.

28. The University of Michigan, however, provides an exceptionally comprehensive program in multicultural work for students of education. All prospective teachers are expected to complete three such courses prior to student teaching. (Gwendolyn C. Baker, Chairperson, Multi-Cultural Program, University of Michigan, Ann Arbor. [Private Correspondence].)

29. Michael B. McMahon, "Celebrating Human Uniqueness: Second Thoughts," *Phi Delta Kappan*, p. 621.

30. Rist, "Student Social Class and Teacher Expectations."

31. Jack L. Nelson and Frank P. Besag, *Sociological Perspectives in Education: Models for Analysis* (New York: Pitman

Publishing Corporation, 1970), p. 130.

32. Reported in *Phi Delta Kappan,* p. 636.

33. *See* Sandford W. Reitman, "An Alternative Field Work Model for Prospective Teachers," *Interchange* 4 (1973): 61–78; *idem,* "Role Strain and the Ameri-

can Teacher," *School Review* 79 (August 1971): 543–59.

34. James N. Porter, "Race, Socialization and Mobility in Educational and Early Occupational Attainment," *American Sociological Review* 39 (June 1974): 303–16.

8

The Family and the School

Despite much talk to the contrary, the American family, in one form or another, is probably here to stay. There are at least two reasons for saying this, one based primarily on empirical data, the other on logic.

In the 1970s more men and women than ever before married at an earlier age, and more men and women remarried. Close to four-fifths of all adult males in the United States were married in 1972, compared with only three-fifths of the male population fifty years earlier. The proportion of married females has increased similarly; technically speaking, however, fewer females than males are married, largely because of the greater number of women who become widowed.[1]

Of males and females between the ages of eighteen and twenty-four, 49.9 percent and 83.2 percent, respectively, were married in 1972; comparable figures for 1975 were 49.5 and 81.1, respectively.[2] While the average age at first marriage has increased slightly since 1972, in general people still appear to be marrying at earlier ages than in the past, despite popular notions that more people are postponing marriage.

The divorce rate has also increased, from 0.7 percent for males and 0.8 percent for females in 1920 to 2.9 percent for males and 4.5 percent for females in 1972—an increase of 2.2 percent and 3.7 percent, respectively. However, we should not be misled by these statistics, for several reasons: (1) It is expected that the divorce rate will begin tapering off in the near future.[3] (2) A fair proportion of the divorces today are believed to occur among those who marry early and attempt to raise families prior to obtaining educational and occupational security.[4] (3) The divorce rate seems to be much greater in some socioeconomic groups than in others; for example, it is greater among working-class and poor people than among middle-class people.[5] (4) Because of the early age at which most couples become divorced, about three out of four remarriages involve divorced persons; that is, most divorced persons in this society choose to try marriage again rather than remain single.[6]

At the same time as a greater proportion of the population is marrying, the average size of families in all socioeconomic groups is declining. A relatively short time ago (1965) the average number of children born to white married women between the ages of eighteen and twenty-four was 3.1; for black married women between those ages, it was 3.4. By 1972 the number of children had declined to 2.2 and 2.4, respectively.[7] They have declined even further since 1972, perhaps to a point below the population replacement rate. The trend toward increasingly smaller families is similar to the child-bearing preferences of parents during the Great Depression of the 1930s. However, the population projected in the United States by the Census Bureau for 1990 is between 239,084,000 and 266,238,000—an increase of from 33 to 60 millions since about 1970.[8]

Thus, despite significant changes in the divorce and birth rates— changes that vary according to socioeconomic status, **ethnicity,** age, and other variables—"It seems safe to conclude that more Americans are spending more years in the marital [and family] situation than ever before in our history."[9]

What is the apparent logic behind this statistical refutation of the argument that marriage and the family are dying institutions? When a social institution no longer serves the functions traditionally associated with its operation, it either adapts to meet new sociocultural conditions (a capability known as "ultrastability"[10]) or it perishes. The interrelated institutions of marriage and the family have remained relatively flexible in the face of profound social change in the wider culture. While other institutions have become highly organized and bureaucratized, the institutions of marriage and the family have remained impervious to strict regulation and formalization. They have remolded themselves into new shapes to fit unfamiliar conditions of reality.

Looking at the family from a macro perspective, we see that the following functions of the institution have declined and in part have been assumed by other institutions in the past one hundred years.

• Economic functions, including those of production, marketing, and service, have been transferred to the factory, the store, the office, and other settings outside the home
• Protective functions, including security in old age and personal crisis, and defense of family members and property, have been largely given over to government, private and public welfare agencies, and insurance companies.
• Control by the male household head, and by parents generally, has been gradually reduced as the health, welfare, and civil rights of children have been increasingly attended to by social welfare, education,

and legal agencies that now share the control of children with parents in certain areas.

• Religious functions, which at one time closely involved the family with the church, have declined as society has been secularized.

• Educational functions, except during infancy and early childhood, have been taken over by the school and the peer group, as well as by other child- and youth-servicing agencies. (Even early childhood edution is in the process of becoming a school function.)

• Family recreational functions have been somewhat curtailed and modified as the family has become urbanized and members of the older and the younger generations increasingly go their separate ways.[11]

But the loss, reduction, or modification of the traditional functions commonly, and often nostalgically associated with the American family of the past does not mean that modern families are obsolete.

The family still continues to serve human needs. The one function that no other institution seems able to replace is that of giving members psychological security and love. Even if reproduction and early socialization were to cease being preeminent concerns of the family, it is doubtful that any other institution, including the school, could replace the family as a central agency for giving individuals the feeling of being wanted and needed in an otherwise impersonal and anomic society.

Most American families—whatever functions they still serve or fail to serve—now are responsible for at least three basic tasks assigned by society:

1. Reproduction of the species
2. Socialization and enculturation of the young
3. Developing emotional security

The Pluralistic View of Family Life in America

One common approach to analysis of the contemporary American family suggests that the differences among families are more important than the similarities. The differences between families have significant implications for schooling and teaching, particularly in regard to academic achievement. Boocock says:

> ... there is relatively little difference among families in their valuation of achievement. Most children and their parents value success and recognize

formal education as an important ingredient. What differs is the degree to which a general yearning is translated into a workable set of life goals and strategies for reaching them. Parents of school achievers not only expect more and communicate this to their children, but they also teach them the behavior needed to fulfill their expectations. In sum, what children who fail to "make it" in school lack is role-playing skills, not the desire to succeed, and because they do not know how to play the role of student, they are less likely to do the things that will lead to success.[12]

According to Boocock and other pluralists, differences in ability to succeed in school are a result primarily of differences in socioeconomic status, race, ethnic group, and religion.[13] *Other things being equal*, the child born into an upper-middle-class family tends to have the best chance of succeeding in school, as success in school is ordinarily defined. Ethnicity, or subcultural identity, also makes a critical difference in how children (who can be identified on the basis of ethnicity) perform in different cognitive areas on standardized tests of mental ability. But within specific ethnic groups, children of middle-class families tend to perform significantly higher in all areas than do those of lower-class families. Thus, both ethnicity and social class, as mediated through the family (especially through the mother's interpersonal relations with the child[14]), appear to play an important role in determining how human beings think, and the degree to which a person's thinking style and level correspond to the demands of schools and teachers. Boocock sums up these ideas in Figure 8–1, a model which separates race, ethnicity, and religion.

Although it is useful as a framework for understanding familial differences, the pluralist view may either not go far enough or may stretch reality too far. For instance, the model ignores culturally patterned sex differences in styles and levels of thinking and valuing as they relate to schooling. One psychologist has recently demonstrated that girls are conditioned from infancy by our culture to fail academically.[15] In the early years of school, however, girls tend to outperform boys[16] who are at a disadvantage in a traditionally female-dominated elementary schooling system that supposedly denigrates their masculinity. In high school, girls begin to perform less well than they did in elementary school, due to their desire to avoid success—to be "feminine," i.e., not competitive. This pattern of reduced academic striving is continued in college, particularly in coed classes where female students often do not want to compete overtly with males. The emancipation of women may help to alter such dubious sex-role patterns. A new generation of mothers and fathers are beginning to share in the effort to socialize their own daughters and sons to less stereotypical roles.

Furthermore, the pluralists often ignore different types of marriage, for example, the "Conflict-Habituated," the "Devitalized," the "Passive-

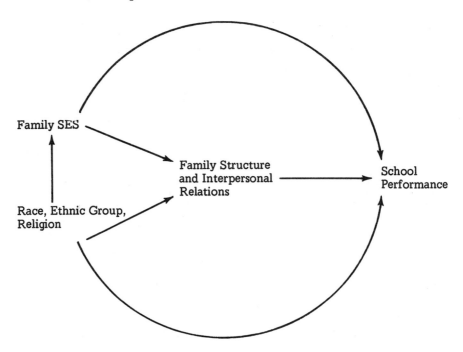

FIGURE 8–1.   *Relationship of Family Variables and School Performance*
From Sarane S. Boocock, An Introduction to the Sociology of Learning
(Boston: Houghton Mifflin, 1972), p. 76. Reprinted with permission of
Houghton Mifflin Company.

Congenial," the "Vital," and the "Total."[17] Although the divorce rate is
increasing, individuals within the same ethnic or class groups marry and
stay married for a variety of reasons besides love (e.g., convenience). The
kind of marriage they develop over time inevitably affects the way in
which parents relate to their children and, in turn, the kinds of values
and thought modes their children possess when they enter school. For
example, a child raised by parents whose marriage has many conflicts is
apt to develop differently than a child reared in a home where the marital
partners have a vital relationship.

      Therefore, when we consider the family in relation to education, we
should be aware that social class *and* ethnicity, as mediated through the
family, are important variables that enter into what a child does in school
and what he obtains from the school experience. Other variables, such as
sex and type of parental marriage, may also make a significant difference
in this experience.

      The pluralistic view, if taken to its logical extreme, infers that
teachers must learn about ethnic, class, and sex groups and their particular family structures, and learn the various languages and dialects of

several subcultures so that they can meet individual needs and learning styles of their students. Teachers will have to find a few organizing principles to transcend major, family-based differences within their classrooms. The unique educational needs of children who are raised differently must be met so that most American parents will be assured that their offspring will have a chance to enter the mainstream—or to stay there.[18]

In a less extreme light, the pluralistic view of the family strongly suggests that we find some coherency of educational thought and strategy for our partially pluralistic society, without reverting to the traditional educational device of trying to melt all youngsters into the same pot. If most parents want their children to succeed in school, but not all children are prepared at home for such success, then perhaps the most reasonable ways for teachers to reach the majority of children and their parents are: (1) to constantly keep in mind that their clients have needs on three fundamental levels—the larger social, the subcultural, and the individual; and (2) to learn to understand the larger social purposes of a school education without forgetting that students are individuals and members of cultural subgroups in the society. Perhaps by actively involving themselves in community affairs, teachers will avoid isolating themselves from the human side of their clients. In addition, all teachers could read the rich ethnic literature of our culture and take elective coursework in ethnic and multicultural studies in order to meet the diverse needs of individuals and the groups to which they belong.

The Emergent Democratic Family and Its Implications for Education

The conventional pluralistic view of the American family emphasizes the differences among families as reflected in children's responsiveness to the experience of schooling. However, many scholars believe that a single modal type of American family is gradually coming into being, which is more similar across class, ethnic, and other boundary lines than it is different.

A Definition of the Democratic Family

In the 1950s social psychologist Urie Bronfenbrenner reported on the results of a study of differences in infant and child socialization practices between middle-class and working class mothers. Since these findings were first reported, attempts have been made to confirm or disprove them, but Bronfenbrenner's results are still reliable, and they continue to be referred to in recent textbooks on the American family.[19] The gist of his findings on infant care in the United States over the twenty-five-year period from 1930 to 1955 is that in the earlier part of that period, middle-class mothers were less permissive in feeding and toilet-training practices than were working class mothers. But since the end of World War II, this trend has been reversed, at least partly by the influence of infant and child development experts such as Dr. Spock, whose books were read by large numbers of middle-class women.

Similar results were found by Bronfenbrenner in regard to continuity of socialization practices from infancy into childhood. As he put it, "... the results depict the middle-class parent as more permissive in all four spheres of activity: oral behavior, toilet accidents, sex, and aggression."[20] He was careful to point out that "it would be a mistake to conclude that the middle-class parent is exerting less pressure on his children.[21] Parents still expect their children to obey and to do well in school, but they are also more relaxed about such matters than they were in the 1930s.

The important point about these studies seems to be that "the cultural gap [between middle and lower classes] may be narrowing. Spock has joined the Bible on the working-class shelf."[22]

The notion that American families are becoming more alike—especially in regard to how children are raised—has obvious implications for school teachers who must reconsider textbook suggestions of using stricter discipline measures for lower-class children than for middle-class ones. In 1948, Ernest Burgess commented on how the "American family presents an external picture of diversity and instability."[23] This is the kind of picture that seems to have impressed extreme pluralists. But when viewed in the larger framework of the ubiquitous social change in our time, "a trend is revealed to the companionship type of family, adapted to urbanization and exemplifying the American ideals of democracy, freedom, and self-expression. The seeming instability of the family is largely a symptom of this transition which may be regarded as a vast social experiment in which adaptability becomes more significant for success in marriage and family living than a rigid stability."[24]

More recently, Philip Slater, has claimed that the "typical" American family has always been more or less democratic, compared with European families. He defines such a "democratic" family as follows:

I mean simply a family system in which the social distance between parent and child is relatively small, the exercise of parental authority is relatively mild, and the child tends not to be seen as a mere parental possession without independent status. It is, in other words, the system

that presently obtains in our own middle class and toward which most of the Western world seems to be moving.[25]

Slater believes that this "democratic family is the most potent expression of democracy, and a necessary condition for its survival. For the very young are, by their very nature, uncommitted":

> *It [the democratic family] assumes that children may adapt better to their environment than did their parents, and that therefore their parents cannot take for granted the superiority of their own knowledge, perceptions, attitudes, and skills. Thus, it not only causes but can only exist under conditions of chronic change.*[26]

In other words, the democratic family (which, according to Slater and Burgess, really means the modal, or characteristic, American upper-middle-class family) has been and is the family type toward which the United States as a whole (and now much of the rest of the world, as well) seems to be moving in its efforts to adapt to massive social change.

Slater, Burgess, and Bronfenbrenner, among numerous other social scientists who hold more or less dynamic views of the family, see the

American family structure as undergoing a transformation that is gradually producing a single type of family uniquely adapted to changing conditions. We no longer can talk incautiously of the "Jewish family," the "black family," the "working class family," or the "Wasp family." Almost all families, despite real differences that remain, are becoming more like the democratic middle-class family in the functions they serve and in their ways of performing these functions.

The democratic family is actually a prototype that has not yet been fully realized. As such, the same sort of cautions apply as did in the discussion of the conventionally pluralist approach. If pluralism is exaggerated, then teachers can easily be led to believe that study of subgroup differences in students and their families is the foundation of effective professional endeavor. Such a single-minded approach would tax even the most dedicated and brilliant prospective teacher. But if pursued with moderation, such an approach to teaching would probably be extremely fruitful. And, if we exaggerate the extent to which American families have actually become similar, then teachers eager to find ready answers to complex problems can easily be beguiled into thinking that all children and their parents can be approached on the basis of relatively simple and unambiguous formulas. This would lead to a regression of American education back to the time when all youngsters and parents were treated as if they were either saints or sinners.

Basic Characteristics of the "Democratic" Family

Some of the democratic family's general features are mentioned in the following paragraphs.

Urbanization.   In values and lifestyle, America is a society of city and suburban dwellers. Even in rural communities, the urban family type is becoming common in terms of such factors as its small size, the father who works outside the home, and so on.

Secularization.   A secular society is reflected in the relative absence of religious interest and focus in the emerging family. The modern family is concerned with the affairs of "this world" almost exclusively.

Instability.   With ubiquitous change and its accompanying dislocations, divorce and confusion about roles and child-rearing norms continue to increase or at least remain at relatively high levels compared with the more certain and settled days of the past when the **primary group** outside the family exerted stronger social controls over family affairs.

Specialization. The emerging and predominantly urban American family is becoming increasingly specialized in function as society grows more complex and differentiated, permitting community agencies other than the family (e.g., the school) to handle many of its former functions. The modern family is specialized in such areas as rearing children who are capable of withstanding the pressures of a society that increasingly compartmentalizes its members' lives. Related to this, the family provides continuous emotional support and affection in a world where secondary social relations emphasize rationality and withholding of any except comparatively superficial and transitory forms of emotional expression. In short, the family is becoming the ultimate primary group in a mass secondary society.

Companionship. The emphasis in the emerging middle-class family is on friendship and companiable relations, which are typical characteristics of the **nuclear family.** These types of family relationships differ from the more dutiful ones of the **extended, or consanguine, family** of the past. Marriage and child rearing are based more and more upon this companionate ideal, clearly differentiating the modern family from the sharply role-structured family of the past.

Democratic Relations. In the companionate nuclear family, relations between the members are becoming more open and democratic than was the case in the past. Emphasis today (at least ideally) is on the freedom of family members to grow and develop creatively in harmony with their own needs, rather than according to clearly defined expectations of parents or significant others in the community. The family is a "sanctuary from the world outside" in which each individual member can find his own personhood and in which all members interact with regard for all others.

Reduced Family Size. Another characteristic of the emerging modern family is its reduction in size. Birth control is widely practiced in a society that no longer demands child labor and is concerned more than ever with the welfare of its individual members. Although the post–World War II "baby boom" temporarily raised the birthrate, growing fears of continuous warfare and increased concerns with problems of pollution and poverty, have caused the birthrate to decline in the 1960s, as it did during the Great Depression.[27]

Changing Marriage Patterns. Until recently, there was a trend toward earlier marriage. Today, parental roles are changing. With the influence of feminism, both women and men often work outside the home to sustain the union. Men and women of all social classes and ethnic groups are beginning to share more equally in rearing children and in earning a living. This seems to be part of the trend toward companionate, democratic families.

Child Rearing.   With increasing uncertainty about child rearing in a changing world, parents rely more on experts. Those with the greatest access to experts—the financially and educationally privileged—rely most upon them, although other socioeconomic groups are now consulting Dr. Spock and his disciples.

Child-rearing methods are more permissive today, although the American family has always reared its children more permissively than is commonly realized. Permissiveness is related to the fact that this society needs flexible individuals who can cope with continuous change. Along with this trend is the fear by many parents, teachers, and other socializing agents—who were reared in slightly less permissive surroundings—that they are losing control and authority over their children. Although reactions to what some consider the excesses of the 1960s have caused some to return to "firm" parenting in the 1970s, most parents today depend far more on appeals to reason (or guilt) than upon direct physical punishment in disciplining children. This is also consistent with trends toward increased education of parents and growing dominance of the middle-class democratic family.

The average middle-class parent still places a relatively strong emphasis upon achievement by their children, in school and on the job. The emphasis on excelling, often reinforced by schools and other social institutions, is not entirely consistent with the emergence of an otherwise leisure-oriented culture; it is also believed to be the source of difficulties between the generations.[28]

Often lamented today is the alleged emergence of a matriarchal society, symbolized by the mythic upper-middle-class suburban experience where father "commutes to work by train early in the morning and comes home late in the evening, often after the children are in bed." Whether such a picture is exaggerated or not, most men are not present in the home as much as they were in the past when divorce was less prevalent and occupations were less distant from the home. Hence, there is some concern for the availability of masculine models for young boys and girls.

The American family, despite some exceptions, can be tentatively described as being in a process of experimental transition—from a structure suited to Pre-Industrial and Industrial societies to one suited to life in a cosmopolitan Post-Industrial civilization.

The Democratic Family as It
Relates to Teaching

From the frame of reference of the democratic image of the family, teachers have somewhat less of a complex problem to deal with in one sense than teachers who subscribe to a strongly pluralistic model. There are fewer family variables (e.g., social class, ethnic, and other subgroup differences) to take into consideration if most of a teacher's students come from increasingly similar home environments.

On the other hand, a teacher's work with children of the emerging democratic middle-class home becomes more complex in the sense that this common background is constantly changing in response to broader social conditions.

Teachers who attempt to become authoritarian or even mildly authoritarian will fail with many children. Such an approach to teacher–student relations succeeded in the past because the community and the extended family—institutions that are waning in influence today—supported restrictive childhood and adolescent behavior. Today's teacher generally has little choice but to be flexible and open-minded in his or her expectation for children; traditional strategies for disciplining are no longer effective. Families have prepared children to be free and involved, and the teacher who attempts to counteract this home experience will be frustrated in his or her attempts to discipline.

But if teachers judiciously allow students who have been "democratically" and "permissively" socialized to move about the classroom occasionally, to communicate casually instead of formally, and to inquire freely, they will usually find that their students are happy in their "second home" of the classroom and eager to learn.

Similarly, if teachers recognize the value placed in expert knowledge by modern parents and become confident child and youth specialists themselves, they will probably find parents more willing to respect and heed their advice about what Johnnie or Janie needs educationally, and will thus create necessary educational support from the parents of their students.

Alternative Family Structures and
Their Implications for Education

Besides the pluralistic and democratic models of American family structure, there are other novel approaches to family life that should be mentioned briefly at this point, even though most of them are incipient. In one sense these new approaches are an extension of the pluralist view of a highly differentiated family institution. They are also often variants of the emerging democratic middle-class family because they are being consciously experimented with mainly by children of the middle class. For all their apparent novelty, alternative family structures are partially mutations of the characteristics ascribed to the emerging democratic family. For example, they promote permissive child rearing and are child-centered, and they emphasize companionship and equality of family members.

Some proponents of alternative family modes differ in belief from the mainstream in that they do not stress achievement, have lost faith in an urbanized life, and desire to bring back the comforting dependency of the extended kin group. The modern rural communal movement is only one of several alternative family structures being tried in American society. Other alternative conceptions of family life that appeal to a number of persons who are disenchanted with prevailing family patterns are discussed in the following paragraphs.[29]

Progressive Monogamy, or Serial Marriage.   This is a form of legalized mating becoming more prevalent in the United States. In this pattern, divorce becomes socially acceptable and "normal" for people who no longer insist that marriage to the same partner for life is realistic or even desirable in a rapidly changing society. If this pattern becomes widespread, teachers will have to deal with many children who have changed homes and acquired new parents, and who have led a disruptive life. Teachers confronted with such children should concentrate on meeting the increased emotional, social, and academic needs of youngsters from relatively unstable families.

Legalized Polyandry and Tribal Marriage.   This is a looser, more relaxed form of mating in which polyandry (one female married to more than one male), polygamy (one male and more than one female), and extended-group relations replace traditional monogamous pairing. There is no state certification of this relatively uninstitutionalized relationship. Polygamy has long been practiced in rural areas of Utah among some isolated members of the Latter Day Saints, although it is not legal any longer.[30] It can also be observed in various rural and urban communes where one sex strongly outnumbers the other. A major difficulty with such patterns has been that members of communes—usually disenchanted middle-class members seeking new and better forms of living—have often found it easier to preach polyandry or polygamy than to practice it. Simple jealousy often interferes with good intentions, with the end result being a reversion to pairing.[31]

Rural communes often run their own schools or attempt to educate their children informally, whether this is legal or not. Urban communalists may send their youngsters to free schools. To the extent that the tribal alternative becomes widespread enough to seriously affect public schools, it may produce novel problems for rigidly traditional teachers, such as discipline problems and rejection of authority figures by youngsters accustomed to relating to adults as friends. Early informal investigations of the behavior and attitudes of children raised on communes suggest that "the children tended to be more open and trusting than is generally found in straight society."[32] If such characteristics are maintained in schools outside of the commune, then well-intentioned, open-minded teachers may encounter unusual receptivity to their instructional strategies by an essentially new population of students.

Dual Marriage.   Margaret Mead[33] proposes a new institutional form of marriage and family life in which young people who are not ready for the responsibilities of bearing and raising children legally marry for a designated period of time. After this trial period ends, they can choose to renew their license or to separate. Only after a couple has been married successfully for a prescribed length of time can they become permanently married and entitled to raise a family. The idea is intended to reduce the guilt and other emotional problems of divorce and to help ensure that children are wanted and have a reasonably stable home in which to be raised.

If implemented in the United States, such a proposal would probably serve to ease relations somewhat between teachers and their clients and to bring home and school more close together than ever, other things being equal. Dual marriage thus may have a stabilizing effect on society and its educational system.

Intimate Networks.   One of the disadvantages of the emerging democratic family is that it represents a loss of extended kin relations and produces an extreme dependency for emotional and social support upon members of the small nuclear group—that is, upon parents, siblings, and spouses. Intimate networks of nuclear families purportedly help highly mobile Americans to find a replacement for the loss of the extended kin group. Three or four families come together regularly, as relatives used to do, and explore their living arrangements, exchange interpersonal intimacies, provide services for each other, and try to work out new and meaningful systems of values and attitudes.

Like the dual marriage, intimate networks of families would probably be stabilizing for education if conventional families are involved and if they offer children a sense of security that facilitates ease of communication and development of a strong self-concept at school. If the networks move significantly away from the mainstream in their exploration of values, this could be reflected in difficulties between highly opinionated school teachers and students from such networks. Teachers need to be open and flexible people in order to cope effectively with divergence from the norm.

The future of these and other alternative family movements arising out of this highly dynamic period and the troubled human relations that accompany it influences the work of a prospective teacher. In particular, today's teacher should have an open mind and a flexible personality in order to respond effectively to these challenges. Contemporary mainstream and ethnic family life already present enormous challenges that require openness and flexibility on the part of teachers. Because of dramatic adjustments in our dominant family patterns, we can already anticipate radical experiments in intimate human living that will require attendant readjustments in our roles and personalities.

How Should Teachers Orient Themselves toward Parents?

Why are some teachers more successful with parents than others? First, teachers cannot expect to receive cooperation from a parent unless the parent believes that the teacher has the child's best interests at heart. This is a sort of trust that is difficult to achieve between middle-class teachers and parents of children from poor backgrounds. In comparison with their dealings with parents of middle-class youngsters, teachers may have to go beyond normal procedures to prove that they really care.

One way is to make "home calls." These should not be made as a ritual; still, they are often best made at the start of a new school year in order to get to know the students' parents and their home environments. If the parents do not have a telephone, and the note you send home with students is thrown out along the way or not able to be read by parents who speak and read in a language other than English, you may, in effect, have to visit the family unannounced. Unless you are with a **home–school liaison person** or are accustomed to such practices from previous occupational experience, this type of visit may be a bit unnerving the first few times.

But, assuming you get up your nerve and drive to the first home, you must then get out of your shiny car, walk down the street past curious neighbors and perhaps milling unemployed street loungers, and then knock on the door, introduce yourself, and state the purpose of your call. This may be the hardest part for the beginner, especially if you happen to have been protected all your life by suburban streets and institutions.

Once in the house, though, you merely need to try to relax and play the role of guest, the role that is expected. After visiting politely for awhile, perhaps enjoying a cup of coffee or tea and talking generally about yourself and the youngster whose family you are visiting—without reference to possible problems at school—you can take your leave.

Your visits to students' homes help to build meaningful communication linkages between you, as representative of the school, and the family of one of your students. These linkages could be the difference between future educational success or failure for your students.

You may choose to visit the family during the year, again on an informal basis. Parents will be far more likely to come to school on "conference day" than they might have been had you not taken the essential first step. After all, the teacher is the one who is the professional, not the parents who are compelled by law to send their offspring to an often seemingly "alien" school.

Middle-class parents also appreciate visits from teachers of their youngsters.

Teachers are sometimes overbearing with parents from low socio-economic groups and, especially in elementary school, they are unduly diffident with upper-middle-class parents. This is largely a result of status discrepancies—real or imagined (fairly frequently the latter, according to researchers).[34] Teachers also often ignore fathers. Men would probably come to school more often than they do, if they did not sense that they were somehow out of place there. This applies to men of all groups. When you meet with parents of either or both sexes at school, it might be worth keeping in mind that you are, indeed, a more or less highly prepared and skilled expert in your particular area of endeavor—education. Parents may not always realize that a beginning teacher is more than "just another young kid doing what any good parent can do." This myth is widespread throughout American society. Therefore, it is important to let parents know that you consider yourself to be a highly qualified and competent person in your work. But this must be done without being defensive or arrogant. Many poor people are afraid of teachers because of frequent negative experiences with schools. In such a situation you need to combine sincere interest in a mutual subject of concern—the child—with a calm objectivity in your interpersonal dialogue. It often helps to tacitly acknowledge the personal dignity of the parents and your respect for them.

Listen to the parents when they speak to you. Respond to questions without being evasive. Give advice confidently when you think it ought to be given. However, do not expect your advice to necessarily be heeded. In the case of a difference of opinion, stand firm on what you believe is best for the child's school education, if you can defend your beliefs on adequate theoretical or empirical grounds. And, at all costs, avoid dis-

playing anger or frustration to parents if they seem uncooperative. Whether they are or are not makes no difference in how you react, if you want to gain and keep their respect.

What if a parent does not like something you are doing and reports you to the school principal? Assuming a three-way conversation among you, the principal, and the parents, it is usually recommended that the teacher speak calmly, truthfully, and unoffensively. Parents are sometimes impetuous when it comes to their children and must be forgiven for their lack of objectivity in this regard. As long as you have done what you can honestly justify as educationally sound, the principal is likely to abide by an unwritten occupational code which mandates that he or she accept the teacher's word in disputes with parents.[35] To break this code, especially today with the increase in teacher militancy often directed against school administrators, is to chance inviting serious trouble with the rest of the staff.

Most skills in working with parents can be anticipated and learned as part of the teacher-preparation program, just as are skills for working with students in the classroom. In working with parents, however, student teaching is not of any significant value at present, since emphasis in such clinical experiences is limited almost exclusively to teacher–student relations. Simulation (role playing) groups are usually the only way a prospective teacher can become confident and proficient in working directly with parents, prior to obtaining a paid position with a school system. Simulation groups, if ethnically heterogeneous and supported by reading, can be especially helpful in preventing, or at least limiting, the culture shock that befalls many beginning teachers of the "disadvantaged."

There is ample evidence that American teachers have never really tapped the full potential of working closely with the parents of their students. Particularly teachers working with disadvantaged children frequently try to exclude parents from involvement with schooling because they believe that parents are not supportive of the school.[36] Many teachers also fear that if parents are allowed to become too closely involved with the school, they will compound teaching problems.[37] In the final analysis, however, the best way to secure the help of parents may be to invite them to visit the classroom informally and to help out with instruction. More parents have become supportive of the school after seeing the day-to-day work of the teachers. This would supplement home calls and constructive teacher–parent conferences.

Parents can be a teacher's ally; at present, there is no institution more closely connected with the success or failure of children and even adolescents in school than the family. The challenge is to link home and school effectively in an age of great change and dislocations of people and institutions, where little can be taken for granted between teachers and the community.*

How Can a Teacher Help the Emotionally Troubled Child?

Young people are growing up in families that have been drastically uprooted from their historic sociocultural and geographical moorings. As a consequence, families are often unable to furnish the kind of positive support needed to ensure success in the larger world—including school— without some unusually sensitive attention by sincerely concerned adults outside the family. The parents of emotionally troubled youngsters often feel completely helpless and frustrated as they watch their children growing up in an anxious world they cannot seem to control.

---

* The idea that teachers need to work closely with the family, particularly "where children lack cultural experiences that support and reinforce schooling" has been challenged recently. Geraldine Clifford has proposed "that family culture per se should be irrelevant and that schools should pay much less attention to cultural reparations than to the business of being schools."[38]

Insecure and hostile children are not ordinarily the victims of cruel, consciously manipulative parents, as they are sometimes portrayed in the mass media. They are "victims of culture,"[39] as culture is mediated through confused parental victims. In a very real sense, all of us living through the ordeal of massive social change are victims of culture, and most of us could profit enormously from some contact with wise and humane friends and mentors. Some young people from infancy on have been unusually traumatized by their environments—which in large degree have consisted of their homes and neighborhoods at this early stage of their lives.

Teachers today can expect to meet in their classes more children from confused homes than teachers of ten, twenty, or fifty years ago. With a minimum of expended time and effort, however, they can play a small part in helping these children and adolescents find themselves as they work with them in mathematics, science, history, art, as well as during recess, between classes, and after school.

Youngsters with problems usually want to talk to some adult whom they can trust. Because parents are usually the last people such youth will approach, they will often turn to the next most available adult in their milieu—their teacher, if he or she displays intelligent and sincere interest in them.

Carl Rogers believes that *all real education is therapy,* and vice versa.[40] In the therapeutic (educational) relationship, the therapist (teacher) elicits thinking of a personally meaningful nature from the client (student) by means of intelligent and concerned questioning. He then attempts to have the client reflect ad expand upon his initial statements by further questioning until the client works out his or her own solution to the problem. This was also essentially the approach used by Socrates. This general mode of eliciting personally meaningful thinking is not only valuable in counseling youngsters on a one-to-one basis, but can be an important general strategy for instruction of subject matter as well.

Although the role of counselor may require that teachers spend extra time with some students, the rewards of seeing children or adolescents become more self-confident in their social relations and more interested and capable in their studies is often well worth the effort. And, a teacher becomes more perceptive in general as he or she learns more about the human side of his or her students from listening to them talk about themselves.

Of course, some youngsters have been so badly emotionally scarred from their early family experiences that no amount of skillful counseling by a teacher can help very much. Some children even become suicidal.[41] Such children need help from qualified experts who have the time to concentrate on their particular problems over a lengthy period. But a teacher's being available to simply listen can often determine if a youngster should be receiving more specialized help.

These thoughts on student counseling apply to teachers of the poor as well as to the highly affluent. Emotional disturbance is far more prevalent among poor children than it is among affluent ones.[42] However, because the well-to-do can afford treatment for their emotional problems, they have been more visible in the statistics on mental illness than the poor.

Whether you work in an inner-city ghetto, an integrated school, or a suburban school, there will always be a few children who have serious personal problems arising out of their family lives. As their teacher, you can help these youngsters either directly or indirectly if you care to and are willing to acquire some basic tactics for effective listening. What other ways can you think of to help the emotionally confused or turned-off child?

Summary

The family is here to stay, although it is becoming modified in form and function in response to basic changes in the rest of modern society. It is still the most influential agent of society in the socialization and enculturation of children and youth. Therefore, it must be carefully considered by those who work professionally in schools. The altered patterning of the family may affect the future of youngsters who are increasingly dependent upon a school education for success in life.

Three basic types of family constellations have been identified as important to modern teachers: (1) the "pluralistic," generally lower-class, ethnic family that operates on the fringes of society. Children from these families have unique needs that require understanding if they are to enter the cultural mainstream and be assured of an equal opportunity in American society. (2) The mainstream and "democratic" middle-class family is emerging as the modal family type in the United States and much of the rest of the world. This family type produces children who require teachers to be more open, flexible, and resourceful than ever before. (3) Different alternatives to family structures are being consciously and unconsciously assumed. Basically, they are variants of the democratic family in search of a future. To the extent that such alternative family styles become more common, teachers will be challenged even more to accommodate changing educational needs.

Teachers often fear the influence of parents. Partly as a consequence as well as because American society has made the mistake of isolating the poor for so long, the modern teacher who wishes to be effective must be willing to "reach out" to parents in an effort to enlist their cooperation in the education of their children. To the extent that teachers take this responsibility seriously and to the extent that they make special efforts to help students immobilized emotionally by harsh familial influences, teachers will be aided in their efforts to acquire the leadership essential for working with their students in a period of fundamental social transformation.

Related Concepts

extended (consanguine) family   The immediate family of procreation (parents and children) plus all relatives—aunts, uncles, cousins, etc.

ethnicity   Having to do with groups bound together and identified by ties of race, nationality, or religion. A term referring broadly to subcultural characteristics that are identifiable within a larger social context.

home–school liaison person   An individual paid by a school system to facilitate harmonious relations between home and school. Such liaison persons are sometimes mothers whose own children attend school in a particular neighborhood; at other times, they are professional social workers or school nurses.

nuclear family   The immediate family of marriage and procreation, consisting of father, mother, and children.

primary group   Intimate, face-to-face groups characterized by affectional and personalized relations over instrumental and relatively objectified ones (e.g., the family, the local neighborhood, some elementary school classrooms, etc.).

Suggested Activity

Obtain permission to sit in on a local teacher's parent conferences on conference day or on open-house night. Or gain permission to make home calls one day with a teacher, school nurse, or home–school liaison worker.

Keep your eyes and ears open to learn about blatant or subtle differences between families and their concerns about school and about possible changes in family patterns and educational expectations compared to when you were a child.

Be ready to report on your findings when you return to your education class.

References and Notes

1. *Statistical Abstract of the United States, 1973* (Washington, D.C.: U.S. Bureau of the Census, 1973), p. 38. According to the 1975 edition of the *Statistical Abstract,* the figures for 1972 declined by about one percentage point.

2. *Ibid.*

3. According to Dr. Paul Glick of the U.S. Census Bureau, as reported in the *Fresno Bee* (March 30, 1976): Cl.

4. Lloyd Baron, "Early Motherhood, Accelerated Role Transition, and Social Pathologies," *Social Forces* 52 (March 1974): 333–41.

5. Robert Parke, Jr. and Paul C. Glick, "Prospective Changes in Marriage and the Family," in Bert N. Adams and Thomas Weirath, eds., *Readings on the Sociology of the Family* (Chicago: Markham Publishing Co., 1971), pp. 453, 454.

6. Hugh Carte, "Eight Myths about Divorce—and the Facts," in William J. Goode, ed., *The Contemporary American Family* (Chicago: Quadrangle Books, 1971), p. 224.

7. *Social Indicators 1973* (Washington, D.C.: U.S. Government Printing Office, 1973), p. 254.

8. *Ibid.,* p. 250.

9. John Scanzoni, *Sexual Bargaining: Power Politics in the American Marriage* (Englewood Cliffs, N.J.: Prentice-Hall, 1972), p. 13.

10. *See* Mervyn L. Cadwallader, "The Cybernetic Analysis of Change," in Amitai Etzioni and Eva Etzioni, eds., *Social Change: Sources, Patterns, and Consequences* (New York: Basic Books, 1974), pp. 159, 160.

11. Ralph H. Turner, *Family Interaction* (New York: John Wiley & Sons, 1970), p. 217, 218.

12. Sarane S. Boocock, *An Introduction to the Sociology of Learning* (Boston: Houghton Mifflin Company, 1972), pp. 75, 76.

13. *Ibid.*

14. See Harry Stack Sullivan, *The Interpersonal Theory of Psychiatry,* Helen Perry and Mary Gawel, eds. (New York: W.W. Norton, 1953).

15. Matina Horner, "Fail: Bright Women," *Psychology Today* 3 (November 1969): 36–38; 62.

16. Patricia Sexton, *The Feminized Male: Classrooms, White Collars, and the Decline of Manliness* (New York: Random House, 1969).

17. John F. Cuber and Peggy B. Harroff, "Five Types of Marriage," in Arlene S. Skolnick and Jerome H. Skolnick, eds., *Family in Transition: Rethinking Marriage, Sexuality, Child Rearing, and Family Organization* (Boston: Little, Brown and Co., 1971), pp. 287–99.

18. Bryan T. Downes and Stephen W. Burke, "The Historical Development of the Black Protest Movement," in Staten W. Webster, ed., *Knowing and Understanding the Socially Disadvantaged: Ethnic Minority Groups,* (Scranton, Pa.: Intext Educational Publishers, 1972), p. 38.

19. Urie Bronfenbrenner, "Socialization and Social Class through Time and Space," in *Readings on the Sociology of the Family*, pp. 111–32.

20. *Ibid.*, p. 121.

21. *Ibid.*, p. 127.

22. *Ibid.*, p. 132.

23. Ernest W. Burgess, "The Family in a Changing Society," in W. Warren Kallenbach and Harold M. Hodges, Jr., eds., *Education and Society* (Columbus, Ohio: Charles E. Merrill, 1963), p. 148.

24. *Ibid.*

25. Philip E. Slater, "Social Change and the Democratic Family," in Warren G. Bennis and Philip E. Slater, eds., *The Temporary Society* (New York: Harper & Row, 1968), pp. 35–42.

26. *Ibid.*, pp. 20, 21.

27. *Social Indicators, 1973*, pp. 252, 254.

28. *See* especially George D. Spindler, "Education in a Transforming American Culture," *Harvard Educational Review* 25 (Summer 1955): 145–56.

29. This discussion of alternative family styles is based on a number of recent writings by sociologists and psychologists. They have been summarized in Herbert Otto, ed., *The Family in Search of a Future* (New York: Appleton-Century-Crofts, 1970).

30. Wallace Stegner, *Mormon Country* (New York: Bonanza Books, 1972), pp. 209–26.

31. *See* Ron E. Roberts, *The New Communes: Coming Together in America* (Englewood Cliffs, N.J.: Prentice-Hall, 1971), p. 46, and Sara Davidson, "The Hippie Alternative: Getting Back to the Communal Garden," in Skolnick and Skolnick, *Family in Transition*, p. 531.

32. David Black, "Commune Children," *New Times* 6 (April 30, 1976): 48.

33. *See* Margaret Mead, "Marriage in Two Steps," in Otto, *Family in Search of a Future*, pp. 75–84.

34. Bruce Biddle, Howard Rosencranz, and Earl Rankin, Jr., *Studies in the Role of the Public School Teacher*, vol. 5, *Own and Attributed Cognitions for the Teacher* (Columbia: University of Missouri Press, 1961), pp. 930–35, and John M. Foskett, *Role Consensus: The Case of the Elementary School Teacher* (Eugene: University of Oregon Press, 1969), p. 115.

35. Howard S. Becker, "Schools and Systems of Stratification," in A.H. Halsey, Jean Floud, and C. Arnold Anderson, ed., *Education, Economy, and Society: A Reader in the Sociology of Education* (New York: The Free Press, 1961), p. 101.

36. Biddle, Rosencranz, and Rankin, *Own and Attributed Cognitions*.

37. Becker, "Schools and Stratification."

38. Geraldine Joncich Clifford, *The Shape of American Education* (Englewood Cliffs, N.J.: Prentice-Hall, 1975), pp. 119 and 123.

39. Harry Laudin, *Victims of Culture* (Columbus, Ohio: Charles E. Merrill, 1973).

40. *See* Carl Rogers, *Client-Centered Therapy: Its Current Practice, Implications, and Theory* (Boston: Houghton Mifflin Company, 1951).

41. For an excellent discussion of the growing problems of suicide by young

people and the need for greater understanding of this phenomenon by teachers, see Donald F. Smith, "Adolescent Suicide: A Problem for Teachers?" *Phi Delta Kap-*

pan 57 (April 1976): 539–42.

42. John T. Hewitt, *Social Stratification and Deviant Behavior* (New York: Random House, 1970).

9

The Peer Group:
Its Implications for
Schools and Teaching

Peers are equals. We are accustomed to the legal phrase "a jury of our peers." Scientists think their scholarly efforts are best understood and judged by their fellow scientists, that is, by their peers. The same concern for peer approval or disapproval is held by artists, by physicians, university professors, assembly line operators, and cab drivers.

We live in an age-graded society. In addition to being ranked by such criteria as vocation and social class, people tend to be automatically assigned slots on the basis of their age. For example, we are now accustomed to bracketing people into those "over thirty" and those "under thirty" the "middle-aged," the "elderly," and the "very young."

A common belief of many Americans is that paid work—one's occupation, vocation or career—is the central source of identity for males and, more often indirectly, for females. To most Americans, an occupation has been the primary basis for forming a family, for religious involvement, for a better life in general. Although the so-called work ethic has been challenged in recent years, the vast majority of Americans continue to believe in it and to bring up their offspring to believe that work is the central source of meaning in life. Many people today, particularly unskilled laborers, are very discontented with their work, so that new ways must be found to engage people in meaningful work as we move into the Post-Industrial age.[1]

Although most Americans think of work as vitally important to personal fulfillment in life—either for its own sake or for the sake of the income it brings—it takes longer and longer to complete one's education and enter the workforce. Today's typical young man or woman attends at least twelve years of elementary and secondary school before going out into the world and obtaining a job in an impersonal corporation or government agency. An increasing proportion of young people believe (correctly or not) that the kinds of jobs they must have in order to obtain success and happiness require a college or graduate degree. Preparation for teaching is a five-year program in some states, such as California, at present.

The average person in modern American society is required to go to school for more and more years in order to just begin to be able to support himself or herself and to raise a family. If an individual at fifteen realizes that he or she has many more years of schooling ahead than his or her parents before being granted adult status by society, then he or she will normally try to adjust his or her conception of the present in order to make this extended period of preparation for adulthood more bearable.

Is it any wonder, then, that there has been a steady, dramatic growth in the importance to young people of a sense of belonging to a separate culture of the young—a subculture of their age-peers that is distinct from that of their parents and other members of the older generation? A youth cult has become institutionalized in contemporary society; we are a child- and youth-oriented society in which people over thirty emulate youth fashions, speech, and hair styles. There are also many people who are threatened by some of the more bizarre folkways and mores of the youth subculture and by the more extreme symptoms of alienation in youth, such as disdain for conventional codes of ethics and morality and the refusal to support such longstanding cultural patterns as racism, war, and two-party politics. The peer groups of school-aged children and youth are highly significant forces with which teachers must reckon. Surviving adolescence today is especially difficult. Young people possess most of the biological and social equipment of adults at the same time as they are being exhorted to behave responsibly but without the full privileges of adulthood. Youth has been forced to innovate mechanisms for survival. To try to stand alone during such a trying stage of lengthy and imposed adolescence is to be relatively defenseless in a world in which the most secure gain strength, power, and ultimately personal identity by uniting in groups. The young in our society have merely observed their parents and other adults who have managed to survive and find a modicum of personal identity; they have applied the lessons learned by orienting themselves to a primary reference group of equals. Although parents, teachers, and other well-intentioned adults may also be viewed as significant others at certain times and for certain specific purposes,[2] these adults cannot hope to completely control the values and behavior of the younger generation. This is primarily because this society increasingly restricts entrance to adulthood to those who have been able to acquire the skills and diplomas that certify the right to be labeled an adult.

Thus, the modern peer group of the young serves one latent function for society as a whole: the provision of subcultural patterns that prevent those who are delayed entrance into the adult world from actively rebelling against their elders. In technical terms, modern peer culture serves a "tension-management" function for society.[3] If the peer group occasionally fails to do its job for society, and things get somewhat out of hand as they did in the late 1960s, that is the price to be paid for not coming to grips with the larger problems of our age of basic transition, of avoiding finding a viable solution to the dilemma of what to do with our young when our technology has raced ahead of our values and norms in the realms of education and occupation.

The Functions of Peer Groups

Viewed from the perspective of the young, the functions served by the modern peer group can be readily enumerated. Elkin and Handel list the functions of peer groups for their members:[4]

• The peer group gives the child or youth experience with egalitarian types of relationships, not possible in adult-dominated contexts.

• The peer group is an educational agency. It serves to help the child anticipate his probable future career as a child and, indirectly, as an adult.

• The peer group offers the youngsters a setting within which to develop close primary relationships that are not tied to family or other adults.

In addition to the functions mentioned above, the peer group also facilitates social mobility for some and helps to preserve existing social class positions for others. Occasionally, youngsters from working class and "disadvantaged" backgrounds may be given opportunities in integrated or semi-integrated schools and in organized youth groups to interact with people their own age from middle-class backgrounds. In such cases, they may acquire subcultural learnings useful for gaining entrance into the middle classes.[5] Of course, the opposite may occur, too; that is, middle-class youth may adopt lower-class behavior, although usually only superficially. More commonly, peer groups of childhood and adolescence tend to be restricted to members of the same class and ethnic groups, thus ensuring, at least until college age, that class patterns prevailing in the wider society will be preserved.

The peer group may also provide examples of, and opportunities to try out, new social roles. For example, a child reared in an autocratic family may learn about democratic relationships through his friends in the peer group, and vice versa.[6] Much seems to depend upon the group leader's personality and role, as well as upon how individual groups structure member participation and opportunities for experimenting with alternative roles in areas relating to the accomplishment of group tasks and the resolution of group problems.

In these and many other ways, the peer group helps the child and youth to find a sense of personal identity in a rapidly changing and confused world, a world officially run primarily by adults for adult ends. Many adults are frightened by the tremendous expansion of peer-group involvement at younger and younger ages. Parents feel that their offspring have abandoned them at too early an age to spend most of their free time with friends whom parents often do not know or of whom they do not approve. Teachers complain of lessened respect from their students who are goaded by some peer-group norms to show disrespect for their teachers. Probably both parents and teachers are correct in vaguely sensing that youngsters are more highly attuned to pressures and influences from their age peers than ever before.

Teachers in particular should realize that changing attitudes of young people toward adults in large part are a necessary response by youngsters to heavy stresses and strains from a confused society. Until the problem of incorporating young people (and the very old and the culturally different, as well) more fully into the cultural mainstream is resolved, the separate culture of the young will continue to flourish and proliferate. Prospective school teachers should recognize the reality and significance of this relatively new subculture and the underlying logic of its existence and operation. To resist this reality on grounds that it is a willful and unwarranted display of contempt toward teachers as representatives of the cultural tradition is not productive. Such an attitude also serves to further alienate the student, and the effectiveness of the teacher as a facilitator of learning is severely curtailed.

Characteristics of Different Peer Cultures

The proportion of energy expended by youngsters on official school business (academic learning) and on peer involvements within and outside of the classroom varies according to age, social class, personality, and other factors. In general, elementary school children are less committed to peers than junior high and high school youngsters, although many of the friends they play with at home are made at school. And, some students seem to depend more on their peers than their teachers or the curriculum even with regard to "official business." According to James Coleman:

> ... the relation of school inputs to effect on achievement showed that those input characteristics of schools that are most alike for Negroes and whites have least effect on their achievement. The magnitude of differences between schools attended by Negroes and those attended by whites were as follows: least, facilities and curriculum; next, teacher quality; and greatest, educational backgrounds of fellow students. The order of importance of these inputs on the achievement of Negro students is precisely the same: facilities and curriculum least, teacher quality next, and backgrounds of fellow students most.[7]

In other words, the curriculum and even teachers appear to have less significance for some children (in this case, black children) than do fellow students, even when differences in academic achievement among students are considered. Teacher disinterest in or disdain for lower-class students may partially account for extreme dependence upon peers in school.[8]

Since the school is the major, although not the only, setting for peer-group relations among the young, and since peer group involvement relates to the social life of children and youth, as well as to their academic achievement, the peer group will be discussed in relation to the school setting.

The Well-Integrated Majority

Despite attention given to the negative and bizarre aspects of life among the young, most young people today behave within the bounds of convention. This does not mean that children and adolescents think and behave in ways identical to adults. On the contrary, mainstream America's children are more sophisticated about politics and sex than were their parents, their music is different, boys wear their hair longer than they used to, girls are slightly more liberated in terms of their sex roles than their mothers were, youngsters of both sexes brought up on TV and candid movies are more impatient with teachers who are dull and unimaginative than their counterparts of the 1950s were.

But despite these and other differences between the young of mainstream America today and those of the past generation, the similarities appear to significantly outweigh the differences. Perhaps this is due in part to a receding of student activism on college campuses, which may be relatively permanent or only temporary. Secondary and even elementary school youngsters, however, were much influenced by the highly publicized and often volatile activities of their older reference figures during the late 1960s. Now that the news media are no longer reporting daily on the activities of draft-card burners and confrontations between the police and students, children and adolescents of the mainstream—particularly upper-middle-class youngsters[9]—seem to have settled down to more "normal" youthful activities, like football and dating. They are less openly and pervasively alienated from the "Establishment."

A recent major study comparing the values of American and Danish youth indicates that U.S. adolescents still consider the following peer-group values the most important:*

	U.S.	Denmark
Having a good reputation	78%	53%
Earning money	56%	30%
Being well liked	54%	32%
Being popular in school	46%	45%
Going out on dates	40%	35%

* Data comparing attitudes of Danish and American youth is from Denise B. Kandel and Gerald S. Lesser, *Youth in Two Worlds: United States and Denmark* (San Francisco: Jossey–Bass, 1972), p. 165.[10]

As the data show, modern American boys and girls are somewhat more concerned with the good opinions of their peers than are Danish youth.

When it comes to the home, the results are also instructive. These are the family values considered of great importance to U.S. and Danish youth:

	U.S.	Denmark
Doing things with the family	42%	17%
Helping at home	30%	23%
Respecting one's parents	87%	60%
Living up to one's religious ideals	9%	2%
Pleasing one's parents	34%	52%

U.S. youth of the mainstream are more concerned with respect for their parents than Danish youth, more willing to spend time with them, and more willing to help out at home, but less concerned with pleasing their parents. Note that both U.S. and Danish youth show extremely little interest in organized religion (nor do their parents).[11]

It is in the area of school work that teachers will be most interested. The findings of the above study by Kandel and Lesser confirm to some extent what James Coleman found in the early 1960s in his research on adolescence. Coleman believed that what adolescents wanted most was to be popular with their peers. His interviews with young people led him to conclude that adolescents were not mostly concerned with being a good student:

> What does it take to get into the leading crowd in these schools? This is another way of asking what the dominant values are in these adolescent cultures. According to the adolescents themselves ... it takes a lot of things; but academic success is not one of them. It takes athletic prowess, knowing how to dance, owning a car, having a good reputation, or liking to have fun. It takes being a good date, liking parties, and often not being a prude (for girls) or a sissy (for boys). Good grades and intelligence are mentioned, but not very often, and not as often as any of the other items.[12]

According to Coleman, it is not mainstream suburban adolescents who mentioned intelligence most as a criterion for membership in the leading crowd:

> ... not the plush suburban school with its excellent facilities and staff, but the comprehensive city school. Good grades are valued next highest in the parochial school, populated by lower-class boys whose parents emigrated from eastern Europe. Third in line is the small town school in which the students—sons and daughters of farmers and villagers—spend

much time in nightly study. The plush suburban school, with the sons and daughters of the professionals and business executives, is close to the bottom for the boys, though somewhat higher for the girls, in the value that students place on good grades.[13]

Although upper-middle-class parents want their children to study hard in school, their children do not necessarily care to please them by doing so.

The figures below on first rank school values of adolescents are given by Kandel and Lesser:

	U.S.	Denmark
Preferred school image:		
Brilliant student	33%	55%
Athlete or leader in activities	34%	10%
Most popular	33%	35%
Learning much in school	39%	31%
Working hard on studies	54%	32%
Doing serious reading	28%	21%
Planning for the future	78%	38%

The conclusions drawn from these data by the researchers are as follows:

These differences between the two countries tend to reveal the United States as an achievement-oriented society and Denmark as a more traditional society. Americans value hard work and its supposed immediate rewards: high income and greater opportunity....

American adolescents are more likely than the Danes to emphasize the importance of social interaction, both with peers and with parents. They are more likely than the Danes to emphasize being a leader in activities ... and being well liked by other students....

The American values thus emphasize sociability as a life style for adolescence but hard work and concrete rewards for advancement in one's future occupational and educational role.[14]

Another important study of the values of Canadian adolescents[15] attempted to dethrone the belief held by many American sociologists, including Coleman, that adolescents value athletics, popularity, and academics in that order.[16] The conclusions from the Canadian study are that this prevalent belief is not tenable, even though respondents overwhelmingly indicated preferences for athletics and popularity over academics. David Friesen argues that these choices are illusory because the rewards of proving one's worth to members of a subculture are immediately gratifying:

The adolescent wishes for recognition in his own society; he wants to be accepted, respected, and applauded for his activities. This source of

*gratification, which is near to him and meaningful in his own terms is
also immediate.*[17]

Academic activities are not immediately gratifying to most students, although they are means to more gratifying activities later in life.
Both the Friesen and Kandel–Lesser studies, among other more informal
investigations, show that mainstream youth do not neglect their studies
altogether, even if they do not always emphasize them. From listening to
their achievement-oriented parents, teachers, and counselors, they realize
that school credentials are needed today in order to succeed in the adult
world later on. Meanwhile, students want to have fun and be rewarded
in the only milieu that can really mean much for an essentially segregated
group.

Why are the primary rewards for mainstream adolescents non-
academic? Because the way in which the American school is organized
does not capitalize upon youthful interests to encourage academics. To
Coleman,

> *Such student attitudes are not the direct consequences of classroom
> experience, but they are nevertheless the product of the school and the
> responsibility of the school. They stem from what might be called the
> "social organization" of the school, in contrast to its curriculum organi-
> zation. This social organization has its values and norms; the standards
> are slanted either toward or away from intellectual endeavor.*
>
>   *For some reason, these matters of peer-group standards have never
> become part of an ideology or philosophy of education as have matters of
> curriculum content and style of teaching.*[18]

For Friesen there is hope:

> *Immediate gratification can also stem from the school and society. The
> school, chief educating agent of society, needs to develop an organiza-
> tion or structure that will reward those activities most closely aligned to
> its major function [academics], and use the peripheral activities [ath-
> letics, socializing], to channel the energies of youth toward learning. If
> schools do not plan for effective education, the short-term goals of ado-
> lescents can submerge the real goals of the school.*[19]

The discussion above applies as well to younger children in elementary school, although perhaps to a lesser extent. By and large, the
well-integrated contemporary child of the mainstream is almost as interested in obtaining immediate gratifications from his or her age mates
as is the adolescent.

What are the typical complaints of elementary school teachers?
That children "fool around" too much in class instead of "working"?
But, for a child, who does not have an adult vocation, play *is* work (as
many believe it should ideally be for adults, as well).[20] Most children
like nothing better than to play (or work) with other young children, both

in and out of the classroom. Since they are rarely allowed much freedom to interact with their peers in class, they understandably race outside to the playground at recess time and at any other opportunity, unless they are social isolates who are uncomfortable with their fellow students.

But mainstream American children, like their older brothers and sisters in junior and senior high school, are sufficiently well enculturated by their achievement-oriented elders to make certain they do not endanger their future lives by being placed in the lowest reading or math groups and/or by being labeled as "underachievers." Because elementary school children are younger, they are viewed as having a right to be more play oriented than adolescents, and their parents and teachers are often willing to accede to the demands of childhood by striving to "open" their classrooms. This propensity for openness in the teaching–learning relation is especially pronounced in the primary grades. Especially in mainstream suburban schools, teachers are often willing to go to great lengths to adapt their instructional efforts to the peer needs of their students. It is in the primary grades that the most open and dynamic climates for learning in our modern society will be observed. These grades have been most influenced by progressive education and the open classroom. At about the third or fourth grade, this attention to children's social interests begins to wane as teachers expect more mature behavior from their students. The emphasis on children's social interests returns to some extent in the junior high school or the middle school (for youngsters aged about ten or eleven to about thirteen or fourteen). At this time, adults expect youngsters to undergo a radical transformation in temperament that is so powerful that it must be responded to by catering to the special strains of early adolescence. But, by the time they reach ninth or tenth grade, youngsters are expected to settle down again and to concentrate on their academic work in anticipation of imminent adulthood, an expectation which—as Coleman, Friesen, and Kandel and Lesser have demonstrated—is unduly optimistic.

Despite growing pressures to achieve academically, youngsters of all ages, like adults, want most to express the desire to belong. And, in our age-graded society particularly, they want to belong to groups of people approximately their own age. Insofar as the school, through its social organization, gears its formal program and instructional strategies to this very deep and widespread need, it may hope to develop strong **intrinsic motivation** in youngsters for seeking a school education. As American schools are typically structured at present, however, the incentives to learn tend to be **extrinsic** and directed mainly toward academically oriented students. In order to succeed in later life, where diplomas and degrees mean so much, mainstream children and youth who have internalized society's powerful drive to achieve put forth a sufficient degree of energy to obtain good grades and approval of teachers and parents. But they reserve most of their energy for fun on the playground, on the football field, or in their automobiles with their peers.

The Counter Culture

As suggested earlier, most working- and middle-class youngsters in the United States conform to most social expectations, despite some illusory differences in outward appearance and mannerism. We might say that while the typical mainstream American child and adolescent of the 1970s is somewhat different from his or her counterpart in the 1950s, the differences are not as great as some writers on youth alienation—for example, Kenneth Kenniston and Theodor Roszak[21]—and the mass media may have led us to believe. Although they are somewhat more serious about some matters, which is a reflection of a growing mood of sobriety toward the problematic future of American society, mainstream young people are still generally interested in getting ahead by obtaining grades to go on to college, in finding a good job after high school, and in being popular with their peers.

But it would be a serious mistake to believe that the heavily publicized upheavals among college-aged youth of the 1960s have not left a more than superficial impression on some of their younger sisters and brothers.[22] The "greening of America," as described by Charles Reich in 1970, and the rise of a counter culture anticipated by Roszak in 1969 have not been as fully accomplished as we had then been led to expect. Nonetheless, society's urban and suburban communities and their schools are populated with substantial numbers of young people who are not typical mainstream Americans. The social movements of the 1960s have had their impact on youngsters below the college level. Although still a minority, more young people than ever before identify themselves as atypical in the sense of feeling a distinct allegiance and preference for divergent values and norms, which are representative of a growing subculture known as the counter culture. This subculture includes both dropouts from society commonly known as "hippies" as well as some of the more politically active elements of the New Left.

Some of these young people, the social dropouts or children of dropouts, are living on rural communes that either have their own versions of schools or no schools at all. The majority, however, live in cities and towns, where they either attend public schools or free schools.

McClellan lists a number of psychological and sociological theories as to why modern youth have been or are in revolt. They include:

• *Oedipal theories.* Counter culturists are basically rebelling against their parents.

• *Religious theories.* Modern activists are searching for the sacred in a fragmented and secularized society.

• *Marxist theories.* Students are an historically oppressed "working class" who identify with oppressed groups and who rebel when they become aware of their own oppression.

• *Militaristic theories.* The prevalence of a war-like mentality in this society has produced a reaction since Vietnam and Cambodia.

• *Psychohistorical theories* (combinations of oedipal theories and historical theories). Because of severe problems with parents in early life, coupled with belief that American society (and education, especially) has become alienating, certain sensitive and intelligent young people become disciples of a counter cultural movement.[23]

While admitting that there are grains of truth to each of the above theoretical positions on why youth have been or are in revolt, two broad positions are held by McClellan to be most meaningful as root explanations for the rise of a modern youth counter culture:

• The view that the young are true revolutionaries, "an historical vanguard that is defining a new and better society."[24] This position has received a great deal of attention from alienated youth and intellectuals generally, largely because it postulates that American society needs a social and/or cultural revolution led by the young to save it. This position justifies extreme anti-Establishment activism.

• The other broad position is propounded by those who maintain that American society is becoming transformed from a state of Industrialism to one of Post-Industrialism. Because the emergence of Post-Industrial society represents a fundamental set of changes for our society and its culture—changes that are very difficult for many people to accept and deal with—the "future shock" accompanying profound change produces a "counter-revolutionary movement, a reaction against the more basic forces involved in the growth of a new technological society."[25]

According to McClellan:

> ... a postindustrial society imposes ... a heavy "organizational harness" upon the young: it requires them to study for many years, to acquire highly specialized technical skills, to stay in school, and to postpone gratification well into biological adulthood. Equally important, this new society renders obsolete a large number of traditional values, skills, and outlooks ... those identified with "traditional" fields like the humanities and the social sciences find that their values and skills are becoming increasingly unnecessary, irrelevant, and obsolete ... The ideals of romanticism, expressiveness, and traditional humanism may dominate the contemporary youth culture, but they do not dominate the social structure—the specific institutions that are changing our lives ... the

humanistic young are rebelling because of their latent awareness of
their own obsolescence...
    An ever-larger group of young men and women feel that they have
no place in the modern world, for they lack saleable skills, basic charac-
ter styles, and value orientations that are adaptable to the emergent post-
industrial society...They rebel in a blind, mindless, and generally
destructive way against rationalism, intellect, technology, organization,
discipline, hierarchy, and all of the requisites of a postindustrial society.[26]

Sociologist Willis Harmon thinks the U.S. will be essentially either a
"garrison state" or a "person-centered utopia" within approximately
fifteen years, depending upon what we do now.[27]

    Persons who stress primarily the negative possibilities of such a
society are, as McClellan suggests, apt to be those with "latent awareness of their own obsolescence." Caught up in the confusions and
rhetoric of the times, they fail to perceive that there may be an alternative
to the "garrison state" *within* the Post-Industrial model—that Post-
Industrialism need not be synonymous with complete depersonalization
and loss of human values. Many who drop out more or less completely
from the cultural mainstream and those who become politically radical
do not know for certain that Post-Industrial society will be inhumane.
They have made up their minds prematurely on the basis of insufficient
evidence. Members of the counter culture, however, play an important
role in keeping society aware of the worst features of a Post-Industrial
society. By pointing out to more complacent Americans the danger of
continuing to take this society for granted and of ignoring its many profound problems, they do society a service. Since we are not adequately
dealing with our gravest problems as we move into the future, we are
more likely to accumulate strains and tensions that may eventually produce an authoritarian response—already hinted at by the investigations
into Watergate and the CIA. Our short-sightedness can indeed produce
a "garrison state," and the development of a counter-culture movement
serves to constantly remind us of the gravity of the present situation, to
prevent us from avoiding confrontation of the reality of basic social
transformation.

    Although we are a highly advanced society in terms of our tech-
nology, we are not very farsighted or rational in working out our major
social problems. One outgrowth of our myopia and confusion is the
emergence of a disaffected counter culture. If we were a truly rational
society we would not experience such a subcultural development, but we
are not wholly rational. Ironically, we need people who are alienated
from established society in order to continually oppose the aimless drift
into the future. It would be far better if we planned intelligently and
carefully for the future.

    Although the counter culture has had its major impact upon the
colleges and universities, some of the parents of children in elementary

schools who have themselves been activists or who have sympathized with the activists and the dropouts have an unconventional influence upon their children's minds and hearts. Some older liberal parents also have become disenchanted with the Establishment. The elementary schools of our society are already discovering that some middle-class suburban and urban children do not conform to the expectations of teachers of mainstream children. They are different—not as ethnic children are different, but in terms of their rejection of such traditional middle-class school values as cooperation and competitiveness.

Some of these children have already entered high school where they continue the nonconforming patterns of their elementary school years. They often seek out and locate like-minded peers in high school. They form their own distinctive subcultures within the youth peer culture. They may or may not use drugs freely. They may or may not be politically aware and interested. They often enjoy high-level informal debating, especially between themselves. They are very often known as "brilliant" minds to teachers who do not resent their unwillingness to conform to prevailing **school cultural** norms. But since they do not ordinarily value grades and other traditional symbols of academic achievement, such teachers may still give them C's or D's on their report cards. If such a student finds a particular teacher whom he respects, he or she may study for that teacher and receive outstanding grades as a by-product of honest intellectual effort. Sometimes their report cards look like this:

English—A	History—C
Mathematics—D	Physical Education—C
Government—B	Art—A

Some of these students do extremely poorly in school, simply because they rarely attend or are apathetic when they do. Others do consistently well and receive offices and other honors; they "play the system's game" on an overt level while covertly despising it.[28] More often, those who do well in school do not think of themselves as deeply committed to a counter culture.

Adherents of the counter culture tend to avoid school dances, varsity sports, and similar extra-curricular activities in which most mainstream youth participate. After school, some may leave quickly with their friends and engage in hedonistic activities at home. The more socially committed may work on the school newspaper if it is not too closely controlled by teachers and administrators. Some may join like-minded youth in community youth centers that encourage encounter therapy or "rapping" or which engage in recycling or other ecological activities. Sometimes, they get together with students attending a local free school for an evening of socialization with members of their own and the opposite sex.

In general, those who identify with the counter culture, whether they retreat from society or are active in it, are marginal in their schools —both in regard to academic expectations and to conventional student social life encouraged through its organizational structure. They are tolerated by school authorities if they do not cause trouble, and even are admired by some teachers and non-marginal fellow students. The continuance of this relative equilibrium in the future will probably be dependent upon such factors as: the availability of alternative schools in cities and towns for the severely disaffected; the degree to which school people can adapt to changing and often extremely nonconforming behavior by students; the extent to which American youth as a group feel provoked to withdraw further from the mainstream by future unpopular wars, indefensible racial injustices, loss of hope for eventual gainful employment, and other failures by society to act on the recommendations of bodies such as the 1971 White House Conference on Youth.[29] Also, the extent to which the coming wave of parents who attended college in the 1960s will socialize and enculturate their own children with the skills, values, and norms they acquired during their adolescence and young adulthood will affect the type of student that teachers will encounter.

The Alienated and Underachieving Poor

What are the peer-group characteristics of youngsters from lower-class or lower working-class backgrounds—the poor and near poor?

Many books have been written about social life and education among the "disadvantaged" in recent years.[30] Numerous sociological studies have been made of relations in school among the poor and between the poor and their more affluent mainstream peers.[31] They all bear out what any observant and sensitive teacher knows from first-hand experience: the peer group is at least as influential on the lives of poor children and adolescents as it is on the lives of affluent mainstream youngsters. More importantly, when poor people are partially alienated from the wider society, as are many of the poor in contemporary America,[32] and their children are forced to attend segregated schools as well, their children are apt to react negatively to the school's teachers and program. They may also influence their peers to do the same.

Here is the experience of a first-year teacher on the first day in his ghetto high school:

> *"Please take your seats so we can begin taking attendance."*
> *It seemed like a reasonable way to start. A few heads turned, a few mouths closed. It may have been reasonable, but it wasn't very effective. I raised my voice and called out the names and waited for "here's" and the raised hands.*

> *Incredibly, at the end of the roll call, there were fewer people in the room than I had marked as present. . . .*
>
> *"Are we going to study any black writers?" from the back of the room.*
>
> *"As a matter of fact, most of the writers you see listed there are black." I felt pretty proud of myself.*
>
> *"Then we should have a black teacher," from a student who had dropped his paper onto the ground.*
>
> *I wanted to say something about universal experience, but the noise level had gotten too high for anybody to hear me, and then I saw one of the schedules go gliding beautifully, aerodynamically across the room.*[33]

Inexperienced teachers of lower-class children either learn to channel negative peer dynamics into constructive activities, ignore the students' disinterest in studying, or become dictatorial toward disaffected students and learn to cope with symptoms of "battle fatigue." The only other alternative is to quit!

Anthropologist Murray Wax, in observing Indian children in Oklahoma, the Dakotas, and the Southwest, noted the following patterns of peer-related classroom behavior:

> *. . . if the observer knows what to look for [many who work with the "disadvantaged" do not], he will perceive that the reticence of the Indian children has nothing to do with personal shyness and everything to do with the relationship between the child and his peers in that classroom. For the Indian children exert a quiet but powerful pressure so that no one of them is willing to collaborate with the teacher, as in most cases the teacher has become defined by the children as an outsider, an intrusive troublesome meddlesome authority; and the school-children respond by encasing themselves in the armor of the peer society. They organize themselves to resist the pressures of the educator, so that in confronting the children, he finds himself facing a blank wall.*[34]

Except in a relatively few communities and schools where serious efforts are being made to enlarge the scope of school community to include the parents and the children of the poor,[35] attitudes of students and their peers toward the school as a central arm of the "Establishment" range from highly alienated and distrustful to manipulative to quietly apathetic and resigned. In general, "disadvantaged" youngsters are not enthusiastic about their teachers and their academic programs. They attend school because the law requires them to or because their parents expect them to. But they do not usually became as deeply involved in school curricular and extra-curricular affairs as do their more affluent contemporaries. There are, however, exceptions to this generalization in communities that have begun to meet the needs of poor students by such means as career education and meaningful racial integration.

By and large, the social climate of ghetto schools is dominated by the competing claims to power of rival gangs or gang-like cliques who oppose more highly adjusted students. In both elementary and secondary schools in the ghetto, students are under continuous pressure not to become academically ambitious. This pressure is exerted by apathetic or openly hostile peers who have substantial influence over students in determining how easy or difficult their out-of-classroom lives may be. Good teachers must be cognizant of this pressure.

The comparatively rare student who challenges this informal system risks rejection from these powerful peers. He or she must make the basic choice of whether to be more or less acceptable to the peer group— of whether to have friends or not. The problem is especially difficult because a poor youngster who does well in a teacher's terms still may not get very far in the adult world. If a good job or a college education are not the rewards for succeeding in school—for a poor child, at the expense of friends and his or her emotional security—the disappointment is compounded. In fact, the risks of frustrated academic ambition for the poor can be devastating for their future mental health.[36] As John Hewitt has expressed the problem:

> We can predict . . . that, if the adolescent has been thwarted in his quest for self-esteem in the company of adults [read teachers and would-be employers] the motivation to continue the search in the company of his peers will be strong; second, that commitment to the norms of adult society will be seriously limited. . . .
>   The adolescent will seek others who promise the approval upon which adequate self-esteem can be built, who will tell him he is good, competent, worthy, clean, manly, and desirable. Because no adult provides these evaluations, he is forced to turn to his peers, and he will probably select peers with exactly the same problems.[37]

In sum, poor children or youths who cannot find substantial acceptance by their teachers and other adults—an acceptance made more difficult because their peer culture rejects the school—are open to very real possibilities of becoming juvenile delinquents and of dropping out of school altogether, thus helping to perpetuate the vicious circle of poverty, rejection, and alienation.

Poor minority youngsters attending integrated schools with mainstream youngsters may be better off academically and socially, because they feel psychologically accepted by a comparatively high-status reference group of peers, a reference group that supports academic achievement as a norm, because its members want to succeed in later life.[38]

Of course, all the subtle dynamics of peer relations attendant upon school integration have not yet been studied, because integration has not been substantially achieved as yet. For instance, we do not know whether racial integration of schools would foster more meaningful relations between poor minority youngsters and marginal dominant group youngsters, such as those of the counter culture, or what the ultimate consequences of such friendships would be on academic, social, and individual behavior.

From studies done prior to the civil rights movement, we do know that important activities in comprehensive high schools that draw from a variety of community segments tended to be dominated by the most affluent mainstream boys and girls, and that less affluent youngsters tended to feel "left out of things."[39]

But times *are* changing and somewhat more socially sensitive and sophisticated students and teachers are now attending and working in schools. Problems in human relations are extremely difficult to deal with effectively; but we may expect that positive and harmonious interactions are becoming possible through the efforts of caring and intelligent educators and an increasingly enlightened student body. There is reason to hope that we are finally ready to experiment extensively and intensively with human relations in school.

The Influence of the School Climate upon Peer-Group Values and Behavior

In order for such experiments to have significant meaning, it may be necessary to take the advice of social analysts such as Coleman and Friesen, who tell us that what is most needed in our society is a greater concentration by educators upon the social climate, or organization, of schools.

The key to effectively harnessing the real peer-group needs of youngsters appears to lie in creating a structure of interpersonal relations between students that is conducive to learning. Student relations should not be isolated from the primary goals of education. As Coleman says:

> In the affluent upper middle classes, the family–school environment gives adolescents freedom without the opportunity for responsibility. It thus invites irresponsibility and guarantees an adolescent community with norms that pull away from learning. In the lowest classes, the compliance demanded by the school conflicts with the rest of a child's environment, and his best solution may be to escape to the streets at the earliest moment.[40]

Coleman proposes a general model for altering the school's social environment so as to make this environment more conducive to learning:

1. Students must have the freedom and opportunity to carry out their own actions and to make mistakes.

2. The school environment must be structured in such a way as to allow students to experience their mistakes, to feel the consequences of their actions.

3. Students' actions need to be fairly small, inconsequential, and repeatable so that their consequences will not be so severe as to discourage further actions and that successes outnumber failures.

4. The school social environment must provide obstacles that, in being overcome, induce the desired learning. In other words, in order to "survive" in school, one must learn the desired skills and social roles (as in learning to speak a foreign language by not being allowed to speak at all in English).[41]

According to Coleman, the above elements, which are largely missing in traditional educational programs, are critical in any environment designed for learning. The essential idea underlying his proposals is this:

> *A child will learn those things he must learn to perform effectively in his present environment. He will not learn things that will only be useful in the future, for he cannot project himself into future roles and activities. The construction of such learning environments would involve bringing future roles into the present and requiring a child to perform in these roles, rather than merely in those that naturally befall him as a child or adolescent.*[42]

Anyone who has spent time in an outdoor school setting can see the validity and applicability of Coleman's ideas. In order to survive for a week or so in the mountains away from his parents, a youngster must learn to perform effectively in his present environment. Students learn rapidly not only to clean up after themselves and to dine with grace, but also to recognize a variety of flora and fauna, to utilize mathematics in constructing maps and bridges, and to live harmoniously with adults, including teachers. And, they do these things with pleasure. Only when they have returned to their segmented lives in town do they forget such competencies and attitudes, which no longer seem essential for daily survival.

Since Coleman is aware that the opportunities to infuse academic learning with challenges to survive are extremely limited in the artificial environment of the school, he advocates greater use of socioeconomic games to simulate environments that youngsters cannot otherwise experience.[43] (He is proposing for children what is proposed in Chapter 7 of this text for adults who wish to become teachers and work with children.)

Murry Wax suggests the following policies to make schools more palatable as learning environments to youngsters and their peers:

1. Reorganize the present age-graded system of structuring schools, so children of different ages can come together and interact beneficially with each other (a form of integration).

2. Bring more adult and adolescent teacher aides (para-professionals) from the local community into the schools to help in relating to youngsters.

3. Introduce scholastic competitions among the groups or gangs of pupils . . . and so specify the terms of this competition to encourage these youngsters to work together and teach each other.[44]

Some, if not all, of the above suggestions need not await official policy directives from the school board or the central administration. Most of these ideas for channeling the interpersonal energies of students into forms that are consonant with the primary purposes of schools can be implemented by the individual teacher in his or her classroom. Others such as Wax's scholastic competition, which is a debatable proposal, would perhaps best be handled on an interschool basis rather than in individual classrooms. To do otherwise would defeat the purpose of replacing athletic competitions on the community level, and also there is already too much competition in many classrooms.

In the individual classroom children learn what the society wants them to, or they fail to learn. The school culture as a whole helps shape the outlines of this classroom experience through its values, norms, and role expectations for teachers and students. In Havighurst's and Neugarten's words, "Educators must reckon with the fact that the child and the adolescent have two sets of expectations to meet, the expectations set by the peer group may be as important as any set by adults in understanding school success and failure."[45] It follows that classroom teachers who neglect the peer-group, especially in a period marked by dramatically increasing importance of this reference group to youngsters, fail to take advantage of a major dimension of the social organization of childhood and adolescence.

Very few classroom teachers have been professionally prepared to think and behave in line with the ideas propounded by social scientists such as Coleman and Wax. Most have been trained to think either in terms of large, undifferentiated groups known as classes or in terms of single, autonomous individuals. Few have been prepared to conceptualize the interpersonal and intergroup networks and dynamics that are most at the heart of the learning enterprise in classrooms. Teachers have been trained from the perspective of a different tradition than social workers and other non-school workers who also deal purposefully with people. Tradition has stood in the way of orienting teachers to accept and capitalize upon the social needs of their students for academic purposes.

But, this is exactly what teachers may need most to do, in addition to being familiar with the subjects they teach. Whether or not the school as a whole is reformed to make it a "community within the larger community," as John Dewey, James Coleman, and others have suggested, under any conditions, the individual teacher can create an environment within the classroom in which youngsters can feel that they belong.

In short, teachers can learn to motivate individual and classroom learning. Group dynamics is essential for good teaching today when the peer culture is so highly developed in American society. A solid and positive group climate is vital for successful teaching. Chapter 16 deals with building such classroom environments. For now, we will consider some modest applications of peer-related thinking by teachers using **sociometric** tools.

How Can Teachers Determine Peer-Group Involvements in Their Classrooms?

What do new teachers need to know, over and above the subject they have been assigned to teach? Obviously, who their students are. What kinds of youngsters they are. Who are the peer-clique leaders, who are the followers, who are marginal to peer cliques, who have power among the students, who are considered bright by their classmates, who are the most well-liked by their peers, etc. New teachers should learn as quickly as possible as much as they can about the social organization of the students with whom they are about to work.

If most of your students have attended the same school together for a while, you can expect to learn something fairly early in the year about the way in which the peer culture in your classroom is organized. If the students are mostly new, it may take a few weeks for them to become organized socially. But they will organize, sooner or later. And, generally the younger the children, the more often will their social relationships change. All classrooms develop in time a distinctive social structure. Teachers can consciously influence this structure and provide incentives for learning based on it, if they understand it.

You may learn much about your students' social relations simply by observing students casually as they undertake different activities with different members of the classroom society. You may notice with whom they voluntarily associate on the playground, next to whom they prefer to sit during mathematics, to whom they look when they are seeking approval for an answer to a tough question, etc.

If you are an astute observer, and have the time to observe closely while carrying out your official instructional duties, you can gradually develop a sense of the subtle, as well as the obvious social ties and dynamics structuring your classroom social system. This is especially true if you are the only teacher in a self-contained elementary school classroom where you are with your students all day long, five days a week.

The problem with such informal methods of studying student peer relationships is that what you think you are seeing is not always accurate. Because most teachers are very occupied during the school day, their views of the lives of children may be somewhat distorted.[46] Inaccurate perceptions can affect the way you behave in your overall capacity as a teacher. Unfortunately, this problem is most likely to arise with regard to "exceptional" children, who need the most attention—the troublemakers, the quiet ones, and the like.

In order to help overcome the deficiencies of casual observation methods in crowded, hectic classrooms, it is often useful to employ more formal tools for gaining important information about your students' social networks. Casual observation of student peer-group behavior is fine up to a point, but, if you really want to help all of your students, not only those who seem average in their academic and social behavior, you may want to sacrifice some of the simplicity of casual observation for methods that give a more penetrating insight into the overall structure of your classroom society.

The sociometric tool most widely employed by teachers for gaining sophisticated information about students' social relations is the *socio-*

gram. A sociogram is simply a map of student peer choices. The most common type of sociogram is constructed after asking youngsters to tell orally or in writing whom they like. The teacher asks questions designed to elicit friendship choices, such as "Whom do you want to sit next to on the bus when we take a field trip to the mountains? Pick three persons—a first, second, and third choice." In almost every classroom there will be some children who are unusually well liked, as indicated by the large number of individuals who choose them. There will be students who are actively disliked as well; they can be indicated by asking the class for negative choices.* There are usually one or two social isolates, that is, youngsters who are outside of or marginal to the classroom peer network.

Popularity based on "likeability" is only one of several variables that structure social relations, although this variable has been given the most attention by educators interested in sociometrics. Social psychologists have found that most classrooms are structured according to the following peer dimensions, in addition to that of friendship:

- *The problem-solving dimension:* "Who engages in or carries on what problem-solving functions with whom to accomplish the public task of the classroom group?"
- *The authority-leadership dimension:* "Who is recognized by whom as having the responsibility and power for facilitating the problem-solving conditions necessary for effective decision-making by the class?"
- *The "power" dimension:* "Who possess what means for gratifying or depriving whose needs?"
- *The personal-prestige dimension:* "Who is valued by whom by virtue of contributions made to the welfare of the group and the accomplishment of its goals?"
- *The sex dimension:* "Which class members are attempting to define participation in the group according to differences in sex and ... which members are relating to one another for purposes of gratifying sex needs?"
- *The privilege dimension:* "Who has the right to what gratifications by virtue of the role they hold rather than by virtue of the contributions they make to the class goals?"[47]

There is no single way to map students' social preferences in a sociogram, but Figure 9–1 provides a general idea of what a sociogram should include. As can be inferred from studying this sociogram, only the teacher can determine what to do with the data it provides.

---

* Although more highly refined data can be obtained by asking children to designate peers whom they do *not* prefer, it is best to avoid such questions because of the ethical and practical considerations involved.

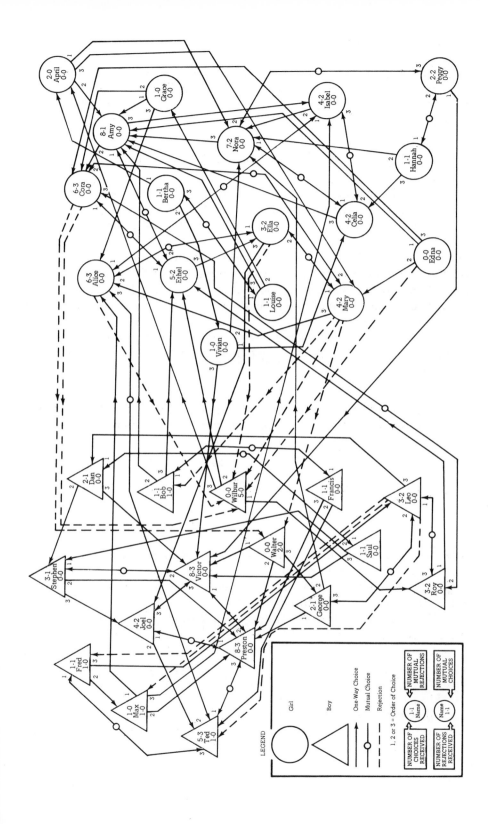

FIGURE 9-1. A Sociogram of an Eighth-Grade Literature Class [From Hilda Tasa and Deborah Elkins, With Focus on Human Relations [Washington, D.C.: American Council on Education, 1950], p. 192. Reprinted with permission.]

Their use will depend upon your classroom objectives and any unique problems you may encounter. The new or confirmed knowledge acquired from the sociogram may lead to a number of concrete actions. For example:

1. Rearranging desks and other furniture to improve classroom communication

2. Assigning certain "housekeeping" jobs to certain students

3. Working more intensively with certain peer leaders

4. Modifying negative attitudes and behavior toward specific students who have irritated you

5. Deciding to have a "heart-to-heart" talk with your entire class on human relations or to do some simulation work with your students

6. Switching plans for a unit in social studies (or math, English, etc.) in response to your new understanding of what the class as a whole seems to need most

7. Arranging a special conference with the parents of one or more of your students in order to enlist their aid in encouraging their child academically or socially.

Perhaps there are other strategies that a refined knowledge of your students' peer-group relations would suggest. Can you think of any?

Summary

The peer group has been assuming an increasingly important role in American life as childhood and adolescence become more highly separated maturation periods in an age-graded civilization that constantly ups the age of entrance into adulthood.

The institutionalization of a separate culture of the young serves to reduce or assuage potentially severe social tensions in young people forced to delay the onset of adulthood, although often biologically and socially ready for it. For the young, peer groups offer opportunities for informal education, friendship, egalitarian treatment, the maintenance or breaking of social-class patterns, and experimenting with new social roles that are more or less independent from adult control.

Neither the well-integrated mainstream majority, the emerging counter culture, or the alienated and underachieving poor and near poor are as vitally involved with the educational aims of schools as most adults would like them to be. Mainstream children and youth, however, take more advantage of the school to meet friends of their own age and enjoy an active social life, while they obtain the credentials necessary for desirable jobs and adult social status in American society.

The school sociocultural climate seems to have a great deal to do with both the relative lack of serious interest in learning by young people at school and with realistic efforts to increase such interests. By understanding and accepting the importance of the peer life of the young as a collective response to social change, and by utilizing informal and formal observational methods to learn about specific peer relationships in their own classrooms, imaginative teachers can harness their students' needs for belongingness and affiliativeness to achieve educational objectives.

Related Concepts

extrinsic motivation   A term often used by psychologists and educators to refer to incentives to learn that are external to the individual. For example, teaching machines that reward a student for the right answers with bubblegum or baseball cards offer an extrinsic motivation to learn.

intrinsic motivation   A term referring to learning based on internal inducements, such as curiosity or desire to belong to a group

school culture   The social heritage accumulated by a particular school or by schools in general. Over time, schools tend to acquire traditions, customs, mores, and folkways unique to them. Revered songs, raising hands to speak in class, dress codes, etc., are elements of school culture.

sociometry   The sociological study and description of human relationships and structure in more or less measurable terms

Suggested Activity

In one of the classrooms in which you are doing fieldwork, make a sociogram of one or more dimensions of student interpersonal relationships.

Study the results and determine the degree to which your previous impressions of the class were accurate.

References and Notes

1. Studs Terkel, *Working: People Talk about What They Do All Day and How They Feel about What They Do* (New York: Pantheon Books, 1974).

2. Denise B. Kandel and Gerald S. Lesser, *Youth in Two Worlds: United States and Denmark* (San Francisco: Jossey-Bass, 1972), p. 165.

3. Alvin Boskoff, "Functional Analysis as a Source of a Theoretical Repertory and Research Tasks in the Study of Social Change," in George K. Zollschan and Walter Hirsch, eds., *Explorations in Social Change* (Boston: Houghton Mifflin Company, 1964), p. 221.

4. Frederick Elkin and Gerald Handel, *The Child and Society: The Process of Socialization,* 2nd. ed. (New York: Random House, 1972), pp. 127–30.

5. Robert J. Havighurst and Bernice L. Neugarten, *Society and Education,* 4th ed. (Boston: Allyn and Bacon, 1975), pp. 163, 164.

6. Robert J. Havighurst and Bernice L. Neugarten, *Society and Education,* 2nd. ed. (Boston: Allyn and Bacon, 1967), p. 174.

7. James W. Coleman, "The Concept of Equality of Educational Opportunity," *Harvard Educational Review* 68 (Winter 1968): 18.

8. Diana H. Kirk and Susan Goon, "Desegregation and the Cultural Deficit Model: An Examination of the Literature," *Review of Educational Research* 45 (Fall 1975): 599–611.

9. Daniel Yankovich, *The New Morality: A Profile of American Youth in the 1970s* (New York: McGraw-Hill, 1974).

10. Kandel and Lesser, *Youth in Two Worlds,* p. 17.

11. *Ibid.*

12. James Coleman, *Adolescents and Their Schools* (New York: Basic Books, 1965), p. 19.

13. *Ibid.,* pp. 19, 20.

14. Kandel and Lesser, *Youth in Two Worlds,* pp. 17–19.

15. David Friesen, "Academic-Athletic-Popularity Syndrome in the Canadian High School Society," in Hershel D. Thornberg, ed., *Contemporary Adolescence: Readings* (Belmont, Calif.: Brooks/Cole Publishing Co., 1971), p. 149–54.

16. *Ibid.,* p. 150.

17. *Ibid.*

18. Coleman, *Adolescents and Their Schools,* pp. 33, 34.

19. Friesen, "Popularity Syndrome," p. 150.

20. *See* Sandford W. Reitman, "An Alternative Field Work Model for Prospective Teachers," *Interchange* 4 (1973): 61–78.

21. *See* Kenneth Keniston, *The Uncommitted: Alienated Youth in American Society* (New York: Harcourt, Brace and World, 1965), and Theodore Roszak, *The Making of a Counter Culture: Reflections on the Technocratic Society and Its Youthful Opposition* (Garden City, N.Y.: Doubleday and Co., 1969). Of interest also is Joseph Berke, ed., *Counter Culture* (London: Peter Owen Limited, 1969). *See also* Charles Reich, *The Greening of America: How the Youth Revolution Is Trying to Make America Livable* (New

York: Random House, 1970).

22.   B. Burlingham, "There's a New New Left," *New Times* (Feb. 20, 1976): 17.

23.   Grant S. McClellan, "The Youth Revolt in Perspective," in McClellan, ed., *American Youth in a Changing Culture* (New York: The H. W. Wilson Company, 1972), pp. 10–15.

24.   *Ibid.,* p. 23.

25.   *Ibid.*

26.   *Ibid.,* pp. 24, 25.

27.   Willis W. Harmon, "Nature of our Changing Society: Implications for Schools," in Philip K. Piele and Terry L. Eidell, eds., *Social and Technological Change: Implications for Education* (Eugene: The Center for the Advanced Study of Educational Administration, University of Oregon, 1970), p. 15.

28.   Keniston, *The Uncommitted,* p. 128.

29.   *Report of the White House Conference on Youth. April 18–22, 1971, Estes Park, Colorado* (Washington, D.C.: U.S. Government Printing Office, 1971).

30.   Evan Hunter, *The Blackboard Jungle* (New York: Simon and Schuster, 1954); Edward R. Braithwaite, *To Sir with Love* (Englewood Cliffs, N.J.: Prentice-Hall, 1960); James Herndon, *The Way It Spozed to Be* (New York: Bantam Books, 1969); Jonathan Kozol, *Death At An Early Age: The Destruction of the Hearts and Minds of Negro Children in the Boston Public Schools* (Boston: Houghton Mifflin, 1967).

31.   August B. Hollingshead, *Elmtown's Youth* (New York: John Wiley and Sons, 1949); James S. Coleman, et al., *Summary Report, Equality of Educational Opportunity* (Washington, D.C.: U.S. Government Printing Office, 1966).

32.   *See* Maurie Hillson and Francis P. Purcell, "The Disadvantaged Child: A Product of the Culture of Poverty, His Education, and His Life Chances," *Eugenics Quarterly* 13 (September 1966): 179–85. *See also* Michael Harrington, *The Other America* (New York: Macmillan, 1962).

33.   Jerome McGovern, "Reaches, Reflections of a First-Year Teacher," *Changing Education* 5 (Winter–Spring 1974): 6.

34.   Wax, "How Should Schools Be Held Accountable," p. 64.

35.   *See* Jane Mercer, with Marrietta Coleman and Jack Herloe, *Racial/Ethnic Segregation and Desegregation in American Public Education.* U.S. Office of Education, OEC-9-72-1137 (Riverside: University of California, 1974).

36.   John P. Hewitt, *Social Stratification and Deviant Behavior* (New York: Random House, 1970).

37.   *Ibid.,* pp. 71, 72.

38.   An excellent summary of the major arguments for and against integrated education, concluding that "only the intergroup [integrated] school has the potential of offering all children an academic and emotional preparation for tomorrow's intergroup world" is Thomas F. Pettigrew and Patricia J. Pajonas, "The Social Psychology of Heterogeneous Schools," in Cole S. Brembeck and Walker H. Hill, eds., *Cultural Challenges to Education: The Influences of Cultural Factors in School Learning* (Lexington, Mass.: D.C. Heath and Company, 1973), pp. 87–106.

39.   *See,* for example, Hollingshead, *Elmtown's Youth.*

40.   Coleman, *Adolescents and Their Schools,* p. 111.

41.   *Ibid.,* p. 108.

42.   *Ibid.,* p. 109.

43. *Ibid.*, p. 106.

44. Wax, "How Should Schools Be Held Accountable," pp. 67, 68.

45. Havighurst and Neugarten, *Society and Education,* 2nd. ed. p. 189.

46. *Ibid.*, p. 466.

47. Gale E. Jensen, "The Social Structure of the Classroom Group: An Observational Framework," in Ronald T. Hyman, ed., *Teaching: Vantage Points for Study* (Philadelphia: J. B. Lippincott, 1968), pp. 240–50.

10

Human Values in Modern Education

In the past several chapters we have been concerned with the relationships between several key social institutions and formal education. In this chapter we turn to the matter of human values, which many leading educators consider even more fundamental for understanding American schools.

General Meaning of the Concept

The concept of "value" has been interpreted in a number of different ways: as something we consider "good," such as love or honesty; as the tendency of a person to show preferences; as general guides to behavior that emerge from experiences; as elusive ideals and compromises with such ideals.[1] One student of values offers the following very broad definition of the concept: "Values to me, simply stated, are the determiners in man that influence his choices in life and that thus decide his behavior."[2] Kurt Baier says that economists distinguish between "the *value* of things and, on the other hand, the *values* of individuals or societies."[3]

Educators are concerned primarily with the preferences and ideals held by people, individually or collectively. Values refer to *ends* believed to be worth striving for by members of a society or group. Although held by individuals, values are always products of culture. People live in societies with unique cultures, and they derive their personally held values, or preferred ends, from their experiences as participating members of sociocultural systems. And they acquire these values primarily through learning, although some degree of personal choice is always associated with such learning.[4] When especially sensitive individuals in a society reject certain extant values and propose new ones, social change is inaugurated. The eventual diffusion of innovations throughout a social system requires that increasing numbers of people choose to adopt new values.

Since values, that is, preferred personal and social ends, are products of culture, it follows that they cannot be challenged except by members of the same culture. One cannot accuse a person of possessing "bad" values, unless one happens to have been brought up within the identical cultural frame of reference. Failure to appreciate this elemental point about cultural relativity and its implications for values has been responsible for much unwarranted hostility between different religious, ethnic, and national groups since the beginnings of recorded history. Ethnocentric thinking still produces friction even among scholars, scientists, and artists representing diverse schools of thought.

In ancient Sparta young boys were carefully trained to steal, with painful sanctions attached to failure in their efforts. Most modern, civilized people look upon this sort of training with abhorrence. They fail to recognize that Sparta was a unique culture with unique problems that may have required—from its members' frame of reference—that stealing be viewed as a worthy end, or value. Can we, as distant moderns, judge their morals as right or wrong? Only fellow Spartans had that privilege.

In America, differences in subcultural values may exist within a classroom. For instance, a teacher who is a middle-class, white, Anglo-Saxon, urban, Protestant may have students from families of lower-class immigrants from rural Mexico or blacks from the rural Deep South. We live in a society that in many ways remains highly pluralistic. This means that different subcultures may possess somewhat different value systems within the larger culture. These differences must be respected by teachers who want to be effective, especially if they themselves are not members of the subculture to which a student belongs.

Thus, values cannot be judged as right or wrong, good or bad, except possibly when the person observing them is an acknowledged member of the same sociocultural system or subsystem as those possessing the values in question. To be morally fair, logically consistent, and socially acceptable, a person is obliged to respect the culturally derived values of others, even if he or she does not believe in them.

Core Values

How is American society to remain structurally integrated, if each of its separate subcultural groups is permitted to adhere to its peculiar values?

A pluralistic and democratic society is held together because all its members acknowledge one supreme value: the value of respecting and tolerating differences in individuals and groups within the society. This toleration extends to all matters other than those judged to be crucial to the society's integrity or survival as a whole, such as patriotism in time of all out, unprovoked war.

In a recent case involving an educational conflict between the state of Wisconsin and the Amish people of that state (*Wisconsin v. Yoder*), the Supreme Court ruled that Amish children were exempted from Wisconsin's state law compelling attendance at school after eighth grade. The Court felt that the Amish community in Wisconsin was able to adequately educate its own children for life within its subcultural structure.[5] The Court respected the unique value system of the Amish, thus reinforcing the overriding principle of democratic pluralism. The Court felt that in allowing the Amish to educate their own children, nothing crucially damaging to the United States society as a whole would result, since the Amish people have lived peacefully in their semi-isolated communities for many years. To have acceded to the educational officials of Wisconsin in this dispute, however well intentioned the state was, might have posed a distinct threat to the autonomy and survival of the Amish subculture, especially since many Amish youth who have lived in states requiring universal education in state-licensed schools have abandoned their subculture of origin.[6]

Whether or not the case of the Amish has ingredients that also apply to every other group claiming to be a highly distinctive subculture —for example, urban blacks, orthodox Jews, Chinese, etc.—is a complex question. It may be that the Amish situation represents an unusually distinctive subcultural pattern not presently shared by other ethnic groups in America. The Wisconsin case should not necessarily serve as a precedent for any and all groups demanding completely separate educational opportunities.

Core Values.   Some cultural values, such as tolerance of differences in individuals and groups in a pluralistic democracy, are so basic to the integration of a society as a whole that the great majority of adult members strive to assure common adherence to the values.

Universal, basic cultural ideals that integrate society are often termed *core values*. In this chapter, we are concerned with core values because schools, as mirrors of society writ large, tend to reflect society's core value structure, whether this structure is stable or changing. A school's structure, its policies, its curricular and extracurricular format, and its instructional processes reflect society's concern for its basic values.

For instance, one of the core values dominating American society has been a widespread belief and faith in "rugged individualism." This belief has been reflected in American schools by their emphasis upon competition for grades and for athletic honors, as well as through a powerful interest in teaching an exclusively heroic version of American history. Nationalism, or patriotism, assumes a leading place in the value systems of most modern societies, including ours. Elementary schools especially have been primary agencies for inculcating a deep sense of nationalistic pride that verges on denigration of other nations, particularly if their economic and political institutions vary significantly from our own. The daily flag salute and the reluctance of teachers and school administrators to offend the American public by teaching about Communism, even in secondary schools, reflects the core value of nationalism in the operation of most schools. Behind official school programs and methods lie deep-seated, emotionally charged values held, at least at one time, by the vast majority of adult members of the society.

Thus, we can say that one of the basic functions of education in schools is to enculturate or acculturate younger members of a society into accepting the core values of that society. Whether the inculcation of such values is done consciously or unconsciously, it is accomplished through subtle and overt processes sanctioned by school officials and other representatives of the dominant groups of society. These groups believe that they have an interest in preserving certain values.

If a society's core value structure is no longer universally agreed upon, then society's schools cannot realistically continue to teach youngsters to uncritically accept a single set of core values. If schools continue to stress obsolete or controversial core values, then they will fail to win advocates and will be passing on values that may later prove to be useless. For example, if a school system seeks to convince youngsters that "rugged individualism" is a cherished value of contemporary society to which they should definitely subscribe, students will inevitably become frustrated when they enter a labor force with a highly specialized division of labor. "Rugged individualism" is an essentially obsolete value in the vocational marketplace. A student brought up on this value will continue to fail throughout his or her career or be forced to concede that the ideal taught at school was not realistic. And, if he or she realizes the uselessness of this value, then he or she is apt to turn against schools and teachers temporarily or permanently. If so, he or she may raise his or her own children to view school in general as a perhaps necessary but a somewhat tedious barrier to overcome before entering the "real world." This last prospect may produce another problem for schools anchored too tightly to the past in a period of basic sociocultural transformation.

Training youngsters to idealize the value of rugged individualism in a corporate society is one example of a **cultural lag** in modern schools. There is evidence that even two hundred years ago, in the midst of the Revolutionary War, most schools were preparing their students to be British subjects.[7] In short, the school has historically been a repository for traditional values.

In a period characterized by basic social change, such as the twentieth century, a cultural lag in values taught at school can mean that the school is no longer a serviceable institution. These questions, then, remain: (1) Is current change in our society's structure severely affecting a significant number of traditional core values, as well as institutions and other forms of organized human behavior? (2) If so, are modern schools lagging behind the times in the area of core values?

To try to answer these and related questions of crucial import for schools and teachers, it is essential that we understand what is happening to core values in modern America. And, in order to do this, we need to examine three distinct positions on contemporary values held by social scientists, philosophers, educators, and the proverbial person-in-the-street.

Three Value Positions

There appear to be at least three basic positions held by people about the condition of core values in modern American society: (1) values exist; (2) values no longer exist; and (3) values are changing.

The Values Exist Position

One school of thought maintains that core values definitely exist as guides to present and future living and can be fairly readily identified, although they may not always be lived up to.

Holders of this general position stress that of all sociocultural phenomena, core values are among the slowest to become significantly altered, largely because they are deeply imbedded in institutional life. As Inlow explains, most of our core values in the United States are rooted in ancient, medieval, and modern Western history. She specifies four sources:

• *The Western rationalist tradition,* which originated in classical Greece, upholds the supremacy of reason and intellect
• *The Judeo-Christian ethic,* a collective tradition that for thousands of years has depicted man and the universe as endowed with ultimate (teleological) purpose. It sanctifies law, justice, and obedience (Judaism) and salvation and brotherhood (Christianity).
• *The Anglo-Saxon tradition,* a conglomeration of long-standing

Anglo-Saxon political institutions, beliefs, documents, and practices extolling individualism, liberty, equality, and political democracy
   • *Pragmatic faith* in the efficacy of the rationalist, religious, and political traditions, based upon tested experience and abetted by the tremendous rise in the primacy of modern physical and social science[8]

Inlow lists the following as key core values (she calls them "value tenets") that have been dominant throughout the ages and are still upheld in the United States:

   • Life has purpose, or meaning, either of a spiritual character (Idealism) or of a naturalistic one (Realism).
   • Man is rational. This unique trait distinguishes him from the animals and helps him to understand and explain how and why life is purposeful and to exist meaningfully and successfully.
   • The individual is of supreme importance. His (or her) inherent worth warrants that he be free to do what he wants with his own life, as long as he does not infringe upon the individual claims of other free men.
   • Material progress is important. In contrast to the first three essentially idealistic values, this value supports those who manage to progressively accumulate wealth, while it mollifies those who, "by dint of relative lack of will or native ability," 'fail' materially in life. Americans are often said to be an exceedingly materialistic people.
   • Certain basic social institutions are especially esteemed as values: (1) the family has been society's bulwark since the end of the colonial period until at least recently; (2) the church has progressively receded in popular importance since colonial times, but religion in American society has been a central repository for our culture's core values; (3) the political state, which seems to be ascending to an unprecedented height of power. (4) The school has been considered America's great panacea, especially since the decline of religion and, to some extent, of the family. The school is presently being criticized and reevaluated.

Other Beliefs and Values.   Other beliefs and values are important. Among them, Inlow includes: *the Golden Rule,* which says treat others as you want them to treat you (or, in its older form, do not treat them as you would not want them to treat you); *the status of authority,* that is, other things being equal, it is good to respect duly constituted authority embodied in people such as judges, teachers, and parents.
   Chauvinism, or extreme nationalism, patriotism, or ethnocentrism, is considered by Inlow to be a powerful value in American society, one that has been carefully nurtured in our nation's schools for almost two centuries. Considering Communism as an evil is related to chauvinism. This value implies that we must not be too smug about our own eco-

nomic and political system in a highly competitive world, in which our chief competitors in recent years have been the U.S.S.R. and the People's Republic of China.

Independence is a controversial value. Inlow asserts that our culture tends to preach independence more than it practices it. We are rewarded more highly for conforming than for being independent, especially in school:

> *In the world of formal education, despite protests to the contrary, rote learning has much more respectability than teachers will admit. Repetitive responses are more popular than creative ones. And independence truly worthy of the name tends to run headon into adult resistance.*[9]

Still, Inlow feels that because independence is the vital ingredient in social change and since change is the order of the day, independence in U.S. culture is increasing. This opinion is of course not shared by individuals who believe that people were far more independent in our frontier past than they are at present.

Victorian sexual attitudes are prevalent in the traditional view of our culture that marriage is the only proper arena for sexual activity, especially for women. Sexual activity is chiefly a means of reproducing the species, not of pleasure. But important changes in sexual values have been taking place in American society in recent years. It is highly questionable whether these changes have been significantly reflected in school practices, such as in dress codes or permissible behavior between the sexes.[10]

The core values listed by Inlow (rationality, individualism, material progress, importance of political institutions, the Golden Rule, status of authority, chauvinism, evils of Communism, independence, Victorian sexual attitudes) have been cited by other scholars as well. They are considered by many to be the central components of the prevailing cultural system in American society, although they are stated in different ways. For example, one sociologist offers the following list of operational core American values. He calls them "major value orientations."

Democracy.   This value is both political and social, that is, it is used to connote the ethos known as "The American Creed," which includes such values as the importance of the individual, brotherhood, social justice, civic duty, etc.

Freedom.   Two conceptions of freedom—which is related to democratic values—have long been in competition: classical liberalism, or the unfettered freedom advocated by Adam Smith in the eighteenth century and today more or less embodied by the conservative members of the Republican Party and the "new" liberalism, which emphasizes the need for ensuring the rights of all people and advocates government intervention in the affairs of men in order to ensure such rights. The "new liberalism" is often associated with John Dewey and with the Democratic Party.

Achievement and Success.   These values are commonly believed to promote individual initiative and creativity, as well as a spirit of competitiveness.

Efficiency and Practicality.   As a central American value, efficiency is believed to aid achievement and success. Practicality presupposes happy adjustment to the status quo and helps promote the illusion that theorists and iconoclastic geniuses are not well fitted for life.

Science and Secular Rationality.   Science is sometimes said to be a viable substitute for revolution (as is political democracy), and rationality opposes tradition that is maintained merely for its own sake.

Progress.   This ideal implies the possibility of human perfectibility through human effort.

A Moral Orientation.   Americans are often considered an unusually moralistic people, although the term more properly should be "puritanical." This moral orientation is related to the idealization of progress and human improvement in the future, and hence, to creative efforts to improve the individual and society.

Nationalism or Patriotism.   This ideal implies the basic goodness, if not the superiority of American society over all others. It supposedly maintains unity and stability within society.

External Conformity.   This value connotes the accepted, superficial way of relating to people in society. The value suggests the practicality of avoiding conflict in areas of potential disagreement; it may actually produce real behavioral unity to the extent that the pose is maintained. If a person does not act out his true feelings, he will help the group to retain its stability and unity.

Institutional Sanctity.   This overriding value assumes that what has worked in the past should be carried into the present through forms and patterns of culture that pervasively influence life, such as the family, church, state and school.[11]

Most who maintain that values do exist would probably not deny that some of our traditional core values are not consistently upheld by the people who support them most vocally. But, unlike those who think that values have been abandoned altogether, they would not interpret this inconsistency to mean that our traditional value structure is in any real danger of dying. Over thirty-five years ago, Lynd wrote about some of these contradictions in American ideals. Perhaps they are even more obvious today:

1. The United States is the best and greatest nation on earth and will always remain so.

2. Individualism, "the survival of the fittest," is the law of nature and the secret of America's greatness; and restrictions on individual freedom are un-American and kill initiative.

But: No man should live for himself alone; for people ought to be loyal and stand together and work for common purposes.

3. The thing that distinguishes man from the beasts is the fact that he is rational; and therefore man can be trusted, if let alone, to guide his conduct wisely.

But: Some people are brighter than others; and, as every practical politician and businessman knows, you can't afford simply to sit back and wait for people to make up their minds.

4. Democracy, as discovered and perfected by the American people, is the ultimate form of living together. All men are created free and equal, and the United States has made this fact a living reality.

But: You would never get anywhere, of course, if you constantly left things to popular vote. No business could be run that way, and of course no businessman would tolerate it.

5. Everyone should try to be successful.

But: The kind of person you are is more important than how successful you are.

6. The family is our basic institution and the sacred core of our national life.

But: Business is our most important institution, and, since national welfare depends upon it, other institutions must conform to its needs.

7. Religion and "the finer things of life" are our ultimate values and the things all of us are really working for.

But: A man owes it to himself and to his family to make as much money as he can.

8. Life would not be tolerable if we did not believe in progress and know that things are getting better. We should, therefore, welcome new things.

But: The old, tried fundamentals are best; and it is a mistake for busybodies to try to change things too fast or to upset the fundamentals.

9. Hard work and thrift are signs of character and the way to get ahead.

But: No shrewd person tries to get ahead nowadays by just working hard, and nobody gets rich nowadays by pinching nickels. It is important to know the right people. If you want to make money, you have to look and act like money. Anyway, you only live once.

10. Honesty is the best policy.

But: Business is business, and a businessman would be a fool if he didn't cover his hand.

11. America is a land of unlimited opportunity, and people get pretty much what's coming to them here in this country.

But: Of course, not everybody can be boss, and factories can't give jobs if there aren't jobs to give.

12. Capital and labor are partners.

But: It is bad policy to pay higher wages than you have to. If people don't like to work for you for what you offer them, they can go elsewhere.

13. Education is a fine thing.

But: It is the practical men who get things done.

14. Science is a fine thing in its place and our future depends upon it.

But: Science has no right to interfere with such things as business and our other fundamental institutions. The thing to do is to use science, but not let it upset things.

16. Women are the finest of God's creatures.

But: Women aren't very practical and are usually inferior to men in reasoning power and general ability.

17. Patriotism and public service are fine things.

But: Of course, a man has to look out for himself.

18. The American judicial system insures justice to every man, rich or poor.

But: A man is a fool not to hire the best lawyer he can afford.

19. Poverty is deplorable and should be abolished.

But: There never has been enough to go around, and the Bible tells us that "The poor you have always with you."

20. No man deserves to have what he hasn't worked for. It demoralizes him to do so.

But: You can't let people starve.*

What are the general implications of the "values exist" position for schools in this society? The answer is fairly obvious. This position implies the availability of powerful core values for Americans to be guided by now. Some of these values are essentially productive of social unity and stability (such as efficiency or practicality), and others are productive of social diversity and change (such as progress and personal initiative). The values exist position conforms to the Enlightenment idea

---

* Selection from Robert S. Lynd, *Knowledge for What? The Place of Social Science in American Culture.* Copyright © 1967 by Princeton University Press; Princeton Paperback, 1970). Reprinted by permission of Princeton University Press.[12]

of the gradual evolution of human civilization, in which values productive of innovations in society and culture are counterbalanced by values provoking resistance to change.

The ultimate task of American schools from this frame of reference is to facilitate harmonious social evolution by preparing people to accept a status quo that extols gradualism rather than immediate alteration of human affairs. For those who uphold this essentially conservative position, there is no problem in locating a structure of values for schools to reflect. Those who do not search on their own for core values such as have been mentioned here must intuit the major themes on the basis of their personal experiences in society, and then attempt to pass on the results of this experience officially and unofficially as they go through their day-to-day routines in their classrooms. For instance, since almost every aspect of the American experience supports Lynd's characterization of our idealization of sexism, it is possible for "well-enculturated" male and female teachers to continue practicing sexist norms in school, regardless of Feminist movement urgings to the contrary and regardless of HEW's recent order that schools become more equalitarian in their treatment of males and females. Boys can continue to be urged to study science and mathematics, while girls take courses in homemaking and literature. On the more positive side, however, upholding the traditional value position places a special burden on teachers in our society to practice behaviors that help actualize such worthy goals as equality of opportunity, generosity, and fair play.

The NEA Educational Policies Commission published a mid-century list of ten core values intended to help American teachers and other educators better dedicate themselves to the ultimate objectives of their work with children, and to avoid being dependent solely upon the vagaries of intuition. The first and preeminent value they list is individuality; all others are deeply rooted in the historic tradition of American culture:

1. Human Personality—The Basic Value
Among the values here proposed, the *first* is fundamental to all that follow. The basic moral and spiritual value in American life is *the supreme importance of the individual personality.*

2. Moral Responsibility
If the individual personality is supreme, *each person should feel responsible for the consequences of his own conduct.*

3. Institutions as the Servants of Men
If individual personality is supreme, *institutional arrangements are the servants of mankind.*

4. Common Consent
If the individual personality is supreme, *mutual consent is better than violence.*

5. Devotion to Truth

If the individual personality is supreme, *the human mind should be liberated by access to information and opinion.*

6. Respect for Excellence

If the individual personality is supreme, *excellence in mind, character, and creative ability should be fostered.*

7. Moral Equality

If the individual personality is supreme, *all persons should be judged by the same moral standards.*

8. Brotherhood

If the individual personality is supreme, *the concept of brotherhood should take precedence over selfish interests.*

9. The Pursuit of Happiness.

If the individual personality is supreme, *each person should have the greatest possible opportunity for the pursuit of happiness, provided only that such activities do not substantially interfere with the similar opportunities of others.*

10. Spiritual Enrichment.

If the individual personality is supreme, *each person should be offered the emotional and spiritual experiences which transcend the materialistic aspects of life**

The values exist position offers American teachers an idealistic and reliable guide to direct their efforts on behalf of their students. The vital question we must frankly ask is whether or not this reliable guide is adequate today.

Values Are Gone: A Culture in Crisis

Not everyone would agree that the contradictions in values discussed by Lynd are minor. Some people see these inconsistencies as symptomatic of tensions and strains lying deep within the fabric of American culture. If these strains were intensified by forces such as unwanted wars, economic recessions or depressions, or a significant rise in extremist group activity, a challenge to the meaningfulness of the entire value structure would be posed.

The Counter Culture.   Some thinkers feel that the structure has already collapsed—that our culture is now so fragmented by ubiquitous change

---

* From N.E.A. Educational Policies Commission, *Moral and Spiritual Values in the Schools* (Washington, D.C.: National Education Association, 1951). Used by permission.[13]

unaccompanied by serious efforts to control the institutional effects of such change that we have become what Erich Fromm and others have termed a "sick society."[14]

How does the counter culture, comprised of young and some older political activists and alienated non-activists feel about the values of contemporary American society? Drews and Lipson claim that "social philosophers, most creative intellectuals, large numbers of the young, and many ordinary people, are now sensing that there must be something wrong with the values by which we live."[15] Other writers are more blunt. As Joseph Berke, speaking for the new radicals, puts it:

> *America is the end product of two thousand years of EUROPEAN–CHRISTIAN culture now synonymous with what is called THE WEST. For our very survival AMERICA must be destroyed.*
> *The destruction/DE STRUCTURING of America has begun. At this moment many cracks in the monolith are evident. Their presence has been announced by the spontaneous development of MICRO-REVOLU-TIONARY groups throughout the WEST—'COUNTER' INSTITUTIONS whose existence subverts the social-economic-political roles prescribed by advanced bourgeois society for itself. These will lead to the creation of an ALTERNATIVE and COUNTER CULTURE.*[16]

In her study of American values and education, Inlow asserts, with Harold Taylor, that the New Left espouses "the prestige of the negative," and has accordingly incorporated negative positions into its platform. (The reader should carefully note that the term "negative," as used by Inlow, describes the value held by some Americans; it is not necessarily judgmental.) According to Inlow, the counter culture is antirational—in complete opposition to the central component of the traditional value system that extols reason. It is also anticonformist. Everyone is "to do his own thing." It is antimaterialist and anti-elitist. Ultimately, it wants a classless society. It is anti-liberal. Thus, radical leftists have something in common with the reactionary right. In Inlow's words, the New Left, is "antiwar, antidraft, anti-imperialist, anti-*in loco parentis* in college and university life, anti-pollution, antiracist, anti-poverty, antihypocrisy, and anti-police brutality—as well as nihilistic."[17]

Some of the above "negative" values are not firmly opposed to many of society's historic core values. Rather, some of the counter culture's values are actually powerful endorsements for the actualization of certain traditional values. For instance, no traditionalist will admit that conformity is one of his or her values, any more than he or she will accept being labeled a conscious elitist. Both traditionalists and counter culturalists in this society claim to value independence and **populism,** even if they do not always practice what they preach.

When the "positive" side of the question is considered, the values for which the New Left crusades are partly in opposition to tradition and partly more strenuous endorsements of traditional ideals. They want:

- Planned changes in the social order
- Social justice for everyone, poor as well as rich
- Power for the people
- A greater role in decision making for the young
- Greater autonomy in people's personal lives
- Immediate cures

Gradualism, an ultimate outcome of the traditional value structure, is no longer acceptable.[18] As Jerry Rubin says, "Do it NOW!"[19]

For most members of the counter culture who are radical political activists, the school probably plays a rather minor role in major socio-cultural alteration. To date, the nation's public schools (not its colleges and universities) have received little attention from the New Left. This is not inconsistent with Marxist philosophy of education as convention-ally espoused;[20] political revolutionaries normally view change in educa-tion as an eventual consequence of successful structural overhauling of society in other institutional areas. Once the political, economic, and other central institutions have been successfully overturned, then and only then do most social revolutionaries believe the school has any useful part to play. As has been the case in Russia, China, Cuba, and other revolutionized nations, the schools have been used primarily as a tool of the new social elite for perpetuating their ideas, not for creating and diffusing the ideas in the first place. This task is generally considered to be the province of intellectuals unaffiliated with institutions and of charismatic movement leaders and their disciples.[21]

Some counter culturalists, either of a nonpolitical bent who prefer to withdraw from the "Establishment" altogether, or those of a political bent who do not believe in the Marxist ideology of materialistic deter-minism, have been more willing to employ education and schools to lead in achieving their values. They envision this occurring either in pri-vate free schools or in informal educational enterprises.

The Self-Actualization Model.   One proposed remedy for the impover-ishment of modern values has been sufficiently in tune with existing cultural norms to have been given widespread publicity over the past few years. It places its emphasis, as do traditionalists, upon the develop-ment of individuals and refrains from proposing the imposition of any overt ideological controls on students. This is what might be called the "self-actualization" model of education for value change, advocated by psychologists such as Abraham Maslow and Carl Rogers, as well as by Existential philosophers of education. As Drews and Lipson summarize this remedy for social sickness:

...we shall need ... different kinds of education ... All young children unquestionably could develop sensitivities and capacities that are largely unknown and at very much faster rates than is now customary. This would be true if we encouraged them to learn at their own pace and in their own style and to follow their own interests as these unfold. Our systems of education might be designed to allow this talent to emerge, to foster and encourage it.

The self-actualizing individuals, who would emerge ideally ... are distinguished by many qualities which have been best described by Maslow. Their creative imagination impels them to innovate, while energy, enthusiasm, and peak experiences, flow forth from their exhuberant joy in living. Being psychologically healthy, they revel in the exercise of stretching their spiritual muscles. For them, work is not drudgery, but excitement; perseverance is not pain, but a vital force. Tolerant of diversity, they seek to include all differences in the unity of knowledge. Open to the world, and large and generous in spirit, they are able to resist the pressures to conform; and, although supremely sure of their own gifts, their awareness that the universe always will remain essentially a mystery endows them with true humility.[22]

The Community of Persuasion Thesis.   One major educational theorist anticipated the counter culturists' characterization of American society as requiring a new set of values.[23] Stanley represents a branch of the school of **Social Reconstructionist** thought applied to education. (*See* Chapter 11 for a more detailed discussion of Social Reconstructionism.) Stanley's version is sometimes referred to as the "community of persuasion" position. In the early 1950s, he believed that American culture was deeply fragmented but could be reintegrated primarily by using schools to teach a "methodology of practical intelligence" for developing new core values.[24] Stanley feels that America (and the rest of the world, as well) is so disordered and divided in its values, norms, and institutions that the primary job of the public schools is to help reconstruct, or reintegrate, the culture.

> *...societies faced with an advanced stage of social disintegration are compelled, on pain of grave social disorder, to direct their energies to restoration of social consensus.*[25]

In Stanley's view, the educational profession has only two alternatives: to passively accept the mandate of the controlling groups in society, or to take the lead in developing a viable democracy by adapting our worthwhile core values to the atomic age and by adding a new set of values. At the present time, the school is probably able to do little else than operate as a guide to development of the capacity to discuss controversial matters democratically (that is, critically and with tolerance), since the interest groups controlling the educational institution will not permit the school to associate itself with one or another specific position.[26]

The long-range hopes held by Stanley for society include an international, social and political order, economic socialism, meaningful equal opportunity, and a modified intellectual and moral order. The ultimate objectives for the world cannot at this time be attacked directly and the schools cannot yet be expected to promote Stanley's values since they are not supported by a consensus of power groups.

The immediate job of the schools in the most general sense, then, is to "help its students achieve order and clarity through such deliberate and intelligent reconstruction of the values and principles inherent in the democratic tradition as will clarify their meaning and restore their integrative power in the contemporary world."[27] Of course, their long-term task is perfecting society by working to further understand the problem of social change and how it may be resolved.

Stanley and others propose a social-problems curriculum for schools:

> ... the curriculum should be organized among the problems encountered by a democratic society, compelled by profound scientific and technological changes to adapt its thinking and its institutions to the requirements of a highly interdependent and industrialized world order ... the school must become a laboratory engaged in the analysis and study of the issues and problems involved in social reconstruction through democratic, as opposed to authoritarian and violent means.[28]

Such a program is not proposed as a means for having children redesign the world or go out and directly reintegrate their confused parents; rather, it would help students learn to think in a way that is necessary if they are to participate in redesigning the world in the future. Stanley believes that schools can actually do something beyond teaching children how to read, write, and figure. They can help make people more intelligent than they are.[29] (John Dewey believed essentially the same thing, but he did not always emphasize the school's capacity to make people intelligent about social problems.)

Largely through group methods of deliberation, the schools and their personnel cannot be expected to be neutral, although they are to be scrupulously fair, as befits a democratic education. Stanley and his colleagues explain the matter carefully:

> ... the educator must impose certain conclusions upon the students. ... The selection of issues for study, the choice of methods of study, and, above all, the atmosphere and discipline of the school represent subtle but significant ways in which the school inevitably shapes the mind and personality of the young. Students can be asked to participate in the determination of these matters to a certain extent, and at an appropriate age they may be encouraged to examine the principles upon which their choices were made. Such considerations should not be allowed to conceal, however, the inexorable fact that to educate at all entails decisions and choices, which are imposed upon students and which inevitably operate to influence their behavior, attitudes, and beliefs.[30]

The community of persuasion solution to the problem of fragmentation of the moral order is to use schools to try to reconcile deep differences among the American people. Teachers would lead in building a program of "practical intelligence," and, if necessary, in promulgating a definite platform of preferred values in the classroom.

The Transitional View:
Values Are Changing

This position views our culture's dominant values as being in a process of overall transformation. According to this position, values are not stable guidelines, as the traditionalists believe; nor are they useless fragments of a sick society, as the counter culturalists and the Social Reconstructionists believe.

According to Rescher, the core values that guided Americans in earlier years are not necessarily permanent; their intensity declines, often with some substantial changes. Rescher believes that some of our "historic American values ... will in all likelihood be subjected to severe stresses and strains in the remaining years of this century ... that will in some cases eventuate in a probable upgrading and in others down-grading."[31] He lists the following as "upgrading values":

- mankind-oriented values (humanitarianism, internationalism)
- the intellectual virtues
- reasonableness and rationality
- the civic virtues
- group acceptance
- social welfare
- social accountability
- order
- public service
- aesthetic values

"Downgrading values" include:

- nation-oriented values (patriotism, chauvinism)
- the domestic virtues
- responsibility and accountability
- independence (in all its senses)
- self-reliance and self-sufficiency
- individualism
- self-advancement
- economic security
- property rights (and personal liberty generally)
- progressivism (faith in progress)
- optimism (confidence in man's ability to solve man's problems).[32]

He also makes the following caution:

> *It should be noted that we have been dealing with phenomena in the*
> *mainstream of American values. The possibility of radical divergencies*
> *from and reactions to some of these developments on the part of radical*
> *and disaffected minorities (political minorities, beatniks and teenagers,*
> *intellectuals, etc.) is not only not to be ruled out, but can actually be*
> *expected to come about.*[33]

Although it has some possible predictive inaccuracies, another useful formulation of the transitional view of American core values was developed by educational anthropologist George Spindler.[34] In simplified terms, this formulation may be restated as follows: Our society's culture is gradually changing from what Spindler terms a "traditional" value orientation to an "emergent" one. This cultural transformation has been going on for some time now, but has intensified particularly since the end of World War II. Many people are resisting this basic transformation because basic values are highly resistant to change. Nonetheless, the transformation is very real and very significant.

During this changing period, many of our older values continue to be clung to by certain more traditionally raised members of the society —at the same time as the newer values are being adopted by many of the younger members. Sometimes, the same individual accepts some or all of both the traditional and the emergent values. (See Table 10–1.)

Not all persons closely associated with schools are at the same point along the value continuum from Traditional to Emergent, as hypothesized by Spindler. The different relative positions of school board members, administrators, the general public and parents, and students are depicted in Figure 10–1.

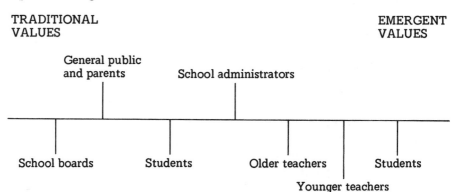

TRADITIONAL VALUES   EMERGENT VALUES

General public and parents   School administrators

School boards   Students   Older teachers   Students

Younger teachers

FIGURE 10–1.   *Placement of School Officials and School Clients along a Continuum from Traditional to Emergent Values (From George D. Spindler, "Education in a Transforming American Culture," Harvard Educational Review 25 [Summer 1955]: 151. Copyright © 1955 by the President and Fellows of Harvard College.)*

Table 10–1. Traditional and Emergent Values in America

Traditional Values	Emergent Values
Puritan morality (Respectability, thrift, self-denial, sexual constraint; a puritan is someone who can have anything he wants, as long as he doesn't enjoy it!)	*Sociability* (.... One should like people and get along well with them. Suspicion of solitary activities is characteristic.)
Work-Success ethic (Successful people worked hard to become so. Anyone can get to the top if he tries hard enough. So people who are not successful are lazy, or stupid, or both. People must work desperately and continuously to convince themselves of their worth.)	*Relativistic moral attitude* (Absolutes in right and wrong are questionable. Morality is what the group thinks is right. Shame, rather than guilt-oriented personality, is appropriate.)
Individualism (The individual is sacred, and always more important than the group. In one extreme form, the value sanctions egocentricity, expediency, and disregard for other people's rights. In its healthier form the value sanctions independence and originality.)	*Consideration for others* (Everything one does should be done with regard for others and their feelings. The individual has a built-in radar that alerts him to other's feelings. Tolerance for the other person's point of view and behaviors is regarded as desirable, so long as the harmony of the group is not disrupted.)
Achievement orientation (Success is a constant goal. There is no resting on past glories. If one makes $9,000 this year he must make $10,000 next year. Coupled with the work-success ethic, this value keeps people moving, and tense.)	*Hedonistic, present-time orientation* (No one can tell what the future will hold, therefore one should enjoy the present—but within the limits of the well-rounded, balanced personality and group.)
Future-time orientation (The future, not the past, or even the present, is more important. There is a "pot of gold at the end of the rainbow." Time is valuable, and cannot be wasted. Present needs must be denied for satisfactions to be gained in the future.)	*Conformity to the group* (Implied in the other emergent values. Everything is relative to the group. Leadership consists of group-machinery lubrication.)

George D. Spindler, "Education in a Transforming Culture," *Harvard Educational Review* 25 (Summer 1955): 149.

American school teachers are caught in the middle of this cultural transformation. They are at the focal center of society's conflicts and transitions in values. Because of their central social position and because they have been professionally prepared in diverse and often contradictory ways, many teachers are under unusual strain today. The ways in which teachers adapt to role strains related to value conflicts differ according to a teacher's early upbringing in the home; the values learned there may agree or disagree with the values acquired during professional preparation and later on the job.

In general, three characteristic types of adaptation are prevalent:

• Ambivalent. A teacher vacillates inconsistently between authoritarian and laissez-faire attitudes in the classroom as a defence against threat of loss of control.

• Compensatory. Teachers overcompensate by becoming either what Spindler terms a "group think" cultist or a rigid authoritarian.

• Adapted. While relatively anchored in either traditionalism or emergentism according to upbringing, an adapted teacher has come to terms with his or her value conflicts and thus can be fairly flexible in behavior and less extreme in his or her efforts to adhere to either value orientation.

An adapted teacher is more autonomous and authentic as a human being and as an educator than either the ambivalent or the compensatory teacher. In the long run, this teacher is apt to accomplish the most with his or her students, whether he or she is relatively "Traditional" or relatively "Emergent" in values orientation.[35]

Which Value Position is Most Valid?
A Brief Assessment

To some extent, all three value positions appear to have some merit, although the transitional view warrants our most serious consideration.

Let us consider the values exist position. Contrary to what we may have been led to believe since the turbulent 1960s, most Americans still seem to value democracy, freedom, science and rationality, a moral orientation, and many other historically sanctified values. To the extent most Americans do in fact agree on certain core ideals, the schools continue to have a mandate to help develop these values.

However, in agreement with some of the ideas held by supporters of the position that American society is "sick" and in a state of crisis, it must be admitted that a great deal of confusion and conflict does indeed presently permeate life. This confusion is related to the efficacy of such older values as efficiency, nationalism–patriotism, conformity, institutional sanctity, progress, virile independence, and to some extent science and rationality (especially in the nonmaterial realms of life). To the degree that these confusions and conflicts persist, our schools lack clear guidelines as they attempt to prepare youngsters for life in the Post-Industrial age.

Traditional values such as puritanical morality, the work–success ethic, extreme individualism, a future–time orientation (not to be confused with futurism, the critical study of the future), and other once-revered ideals are giving way gradually to such values as a relativistic moral orientation, a leisure orientation, group centeredness, a present-time outlook, and a public service–welfare ethic. This transformation is especially notable among the young.[36] As modern society is being carved out and continues to evolve, its most crucial axis of support—its system of core cultural values—must become modified. The present generation of adults and children must decide how to construct its Post-Industrial future. It cannot long tolerate confusion and it cannot return to the "good old days."

Society can decide to build a future founded upon some of the best and most widely accepted traditional values, for example, respect for human differences and belief in human improvement. At the same time, society must be aware of the necessity to adopt some new values in response to new behavioral and attitudinal demands. This is the course to be taken if we wish to become a stable but flexible and self-renewing society.

Whichever course society takes on the fundamental question of values, our schools in one way or another will reflect this course, as they have reflected core values in the past. The schools and their teachers will either serve as apologists for a status quo, as promulgators of social divisions and wholesale confusion, or as healthy sources for the combined evolution and creation of sound universal cultural ideals in a new, democratic and pluralistic social order.

Coping with Relevance
Can Teachers Avoid Teaching Values?

Values undergird everything that is done in school, both in and out of the classroom. During highly stable periods of history as well as during periods of dynamism and flux, teachers have unconsciously and consciously behaved so as to inculcate cultural values in their students. Historically, most value inculcation has been subtle or overt. Unless the values are new and controversial, the indoctrination activities of teachers have been sanctioned by society through its leading school-control groups. These activities have been taken for granted to the extent that most teachers and other people have not been aware that what was going on was indeed indoctrination. But, "because schools have been asked to do certain tasks does not mean that they have succeeded."[37]

Indoctrination of values usually becomes a problem for schools and teachers only when newer values are competing with traditional ones. This is likely to occur primarily under conditions of exceptionally great social turbulence and basic cultural change. We are experiencing such conditions in contemporary American society; therefore, the question of how to handle values in the classroom is receiving unprecedented attention from educators.

If teachers are uncritical about which values they impose upon students—particularly the youngest ones—in the present period of profound transformation, they will be responsible for creating a faith in influential traditional ideals that may not be shared by other people with whom their students must live outside of school. Teachers do not help students by educating them for early obsolescence when they teach obsolete values during a period of great change.

On the other hand, if teachers attempt to impose newer and highly disputed values upon students—especially values in conflict with those held by parents and peers—then they do students an equal disservice by preparing them to merely parrot ideals which, whether worthy or not, are not necessarily held by their significant others. Chances of being successful in inculcating new and disputed values are almost negligible, because teachers possess no public mandate to do so.

If teachers attempt to remain neutral, which is probably impossible in such an emotionally laden area as values, they only act as models of inconsistency and confusion for students. Teachers, however, at least unconsciously support either traditional or emergent values. If they do so uncritically, they are allowing youngsters to obtain their values haphazardly. Even if most teachers were willing to abdicate their professional responsibilities in the area of values, the public would never permit them to do so. The public is concerned that the next generation will be guided in school toward worthy conceptions of life.

Research in the area of values education is growing rapidly, and materials for teachers are more widely available.[38] The general solution to the problem of teaching values may be for teachers to concentrate on helping students to develop and clarify their own values—"to help each student build his own value system."[39] This should help to keep the school's functions educational instead of political and facilitate a relatively smooth transition into a humane Post-Industrial era. There are no guarantees that an open, freely inquiring education will produce the most worthwhile ends. There is only the expectation that freedom of inquiry may enlighten students and thus enable them to make the wisest decisions possible for the times in which they happen to live.

A teacher's job in elementary or secondary schools in helping youngsters to develop and to clarify their own values is very important. Once acquired, values are not easy to change (in comparison with cognitions and skills).

Values Clarification.   According to Raths, there are two essential requirements for all effective values clarification: (1) the establishment of a climate of psychological security, and (2) the application of a clarification procedure.[40] In general, you establish a climate of psychological security, so necessary in the honest study of emotions and values, by creating a "transactional classroom" in which all members—teachers and students alike—feel important and worthwhile participants in a group interested in educational outcomes. Raths suggests that teachers learn to hold nonjudgmental attitudes, to express concern for the feelings and ideas of students, and to offer many opportunities to share ideas.[41] The idea is essentially to elicit thoughtful student judgments about themselves and others in a variety of human contexts by asking what are known as "divergent" and "evaluative" questions. These questions are thought- and feeling-producing questions, whereas "convergent" questions produce factual answers. The student's responses should be accepted without a moral judgment, and with an indication that you have listened caringly.[42]

Obviously, there is a great deal more involved in helping youngsters to develop and clarify their values. For example, students can compare and contrast the values of different groups in social studies work. Teachers can take advantage of common school conflict situations, such as name-calling incidents and challenging of the school rules, to discuss values. You can undoubtedly think of other ways to help students develop and clarify their values.[43]

Underlying all of the various strategies for teaching values are the principles of establishing a psychologically secure climate in class and applying a clarification procedure that elicits significant student inquiry into their own and others' feelings and behaviors.

Summary

Although not consciously realized by most people, values are a primary concern of schools. Core values, particularly, are the heart of culture. Schools are established first and foremost in order to ensure the preservation of the society that supports core values. Schools are also responsible for teaching students to cope effectively with their culture.

Three value positions may be said to be in contention for the allegiance of Americans today: (1) the position that this society continues to possess a coherent body of core values by means of which educators may be guided (the value-exist position); (2) the belief held by both counterculturalists and Social Reconstructionists that our society is impoverished at its core, thus leaving an educational vacuum in the realm of values to be filled (the notion that values are gone); and (3) the position that our basic values are gradually undergoing inexorable transformation (the values-are-changing position). While each of these important positions appears to have a greater or lesser degree of validity, the values-are-changing position warrants our most serious attention because it includes both traditional and newly emergent values.

Any program in the school should start with the recognition that all incentive to learn is a matter of valuing something in the culture to which students aspire to belong as participating members. A successful teacher interweaves value teaching of an exploratory and clarifying nature throughout the day and the year and thereby stimulates youngsters to seek cultural identity through learning. Such teaching is especially important in a period as fraught with widespread individual alienation and anomie and collective fragmentation as the present one.

Related Concepts

cultural lag   A term originated by sociologist William F. Ogburn to refer to the inability of the "non-material" portions of a culture (e.g., values) to stay abreast of the "material" parts (e.g., technology) during the process of evolutionary sociocultural change. This view has been largely discredited as being unduly deterministic. Social change theorists now acknowledge with Max Weber that cultural "lead" and "lag" can take place in "material" parts of a culture, as well as in "non-material" parts, depending upon time and place.

populism   Originally, the theory and policies of the "People's Party" in American politics (1891–1904), which advocated public ownership of utilities and an income tax. Now the term is also used to connote social and political movements oriented to improving the power and welfare of the average person and the poor.

Social Reconstructionism When applied to education, a social philosophy which advocates using the public schools to lead modern society in radically overhauling itself. Its major spokesperson since the

1950s has been Theodore Brameld. Other important proponents have included George Counts, Harold Rugg, and William O. Stanley.

Suggested Activity

Devise a list of traditional and emergent values from the lists on pages 260–273 and check off those values to which you subscribed as a child and those to which you subscribe at present. Candidly ask yourself which of the values that you checked off you would be most likely to retain if a test of your deepest convictions were forced upon you.

References and Notes

1. Gail M. Inlow, *Values in Transition: A Handbook* (New York: John Wiley & Sons, 1972), pp. 1, 2.

2. *Ibid.*, p. 2.

3. Kurt Baier, "What is Value? An Analysis of the Concept," in Baier and Nicholas Rescher, eds., *Values and the Future: The Impact of Technological Change on American Values* (New York: The Free Press, 1969), p. 36.

4. Herbert Blumer, *Symbolic Interactionism: Perspective and Method* (Englewood Cliffs, N.J.: Prentice-Hall, 1969).

5. Joe Young, "Relevant Court Cases Summarized," in bulletin of *Study Commission on Undergraduate Education and the Education of Teachers* (Lincoln: University of Nebraska, 1974), p. 9.

6. *See* Joe Wittmer, "An Educational Controversy: The Old Order Amish Schools," *Phi Delta Kappan* (November 1970): 142–45.

7. R. Potter, "The Role of the School in a Transitional Society," *Dissertation Abstracts* 15 (1954): pp. 78, 79.

8. Inlow, *Values in Transition*, p. 20.

9. *Ibid.*, p. 36.

10. *Ibid.*, pp. 21–38.

11. Robin Williams, *American Society* (New York: Alfred A. Knopf, 1951), pp. 415–70. *See also* the listing made recently by Nicholas Rescher, "What is Value Change? A Framework for Research," in Baier and Rescher, *Values and the Future* pp. 92–95.

12. Robert Lynd, *Knowledge for What?* (Princeton, N.J.: Princeton University Press, 1939), pp. 60–62.

13. N.E.A. Educational Policies Commission, *Moral and Spiritual Values in the Public Schools* (Washington, D.C.: National Education Association, 1951), pp. 18–30.

14. Erich Fromm, *The Sane Society* (New York: Holt, Rinehart, 1955).

15. Elizabeth Monroe Drews and Leslie Lipson, *Values and Humanity* (New York: St. Martin's Press, 1971), p. 148.

16. Joseph Berke, "The Creation of an Alternative Society," in Berke, *Counter Culture* (London: Peter Owen Limited, 1969), p. 14.

17. Inlow, *Values in Transition,* pp. 137–39.

18. Inlow, *Values in Transition,* pp. 139–41.

19. Jerry Rubin, *Do It! Scenarios of the Revolution* (New York: Simon and Schuster, 1970).

20. Robert S. Cohen, "On the Marxist Philosophy of Education," in Fifty-fourth Yearbook of the National Society for the Study of Education, Part I, Nelson B. Henry, ed. (Chicago: University of Chicago Press, 1955), pp. 175–214.

21. *See* Sandford W. Reitman, "An Evaluation of the Reconstructionist Conception of the School's Capacity to Make Sociocultural Changes," unpublished Ed.D. dissertation (Cleveland, Case Western Reserve University, 1969).

22. Drews and Lipson, *Values and Humanity,* pp. 149, 153.

23. William O. Stanley, *Education and Social Integration* (New York: Teachers College, Columbia University, 1953).

24. *See also* R. Bruce Raup, *The Improvement of Practical Intelligence* (New York: Harper and Bros., 1950).

25. Stanley, *Social Integration,* p. 38.

26. *Ibid.,* pp. 12, 13.

27. *Ibid.,* p. 173.

28. B. Othanel Smith, William O. Stanley, J. Harlan Shores, *Fundamentals of Curriculum Development* (New York: Harcourt, Brace and World, 1957), p. 628.

29. *Ibid.,* p. 638.

30. *Ibid.,* p. 645.

31. Rescher, "What is Value Change?" p. 88.

32. *Ibid.,* p. 89.

33. *Ibid.*

34. George D. Spindler, "Education in a Transforming American Culture," *Harvard Educational Review* 25 (Summer, 1955), 145–56.

35. Spindler, "Transforming Culture," pp. 154, 155.

36. Daniel Yankelovich, *The New Morality: A Profile of American Youth in the 1970s* (New York: McGraw-Hill, 1974).

37. Glenn Smith and Charles R. Kniker, eds., *Myth and Reality: A Reader in Education,* 2nd ed. (Boston: Allyn and Bacon, 1975), p. 99.

38. Douglas Superka, "Approaches to Values Education," Social Science Education Consortium *Newsletter* 20 (November 1974).

39. James Raths, "A Strategy for Developing Values," in James Raths, John R. Pancella, and James S. Van Ness, eds., *Studying Teaching* (Englewood Cliffs, N.J.: Prentice-Hall, 1967), p. 318.

40. *Ibid.,* pp. 318, 319.

41. *Ibid.,* p. 319.

42. *See* Ned A. Flanders, *Teacher Influence, Pupil Attitudes, and Achievement,* Cooperative Research Monograph No. 12, Office of Education, U.S. Department of Health, Education and Welfare (Washington, D.C.: U.S. Government Printing Office, 1965).

43. For a classification of various approaches to values teaching, *see* Superka, "Approaches to Values Education."

11

The Goals of Education in a
Transitional Age

In previous chapters, some of the dominant characteristics of our transitional society and culture have been described. In this chapter, we shall synthesize our findings.

This chapter will consider what schools *ought* to do—a value question of the first order. First, we will discuss educational values of scholars and practitioners that can be viewed as competing philosophic conceptions of what the schools' social purposes should be. Then we will review what the schools are doing, as well as what they may do in the future. The purpose of this review is to compare the educational ideals of philosophers with the actual social capacity of the American school. Finally, we will consider the question of whether it is essential for teachers to possess their own philosophies of education.

Divergent Conceptions of Educational Purpose

There are five broad and more or less distinctive "systems" of social philosophy in greater or lesser favor among educators. Several of these systems of thought were discussed earlier in a context broader than education (*see* Chapter 2). They are Perennialism, sometimes known as "Scholasticism" or "Thomism"; Essentialism, that is, loosely speaking, Realism and Idealism applied to contemporary education; Instrumentalism, popularly known as Progressivism, Experimentalism, and Pragmatism; Social Reconstructionism, a variation of this idea being the "community of persuasion" notion discussed in the previous chapter; and Existentialism.

These are more or less coherent systems of philosophical thought applied to education. While some people subscribe to one system completely, it is also common for educators to be **eclectic** in their educational philosophy. Some purists are critical of eclecticism because they feel that it is the result of sloppy thinking and lack of a coherent and well-developed philosophic stance about life and education. Others are more tolerant of such a stance. Some believe that a well-conceived eclecticism may be preferable to a rigid adherence to a single philosophic system, especially in a time of great social disequilibrium demanding flexibility in thought and feeling. There are, of course, philosophers and lay people who reject, on principle, any and all systems of thought. There are also people who grant others the right of accepting one system, but who do not personally subscribe to any of them. Still others may opt for another system, such as **educational Marxism** or **analytic philosophy.**

The systems mentioned above represent the most prevalent thinking to date by leading writers in the field of social values and philosophy. Therefore, they have been singled out for presentation in this chapter on educational goals.

Perennialism

Perennialists maintain that the United States is a troubled, crisis-ridden society. They hold that the only real hope for sound education and a re-stabilized culture lies in a restoration of the liberal spirit that dominated education during the Middle Ages and further back. They are interested less in transmitting the Western cultural heritage than in helping the young to acquire, through disciplined rationality, the "eternal" principles of truth, goodness, and beauty that are believed to be outside space and time—in short, those truths that are perennial.

The medieval system of education essentially was a search for eternal "first principles" primarily in the spiritual realm of the Church, although supported by classical Greek secularism.

The aim of such an education was to discover absolute truth by logical analysis and intuition. By using logical analysis, the truths, or axioms, would appear self-evident to anyone possessing the necessary intellectual equipment by birth and training.

Modern Perennialists, who are frequently associated with schools and colleges established by the Catholic Church, believe that most formal education in the U.S. has become corrupted by its gradual departure from this medieval emphasis on deductive logic and certainty. According to them, this has adversely affected society and weakened its leadership. Hence, Perennialists assert that the major aim of all education—from primary school through the university—should be to train those who are innately intelligent as intellectual leaders. If properly applied, the perennial principles will help society to achieve a rationally determined moral order.

Because they were concerned primarily with the especially "gifted" student, Perennialists have been attacked as elitists. To counter this charge, they have recently claimed that everyone can profit in varying degrees from a rigorous formal education.

Perennialists are especially critical of the system of educational philosophy known as Instrumentalism, or Progressive Education. In recent years, however, they have listed *Democracy and Education,* John Dewey's famous book, with the world's one hundred greatest books of all time.[1] (Dewey was the leading formulator and articulator of philosophical Instrumentalism applied to formal education.)

Essentialism

If Perennialism can be considered reactionary, Essentialism (in most of its variants) is at least conservative. Insofar as it can be linked with Essentialism, Skinnerian behaviorism may be an exception. The term Essentialism has been loosely used in educational circles since the late 1930s to connote conservatism in educational policies, programs, and methods propounded and practiced by both philosophical Idealists and by Realists. To date, most behavior modification efforts, which are based on Skinnerian Realism, have been employed to condition students to the status quo, although Skinner himself is interested in social change.

In general, adherents to both schools of thought tend to agree that basic formal education must be grounded first and foremost upon the "essentials" of historically acquired knowledge; that is, upon the tested heritage of skills, facts, beliefs, and values of the last three or four centuries. Accordingly, Essentialists believe that formal education should be built largely upon the foundations of a traditional curriculum. Such a curriculum is not dominated by the medieval spirit of deductive logic and intuitional absolutism, as is the case with Perennialism, but rather by a preference for knowledge accumulated in a variety of areas in the culture and passed down gradually to moderns.

This storehouse of wisdom today consists of such subject matter conventions as science (not social or psychological science so much as natural science which, being older, possesses more esteem); history; the

"3 Rs"; and European and American literature. In short, most of the types of subject matter presently preoccupying the average school person and parent in the United States and Western Europe are those esteemed by Essentialists.

To the prototypical Realist–Essentialist, the mind of the student is an empty vessel (John Locke's *tabula rasa*). The school must provide the student with as much organized information about the objective world via the senses as the student's "vessel" can contain. In the case of Idealism, the mind is often viewed as a means for appropriating and organizing the subjective interpretations of more knowledgeable minds regarding the empirical world and, more important, for apprehending transcendental Ideas. In either case, the fundamental process of learning appears to entail a good deal of what we might call absorption.

The teacher's main instructional role is to serve either as a mediator between the storehouse of knowledge contained in the outside natural world and the mind of the student or as a model of some more nearly universal Truth, or Absolute Idea (perhaps God). Examinations and similar judgmental devices are means by which schools measure the quantity and evaluate the quality of content held by the student's "mental receptacle." To many Essentialists, as to many Perennialists, Progressive education has been viewed as a scheme of non-education that encourages superficial innovations that should properly be no more than extracurricular offerings. During the late 1950s and the first half of the 1960s, Essentialist educational writers such as Arthur Bestor, James Conant, and Hyman Rickover wrote prolifically, and sometimes stridently, attacking American education for its "dangerous anti-intellectual tendencies," which were allegedly attributable to the influence of Dewey and his disciples.[2] Since then, a number of educational "humanists," or neo-Progressivists, such as John Holt, Herbert Kohl, Neil Postman, and Charles Weingartner[3] have come to the fore as critics of Essentialistic policies and practices in our nation's schools.

Instrumentalism (Experimentalism)

Progressivists, as proponents of Instrumentalism are commonly called, hold that the primary purpose of education is to help people to live harmoniously in the world as it changes, primarily by stimulating them to think effectively. This means to analyze, criticize, and select from among alternative courses of action—in brief, to solve personal and social problems. Progressivists believe that the scientific method is applicable to all areas of intelligent living. They view learning as a five-step process, involving certain strategies:

1. A "felt" difficulty arises to confront a person as he or she experiences life. For example, a high school youth is asked to go out with his buddies on the night before he has an important test.

2. The problem is *analyzed and clarified* on the basis of available pertinent data. The youth deduces from previous experiences and known facts that his pleasure in going out with his friends is being compromised by his apparent need to stay home and study for future benefits.

3. Numerous suggestions, or hypotheses, are generated and allowed to surface, in the form of possible alternative solutions to his dilemma. For instance: he can forget the test, and go out with his friends; he can forget the pleasures of going out, and grind away at his studies; he can study before dinner, and still go out with his friends; he can go out, and study late at night when he returns home.

4. Formally or informally, the probable consequences of the hypotheses are evaluated one at a time. If he studies instead of going out, he will probably do well on the test but lose an opportunity for peer-group fun, which is important for an adolescent. If he goes out and does not study, he may pass the test or may fail, but at least he will probably have a good time; however, the price in terms of his future may be excessive. If he studies before dinner, he will be forced to move at a rapid pace that may or may not allow him to adequately learn the material on which he expects to be tested next day; but at least he is likely to be more relaxed tomorrow for the test because he studied some material and because he enjoyed himself the previous evening. If he goes out and tries to study later at night, he may be too tired to do well on the test.

5. The hypotheses that are rejected because of their probable unfavorable consequences are abandoned. The remaining choices are tried out experimentally. (Of course, in life one may have only one chance to test one's hypothesis, and the results can be either very satisfying or disastrous. Therefore, Instrumentalists want schools to give students many opportunities to fail and succeed in a secure environment). In the present instance, let us assume that the adolescent made some compromises. He decided to study for an hour before dinner, then went out with his friends, made sure he got home by 11 PM, and then studied for another hour before going to bed. He gambled that two hours of study would be sufficient even if he were slightly tired during the second hour. In making the decision, he concluded that he could "have his cake and eat it too." He will find out whether this is, indeed, true when he receives his grade on the test (thus, confirming or disconfirming the hypothesis that he tried out experimentally).[4]

The above case illustrates the Instrumentalist conviction that intelligent behavior results from being able to adjust and readjust to the natural and social order of which the student is an integral part, not merely a passive spectator. Of course, the example used was trivial in comparison with those problems used in schools, such as problems of community improvement, of vocational decision making, of race relations, or of civic responsibility. The study of these problems might take weeks or months of individual or group work and research in the public school setting.

No one ever completely fulfills himself or herself in this way but is always in a *process of becoming,* of progressively "climbing mountains" that lead to higher mountains. To Instrumentalists, life is the process of intelligent becoming—no more, no less. Thus, life is education, and vice versa.

Schools, then, should be the chief agencies by means of which children and youth learn to live intelligently, to approach life critically as scientific thinkers and doers. True democracy requires intelligent thought and action on a collective level, and schools should be micro-centers of democratic living and learning. They should provide continuous opportunities to meet and solve dynamic, timely problems through cooperative participation by the involved "student–citizens," who utilize the general scientific method of thinking outlined above. The program of the school ideally should not be dependent upon preestablished subject matter, as in the traditional school, but rather upon increasingly difficult challenges to be coped with as student-citizens undergo the process of becoming—in the micro democracy known as school. Since such an ideal is probably too much to expect at the present time, whatever formal subject matter is imposed upon students should at least be handled by teachers in such a way as to elicit problem-solving responses; teaching should not merely strive to "fill up" the minds of students indiscriminately, without cultivating intrinsic motivation, as Essentialists are alleged to do.

Social studies, for example, should be taught by a "unit method," in which students become deeply involved in research, construction activities, and similarly enjoyable but meaningful experiences with subject matter. For the most part, teachers are to be partners and fellow explorers with their students in the common educational enterprise. Essentially, teachers should act as guides or "research directors" in a learning process that takes place as spontaneously as possible through active involvement in the personal and social experience of life and its challenges in the modern world.

At present, most of the progressive educational work in this country is done with young children, especially in early-childhood-education programs. Adults taking graduate work that entails much personal involvement in problem-oriented research also have a Progressive educational experience. The Progressive movement in the U.S. was strong during the first half of this century and may be revived on a broad scale with the current trend toward open classrooms and multicultural education, which constantly investigates contrasting values and life styles.

Social Reconstructionism

This is actually an offshoot of Instrumentalism, which began to take form during the Great Depression of the 1930s when some Progressivists became disenchanted with the gradualistic, individual-centered tone of Progressive Education, which was then in its heyday. The Social Reconstructionists urged that the American school and its teachers dare to lead in the creation of an entirely new and more viable social order.[5] The movement reached its pinnacle of influence in the 1950s and early 1960s as a result of the prolific writing of Theodore Brameld, still its preeminent spokesman.[6] Recent discussions of Reconstructionism in textbooks, scholarly journals, and at conferences of educators suggest that it could conceivably be revived as a leading educational philosophy, at least among educational intellectuals.

On one point, this philosophic system agrees with Perennialism: There is an urgent need for clarity and certainty today because our civilization is extremely confused and bewildered. It radically disagrees, however, with the solution offered by Perennialists to the problem of a "crisis culture." Rather than return to the medieval ideal of an educational program devoted to training the mind to logically deduce eternal verities, Social Reconstructionists wish to attempt to completely reconstruct modern Western civilization by means of novel schooling. They want to build a new and better society based upon a broad consensus of educators and the public concerning the aims that should govern humankind in the short and long-term future and the means of attaining those aims.

It is generally believed that these ends and means can be discovered through cooperative social problem-oriented research (especially of an anthropological character) undergone in elementary and secondary school and continued in colleges and universities. The Reconstructionists claim that there already is a growing consensus about the basic characteristics of these aims. They believe there is increasing agreement among Westerners that the future should be ruled by the people, that society should be broadly collectivized, that nationalistic interests should be subordinated to the principle and practice of world government, and that a new morality based on humane ideals be consciously developed.

The job of the teacher in promulgating the reconstruction of society is to act as a "missionary" on behalf of the cause espoused, albeit a sophisticated missionary who subtly inculcates new values and strategies for achieving them in collaboration with others. Reconstructionists claim that democratic inquiry similar to that advocated by Instrumentalists, although more intentionally directed at social objectives, should be used to develop values.

One of the Reconstructionist emphases in the realm of instructional methodology is interpersonal "interpersuasion" (Stanley's "community of persuasion"). Through carefully directed group dynamics in the classroom—a process that purports to join reason, anthropological insights, mutual feeling, and value commitment in social, goal-directed learning—Social Reconstructionists hope that increasing consensus about the future will be achieved. The school, the last hope of a befuddled and corrupted world, will finally serve society as it should—by leading it to a higher plane of civilized community life.

Existentialism

In this position are frequently included both serious philosophers and many popular humanist writers. Adherents to this increasingly prominent philosophical view of reality, knowledge, and ethics maintain that the main purpose of education and schooling should be to help develop self-actualizing personalities, each capable of creating his or her authentic destiny. In so doing, individuals will take responsibility for life in a lonely world with no necessary meaning or after life; a world in which a person has no recourse but to make the best of things from birth until death. The Existentialist does not use the environment to rationalize his or her actions.

Since schools are commonly considered one of the major sources of group conformity, the Existentialists (to whom conformity is anathema) want to persuade those who run educational establishments that efforts to perpetuate the myth of collective responsibility are wrong. All that schools should do is to help individuals to make responsible choices freely, choices based on the meanings they have personally inferred or created as a result of engagement in the educational process.

Teachers should foster student self-discipline and allow students to freely select topics for study. The basic role of the teacher is to act as a resource person and friend to the student when called upon for help. The Existential teacher does not direct learning or behave as an authority figure representing the adult community.

Because of the stress of the social sciences upon cultural reasons for human behavior, they have been held in special contempt by Existentialists. (This may change, as Existentialists refine their outlook.) Van Cleve Morris, one Existential proponent, has expressed it this way:

> However much the sociologist and anthropologist turn him into a cultural product man can still oppose his culture. He cannot lay his faulty values, his barbaric politics, or even his personal psychoneurosis to his member-

*ship in a given human group—family, community, or national society—
for he could have had it otherwise. Man can choose which way he will
take; and this freedom to choose distinguishes him from all other phenomena in the universe. To be a man is to be undetermined, to be free.*[7]

Although Existentialist educators prefer a **Summerhillean** free-choice
program, most schools must impose some kind of curriculum. If a curriculum is necessary, the Existentialists would root it in the humanities,
which supposedly stress and encourage individualism and courage. Let
philosophy, art, literature, and music hold the dominant place in formal
education programs now improperly held by the objective disciplines,
such as the sciences.

In a relatively free academic arena, the encouragement of self-
discipline and the teaching of the subject matter of the humanities
by open, non-authoritarian teachers will facilitate development of
strong character and of tendencies that enable a person to recognize
truth and to remain free in a world populated primarily and increasingly
by conformists.

Despite major differences in its ontology and **axiology,** Existentialism seems to have in common with Perennialism (and, to some extent
with Idealistic Essentialism) a strenuous epistemological faith in the
capacity of individuals to become disciplined to intuit first principles and
thereby find what the religious might call personal salvation.

In spite of such a trust in the essential humaneness of people, however, no assurances are offered that such a philosophy of educational
freedom will be easy and comfortable to live with and to implement with
students. As Greene says:

> *The existential teacher recognizes that he cannot tell another person how
> to live; nor can he demand that his students exercise their will and be-
> come, in their own way, volunteers. But he can set up classroom situa-
> tions that make it difficult to maintain "peace of mind." He may use
> literature and the arts; he may focus on crisis situations—such as a
> Peace Moratorium; he may engage students in concrete questioning and
> confrontation; he may urge them to take stands. The task will not be easy
> for such a teacher, anymore than it will for his students because they are
> forever condemned to the freedom that requires them to create them-
> selves over and over without a sense of comforting constraint or a priori
> norms.*[8]

Existentialism is not a philosophy for those concerned with emotional
security, but one does wonder whether a teacher in today's crisis-torn
world can expect great emotional security anyway.

Each of the philosophic systems of education briefly outlined above
has long been the object of intensive and extensive inquiry, explication,
and debate by leading educators.[9] See Table 11–1 for a summary of these
philosophies, their proponents, and their beliefs.

Table 11–1. The Main Elements of Major Philosophic Systems of Education

		Leading Proponents	Basic Philosophical Assumptions	The Learner
TRADITIONAL — "Essentialism" / "Perennialism"	Idealism	Plato Theodore Greene Herman Horne Robert Ulich J. Donald Butler	A world of Mind; universe evolves in accordance with ultimate plan as interpreted by speculative thinkers	Learner as microcosmic mind
	Realism	Aristotle Frederich Breed Harry Broudy John Wild (B. F. Skinner)	A world of Things; universe evolves in accordance with natural law as interpreted by scientists	Learner as sense mechanism
	Secular	Aristotle Mortimer Adler Robert Hutchins	A world of Reason and Being/God; reality is dualistic, composed of two essences: matter and ideas (or spirit and form).	Learner as rational
	Sacred	Thomas Aquinas William McGucken, S. J. Jacques Maritain	Knowledge secured by scientific method; ideas and values by reason, intuition, revelation, or faith	and spiritual being
MODERN	Instrumentalism	Boyd Bode John Childs John Dewey William H. Kilpatrick	A world of dynamic, human, testable experiencing and valuing	Learner as inquiring, experiencing, creative organism
	Reconstructionism	George Counts Theodore Brameld Harold Rugg Wm. O. Stanley	Essentially same as Instrumentalism, with greater emphasis placed on social/cultural implications	Same as Instrumentalism
	Existentialism	Ralph Harper Van Cleve Morris George Kneller Maxine Greene	A world of existing; offers unlimited freedom of personal choice for the daring individual	Learner as ultimate and responsible choicemaker

Adapted from Van Cleve Morris, "Schematic Summary of Views," in *Philosophy and the American School: An Introduction to the Philosophy of Education* (Cambridge, Mass.: The Riverside Press, 1961), p. 467. Copyright © 1961 by Houghton Mifflin Company. Adapted by permission of the publisher. Also from Ralph L. Pounds and James R. Bryner, "Contemporary Conflicting Philoso-

Table 11–1. *Continued*

	The Teacher	The Curriculum	The Method	Social Policy
TRADITIONAL — "Essentialism"	Teacher as paradigmatic self (a model of ideals)	Subject matter of symbol and idea (literature, history, etc.)	Absorbing ideas	The "trailing edge": Conserve the moral and intellectual heritage accumulated over past several hundred years
	Teacher as demonstrator or conditioner	Subject matter of the physical world (mathematics, the physical sciences, etc.)	Mastering facts and information	The "trailing edge": Transmit settled knowledge to help students live in the present
TRADITIONAL — "Perennialism"	Teacher as mental disciplinarian and spiritual leader	Subject matter of the intellect and spirit (mathematics languages, logic, Great Books, Dogma, Doctrine)	Training the intellect	None. Since basic values, principles, and assumptions do not change, schools should help students to find perennial truths, which may then be applied to current mundane problems
MODERN	Teacher as individual and group project director	Subject matter of personal and social experience (social studies, projects, etc.)	Scientific problem solving	The "growing edge": Teach how to manage ubiquitous change
	Same as Instrumentalism	Subject matter of social and personal experience (social studies, community projects, problems, etc.)	Similar to Instrumentalism with greater emphasis on hypothesis as predeterminant to solution of problem	The "Utopian Future": Teach to radically reconstruct the crisis-ridden social order
	Teacher as unfettered provacateur of the personal self	Subject matter of subjective choice (the arts, moral philosophy, ethics)	Finding the authentic self	?

phies Compared," in Pounds and Bryner, *The School in American Society*, 2nd ed. (New York: Macmillan, 1967), pp. 486, 487. Copyright © 1969 by the Free Press, a division of The Macmillan Company. For further amplification, *see* Morris and Young Pai, *Philosophy and the American School*, 2nd ed. (Boston: Houghton Mifflin, 1976).

The Social Scientific View
of the School's Functions

Philosophers are primarily concerned with what they believe ought to be. However, what ought to be is not always what can be. What *should* be depends in part upon what is possible. Because there are real limits to what can be made possible, social philosophies of education, such as those presented above, may not be entirely realistic, although they may provoke critical thought.

Before further evaluating philosophic systems, we will review some of the key social functions that our schools are expected or permitted to perform, keeping in mind that schools are established by adult members of society in order to secure purposes that *they* respect, regardless of what educational philosophers believe they *should* respect. Even the manifest functions assigned to schools are not necessarily always performed. People often discover that manifest functions such as providing equal opportunities are not being adequately fulfilled, while latent functions such as babysitting are.

What are the manifest functions discussed in Chapter 3 that can be considered to still dominate the expectations of most people for the American school?

1. Selecting and sorting people for various adult roles
2. Building and maintaining nationalism and citizenship
3. Transmitting traditional culture
4. Socialization and enculturation
5. Acquisition of basic skills
6. Vocational preparation

Most of these are what may be termed pattern-maintenance functions.[10] Schools have always been chiefly concerned with helping to preserve extant sociocultural patterns through the learning process.

What about functions that are emerging?

1. Personal and social problem-solving (within basic values)
2. Social competence for a secondary society
3. Diffusion of new knowledge
4. Providing equality of opportunity for a social position
5. Sex and family life education
6. Extended functional literacy
7. Development of cosmopolitan attitudes
8. Existential creativity

These are what may be considered adaptive functions, or functions that relate to helping individuals and, within limits, groups to make accommodations to changing conditions in their milieux.[11] While adaptive functions are still often controversial or less universally supported than pattern-maintenance functions, they are within the parameters of the school's capacity. They do no more than seek to help people achieve already predetermined core values, or ends in process of being determined by society at large. They do *not* seek to formulate new goals for society, a type of function belonging to the political institution.[12] We live in a period of when *adaptive* educational functions are increasingly replacing and will undoubtedly continue to replace pattern-maintenance functions, but in which goal-attainment functions still belong to the political institution, not to the schools.

Some important additional adaptive functions mentioned in Chapter 5 as basic needs for all people growing up in an emergent Post-Industrial society are:

1. The general improvement of human relations
2. The ability to cope with new ideas, values, and problems
3. The human use of new technologies
4. The ability to create and cope with new lifestyles

All the above adaptive functions are related to the concept of "ultra-stability," or "self-renewability." The ultimate concern of educators must be to create an educational system capable of responding to changes in the environment. Specific educational purposes are to be determined as particular new social and individual conditions arise or are anticipated.

What Can Realistically Be Expected of Schools?

The school has limited capabilities because it is a social institution controlled by people with vested interests. Historically, schools have served primarily pattern-maintenance (conservative) functions for comparatively slowly changing societies. They have also served the functions of helping to keep local communities integrated and adolescents relieved from the tensions of delayed adulthood by means of such nostrums as high school athletics. Schools have also served some important latent functions such as babysitting for mothers who have, in increasing numbers, wanted to be gainfully employed outside the home. The school has never served the function of leading in radical social change nor, according to what is known about social systems, can it ever realistically be expected to serve such a function. If anything, the school has always been one of society's more conservative institutions.

In today's condition of unusually rapid and pervasive change, institutions that continue to operate much as they did in the past become outmoded, since the functions served by these institutions are no longer relevant to what actually goes on in society. The modern school is being criticized for being out of touch with the modern world. There is little question that it continues to emphasize the essentials of historical periods now long gone, instead of the essentials of life in an emergent Post-Industrial society. The school continues to celebrate history instead of sociology, classical literature instead of twentieth-century writing, Rembrandt instead of Picasso, reading print instead of speaking and interacting. In the fast-emerging age, traditional philosophic systems such as Essentialism and Perennialism are probably best dispensed with as key positions undergirding school policy, curriculum, and methodology.

What is relevant in the other systems discussed here? In its pure form, Social Reconstructionism is a utopian political philosophy, not an educational one. (Formal education, of course, cannot be completely divorced from politics.) Schools and school teachers never have been and probably never will be agencies and agents of significant social reconstruction. Social reconstruction by educational means inevitably follows social change occurring in other institutions or in the society at large. The schools have not been given the function of setting goals for society, nor in all probability are they going to be; this is a prerogative of the political system.

What about Existentialism? In a time of basic change, this philosophy promises some hope for helping the lonely individual retain his or her individuality. It offers a chance to acquire and retain personal identity in a world that confuses many people. But do the schools have the assigned function of helping individuals to find themselves in such a period as the present? Only peripherally. Even if they were granted this function as a central charge, would Existential philosophy, with its disdain toward the need to belong and its insistence upon the meaninglessness of all systems, be able to accomplish what it promises? Probably not.

Instrumentalism is probably most akin to a refashioned Existentialism. In a period of great social upheaval for a pluralistic democracy, a philosophy that offers people a chance to learn to reason inductively and deductively in order to solve some of their problems and that shows the way to problem-solving success at the group level, should be seriously considered. But does this philosophy, as articulated by its leading spokespersons, have the whole hearted mandate of the power groups that largely determine the school's functions? Does Instrumentalism appreciate the substance and tenuousness of modern collective and individual life and the sense of urgency to improve life? Probably not, although there is great potential for strengthening this particular philosophy in both regards.

Educators readily admit indebtedness to each of the seminal contributions to modern educational philosophy (Reconstructionism, Existentialism, and Instrumentalism). While each contributes something valuable, the school's finest contribution to our age probably will not be in terms of their separate identities, however. Cast in conventional philosophical terms, what American education may most need now is a combination of the best elements of Instrumentalism, Existentialism, and Reconstructionism; in other words, a well-constructed eclectic synthesis. This always has been the basis for meaningful creativity generally, since creativity and innovation almost always emerge from the synthesis of diverse elements.[13] Eclecticism is a necessary ingredient for creative change. A vital, dynamic society requires an eclectic philosophy or education so that its schools may function in the best interest of an open and continuously renewing cultural system.

The blend of Reconstructionist, Instrumentalist, and Existentialist themes in a new adaptive school function for convenience may be labeled "transactional," because the main concerns are with promoting a dynamic transaction between individuals and the social collective; between the past, present, and future; between the tensions separating reason and emotion; and between other dualities that must be bridged in order for education to make creative adjustments to the changing environment.

A transactional school would serve society's members by helping them to cope intellectually with the implications of basic social transformations by using scientific modes of deduction and induction (part of the Instrumentalist dimension). It would also facilitate freely chosen nonintellectual approaches to the problems of life in the realms of aesthetics, values, and feelings (the Existential dimension). And, since the needs for individual and social adaptation and actualization are very great in this society, the urgency of Reconstructionism is a vital and integral element of this eclectic view of school function.

The overriding goals to be achieved by the schooling process in this emerging era appear to be greater intellectual and affective capabilities by men and women on a large scale. In Parsonian language, these functions are instrumental (with a logical means and end), as well as expressive (or emotive).[14] This contrasts with the traditional school's concentration on instrumental functions to the exclusion of the affective component of human life.

Why Should You Develop a
Coherent Philosophy of Education?

Any responsible educator would urge you to philosophize because it is an important way to learn to live and to help your students learn to live. After you have learned theories and facts, the contemplative effort to comprehend the meaning of life and education will lead to implications for action that will strengthen your teaching.

Can it be denied that without a fairly coherent conception of your own purposes in working with students that you will be little more than an automated robot, employed to carry out orders for a system you neither understand nor can really hope to care about? Without a personal philosophy would you not be as alienated as the Existentialists and Marxists claim modern men and women are?

Philosophizing would perhaps produce a sense of personal responsibility for yourself and for your work. It also may be absolutely essential to your long-term personal sense of well-being and connection with the world and to your development as an educator—not simply as an employed technician with specialized knowledge.

As you philosophize about life and education, you may find yourself in significant disagreement with other greater or lesser authorities. No position is sacrosanct; every belief is open to criticism. The views presented in this chapter on what education and teaching should become were not intended to persuade you, but rather to provoke you to think and to react to them. All philosophical positions are open to challenge and improvement.

As a future educator, your views on education are worth a great deal. Keeping in mind the admonition to search for ideas that promote self-renewal in educational matters and that recognize the functional limitations of schools in our society, as a prospective teacher, you should philosophize about the ends of education and schooling in the world you and your students have inherited, at the same time you consider the means by which you and other teachers may hope to realize these ends.

Summary

Normative philosophies of education are more or less coherent expressions of key values about the ultimate purposes of life and learning. As such, everyone has a philosophy of education, although it may not always be clearly and explicitly articulated.

Among the more widely debated philosophic systems propounded by American educators are Perennialism, a philosophy of eternal verities to be inculcated by schools; Essentialism, a conservative system advocating the passing down of the cultural heritage to the young; Instrumentalism, a philosophy of tested experience and critical thinking; Social Reconstructionism, a system proposing radical overhauling of modern society under school leadership; and Existentialism, a system denigrating systems in general and eulogizing the present and the individual's personalized search for truth.

Philosophies of education deserve to be considered as expressions of personal preference, separate from pragmatic considerations. They also warrant being viewed as normative positions that may or may not be capable of working if put to the test within the real functional limitations of schools.

Because modern society requires and increasingly permits schools to take on adaptive functions, any philosophy of education that is to be considered tenable at the present time cannot only focus on pattern-maintenance or revolutionary goal-setting functions. Perhaps an eclectic synthesis of the urgency of Reconstructionism, the logic of Instrumentalism, and the person-centeredness of Existentialism is in order today.

Whether or not this is so, any philosophy of education developed for application to modern schools needs to be open to modifications as sociocultural conditions change in the future. It must respect the principle of self-renewal in education and society at large.

Teachers should be philosophers of education and "do" philosophy as they work with children and others in the classroom and outside of it.

Related Concepts

analytic philosophy   Also called Linguistic Analysis, this is a contemporary philosophy that maintains that careful study of language and linguistic propositions is of paramount importance in resolving educational dilemmas

educational Marxism   The philosophic application of Karl Marx's principles of economic determinism and social stratification to educational endeavors

eclecticism   Selection of ideas from several sources

Summerhillean   An adjective sometimes used to connote adherence to the philosophy of student freedom advocated by A. S. Neill, founder of the famous Summerhill boarding school in England

axiology   In philosophy, the study of the nature of ethics and of
values

Suggested Activity

In discussing the several philosophies presented in this chapter, the word
utopian was used in reference to one of them. Utopian thought (not to be
confused with more modest consideration about the future) is often believed to be impractical. However, by virtue of its sharp contrast with
prevailing ideas and practices, such thought can provoke interesting and
creative conceptions of life and strategies for improving it. Other than
science fiction, comparatively little has been written about utopias in education in the twentieth century. Plato's *Republic* is the famed classical
writing on educational utopianism and many scholarly books have been
written in recent years about utopias in realms broader than education.
One contemporary student of educational utopias is Howard Ozmon,
whose book *Challenging Ideas in Education* explores major utopian writings of the past and present related to the institution.[15]

Read this book and ask yourself if some of the ideas expressed can
be applied to contemporary education either as they stand or in somewhat modified form. If not, ask yourself why not.

Since the study of educational futures is beginning to be taken seriously by non-utopian scholars, you may want to extend your reading on
this important topic. Two suggestions for reading: Louis Rubin, ed., *The
Future of Education,* and Harold Shane, *The Educational Significance of
the Future.*[16]

References and Notes

1. John Dewey, *Democracy and Education: An Introduction to the Philosophy
of Education* (New York: Free Press,
1966).

2. For instance, see Arthur Bestor, *Edu-
cational Wastelands: The Retreat from
Learning in Our Public Schools* (Urbana:
University of Illinois Press, 1953); James
B. Conant, *The American High School To-
day: A First Report to Interested Citizens*
(New York: McGraw-Hill, 1959); Hyman

Rickover, *American Education, A Na-
tional Failure: The Problem of Our
Schools and What We Can Learn from
England* (New York: E. P. Dutton, 1963).

3. John Holt, *How Children Learn* (New
York: Pitman Publishing Corporation,
1967); Herbert Kohl, *The Open Classroom: A Practical Guide to a New Way
of Teaching* (New York: A New York Review Book, distributed by Random
House, 1969); Neil Postman and Charles

Weingartner, *Teaching as a Subversive Activity* (New York: Delacorte Press, 1969).

4. Dewey, *Democracy and Education*, pp. 152–63; F. S. C. Northrop, *The Logic of the Sciences and the Humanities* (Cleveland: The World Publishing Company, 1959), pp. 12–18. Dewey's most elementary formulation consists of only four conceptual steps: (1) experience (2) data (3) ideas (4) testing of ideas. The "felt difficulty" encountered as a result of undergoing experience in step 1 has been treated with great clarity in Dewey's *Interest and Effort in Education* (Carbondale: Southern Illinois University Press, 1975), pp. 46–64.

5. George Counts, *Dare the School Build a New Social Order?* (New York: John Day Company, 1932).

6. Brameld has written over ten books espousing his philosophy of Reconstructionism. One of his earliest expositions is Theodore Brameld, *Ends and Means in Education: A Midcentury Appraisal* (New York: Harper and Brothers, 1950).

7. Van Cleve Morris, "Existentialism and Education," in Van Cleve Morris, ed., *Modern Movements in Educational Philosophy* (Boston: Houghton Mifflin, 1969), p. 364.

8. Maxine Greene, *Teacher As Stranger: Educational Philosophy for the Modern Age* (Belmont, Calif.: Wadsworth Publishing Company, 1973), pp. 281, 82.

9. Currently, the leading scholarly journal for philosophers of education is *Educational Theory*, associated with the John Dewey Society and the Philosophy of Education Society.

10. *See* Alvin Boskoff, "Functional Analysis as a Source of a Theoretical Repertory and Research Tasks in the Study of Social Change," George K. Zollschan and Walter Hirsch, eds., *Explorations in Social Change* (Boston: Houghton Mifflin Company, 1964), p. 221.

11. *Ibid.*, p. 220.

12. *Ibid.*

13. The noted anthropologist Ralph Linton expressed this idea in terms of the culture concept years ago when he said:

Although the knowledge incorporated into a new invention may derive in part from a fresh discovery, most of it always derives from the culture of the inventor's society. Every inventor, even the one who produces a basic invention, builds upon this accumulation of previously acquired knowledge, and every new thing must grow out of other things which have gone before...

(Ralph Linton, "Discovery, Invention, and Their Cultural Setting," *The Study of Man* New York: Appleton-Century-Crofts, 1936, reprinted in Amatai Etzioni and Eva Etzioni, eds., *Social Change: Sources, Patterns, and Consequences* (New York: Basic Books, 1964), p. 433.

14. *See* Talcott Parsons, *The Social System* (Glencoe, Ill. The Free Press, 1951).

15. Howard Ozmon, *Challenging Ideas in Education* (Minneapolis: Burgess, 1967).

16. Louis Rubin, ed., *The Future of Education* (Boston: Allyn and Bacon, 1975) and Harold G. Shane, *The Educational Significance of the Future* (Bloomington, Ind.: Phi Delta Kappan, 1973).

How Can the Purposes
of Education Be Realized?

Power and Control in Education

12

The Structure of Authority in Formal Education

Contrary to what most Americans have long believed, elementary and secondary schools, as well as most colleges and universities, have always been involved in struggles for power over the ends and means of education. Today, they are increasingly forced to compete with other agencies of government for scarce financial and other resources. Schooling in American society has been a major political endeavor since colonial times, although popular mythology would have it otherwise. Educators, journalists, and public officials have promulgated this mythology. The following is a newspaper editorial written in 1970, shortly after Wilson Riles took office as State Superintendent of Public Instruction in California, following his political victory at the polls over conservative incumbent Max Rafferty:

> California schools have been hurt over the last decade by being caught repeatedly in partisan political crossfires. One of the heartening aspects of the election of Wilson Riles as state superintendent of public instruction is that his election will contribute to the de-politicalization of education problems.
>
> The quality of schooling provided the state's youngsters will remain the chief issue facing California, but it should not be a partisan one. Merit alone should decide issues, not politics.
>
> In a postelection statement, Riles pledged to work as superintendent on the nonpartisan basis Californians and their state Constitution demand. This newspaper has been strongly critical of Riles' predecessor for involving education in politics, but the responsibility has not been his alone. Other office-holders also have been guilty of using schools as a political football.

> *All should take to heart this nonpartisan philosophy voiced by Riles:*
>
> *"I am going to approach the whole task in a spirit of unity and reconciliation, and I expect that in return. Too much is at stake. The whole school system is at stake. The education of the children in this state is at stake. I don't think the public would look kindly on political infighting."*
>
> *The answer to California's school problems does not consist simply of more money. A wide variety of changes are needed to improve the system. Both major parties should be interested in seeing that they are provided. There is no Democratic solution to educational problems any more than there is a Republican solution.[1]*

The writer of the above editorial does not regard Riles as a politician (whom we shall define here as anyone who engages in struggles to obtain or keep power in any public domain). Nor does Riles conceive of himself as a politician, as indicated by his statement quoted above. However, like political winners in every sphere and on all levels—from city mayors to U.S. presidents—Riles did in fact win his office by publicly campaigning in opposition to what many considered the reactionary incumbent, Max Rafferty. The difference here is that there is a common myth on the side of schoolman Riles; unlike other government affairs, schooling is inherently a nonpolitical matter, and everything possible should be done to keep it that way. The existence of such a myth does not prevent school politicians from doing exactly what Riles publicly denounces—engaging in political infighting while pretending to others and very often to themselves that they are doing no such thing, thereby sanctifying their struggles with what Laurence Iannaccone and Frank Lutz view as a nineteenth-century aura of the "sacred." As they say in their recent study of local school politics:

> *American school districts with their peculiar social organizations, traditional behavior, and particular ethos tend to resemble the sacred rural community even in suburban metroplexes. Not withstanding the secular urban context of New York City, the governmental process and decision-making patterns of that city's school district tend to reproduce the sacred rural community values for educational policy and for political behavior in the city's school government. Nor does New York City stand alone in this, for Los Angeles, Chicago, San Francisco, Atlanta, and St. Louis seem, at least at the school board level, to have found greater success in displaying the sacred nineteenth century small town American orientations toward education and its government than a secular twentieth century urban outlook. Not a few of the unresolved problems of urban education remain unresolved, becoming increasingly unmanageable partly because of this curious development of the ground rules and flavor of the sacred society in the politics of urban education.[2]*

Iannaccone and Lutz enunciate a major fact about education in American society: While the society as a whole is moving into the

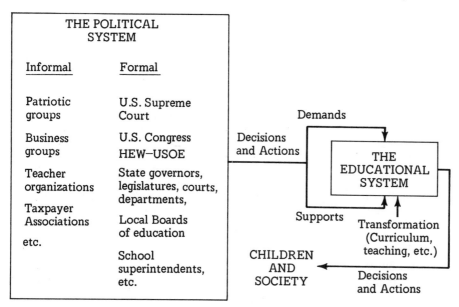

FIGURE 12–1. *A Flow Model of the Political System of Formal Education*

twenty-first-century, schooling remains essentially a nineteenth-century institution politically. This institution has been wrought largely out of the effort to educate large masses of foreign-born and newly urbanized people during the period of emergent Industrialism.

One of the factors chiefly responsible for the comparatively slow transformation of the American school into a vehicle for enculturating and socializing children and youth for life in a new society may be the long-held myth that the school is somehow above politics. Such a myth fosters a widespread ethos extolling consensus in matters educational, rather than a dissensus. Throughout the rest of society, dissent has been valued as a primary source of innovation, preventing social institutions from becoming obsolete. In education, however, dissent is seen almost as disloyalty to the great opportunity system which Horace Mann, Henry Barnard, and other notables of the mid-nineteenth century worked so hard to establish for the benefit of "the multitudes of ignorant people eager to find a place in the land of opportunity."

As we shall learn in the following chapter, dissent by school teachers has been especially discouraged. The lay public, school administrators, and professional teachers generally believe that they should not express opposition to the ideas of those who pay their salaries or of those who carry out the will of the public. At the heart of the educational enterprise, teachers have traditionally been expected to take on the role of servant to the public and its elected or appointed school policy-makers and managers. They are not expected to become significantly involved in high-level decision making directly affecting their work in the classroom.

Richard Pratte disagrees with this conception of the teacher's accountability:

> ... while the public appoints the teacher, in terms of teaching activities the public does not have the right to command him, except to fulfill his teaching activities. The teacher's duty is to his profession and not to his electors. When one realizes the import of this, it is obvious that the principle runs counter to the popular view [substitute "myth"] that in a democracy public school teachers are the servants (the agents) of the public (the voters). It is only in his duty to the office of teacher (teacher accountability) that the teacher is the servant (the agent) of the public (the voters).[3]

If Pratte's analysis is correct, the implications for the politics of education are enormous. In order for the teacher to fulfill his duty to his profession, it may at times be necessary for him to abandon his traditional posture of acquiescence. A teacher may feel that it is in the best interests of the public's children and the future of society to dissent. Dissent here means to enter into creative conflict with others with whom an individual or an organized group disagrees, to enter the political arena openly and honestly. Only in very recent years has there begun to be an understanding of this vital principle of democracy on the parts of American teachers. A concomitant development of movements in this society by organized and unorganized teachers may alter, or at least modify, the American mythological ethos extolling a consensus at all costs in educational matters.

American schooling is and always has been a political endeavor. The rural romanticism of the nineteenth century, however, perpetuates the myth of the school as a nonpolitical institution "in contrast to the rest of American governmental life."[4] The notion that the local school district is the last stronghold of direct, nonpartisan democracy in American life obscures two very real facts: (1) that power struggles occur internally in school systems, particularly between superintendents and boards of education, in which the former is more often than not the actual leader;[5] (2) that such struggles occasionally break out of the control of professionals involved when an issue is unusually volatile and becomes a genuine public, or external, concern.[6]

The idea that schooling is outside of the parameters of politics, coupled with the romantic notion of rural localism, retards the development of a realistic awareness on the parts of school people and the public (1) that public education is, by constitutional mandate, a distinct function of state government—not of local communities. Hence, the authority traditionally delegated to local school districts can be taken away at any time by state legislatures and (2) public (as well as private) education in this country is increasingly being financed—and therefore controlled—by the federal government. The implication of both of these points seems to be that far more political sophistication is needed by individuals and groups concerned with the future of public education. This is especially true today as education becomes increasingly complex and removed from the citizenry.

Because formal education is a somewhat closed political system, acknowledgement of its political nature may be difficult to secure. One political scientist thinks that high-ranking administrative bureaucrats really control school politics in American society and that this is unfortunately reflected in the classroom:

> It is in the classroom . . . that they [teachers] exert their greatest influence. Here the student learns that the schools are sacrosanct, that any criticism of public education is an attack on the foundations of the republic. Here he learns, too, that government (particularly city government) is a sorry business and politics unclean. It is in the classroom, in short, that the antidemocratic freight of the schoolmen's doctrine makes its greatest impact on the young citizen. The destructive consequences of this antigovernment attitude could have been foretold with complete assurance; unhappily, they are now a matter of record. They are to be seen in citizen ignorance of public issues, in absence of interest in public affairs, in failure to take part in the democratic process, in scorn of government and contempt of politicians.[7]

Informal Aspects of Control: The Major Forces of Educational Power and Influence

Contrasting Human Values

Since schooling is a highly political endeavor, people interested in schooling and in other public affairs vie with each other for personal benefits, such as higher salaries; greater or lesser support for curricular or extra-curricular offerings and the attendant personal advantages accruing to those who gain such support, such as seeking financial support for more language programs rather than more varsity athletics and the jobs resulting from gaining one kind of program over the other; increased or decreased funding for capital outlays for new buildings or updated textbooks; and increments or decrements in operational expenditures affecting class size, for example. School politics, like all politics, evolves out of the reality that different people want different things from the schooling process.

The illusion that education is above politics in no way alters the fact that people contend for what they want for schools, just as they do for other important social agencies, such as police departments, fire departments, and social welfare agencies. Perhaps the political fighting is often more gentlemanly and obscured from the clear vision of most people, but it is very real. It goes on in closed or executive sessions of local school boards prior to public meetings when school board and superintendent put up a front of consensus; in "smoke-filled rooms" when state educational organization lobbyists bargain with state legislators for special favors; in the streets of cities and towns when literature for candidates for the school board is passed out by campaign workers; and during meetings in the homes of members of ad hoc committees created to stabilize property taxes by preventing the passage of new bonds in upcoming elections.

Federal officials from the United States Office of Education have political contact with school superintendents who have been slow in obeying federal court orders to desegregate their districts. Political leverage is used to force compliance by withholding federal financial assistance until school districts comply with federal desegregation requirements. Political activity is obviously engaged in when representatives of teachers' unions meet with school boards to consider demands for increased salaries and improved working conditions and when teachers picket and refuse to go back to work. Congress is involved when a bill with implications for future educational spending is being considered. The U.S. Supreme Court hears cases dealing with student claims of loss of First Amendment free-speech rights. These are only a few of the ways in which the politics of education is pursued in American society today. As these examples suggest, educational politics are evident at all three major levels of government in the United States—the local, the state, and the federal.

Educational politics occurs because all people do not share the same educational values. Because American society is pluralistic and undergoing great change, there is no clear consensus about what schooling should be. With the exception of some childless and older people, schooling in America is almost universally believed to be vitally important to the progress of society and to the personal benefit of the youngsters now growing up in it. Differences in the values held by people about formal education tend to produce emotional reactions in individuals who feel that they or their children are affected by this institution.

For instance, members of racial and ethnic minorities want the positive contributions of their popular heroes to be presented to their children and to the children of members of dominant social groups in history textbooks and by classroom teachers. Members of the dominant culture might be offended by textbooks and teachers who break with tradition by presenting too much about newer groups, at the expense of the "true heroes who built America." For example, when a new eighth-grade social studies textbook, *Land of the Free,*[8] was adopted by several states a few years ago, many citizens groups emerged to fight the "un-Americanism" and "excessive" amount of space given to the contributions of blacks and other minorities. In many communities, citizen committees demanded that the new text either be modified or withdrawn from the schools altogether. The issue was highly charged because basic value differences were at stake, or perceived to be so. In West Virginia, angry citizens backed by fundamentalist clergymen attempted to prevent the schools of the state from using certain "un-American," "immoral," and "un-Christian" textbooks in the schools. Sometimes the issues involve school teachers or superintendents and their alleged left-wing interests or activities. In some recent instances, homosexuality of teachers has been the cause for concern. The notion of having a homosexual teacher in charge of little children in elementary school arouses strong feelings in many Americans, because of the unproven presumption that such tendencies will influence the pupils. These examples illustrate the emotionally laden valuational base of school politics.

Interest Groups

Although they have a great deal of concern about schools, most people do little to effectuate desired changes in them or to ensure that schools and their programs remain essentially as they have been in the past.[9] If a particularly volatile issue is brought to the attention of the public, such as a bond proposal for increased spending on schools, they may take the time to vote for or against it. Many bond requests have been turned down by the voters across the country in recent years, as Tables 12–1 and 12–2 show.

Other than voting in bond elections or for school board members—where voter turnout is generally quite low (20 to 30 percent)[10] compared to other local, state, and national elections, the average man or woman in the street *is* part of a silent majority where formal educational affairs are concerned. As a series of recent Gallup Polls of popular attitudes toward education has clearly demonstrated, most people hold definite opinions about what schools and teachers should be doing in such areas as discipline, curriculum, financing, student dress, etc.[11] But the average person is unlikely to do very much about his or her attitudes as an individual, except possibly to call a board member or the superintendent of schools or to complain to his or her child's principal or teacher.[12]

Efforts to implement educational values through political activity—by community members seeking reduced taxes, by professional educators attempting to modify the curriculum, or by people generally interested in education—are usually group, not individual, efforts. In this society, a variety of interest groups engage in the politics of education, as in other human affairs. Those in positions of power rarely listen to a single individual, unless the individual is a representative of a potentially powerful group, such as the local Chamber of Commerce, or unless he or she possesses unusual political clout due to financial or social resources that allow access to key decision makers. Studies of educational power in the 1950s and early 1960s suggest that educational politics, especially in large urban and suburban districts, are run from a base of **power pluralism.** Other communities are controlled by **power elites,** especially small, conservative rural communities.[13] However, few generalizations can be made with great certainty about the precise types of communities possessing elitist power structures or pluralistic ones, since the study of school politics by political scientists and sociologists is still in its infancy.

Numerous special-interest groups at many levels work to implement their particular educational concerns through the political process. One cannot bring about important changes in the educational system solely by working in one's classroom.

Educational interest groups are either permanent, such as parent–teacher associations, or temporary, such as an ad-hoc citizen group established to fight a tax increase. Raywid calls them "legitimate" or "illegitimate," according to the extent to which they abide by three broad sets of rules in making and pressing their claims. These rules are (1) rules of

Table 12–1. Number of Public Elementary and Secondary School Bond Elections Held and Number and Percentage Approved for Fiscal Years 1964–1973

Fiscal year ending June 30	Number of elections—		Approved (in percent)
	Held	Approved	
1964	2,071	1,501	72.5
1965	2,041	1,525	74.7
1966	1,745	1,265	72.5
1967	1,625	1,082	66.6
1968	1,750	1,183	67.6
1969	1,341	762	56.8
1970	1,216	647	53.2
1971'	1,086	507	46.7
1972	1,153	542	47.0
1973	1,273	719	56.5

Irene A. King, U.S. Department of Health, Education, and Welfare, Office of Education, *Bond Sales for Public School Purposes, 1972–1973* (Washington, D.C.: U.S. Government Printing Office, 1974), p. 2.

evidence (is the truth being sincerely sought after and exposed when found?); (2) rules of democracy (is the group open and above board about its motives and methods?); (3) rules of common decency (does the group avoid smear campaigns and slanderous literature?)[14]

Writing primarily about state educational politics, Bailey separates interest groups into two basic types: those more or less pro-school and those in opposition to schools. In the pro-school category he includes (1) educational academics (teachers of teachers) who are very important in initiating debate on many political issues; (2) state educational and political officials (state board members, members of state education departments, governors and legislators, special citizen commissions, etc.), who bargain with lobbyists, pass laws, and issue directives; (3) professional educators (organizations of teachers and of superintendents, principals, board members, etc.); and (4) "surprise" actors, that is, coalitions (usually devised by schoolpersons) of citizens who align with schools for various reasons. "Each group develops quite different characteristics, holds different motives and plays different parts."[15]

According to Bailey, groups tending to oppose public school interests include: (1) the Roman Catholic Church, although this may be changing as increased federal funding for private schools is granted under the auspices of legislation such as the National Defense Education Act of 1958 and the Elementary and Secondary Education Act of 1965; (2) tax-minded business groups such as the state chambers of commerce or units

Table 12–2. Par Value of Public Elementary and Secondary School Bond Issues Proposed in Elections Held, Par Value of Those Approved, and Those Approved as Percent of Proposed for Fiscal Years 1964–1973

Fiscal year ending June 30	Par value of bond issues (in millions of dollars)		Approved (in percent)
	Proposed	Approved	
1964	$2,672	$1,900	71.1
1965	3,129	2,485	79.4
1966	3,560	2,652	74.5
1967	3,063	2,119	69.2
1968	3,740	2,338	62.5
1969	3,913	1,707	43.6
1970	3,285	1,627	49.5
1971	3,337	1,381	41.4
1972	3,102	1,365	44.0
1973	3,988	2,256	56.6

Irene A. King, U.S. Department of Health, Education, and Welfare, Office of Education, *Bond Sales for Public School Purposes, 1972–1973* (Washington, D.C.: U.S. Government Printing Office, 1974), p. 2.

of the National Association of Manufacturers; (3) rural groups—farmers' associations such as the Grange, which tend to oppose increasing state involvement in education; (4) conservative politicians and state officials, whose pressures and exposure in the mass media often prevent additional spending for education; and (5) schoolmen themselves. With regard to the last group, Bailey says:

> *Effective organization is exceptional. Most of the time in most of the states disorder and naivete are the schoolmen's outstanding characteristics...*
> *The number of special educational interests stirs up a vast—and often infuriating—buzzing in a lawmaker's ears. The wily lawmaker finds it easy to ignore educators disunited—or to play one educational group off against another...*
> *Schoolmen have handicapped their own political success by their failure to understand, develop, and use political machinery available within their own ranks.*[16]

Political scientists often cite the following kinds of local groups as especially interested in school politics: local teachers' organizations (largely pro-school except when opposing other school people to improve their status and their working conditions); civic organizations, such as the League of Women Voters (largely pro-school); combinations of school and lay interests, such as the Parent–Teacher Association (largely pro-school and controlled by school administrators); civil rights organizations such as the local branch of the NAACP (largely pro-school, although often in search of reforms in education); local chambers of commerce and branches of the National Association of Manufacturers (often opposed to school financial interests); and ad-hoc groups of budget-minded taxpayers (also generally opposed to increases in school budgets).[17]

The federal level is a relatively new educational political focus that is bound to extend the participation of all types of interest groups, as well as produce situations leading to the creation of new ones. We will undoubtedly continue to observe enlarged interest in educational affairs by major religious organizations, by labor unions, and by civil rights organizations. This has come about as the federal government has stepped further and further into the educational arena, which in the past paid relatively scant attention to Catholic, labor, and minority-group interests. As these interests become more articulate and organize more widely, this society will become more responsive to the educational claims of all groups.

Most of the political interest groups mentioned above are considered legitimate in Raywid's terms because whatever their particular stance on an issue or however critical their attacks on schools and teachers, they usually strive to adhere to the three sets of broad criteria for legitimate interest groups listed earlier: rules of evidence, democracy, and common decency.

Raywid also identified a large number of illegitimate educational interest groups.

> In this country there are approximately a thousand groups that are highly critical of public education. Yet even with a daily heightening of their vocalism in newspapers, books, and magazines, there persists the lethargic assumption that it is the sound of a noisy little group of disgruntled professors, publicists, and admirals. But by virtue of numbers alone, the critics of educational policy and practice are a force to be reckoned with.[18]

Illustrative of the "illegitimate groups" are the American Coalition of Patriotic Societies, the Anti-Communist League of America, the Christian Nationalist Crusade, Defenders of the American Constitution, the Liberty Lobby, and the World Union of Free Enterprise National Socialists formerly headed by Lincoln Rockwell.[19] Each of these groups is concerned with at least one or more of the following conditions that they allege exist in American public schools: subversive textbooks or other unsuitable text material; teacher disloyalty and lack of patriotism; un-Americanism; impractical curricula; immoral beliefs and activities; Progressive educational methods; aims contravening the American tradition or other "improper" educational aims; godlessness in schools; sectarianism in schools; inadequacy of teacher preparation; excessive amounts of money spent on schools or money spent on the wrong things; unsound administrative practices and administrative aimlessness; indifference to sound education or to the American tradition; desire by schools to control society; and domination by anti-intellectuals.[20]

Raywid's study was made shortly after the Cold War period of McCarthyism and the concern for improved educational standards provoked by the launching of Sputnik. Raywid was understandably preoccupied with the far right wing. After her results were published in the early 1960s, another reaction set in against schools, this time led by liberals and the Far Left. Although few, if any, serious studies of left-wing educational organizations have been made, there is little doubt that certain more prominent neo-Marxist or similar groups such as Students for a Democratic Society and the Weathermen, and perhaps some of the more extreme segments of the free school movement have employed "illegitimate" tactics in seeking their ends. Usually, however, the Far Left has not had marked concern for schooling, preferring to concentrate upon economic priorities.

In general, strong left-leaning critics of the schools have made their attacks as individual writers and speakers, not as leaders or followers of organized interest groups. Or, as in the case of the free schoolers, they have elected to separate themselves completely from public school concerns and to seek their educational objectives in previously untilled fields. Most illegitimate school pressure groups have been highly conservative or even reactionary in orientation, rather than liberal or radical in outlook. However, this assertion is not meant to infer that no right-wing groups can be considered legitimate in their tactics or that no left-wing group is illegitimate.

Whatever their basic orientation, illegitimate groups can be extremely damaging to the cause of the public schools in the United States. In a fight governed by strict rules and carefully supervised, an unethical fighter loses points or is disqualified. On the other hand, in a street fight no one expects any rules to be followed, so all contenders at least know what they are getting themselves into before they even start. But in a fight in which no ground rules are established beforehand and one fighter is clean while the other is not, the clean fighter generally loses. American school politics go on without widely known ground rules. Largely because of the myth that schooling is nonpolitical, the rules are highly ambiguous, unlike politics in other spheres of government.

This example can be applied to illegitimate educational interest groups; in their willingness to do anything to win, they are likely to emerge victorious in political conflict ungoverned by well-known and rigidly adhered to norms and laws. Schooling in a transitional society must recognize its political base and establish rules of the game so that all participants know exactly for what and with whom they are fighting.

Teachers should be highly conversant with this crucial dimension of their occupational and, indirectly, of their personal lives, and, through their own interest groups, work legitimately to clarify the rules where they exist vaguely and ambiguously and to create new rules.

Formal Aspects of Control: The Official Structure of Educational Control

Compared to the process of educational politics (the informal aspects of school control), the actual governing structure that organizes education is fairly easy to describe. Students of politics and government both outside and within the ranks of school people have written extensively on this topic, and there is much statistical data available.

The United States Constitution makes no mention of education. This omission was early interpreted to mean that the several states of the union were to be responsible for this particular social enterprise under the "reserved powers" of the states. But long before the Constitution was written, most of the colonies had already evolved a tradition of local control of schools. The tradition of local responsibility for schooling continued after independence and remains with us, although it is increasingly vestigial as more and more states are being called upon to take a more active role in at least the financing of education for equal opportunity of all state citizens. (A precedent-setting case in this regard was California's *Serrano v. Priest* (1971) in which the plaintiff argued successfully at the state level that the local tradition of using the property tax to finance schools prevented children of low-income school districts from obtaining an education equivalent to that offered children in high-income districts.) The vestigial nature of this tradition is more apparent as the federal government becomes more influential as a source of revenue for schools and as a protector of the Constitutional rights of school clients under the First, Fifth, and Fourteenth amendments.

Although most Americans still think the schools operate at a grass-roots level, in actuality they never did. They were and are creatures of the several states that have historically (with the exception of Hawaii which maintains control at the state level) delegated authority over school matters to local communities. This delegated authority is being withdrawn further and further as the constitutional responsibility for education is reinterpreted:

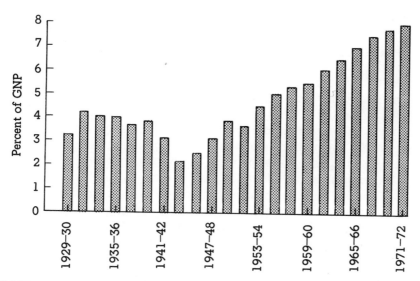

FIGURE 12–2.   *Total Expenditures for Education as Percentage of the Gross National Product for the U.S. (From Kenneth A. Simon and W. Vance Grant, Digest of Educational Statistics [Washington, D.C.: U.S. Government Printing Office, 1973], p. 24.)*

The Constitution of the United States has proved to be a flexible instrument of government in the hands of the executive, legislative, and judicial branches. The Constitution has undergone a great variety of interpretations by the agencies which were created by it. These interpretations have affected the lives of our citizens in ways which could not possibly have been foreseen by the Founding Fathers . . . The school, as a most vital institution in our society, has not escaped these interpretations of its role and function.[21]

The Federal Government and Education

The United States government is divided into three main branches, as are the state and local governments: a legislative branch, an executive branch, and a judicial branch. In recent years each of these branches has made a profound impact upon the formal education institution in our society.

The Legislative Branch.

The Congress hereby finds and declares . . . that the security of the Nation requires the fullest development of the mental resources and technical skills of its young men and women. . . The national interest requires . . . that the federal government give assistance to education for programs which are important to our national defence.[22]

Thus began the preamble to the National Defence Education Act of 1958, an act by the United States Congress passed largely in response to a fear of losing the Cold War created by the launching of the Sputnik a year earlier. Thus, nationalistic concerns for defence were the prime movers of significant educational change. The NDEA was the prelude for federal involvement in education, and specifically set the stage for the massive funding of the Elementary and Secondary Education Act of 1965. According to Sundquist, the impetus given by these two acts multiplied federal expenditures for education "more than ten-fold in a decade— from $375 million in 1958 to an estimated $4.2 billion. The federal share of all expenditures for education by all levels of government had risen during the decade from less than 3 percent to about 10 percent."[23] By 1973 this share had increased to over 10 billion dollars and over 11 percent, as Table 12–3 indicates.

The long-range outlook is for continued increases in the amount and percentage of money spent on education by the federal government, although galloping inflation throughout the 1970s may temporarily threaten education's share of the federal budget.

NDEA authorized grants for loans to college students, language-

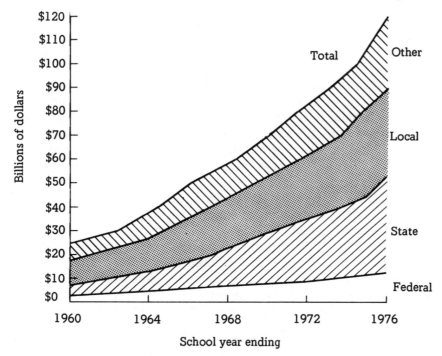

FIGURE 12–3. *Expenditures of Federal, State, and Local Governments on Education (Education Division, Department of Health, Education, and Welfare, The Condition of Education [Washington, D.C.: U.S. Government Printing Office, 1976], p. 27)*

development centers, the preparation of college teachers in areas deemed relevant to national security, such as the sciences and engineering, and the improvement of guidance, counseling, and testing programs.[24] The passage of NDEA created the necessary conditions for "probably the greatest landmark in the history of federal aid to education,"[25] the Elementary and Secondary Education Act of 1965 (ESEA).

Originally conceived during the Kennedy administration and enacted under the Johnson administration, the bill initially contained five titles to which several amendments have been added. The essence of the bill and its titles are summed up by Bailey:

> The positive goals were innovative and exciting: to focus federal attention on the children of poverty, those in greatest need of education, who were seldom getting it; to induce the rubbing of shoulders of educators and non-educators in the search for educational improvements; to create inducement for public and parochial schools to work together; to break down the "fortress school" concept so that schools would serve the larger community before and after hours and around the calendar; to promote research and experimentation in curriculum, method, and educational evaluation.[26]

319

Title I, the heart of the bill, provides for grant money through states to local districts for the purposes of upgrading programs and facilities specifically for "deprived" children. Project Headstart for poor pre-kindergarten children is funded by Title I.

Title II authorizes funds to states for school library resources, textbooks, and other printed instructional materials for use in both public and private (primarily Catholic and Lutheran) elementary and secondary schools. Title III provides for supplementary centers and services such as counseling, remedial instruction, vocational guidance, experimental teaching, creative use of mass media, courses in the creative arts, etc. This title was aimed especially at possible educational reforms. Title IV bypasses the states in its provisions for support of educational research and dissemination projects. Title V provides funds to strengthen state departments of education.[27]

In 1969 two other titles were added, one to provide funds for bilingual education programs for children from homes in which a language other than English (usually Spanish) is spoken, and one for dropout prevention programs. In 1974, Congress approved new ESEA legislation designed (1) to make Title I programs of compensatory education for the "disadvantaged" more equitable by placing greater emphasis on family income and less on aid-to-dependent-children criteria; (2) to consolidate titles of ESEA and NDEA pertaining to aid to libraries, equipment, guidance, counseling, testing, innovative programs, aid to state education departments, dropout prevention, and health and nutrition; (3) to provide new programs for metric, arts, career and consumer education, community schools, women's equality, and "gifted" students; and (4) to provide major new programs concerned with reading and the handicapped.[28]

Table 12–3. Estimated Expenditures of Educational Institutions by Source of Funds for 1967–68 to 1972–73

(Amounts in billions of dollars)

Source of funds, by level of institution and type of control	1967–68		1969–70		1970–71		1971–72		1972–73	
	Amount	Percent	Amount	Percent	Amount	Percent	Amount	Percent	Amount	Percent
1	2	3	4	5	6	7	8	9	10	11
All levels:										
Total public and nonpublic	$57.2	100.0	$70.0	100.0	$76.9	100.0	$83.8	100.0	$90.2	100.0
Federal	6.8	11.9	7.7	11.0	8.4	10.9	9.1	10.8	10.2	11.3
State	16.8	29.4	22.5	32.1	24.8	32.3	27.2	32.5	29.4	32.6
Local	18.6	32.5	21.9	31.3	24.1	31.3	26.3	31.4	27.6	30.6
All other	15.0	26.2	17.9	25.6	19.6	25.5	21.2	25.3	23.0	25.5

Kenneth A. Simon and V. Vance Grant, Office of Education, National Center for Educational Statistics, *Digest of Educational Statistics, 1972* (Washington, D.C.: U.S. Government Printing Office, 1973), p. 22.

The extent of federal involvement in formal education in recent years is indicated by the list of national legislation (in addition to NDEA and ESEA) that is now in effect and is specifically educational in nature. The amounts funded for the year 1973 are also given:

- School assistance in federally affected areas (Indian lands, military bases, etc.): $478,347,000
- Higher Education Act (especially equal opportunity grants and student loans): $1,056,388,000
- Higher Education Facilities Act (especially community colleges): $139,761,000
- Vocational Education Acts: $463,652,000
- Educational improvement for the handicapped (including teacher education and recruitment): $113,211,000
- Research and development: $150,537,000
- Adult basic education: $57,480,000
- Civil rights activities: $19,000,000
- Land-grant colleges: $2,600,000
- Education revenue sharing: $110,000,000
- Special foreign currency program for training, research and study (grants to American institutions overseas): $3,627,000
- Educational broadcasting facilities: $12,152,000
- Follow-through (for former Headstart pupils): $34,700,000
- Emergency school assistance: $381,000,000
- Office of Education salaries and expenses: $74,380,000.[29]

In summary, Bailey says:

> *The fact is that education has now become a large element in the congressional pork barrel... Educational interests are far-flung; educators are frequently powerful public opinion formers; the costs of education are mounting; ... Every senator and most congressmen have both elementary and secondary schools and the public or private institutions of higher education in their bailiwicks. There is no reason to believe that local protests against higher levies on property and sales taxes for education will diminish, or that states will move toward massively increased revenues for education with any delight. The number of local, state, and university lobbies in Washington is mounting in almost direct proportion to the increase in federal spending for Great Society programs.[30]*

The Executive Branch and the U.S. Office of Education.   If the special educational role of Congress is to pass new legislation, the role of the U. S. Office of Education is, especially since ESEA of 1965, to administer federally legislated programs and often to help prepare legislation for congressional enactment.

Prior to 1950, however, the U.S. Office of Education (USOE) was a

Table 12–4. Summary of Expenditures for Public Elementary and Secondary Education, by Purpose, from 1919–20 to 1969–70

Purpose of expenditure	School Year			
	1919–20	1929–30	1939–40	1949–50
1	2	3	4	5
	AMOUNTS IN THOUSANDS OF DOLLARS			
Total expenditures, all schools	$1,036,151	$2,316,790	$2,344,049	$5,837,043
Current expenditures, all schools	864,397	1,853,377	1,955,166	4,722,288
Public elementary and secondary schools	861,120	1,843,552	1,941,799	4,687,274
Administration	36,752	78,680	91,571	220,050
Instruction	632,556	1,317,727	1,403,285	3,112,340
Plant operation	115,707	216,072	194,365	427,587
Plant maintenance	30,432	78,810	73,321	214,164
Fixed charges	9,286	50,270	50,116	261,469
Other school services	36,387	101,993	129,141	451,663
Summer schools	(2)	(2)	(2)	(2)
Adult education	3,277	9,825	13,367	35,614
Community colleges	(2)	(2)	(2)	(2)
Community services	(1)	(1)	(1)	(1)
Capital outlay	153,543	370,878	257,974	1,014,176
Interest	18,212	92,536	130,909	100,578
	PERCENTAGE DISTRIBUTION			
Total expenditures, all schools	100.0	100.0	100.0	100.0
Current expenditures, all schools	83.4	80.0	83.4	80.9
Public elementary and secondary schools	83.1	79.6	82.8	80.3
Administration	3.5	3.4	3.9	3.8
Instruction	61.0	56.9	59.9	53.3
Plant operation	11.2	9.3	8.3	7.3
Plant maintenance	2.9	3.4	3.1	3.7
Fixed charges	.9	2.2	2.1	4.5
Other school services	3.5	4.4	5.5	7.7
Summer schools	(2)	(2)	(2)	(2)
Adult education	.3	.4	.6	.6
Community colleges	(2)	(2)	(2)	(2)
Community services	(1)	(1)	(1)	(1)
Capital outlay	14.8	16.0	11.0	17.4
Interest	1.8	4.0	5.6	1.7

Table 12–4. *Continued*

	School Year					
	1959–60	**1961–62**	**1963–64**	**1965–66**	**1967–68**	**1969–70**
	6	7	8	9	10	11
AMOUNTS IN THOUSANDS OF DOLLARS						
	$15,613,255	$18,373,339	$21,324,993	$26,248,026	$32,977,182	$40,683,428
	12,461,955	14,923,363	17,645,973	21,701,584	27,743,581	34,853,578
	12,329,389	14,729,270	17,218,446	21,053,280	26,877,162	34,217,773
	528,408	648,372	744,770	937,646	1,249,028	1,606,646
	8,350,738	10,016,280	11,750,469	14,445,484	18,375,762	23,270,158
	1,085,036	1,283,085	1,445,845	1,762,745	2,074,638	2,537,257
	422,586	477,346	539,186	623,581	789,760	974,941
	909,323	1,077,278	1,343,684	1,700,965	2,388,286	3,266,920
	1,033,297	1,226,909	1,394,492	1,582,858	1,999,689	2,561,856
	13,263	21,326	28,994	70,310	105,894	106,481
	26,858	29,536	74,872	120,874	151,864	128,778
	34,492	71,252	245,433	301,545	390,069	138,813
	57,953	71,979	78,229	155,575	218,592	261,731
	2,661,786	2,862,153	2,977,976	3,754,862	4,255,791	4,659,072
	489,514	587,823	701,044	791,580	977,810	1,170,782
PERCENTAGE DISTRIBUTION						
	100.0	100.0	100.0	100.0	100.0	100.0
	79.8	81.2	82.7	82.7	84.1	85.7
	79.0	80.2	80.7	80.2	81.5	84.1
	3.4	3.5	3.5	3.6	3.8	3.9
	53.5	54.5	55.1	55.0	55.7	57.2
	6.9	7.0	6.8	6.7	6.3	6.2
	2.7	2.6	2.5	2.4	2.4	2.4
	5.8	5.9	6.3	6.5	7.2	8.0
	6.6	6.8	6.5	6.0	6.1	6.3
	.1	.1	.1	.3	.3	.3
	.2	.2	.4	.5	.5	.3
	.2	.4	1.2	1.1	1.2	.3
	.4	.4	.4	.6	.7	.6
	17.0	15.6	14.0	14.3	12.9	11.5
	3.1	3.2	3.3	3.0	3.0	2.9

Kenneth A. Simon and V. Vance Grant, U.S. Department of Health, Education, and Welfare, Office of Education, National Center for Educational Statistics, *Digest of Educational Statistics, 1972* (Washington, D.C.: U.S. Government Printing Office, 1973), p. 63.

rather minor government agency, chiefly involved in accumulating and disseminating educational statistics, preparing reports, and providing consulting services to state and local educational agencies.[31] Between 1950 and 1965, the Office began to grow and change markedly as a result of Cold War interests in national defense that culminated in passage of the NDEA in 1958 and of the Great Society movement of Kennedy and later Johnson.

With the drafting of legislation to eliminate poverty and provide federal aid to education that became the ESEA of 1965, the USOE, under the leadership of U.S. Commissioner of Education, Francis Keppel, began to participate actively. Once the legislation was passed, the USOE had to administer it, a job requiring major alterations in its structure, inaugurated under the leadership of Keppel.

Today the USOE is an important component of the huge federal bureaucracy. It has an annual operating budget for salaries, expenses, and technical services of over seventy-five million dollars.[32] Although still a department of the United States Department of Health, Education, and Welfare, it has been suggested that USOE has grown so much that it should become a cabinet department. Fifty states and thousands of individual school districts depend on the USOE for financial support based largely on grants-in-aid on which they rely more and more at a time of increasing reluctance by local taxpayers to meet the spiraling costs of constructing and operating schools (see Table 12–4).

The USOE has enormous leverage which it uses to regulate and possibly alter the course of formal child and youth education. The occupational lives of prospective teachers will probably be increasingly influenced by actions taken by key decision makers in the United States Office of Education.

The National Institute of Education (NIE) was created in 1972 by the Nixon administration to provide national leadership and support to educational research and development. Thus far, the NIE has funded grants in five priority areas: essential skills, such as reading; improving the productivity of the nation's education system; career education; resolving local educational problems; and "cultural diversity."

The Judicial Branch.   The third major branch of the federal government that has affected formal education significantly in recent years has been the judicial branch, notably the United States Supreme Court, the ultimate authority in all matters of law in American society.

In our system of checks and balances, it is the role of the federal courts to try individual or **class action** cases in light of constitutional provisions and precedents set in previous cases. Although the Constitution makes no specific reference to educational guarantees, some of its provisions insist upon certain basic civil rights for all citizens, including teachers and children. The Tenth Amendment, which reserves certain powers for the states, is superceded in cases involving civil rights. Most of the cases involving educational issues in recent years have concerned some question relating to First Amendment (freedom of speech, press, and religion) or Fourteenth Amendment (due process and equal protection) rights.

Since the end of World War II, the U.S. Supreme Court and the lower federal courts have rendered a number of landmark decisions in the educational realm. These cases include *Brown v. Board of Education of Topeka, Kansas* (1954), which held that racially segregated schools violated the Equal Protection clause of the Fourteenth Amendment; *Tinker v. Des Moines Independent School District* (1969), which upheld the First Amendment right of freedom of expression by students; and *Engel, et al. v. Vitale et al.* (1962), *School District of Abington Township, Pennsylvania, et al. v. Schempp, et al.,* and *Murray, et al. v. Curlett* (1963), all of which ruled that school prayer and school religious ceremonies were unconstitutional.[33] These precedent-setting decisions have far-reaching implications for the quality of schooling and the rights of school clients and teachers. They also emphasize the growing influence of the federal government upon all aspects of education.

The State Government and Education

The three levels of government in our society—national, state, and local —are organized in quite similar ways for educational purposes (*see* Table 12–5).

Each state has a **bicameral** legislature that passes increasingly detailed laws pertaining to education. The laws are conceived within the framework of the state constitution and federal constitutional limitations. These laws are usually contained in a rather ponderous state education code, which limits permissible activities in schools throughout the state. Most of the legislature's members, other than a few key figures, are usually powerless, in comparison with members of the United States Congress. They tend to lack great prestige and coordination.[34]

The state governor, as chief executive at the state level, is often extremely powerful, although, for example, if he or she is a Democrat who comes into conflict with a rural-dominated legislature, this power may be somewhat reduced. In most cases, the governor is the key to the extensive bargaining that goes on between spokespersons lobbying for organized educational interests, such as the state teachers association or union or the state chamber of commerce. Bargaining between interest groups and elected or appointed officials is the quintessence of state educational politics.

Table 12–5.   Organization of Educational Policy Making in the United States

	NATIONAL	STATE	LOCAL
General Legislative	Congress	State Legislature	Common Council
Educational Legislative	President	State School Board	Local School Board
Executive	President	Governor	Mayor
Administrative	HEW-USOE	State Dept. of Education	School Superintendent
Judicial	Supreme Court	State Supreme Court	Federal or State District Court
Professional Interests	NEA [and AFT]	State Teachers' Association [Union]	Local PTA
Other Private Interests	U.S. Catholic Conference	State Chamber of Commerce	John Birch Society Chapter

Adapted from Stephen K. Bailey and Edith K. Mosher, *ESEA: The Office of Education Administers a Law* (Syracuse, N.Y.: Syracuse University Press, 1968), p. 232. By permission of the publisher.

The governor usually appoints a comparatively weak and titular state board of education to legitimize the interests of the party in power at a given time. The state board of education is charged ostensibly with encouraging minimum standards for programs of public education in the state, and sometimes with administering the licensing of school personnel and apportionment of state funds to local school districts.

A state department of education is somewhat comparable to the USOE, but it is smaller in scale and comprised mainly of professionals, some of whom have ties to the governor and key legislators. It is responsible for implementing state educational policy based on legislation and administrative rulings, particularly in regard to state financial aid to local districts. State departments of education have been gradually strengthened in recent years, especially through grant funds based upon Title V of the Elementary and Secondary Education Act. Their role has also increased because local levels have greater problems obtaining adequate funding in an inflationary economy.

The state education department is headed by an elected or appointed state superintendent of public instruction, or more often a commissioner of education, who is normally a professional educator.

In addition to the official structure of educational governance in most states, special commissions of important citizens and occasionally educators are often appointed by the governors, legislative party leaders, or even state superintendents of education. Their major functions are to act as a bridge between various actors in the arena of state educational politics and to explain to the public politicians' positions on sensitive areas and issues, such as financing of schools and curricular or personnel reforms.

The state supreme court has jurisdiction over questions of legality at that level. Of course, its decisions are guided by the state constitution and its education code and by federal constitutional requirements, as defined by the United States Supreme Court. An important example of state court influence over education was the 1971 case of *Serrano v. Priest* in California. Although the precedent of this case was later offset by an adverse ruling by the U.S. Supreme Court in *San Antonio Independent School District v. Rodriguez* (1973), since the 1971 *Serrano* case, many of the newly passed state laws give a more realistic basic level of funding for all children in the state, not merely those who are fortunate enough to live in wealthy districts. Guthrie says:

> *Despite the April, 1973 Supreme Court decision in Rodriguez v. San Antonio, substantial school reforms are likely throughout the remainder of the 1970s. The school expenditure and property tax inequalities uncovered by the courts have received widespread publicity. Public officials and laymen now realize that previously unquestioned school-finance labels such as "equalization aid" and "minimum foundation programs" are hollow rhetoric; most state school-finance arrangements have never provided equality or satisfactory minimum school programs.*[35]

And, according to Berke, "The state courts have and will increasingly become the forum in which constitutional litigation will proceed."[36]

Public elementary and secondary education in the United States is clearly the legal responsibility of the state. Most of the money collected for the support of schools does still come from local revenue sources, particularly the property tax. However, the role of the states in governing and financing education will become increasingly important, as will the role of the national government, while the delegated role of the local districts will become smaller and less significant. Since state educational politics and government are the most complex, amateurish, and disordered of the three levels at the present time,[37] it would seem that as this level of control becomes increasingly visible in the future, persons concerned with educational governance should take a meaningful look at its structure, with a view to possibly reforming it in pursuit of more effective functioning.

The Local Government and Education

Local communities still have a part to play in the determination of their children's educational fates. Most of the money spent on education in the United States still comes from local community coffers, and much of the authority to make decisions about the way in which these funds will be spent continues to be delegated to the 15,000 local districts across the land. In many ways, education is still a grassroots affair, even though it seems to be becoming less so every year. It will be a long time before public education in the United States is entirely removed from local control, if ever. Therefore, it is important to understand how this level of control operates, since most of what a teacher does will be determined at least immediately by events and people at the local level—where he or she performs daily work with youngsters.

The School Board.   Local school districts are the results of custom reaching back to colonial days and of special state constitutional arrangements made in the eighteenth and nineteenth centuries to facilitate the administration of schooling in this society.[38] Their geographical boundaries may or may not be coterminous with those of surrounding municipalities. Often, they are, of course; school districts such as Cleveland have boundaries the same as those of the city proper. School districts are usually governed by locally elected representatives of the people in the district. These lay representatives constitute a local school board that possesses the lawful authority to meet and make broad policy decisions concerning personnel, programs, and financing of local schools.

School board members are officially elected on a nonpartisan basis to serve all the people of a community, not special interests. However, the behind-the-scenes machinations required to develop coalitions strong enough to get a candidate into office may often mean that *unofficially* partisanship is an integral part of school board election campaigns. Study after study following George Count's seminal effort in the 1920s[39] shows that there is unequal influence among citizens in school matters, as in other political affairs. Businessmen tend to hold most of the positions on local school boards, followed by professionals, such as physicians, then by well-to-do housewives and farmers, and other representatives of middle-class America. In large cities, representatives of labor, of minority groups, and occasionally of formal education may also serve on school

boards. Affluent businessmen have been moving away from central cities to suburban bedroom communities, where they may become involved in suburban school politics.

The real power of school boards to make important policy decisions on their own has apparently been dwindling over the years as more and more boards have been forced to recognize the increasing complexity of educational matters and the attendant need for expertise to arrive at decisions. In some small rural districts with strong cultural traditions and great social stability school boards may still make important decisions on their own.[40] But in most modern urban and suburban communities, school boards have gradually come to play less active roles in school governance than is commonly recognized. They allow major decisions to be made by relatively highly paid school superintendents and their staffs of professional administrative experts.[41] Sociologist Norman Kerr says that most

> school boards chiefly perform the function of legitimating the policies of the school system to the community, rather than representing the various segments of the community to the school administration, especially with regard to the educational program (with which board members tend to possess the least familiarity and understanding). This unintended func-

tion of school boards may be viewed as an organizational defence which counteracts the threat to the school system's institutional security inherent in local control by laymen.[42]

According to Kerr and others, school boards generally do not set policy and then hire school superintendents to execute their policies. Rather, the reverse process holds; school boards hire school superintendents, often from outside the community, who are professional experts in the field of formal education. They set policy for the community's school system. Once a school board is reasonably certain of the superintendent's willingness to fit into the prevailing patterns of the system, it tends to follow his advice on most educational matters.

The public sees the board operating in relative consensus at regularly scheduled open meetings, but the *real* decision making, which is led by the superintendent, normally goes on in closed, or executive, sessions. Here, the superintendent presents a budget that his central office staff has drawn up, tells the board who should be hired, what kinds of programs should be implemented, and so forth. The relatively great power of the modern school superintendent, in relation to boards of education and lower administrative staff has been studied by Rosenthal in five major cities. Although these cities are not necessarily completely representative of the country, the results obtained by Rosenthal are at least indicative of the key role that superintendents often play in making local educational policy. These results are summarized in tables 12–6 and 12–7.

The School Superintendent.   The role of the superintendent behind-the-scenes places him in a rather precarious position vis à vis the board members with whom he must get along in order to retain his job and with teachers whose militancy has been growing in recent years. As the top professional in the system, the superintendent is expected not only to be an agent of the board, but also an educational leader and morale builder of the personnel working in the system.[43] As American teachers increasingly identify themselves as professional labor, in fundamental opposition to management (which includes school administrators and board members), the problem of with whom the superintendent shall side in conflicts between labor and management becomes intense. The growing precariousness of especially the urban school superintendent's position is illustrated in the following satirical composite of his typical day, compiled by a sympathizer with his plight.

6:00 AM   Rises, drinks coffee. Calms wife.
6:45 AM   Arrives at office. Reviews appointment calendar. Scans security report of yesterday's bomb threats, vandalism, fires, and student shakedowns. Dictates memos and letters.

Table 12–6.   Relative Power of the Superintendency Compared to the Board of Education

Policy Domain	New York	Boston	Chicago	San Francisco	Atlanta
Salary	−0.20	−0.55	+0.30	−0.65	+0.05
Personnel	+0.44	+0.05	+0.83	+0.33	+0.40
Curriculum	+0.74	+0.58	+1.03	+0.61	+0.52
School System Organization	+0.04	−0.05	+0.44	+0.12	+0.24

A plus indicates that the difference between the relative power indices of the board of education and the superintendent runs in the direction of the superintendent; a minus indicates the opposite.

Alan Rosenthal, *Pedagogues and Power: Teacher Groups in School Politics* (Syracuse, N.Y.: Syracuse University Press, 1969), p. 141. By permission of the publisher.

Table 12–7.   Relative Power of the Superintendency Compared to the Administrative Buraucracy

Policy Domain	New York	Boston	Chicago	San Francisco	Atlanta
Salary	+0.88	+0.10	+1.57	+1.21	+0.87
Personnel	+0.42	+0.23	+0.72	+0.32	+0.70
Curriculum	+0.03	+0.16	+0.32	+0.43	+0.28
School System Organization	+0.43	+0.26	+0.72	+0.64	+0.62

A plus indicates that the difference between the relative power indices of the superintendent and the administrative bureaucracy runs in the direction of the superintendent.

Alan Rosenthal, *Pedagogues and Power: Teacher Groups in School Politics* (Syracuse, N.Y.: Syracuse University Press, 1969), p. 142. By permission of the publisher.

7:30 AM	Has breakfast with teacher association salary committee, which demands 20% increase for next year.
8:30 AM	Meets with assistant superintendents on budget problems.
9:00 AM	Meets with teen-age militants who display switchblades when he refuses to reinstate a pal of theirs.
10:00 AM	Meets with parent group, which calls for his resignation on the ground that he is a Communist because students are reading *1984* and *Brave New World*.
10:30 AM	Meets with a disgruntled architect who failed to get new high school job.
11:00 AM	Answers 10 urgent phone calls from news media.
12:00 PM	Meets with school board president who wants answers to a dozen questions.
12:30 PM	Has lunch with labor leaders, who protest low salaries of lunchroom workers.

1:30 PM   Meets with chairman of bond campaign committee, who fears taxpayers' revolt.

2:00 PM   Meets with PTA leaders who demand new junior high school.

2:30 PM   Meets with school board in executive session on next year's budget; also considers case of the beautiful art teacher whose miniskirt is out of bounds, according to her principal. Matter tabled indefinitely.

3:30 PM   Attends open board meeting, where he is insulted, in turn, by a mother whose boy was expelled for selling dope and threatening a vice-principal with a revolver; by the minister of an obscure sect, who wants hymns sung at every student assembly; by a taxpayer, who objects to administrators' "high" salaries; and another who objects to hiring architects to plan new school buildings.

5:00 PM   Returns to office with board member, who objects to his son's football coach.

5:30 PM   Dictates letters.

6:00 PM   Meets with a father, whose son has been beaten up by another student a half mile away from school. Parent punches superintendent in jaw. Parent is thrown out of office.

6:30 PM   Attends sports winter banquet. Makes brief remarks on fair play and importance of keeping fit.

8:00 PM   Attends a PTA carnival at an elementary school. Wins two goldfish.

9:30 PM   Enters car in parking lot. Windshield broken.

10:00 PM   Arrives home. Answers "hate" calls until 10:30, then pulls phone from jack.

10:30 PM   Has Scotch and water. Reads *Phi Delta Kappan*.

11:00 PM   Goes to bed. Sleeps fitfully.*

To sum up this section, educational governance at the local community level centers largely around the activities of two sets of key actors: (1) elected lay board members who require advice from professionals, and (2) the superintendent who works with the school board to accomplish what he and his professional colleagues at large and in the community believe is warranted and possible—given prevailing local conditions and changing external realities. In order to accomplish their ends, the school board and professional educators (the superintendent and his staff of administrators) try to achieve

> a consensus among interested parties prior to official and public confrontations at school board meetings. As a result, the politics of education has traditionally been a politics of low visibility and informal agreement. School district-wide discussion and debate of educational issues, es-

---

* From Carroll Hanson, "In the Eye of the City," *Phi Delta Kappan* (October 1970). Reprinted by permission.[44]

pecially discussion on the values to be emphasized or de-emphasized by the schools, are discouraged because of the characteristic consensus politics of education.[45]

But sometimes discussion of values cannot be contained within the internal, informal mechanisms developed by superintendents and board members. A current example of loss of control over educational policy-making at this level is desegregation of schools. The federal government, acting through HEW and its Office of Education, now requires that schools in racially mixed communities substantially desegregate their schools. To accomplish school desegregation by means of busing offends many people, including parents of school children who sincerely believe in the neighborhood school concept, a long-held tradition in American society. As a result of the controversial nature of desegregation, superintendents and boards are finding themselves at the center of deep social tensions and conflicts. They often fear that their decisions and actions will hurt them, if the public strongly objects. Consequently, boards and superintendents sometimes fail to act at all, until backed to the wall by HEW, and then often do only the minimum required by that agency. Since school superintendents often have a great deal more to lose in the way of salaries and future career opportunities by coming out vocally in favor of desegregation (than do most school board members who are not paid for their school work), many school superintendents have become merely administrative agents of boards when controversial public issues have arisen. This leaves the center of public attention to the community's officially elected leaders and, at least temporarily, validates the traditional belief that schools are controlled by the citizenry.

In more stable times, superintendents and board members operate, based upon a model of board legitimation of professional decision making that is illustrated in Figure 12–4.

Why Should Teachers Be Aware of the Political Aspects of Education?

Next to students, for whom systems of education are established, teachers are the central figures in the educational process. Although some extremists have been urging in recent years that students do not need teachers in order to learn, most young and inexperienced people need some guidance in the learning process from older, more experienced human beings, if only to help them locate resources in the environment with which to help themselves.

According to research and discussions with prospective and prac-

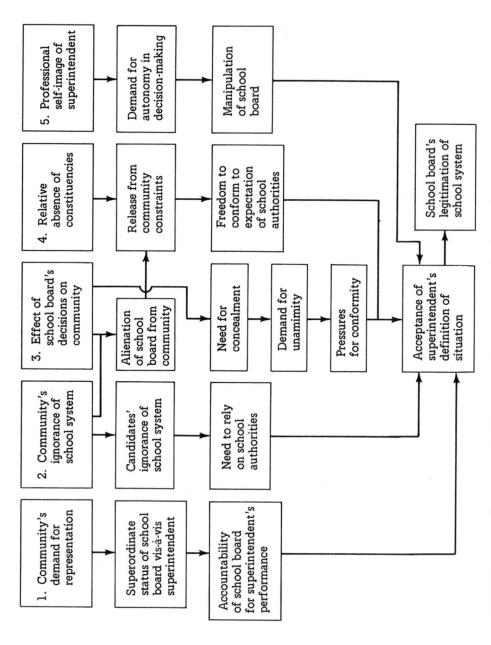

FIGURE 12–4. Summary of Influences That Convert School Boards into Legitimating Agencies [From Norman D. Kerr, "The School Board as an Agency of Legitimation," Sociology of Education 38 [1964]: 58. Reprinted with permission.]

ticing teachers, many American teachers believe the myth that schooling is a nonpolitical affair.[46] They think that all they have to do is carry out the will of "higher" authorities, and the children with whom they work in the classroom will somehow turn out to be good citizens and successful workers. In placing their faith so naively in the good judgment of these "higher" authorities, however, school teachers may directly help to sustain an outmoded system of education.

Furthermore, by their unquestioning acceptance of a consensus view of educational control, teachers may unwittingly allow themselves to become dependent upon others in the educational system for advances in their salaries and improvements in their working conditions. Whenever individuals rely exclusively upon the good will of others for their welfare, they take a chance that the others actually possess the generosity and broad vision that they may appear to possess. In a secondary society such as ours is, where personal contact within institutions is minimized, this becomes an especially great problem. In the case of teachers, their welfare may have been materially improved less than that of others in society because they have not successfully used the political process to demand improvements in salaries and working conditions. This is a possibility that might be worth exploring in depth as you progress with your studies in the foundations of education.

Once you have seen through the defeating myth of nonpoliticalization of schooling and have begun to comprehend how the myth desensitizes teachers to objective diagnosis of some of their students' *genuine learning* needs, you have a reasonable chance to go forward realistically on behalf of the ideal interests of your students and yourself.

Armed with the realization that sophisticated interest groups possess political clout in this society, you can, if you wish, become part of organized interest groups now in the process of developing political power.

Significant learning occurs in environments that nourish freedom of inquiry and speaking of one's mind from the earliest years. This is the kind of environment that ideally an open political structure should be. You can, if you desire, work outside of class with others to unlock the educational control system, and in class to reflect the opened system by releasing your students from constraints of obsolete rules and traditions that inhibit divergent thinking and the expression of personal feelings, both so important to authentic learning.

Aside from realizing the necessity to become organized with fellow teachers on behalf of yourself and your students and to reflect a truly democratic conception of the learning process within your own classroom, the acknowledgment that formal education is a highly political endeavor may simply help make you more sure of who you are and where you stand in relation to others concerned with education. A liberal education is said to help emancipate individuals from unjustifiable convention and tradition so that they may pursue their varied objectives in life with greater intelligence and autonomy. Is it conceivable that one of the most liberalizing educations any teacher (or lay citizen, for that matter) can receive at present is an education concerned about how social life is controlled, by whom, and why?

Summary

Americans have historically been encouraged to believe that formal education is, or should be, above politics. This belief is a myth that confuses the entire issue of control and authority over public schooling. Control and authority are almost always gained through power struggles involving campaigning and bargaining between "legitimate" and "illegitimate" interest groups with opposing values. The struggle for power in the field of education is no exception, although this struggle is clouded by the widespread acceptance of the myth that school affairs are nonpolitical by teachers, parents, and other people concerned with schooling.

The struggle for power over public education in the United States takes place largely within the organized structure of our three levels of government: the federal level, where the Congress, the U.S. Office of

Education, and the Supreme Court have become more active and influential since the 1950s; the state level, which is legally responsible for public education in this society and where intensive bargaining by organized interests goes on between legislators, the relatively powerful office of governor, and state boards, departments of education, and special commissions; and the local community level, which is delegated authority by the state to administer school districts, an authority increasingly questioned and compromised. The politics and governance of schools at the local level are largely the domain of lay school boards elected to determine policy locally and, particularly, of the professional experts hired as agents of the boards to superintend the district schools and to prepare the annual budget.

In a transitional period of history such as the present, school teachers need to possess a keen and realistic awareness and understanding of the political nature of educational authority. They can thereby participate actively and successfully in efforts to increase the responsiveness of the school to the changing learning requirements of students and also upgrade their own occupational status.

Related Concepts

bicameral   Referring to a legislature with two branches, such as the U.S. House of Representatives and the U.S. Senate

class action   A law suit filed on behalf of several individuals possessing a common grievance such as a group of disgruntled taxpayers

power elitism   A situation in which political power and government authority are not widely distributed in a social system, but rather possessed by a few influentials operating informally and outside of the formal government structure

power pluralism   A situation in which political power and government authority are distributed fairly evenly among a variety of individual groups in a social system, according to their respective interests and formal positions

Suggested Activity

In today's world, it is important that educators keep abreast of the developments affecting the educational institution. Most educational news is reported in daily newspapers. Make it a point to spend some time each day searching for information in newspapers about influential court decisions, legislation, new policies and programs in your community's schools, demands by educational interest groups, and other events related to education. You can begin to keep your own record of news items by compiling a scrapbook of current events in education.

References and Notes

1. *The Fresno Bee* (Nov. 9, 1970), p. 16A.

2. Lawrence Iannaccone and Frank W. Lutz, *Politics, Power and Policy: The Governing of Local School Districts* (Columbus, Ohio: Charles E. Merrill Publishing Company, 1970), pp. 34, 35.

3. Richard Pratte, *The Public School Movement: A Critical Study* (New York: David McKay Company, 1973), pp. 156, 157.

4. Iannaccone and Lutz, *Politics, Power and Policy*, pp. 14, 15.

5. For an excellent discussion of the functions of school boards and superintendents, *see* Norman D. Kerr, "The School Board as an Agency of Legitimation," *Sociology of Education* 38 (1964): 34–59.

6. *See* Roscoe Martin, "School Government," in Michael W. Kirst, ed., *The Politics of Education at the Local, State and Federal Levels* (Berkeley, Calif.): McGutchan Publishing Corp., 1970), pp. 146–66.

7. Roscoe Martin, *Government and the Suburban School* (Syracuse, N.Y.: Syracuse University Press, 1962), p. 63.

8. John Caughey, *Land of the Free* (Pasadena, Calif.: Franklin Publications, 1965).

9. Martin, *Government and the Suburban School*, pp. 54, 55.

10. Marilyn Gittell, T. Edward Hollander, and William S. Vincent, "Fiscal Status and School Policy Making in Six Large School Districts," in Kirst, *Politics of Education*, pp. 60–67.

11. Stanley Elam, ed. *The Gallup Polls of Attitudes Toward Education 1969–1973* (Bloomington, Ind.: Phi Delta Kappa, 1973).

12. Martin, *Government and the Suburban School*, pp. 55, 56.

13. Floyd Hunter, *Community Power Structure: A Study of Decision Makers* (Chapel Hill: University of North Carolina Press, 1953); Robert Dahl, *Modern Political Analysis* (Englewood Cliffs, N.J.: Prentice-Hall, 1963).

14. Mary Anne Raywid, *The Axe-Grinders: Critics of Our Public Schools* (New York: Macmillan, 1962), pp. 22–24.

15. Stephen K. Bailey, Robert T. Frost, Paul E. Marsh, and Robert C. Wood, *Schoolmen and Politics: A Study of State Aid to Education in the Northeast* (Syracuse, N.Y.: Syracuse University Press, 1962), p. 23.

16. *Ibid.*, pp. 52, 53, 55, 56.

17. Gittell, Hollander, and Vincent, "Fiscal Status," pp. 33–73.

18. Raywid, *Axe-Grinders*, p. 3.

19. *Ibid.*, pp. 13–17.

20. *Ibid.*

21. Daniel Selakovich, *The Schools and American Society*, 2nd ed. (Lexington, Mass.: Ginn and Co., 1973), p. 139.

22. Quoted in James L. Sundquist, *Politics and Policy: The Eisenhower, Kennedy, and Johnson Years* (Washington, D.C.: The Brookings Institution, 1968), pp. 179, 180.

23. Sundquist, *Politics and Policy*, pp. 216, 217. Center for Educational Statistics, *Digest of Educational Statistics, 1972* (Washington: U.S. Government Printing Office, 1973), p. 22.

24. Kenneth A. Simon and Martin M. Frankel, U.S. Department of Health, Education, and Welfare, Education Division, Office of Education, National Center for Educational Statistics, *Projections of Educational Statistics to 1981–82* (Washington, D.C.: U.S. Government Printing Office, 1972), p. 179.

25. Stephen K. Bailey, "The Office of Education and the Education Act of 1965," in Kirst, *Politics of Education*, p. 357.

26. *Ibid.*, p. 364.

27. *Ibid.*, pp. 364–66.

28. George Neill, "Washington Report," *Phi Delta Kappan* 56 (September 1974): 80.

29. Simon and Frankel, *Projections*, pp. 177–79.

30. Bailey, "Office of Education," p. 380.

31. *United States Government Organizations Manual 1965–1966* (Washington, D.C.: U.S. Government Printing Office, 1965), p. 254.

32. Simon and Frankel, *Projections*, p. 179.

33. *See* James W. Noll and Sam P. Kelly, eds., *Foundations of Education in America: An Anthology of Major Thoughts and Significant Actions* (New York: Harper & Row, 1970), pp. 447–59; and Richard L. Berkman, "Students in Court: Free Speech and the Functions of Schooling in America," *Harvard Educational Review* 40 (November 1970): 567–95.

34. Phillip Moneypenny, "A Political Analysis of Structures for Educational Policy Making," in William P. McLure and Van Miller, eds., *Government of Education for Adequate Policy Making* (Urbana: Bureau of Educational Research, College of Education, University of Illinois, 1960), p. 7.

35. James W. Guthrie, "School Finance Reform: Acceptable Remedies for *Serrano*," *School Review* 82 (February 1974): 207.

36. Joel S. Berke, "Recent Adventures of State School Finance: A Saga of Rocket Ships and Glider Planes," *School Review* 82 (February 1974): 192.

37. *See*, for instance, Bailey, et al., *Schoolmen and Politics;* and Lawrence Iannaccone, *State Politics and Education* (New York: The Center for Applied Research in Education. Published by CARE, Inc., 1967).

38. Iannaccone and Lutz, *Politics, Power and Policy*, pp. 8–11.

39. George Counts, *The Social Composition of Boards of Education* (Chicago: University of Chicago Press, 1927).

40. Iannaccone and Lutz, *Politics, Power and Policy*, pp. 29–51.

41. *Ibid.*

42. Kerr, "School Board as an Agency of Legitimation," p. 35.

43. Educational Policies Commission, *The Unique Role of the Superintendent of Schools* (Washington: National Education Association, 1965).

44. Carroll Hanson, "In the Eye of the City," *Phi Delta Kappan* (October 1970): 116–17.

45. Iannaccone and Lutz, *Politics, Power, and Policy*, p. 20.

46. According to some, the political realities of public education are especially apt to be resisted by women, who presently make up over 70 percent of the teachers in schools below the college level. In the words of one woman writer, "Women are generally more disapproving of or passive toward the processes by which conflicts are generated or exposed, debated, and resolved, than are men." (Geraldine Jonich Clifford, *The Shape of American Education* [Englewood Cliffs, N.J.: Prentice-Hall, 1975], p. 26). Let us hope that the Feminist movement will influence the women who work in schools so that in the years to come they will become more actively engaged in political action.

13

Challenges by Teachers to Traditional Authority

Not so very long ago, boards of education and school administrators from the superintendent to the school principal, acting as agents for the board, told teachers what to do inside and outside the classroom, and teachers did what they were told. In the brief span of time since 1961, the year that New York City teachers first voted to be solely represented in their dealings with school officials by a union—the United Federation of Teachers (UFT)*—domination over the lives of teachers both within the classroom and without by external power groups has declined considerably. The civil rights of teachers are being respected, and their occupational and personal status has risen significantly.

Changing Expectations of American Teachers

Consider some of the expectations most modern teachers take for granted, as contrasted with what their counterparts of about one hundred years ago might have been allowed to expect.

The Right to Marry and Raise a Family. The great majority of contemporary school teachers are married and have children; one hundred years ago, this was generally out of the question, particularly for women.

---

* The name has since been shortened to United Teachers.

The Right to Reside Where One Desires.   Today teachers live where they desire, often considerable distances from their workplaces. One hundred years ago, most teachers, who were generally unmarried, boarded with families who lived within walking distance of the schools in which they were employed. This sort of arrangement greatly inhibited any individuality a teacher might have wished to express in his or her personal life.

Personal Habits.   Although not yet completely free to dress and wear one's hair as one chooses, most teachers today have far more latitude in regard to appearance than did their occupational counterparts of a century ago. One hundred years ago, smoking and drinking (as well as dancing, gambling, "courting," and many other "sinful" or "distracting" activities) were prohibited for teachers. And, in some cases, their prohibition was stipulated in formal provisions written into contracts prepared by local boards of education.

Expressing Opinions Contrary to Those of One's Superiors.   Although boards of education, superintendents, and school principals still often resent having teachers express differing opinions publicly, and occasionally attempt to terminate or punish teachers who do express themselves freely, the courts in recent years have increasingly sided with teachers who have been "disciplined" for such expressions of honest differences. It would have been inconceivable for a teacher to contest his or her superiors' views or actions either publicly or in private one hundred years ago.

Recess and Lunch Breaks.   As recently as ten or fifteen years ago, teachers in some school systems in the United States had *no* free time during school hours. They literally were on duty from the time of the opening bell until school ended for the day. They were expected to remain with their children when they went outside for recess and, in some cases, when they ate lunch. Today teachers generally have at least a morning recess break and increasingly a duty-free lunch period. One hundred years ago, they had neither.

Salaries.   Teachers continue to be among the more poorly paid of all comparably educated white-collar workers, but for various reasons (to be discussed shortly), the gap between teachers' salaries and those of other highly skilled workers has been narrowing in the past ten years. One hundred years ago, few men with families could consider teaching below the college level (certainly not in elementary schools), except perhaps on a temporary basis prior to attending law school or entering business. Teaching was a "woman's job," partly because usually single

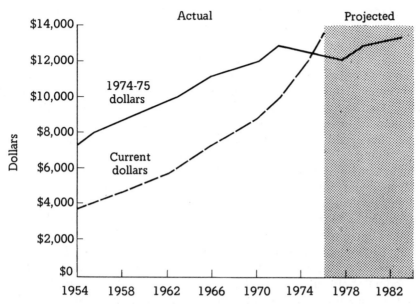

FIGURE 13–1. *Average Salaries of Instructional Staff (Education Division, Department of Health, Education, and Welfare,* The Condition of Education *[Washington, D.C.: U.S. Government Printing Office, 1976], p. 132.)*

women taught in elementary and high schools, and they often had only themselves to support. The predominance of women in the profession also kept the salary levels low. For both men and women, the right to receive a decent financial compensation for their work is being taken for granted by American teachers.

Physical Conditions of Work. One hundred years ago, teachers frequently worked in poorly lighted and poorly heated buildings, whether the latter were one room schoolhouses in the country or brick edifices in the expanding cities of our nation. Sometimes, fires would break out in the poorly constructed buildings, killing many children and their mentors. Today fire code regulations and other safety measures, as well as updated standards of minimal comfort, ensure that the vast majority of teachers and their students—aside from those in inner-city schools—will spend their occupational hours in reasonably secure and comfortable surroundings. As newer buildings replace outmoded structures, air conditioning and carpeting, more aesthetic walls, windows, and ceilings are becoming the norm for growing numbers of teachers and their students.

Social Climate of Teaching. The work atmosphere of teaching tended to be cold, repressive, and overly formalized a century ago, especially in

urban areas. Few prospective teachers of the contemporary age, however, have reason to look forward to such a harsh social environment, although variations in the quality of the social arrangements surrounding
teaching continue to exist, largely contingent upon the influence of the
building principal.* Even the most authoritarian principal today is under
real pressure from both his or her administrative superiors and teaching
staff to promote good human relations in the building. In addition, new
instructional technologies such as team teaching and "open spacing" help
to overcome rigid and overly formalistic patterns and to promote warmer,
more human relations between both adults and youngsters participating
in the activities of modern schools. The social climate of teaching today is
vastly altered from that found in most schools of the past.

Some of these improvements in the occupational and personal lives
of teachers have evolved gradually because they are part of a larger historical pattern; for example, residential separation from the workplace is
largely dependent upon the invention and widespread diffusion of the
automobile and, correspondingly, of better streets and freeways. Others
have come about rather abruptly since the end of World War II and particularly since the decade of the 1960s, such as the increase in salaries of
most teachers and increased freedom of expression for teachers.

The civil rights movement has had a significant impact upon the
sensibilities of teachers, as one of its institutional side effects. In turn, as
teachers have become more self-conscious as individuals and as members
of a group in their own right, they have begun to strongly challenge some
of the traditional assumptions about their proper place in the educational
hierarchy. They have acted largely within existing system boundaries,
particularly through the federal courts. The civil rights of American
teachers are now being reconsidered, and changes both in and outside of
the classroom are beginning to reflect recent precedent-setting decisions
of the courts.

Another more significant source of recent change in the expectations and behaviors of American teachers is the teacher power movement,
a large-scale movement that, to some people, threatens to ruin the system
of schooling. To teachers, the movement promises to allow the occupa-

---

* Students of school culture have demonstrated that the building principal can
  have an enormous influence upon the sociocultural climate of American
  schools. For example, an authoritarian school principal can have either a
  demoralizing effect or, if "benevolently despotic" and paternalistic, he or
  she may produce a contented dependency among members of his or her
  teaching staff. A weak principal with a laissez-faire philosophy can also
  produce staff demoralization or can free teachers to become highly integrated,
  if informal leadership emerges within the faculty ranks. A warm, energetic,
  "democratic" principal may exert real leadership if he or she has a
  moderately professional staff.

tion to become a full-fledged profession, with all the benefits that accrue to professionals and their clients.

These two recent interrelated developments—the growth of concern for the civil rights of teachers and the teacher power movement—are the topics of the remainder of this chapter.

What Are the Civil Rights and Responsibilities of Teachers?

Rights and duties go hand-in-hand. To what extent have American teachers been accorded rights commensurate with the duties expected of them by the community and the schools? Where do teachers stand in relation to most other citizens in respect to their fundamental civil rights?

Teachers' Rights

As the introduction to this chapter stated, teachers in the United States have not always been accorded the same rights as all other adult citizens. Their work has been considered crucial by Americans because they possess a strong faith in the benefits of formal education. Like the clergy, teachers historically have been expected to be paragons of middle-class virtue—as that is defined in a given period—in order that impressionable children will have positive role models. Many of the virtues expected of contemporary teachers have already been abandoned by the adult population at large, demonstrating again that our schools tend to reflect socio-cultural patterns which are no longer universal—which may be defunct. For instance, men's hair styles have changed markedly within the past five years; many men now sport beards and mustaches and allow their hair to grow down to their shoulders. But, despite the prevalence of new hair styles in the population at large, male teachers in many districts are still forbidden to let their hair and beards grow out. In some districts, prospective teachers with excellent university records are refused employment until they have been to a barber to have their hair shorn. The reason typically given for such demands is that unconventionality might unfavorably influence youngsters and offend older adults in the community.

But teachers are only human. Despite the school marm or master stereotype still held by many people, most teachers today want to enjoy the same freedoms as do other members of society. They want to be free to dress and wear their hair stylishly, to participate in political activities,

to express their own opinions about contemporary issues in class, to belong to organizations that have personal meaning for them, and to do as they please in their private lives.

In growing numbers, teachers who believe that their civil rights have been violated are going to court to fight for these rights. However, far too many teachers still do not even know what their civil rights are, so they continue to abide unquestioningly by expectations for their public and private behavior. Many of these expectations limit their opportunities to live normal lives, challenge the claim that schools are centers of democratic living, and, in effect, make teachers second-class citizens.[1]

What are civil rights? Fischer and Schimmel define civil rights as "Constitutional rights that cannot be taken away by official order or policy [hence] cannot be given away in a contract."[2] Specifically, they are rights guaranteed to all citizens—including teachers—by the United States Constitution. In recent years, the due process clause of the Fourteenth Amendment has been frequently invoked in civil rights cases brought before the courts. Section 1 of this amendment is quoted below:

> All persons born or naturalized in the United States, and subject to the jurisdiction thereof, are citizens of the United States and of the State wherein they reside. No State shall make or enforce any law which shall abridge the privileges or immunities of citizens of the United States; nor shall any State deprive any person of life, liberty, or property, without due process of law; nor deny to any person within its jurisdiction the equal protection of the laws.

Civil rights are guaranteed to all citizens of the United States; they cannot be withheld by a state or local community from a "special class" of citizens, such as blacks, women, factory workers, children, or teachers— even though education is a function delegated to the state and its localities. Freedom of speech, a First Amendment right that is guaranteed to all Americans, is thereby guaranteed to all teachers:

> *A teacher is no longer a teacher twenty-four hours a day; he also has a life as a private citizen. As such, he has the same right to freedom of expression as anyone else, subject to the ordinary rules of libel and slander, and the general principles of criminal law.*[3]

What about freedom of speech inside the school? Does it relate to academic freedom? Many educators consider academic freedom to be a special privilege that goes beyond the freedom of speech right. Even during school a teacher is protected by the First Amendment as long as his or her use of controversial statements or materials in class are relevant to the subject being taught, appropriate "to the age and maturity of the students, and not disruptive of school 'discipline'."[4]

Hair style of teachers is also generally protected by the courts, as a form of "symbolic speech." The courts have been inconsistent in their evaluations of teachers' morals. The criteria commonly used by the courts in arriving at a decision are "(1) whether the conduct was personal and private, (2) whether it became public through the indiscretion of the teacher, and (3) whether it involved students."[5] In general, court decisions in the area of teacher morality appear to increasingly reflect more relaxed social mores at large, as long as the conduct involved does not appear to adversely affect the teacher's professional responsibilities and effectiveness with students.

In the area of teacher loyalty, the courts are changing dramatically. They now protect teachers' rights to belong to controversial organizations and to associate and assemble freely. As long as their activities do not interfere with school operations, teachers are increasingly free to participate in controversial politics, as well as to join teachers' organizations that advocate collective bargaining with employers. (The right of public employees to strike, however, has not yet been deemed legal by the courts.) On the other hand, a school board may still demand that teachers take a loyalty oath before being employed if the oath is not excessively vague or negatively phrased.

Modern teachers are rapidly gaining broad protections under the law in matters involving arbitrary or discriminatory action by school authorities, such as dismissal of a female teacher for pregnancy and childbirth. These conditions must now be treated in the same manner as any other temporary disability. Nor can teachers be terminated, reduced in rank or pay, or suspended for arbitrary reasons. Fair procedures in accordance with the due process clause of the Fourteenth Amendment are increasingly being required of school employers in personnel matters affecting untenured, as well as tenured, teachers. (Tenured teachers already have these rights guaranteed by state laws or contract provisions.) In short, the civil rights of teachers are now being respected by school officials and lay people. Growing numbers of modern teachers are learning of their legal rights and standing up to be counted as first-class citizens.

Responsibilities of Teachers

Of course, with rights go certain responsibilities. The teacher is in a responsible position *vis à vis* his or her primary clients, who are impressionable youngsters. If a teacher expressed his or her constitutionally guaranteed right to free speech by using profanity in a class of fifteen-year-olds, for reasons other than to facilitate instruction in literature, such a teacher might properly be considered irresponsible. His or her freedom of speech might offend the sensibilities of some students who are in his or her charge under the laws of compulsory attendance. This is even more obvious wth eight-year-olds in middle-class elementary schools. On the other hand, one could argue that college seniors attend classes of their own volition and ought to be mature enough to handle almost any kind of language used by their instructors. A college professor who occasionally uses informal language in class might not be considered irresponsible in the same way as a high school or elementary school teacher would be.

The courts usually take into consideration factors such as student age and instructional objective, when weighing evidence and arguments in cases involving claims that civil rights of teachers have been abrogated. The *rights* of teachers have been more neglected by the courts and the public than have their responsibilities. Teachers have always been held accountable for their actions. Little concern has been expressed by the public or school officials for their privileges. There is little reason to fear that ensuring the basic civil rights of American teachers will thereby lower their sense of occupational responsibility.

The Teacher Power Movement

Hand-in-hand with efforts in the courts to secure the legal rights of teachers go efforts to upgrade their status as an occupational group and to be granted a larger role in the educational decision-making process.

Major Factors in Its Growth

The civil rights struggle generally takes the form of a single teacher suing a school district for restitution of allegedly denied basic rights. The teacher power movement is a group effort to organize teachers in order to gain valued ends through strategic use of collective power. (Of course, belonging to teacher organizations that retain their own attorneys will also ensure legal counsel if an individual teacher is faced with a court action.)

Teachers throughout American society today are agitated. They are often angry about the way they think they are treated by school administrators, school boards, and the public. Like members of other historically disadvantaged groups, such as blacks and women, teachers have been caught up in the human liberation movement of the 1960s and the 1970s and are demanding a sizable chunk of the action in their particular institutional sphere of concern.

What are some of the factors involved in the new teacher militancy? Here is a lengthy quotation taken directly from a book intended to help school officials quell rising teacher demands. In spite of its purpose, the authors have identified a number of the grievances of teachers quite well:

Inadequate Salaries. *Although teachers have made considerable progress very recently, they are still underpaid in relation to comparable professions for comparable hours worked. Until teachers feel that their salaries are at least equal to those of other professionals, and commensurate with the demands of their jobs, they will continue to insist on higher salaries.*

High Pupil–Teacher Ratio. *As a group, teachers still have a tendency to measure educational progress in terms of class size reduction. And, from the teacher's point of view, little progress has been made in this area. Teachers still feel that they have too many students to instruct effectively, that despite the addition of all types of auxiliary personnel and manipulation of grouping, there are still too many children in a given classroom.*

Lack of Meaningful Teacher Involvement. *The complaint persists that teachers are not consulted on matters which have bearing on what goes on in the classroom. As a group the teachers seem to feel that their advice is vital in many matters having direct or indirect influence on the instructional program.*

Poor Personnel Practices. *Close association with teachers reveals that many of them feel that they are not treated with adequate respect by their superiors and administrators; that supervisors and administrators do not practice good human relations...*

Rapid Urbanization. *For the most part teacher militancy exists only in the population centers of the nation. Therefore, teacher militancy must be analyzed in terms of the total scope of urbanization problems. The center city may face one set of school problems, while the suburbs may face a different set. The population explosion of our cities has gen-*

erated a number of problems which overflow into the classroom: tran-
siency, poverty, grouping problems, crowded conditions, financing
problems, and many more.

Inadequate Supplies and Facilities.   *Although closely related to a
number of other problems, the shortage of instructional materials and
the inadequacy of school facilities continue to be annoying problems for
teachers. Teachers still complain that there is not enough instructional
equipment, and that when new equipment is purchased, it is not kept
repaired...*

Poor Working Conditions.   *One of the main complaints of teachers
has persisted over the years, e.g., that teachers must assume too many
non-teaching and non-professional duties. Next to salary this item seems
of most concern to them. In some ways it is an expression of their desire
to become true professionals. In other ways it is an attempt to achieve
status through the assumption of exclusively professional duties...*

Increased Education of Teachers.   *No longer is teaching a job
carried on in a one room school house by a nice lady who graduated from
a local normal school. Schools today are huge institutions in large cities,
staffed by highly articulate and trained professionals. These teachers are
worldly, and they expect to run their own profession and gain their share
of America. No longer will they accept the old-time paternalism and
benevolence of board members and superintendents.*

Increase of the Teacher–Parent.   *There was a day in many rural*

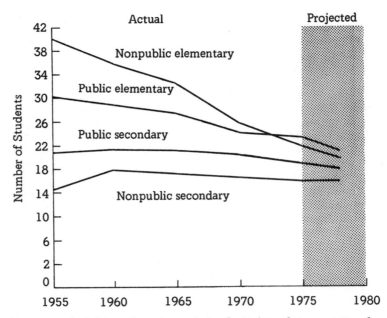

FIGURE 13–2.   *Pupil–Teacher Ratios: Number of Students per Teacher
(Education Division, Department of Health, Education, and Welfare,
*The Condition of Education *[Washington, D.C.: U.S. Government Printing
Office, 1976], p. 129.)*

school districts when a married woman was not permitted to teach. Today, however, the majority of teachers are not only married but are parents, and many are the heads of households. These teachers are responsible for the welfare of their families. Their job is a matter of basic family security. Such teachers are deadly serious in their support of any action which increases their economic well-being. To them, teaching is not just something one does until marriage. Teaching is a career.

Aspirations of Professionalism.   Closely integrated with the other causes of militancy are the goals being sought by the teaching profession. These goals consist of greater control over licensing of practitioners, greater policing of the ranks, improvement of the art, greater remuneration, increased academic freedom, higher status, and more control over policy. Many teachers feel these goals can be achieved only through militant actions.

Collective Negotiation Laws.   In 1962, President Kennedy signed Executive Order 10988, which provided almost all federal government employees with the same basic collective bargaining rights as private employees, with the exception of the right to strike. Within five years a dozen states passed similar legislation covering state and local government employees....There is no doubt that these laws have fostered and accelerated collective negotiations, and thus provided an outlet for teacher militancy.*

Others believe that additional concerns will become the objects of teacher militancy in the near future.[7]

Teacher Tenure.   In light of trends toward collective negotiations, many critics of schools believe that teachers no longer need tenure laws. Furthermore, some claim that tenure laws do little more than protect incompetent or lazy teachers who have only put forth effort to impress administrators for three or four years.[8] Once tenure is granted, some argue, it is almost impossible to remove a teacher from his position except by proving flagrant instances of immorality, incompetence, cruelty, negligence, subversion, or mental illness. Teacher organizations, however, want to police their own ranks while retaining present tenure laws. They allege that tenure is the best protection of academic freedom for good teachers who might otherwise be afraid to express their professional opinions in controversial matters.

Performance Contracting.   A number of school systems in the United States have signed contracts with private corporations to pay so much money to the firm upon furnishing evidence that use of its programs or teaching machines has substantially increased student achievement levels on standardized tests of reading, mathematics, and other subjects.

If such firms are successful in accomplishing what teachers have allegedly been unable to do for many years, quite a few teachers will be put out of business. This of course would be strenuously resisted by teacher organizations. Extravagant claims by numerous private firms have failed to result in materially improved pupil scores on achievement tests.

Differentiated Staffing.   This plan is already in effect in a number of school systems around the country. It provides for different classifications of instructional personnel within a school, with varying salaries and role functions. School personnel with advanced graduate school work might become "master teachers" in charge of a team; the majority might function as teachers possessing a standard credential; other staff members would be interns completing their college work, or teacher aides with a high school or junior college diploma. The idea of differentiated staffing is a step toward merit rating of teachers, to which teacher organizations are strongly opposed on grounds that it is impossible to determine what constitutes superior work in the classroom. Differentiated staffing, then, could become the object of serious concern of militants.

Accountability.   Related to tenure, accountability of teachers for what they accomplish with youngsters has become a troublesome issue. Many lay people want teachers to prove that they deserve their salaries. California already has an accountability law that mandates that all teachers shall write yearly "performance objectives" in all subjects and demonstrate to their principals that these objectives have been reached. Many teachers do not like the idea. They argue that the results of good teaching cannot always be accurately demonstrated. Teachers are apt to resist this expectation if they can.

Goals and Objectives.   The question of what should be the ultimate functions of schooling and teaching has confounded educators for centuries. But in a changing society like ours, the debate over educational ends becomes crucial. Cleavages between teachers who work with youngsters directly and school managers and parents are likely to become extremely deep in the future and find expression in the operations of teacher organizations.

Many of the most militant teachers are males with families to support and careers to build. Their numbers are increasing rapidly. And, since most of the men in teaching today are found in secondary schools (in 1973, close to 54 percent compared to less than 20 percent in the nation's elementary schools[9]), the male high school teacher is likely to be most militant. In an important 1965 study in Oregon, Harmon Zeigler found that "maleness emerges as the essential variable and the male high school teacher is, in a sense, the underclass of the teaching profession, a rebel in a female system."[10] Ronald Corwin's recent study of militant professionalism in the Midwest found that older, as well as younger, males were the militants:

> The fact that older males are militant seems to indicate that militants do not necessarily leave the field of teaching or mellow with age. Moreover, the militant attitudes of the younger men may forecast a new generation of even greater militant tendencies to replace the present one.[11]

As more and more men enter the field of elementary education, which presently wants as many qualified men as it can accommodate, this level of the system may begin to produce a larger share of militants, especially in view of the special status strains for men in our culture who work in a field traditionally dominated by women. As women's liberation begins to significantly affect school teachers, we are likely to witness a dramatic increase in female militancy at all levels of the schooling system, especially among self-supporting women.

Teachers will probably never again be the same, now that they have begun to organize and apply pressure upon school managers by withholding contracts en masse, threatening sanctions, and even striking.

The Leading Organizations of Teachers

The two major organizations presently vying for the allegiance of teachers across the nation are the National Education Association and the American Federation of Teachers.

The NEA
and the "Collaborationist" Ideal

Founded in 1857, the National Education Association had about 1,700,000 members in 1975, making it one of the largest occupational organizations in the world. Its strength has traditionally been in rural areas and smaller cities and suburbs, rather than in highly urbanized centers.

Until recently, it was considered a relatively unaggressive organization whose local affiliates, in Lieberman's sardonic words, typically engaged "in futile efforts to improve their [teachers'] conditions of employment. Other than this, they give teas for new teachers in the Spring, and perhaps listen to a few travelogues in between."[12]

The main reason for such a comparatively unassertive stance in the past on behalf of its members—85 percent of whom have been classroom

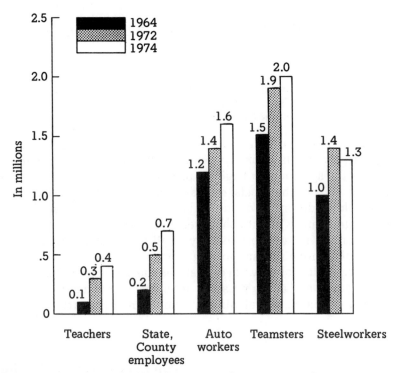

FIGURE 13–3. *Union Membership of Teachers Compared to Union Member-*
ship of Other Occupations (Education Division, Department of Health,
Education, and Welfare, The Condition of Education *[Washington, D.C.: U. S.*
Government Printing Office, 1976], p. 130.)

teachers—can be traced to the fact that historically the NEA's official
membership policy has been to encourage both teachers and administrators and other management-level school workers to join. The NEA believed that everyone engaged in professional educational activities,
regardless of salary or position, is a fellow professional, a member of the
same team. The improvement of public education depends upon the
concerted efforts of teachers and school managers working harmoniously
together, collaborating in a mutual endeavor to raise the status of the
profession in the public's eyes and the conditions under which educators
and students engage in the learning process.

In the past, the NEA's collaborationist posture generally meant that
the majority of its members, teachers, were dominated by a minority of
higher echelon school people—administrators, curriculum specialists—
who actually controlled the organization and its state and local affiliates.
For instance, as recently as 1965, the author, upon receiving a promotion
from classroom teacher to supervisor, was invited to become a member

of the executive committee of a California Teachers Association's (the state affiliate of NEA) local. He discovered that almost all the other members of this local policy-making group were school principals, assistant principals, central office curriculum specialists, and supervisors. These were the people who participated in the decision-making process and lobbied on behalf of the general membership.

In order to advance in the occupational hierarchy of formal education—to become first a middle- and later a top-level educational "executive"—typically depends on the same general sort of process that operates in most other occupations, from those in the private sector to the federal civil service system. Higher executives in the organization tap individuals whom they believe possess unusual talent and organizational loyalty, and promote them when an opening occurs. In the case of the schools, it is advantageous to be in a position, such as that of athletic coach, that offers greater-than-normal access to informal channels of communication with the higher ups in the hierarchy. Even government agencies operating under strict civil service codes that require written tests to determine eligibility for promotion usually use these tests only as initial screening devices. Personal interviews and reliance upon the subjective judgments of one's superiors usually count at least as much in determining which of two individuals receiving identical scores will actually be offered an available promotion.

If an organization is controlled by school managers, as the NEA and its affiliates once were, then teachers are likely to try not to offend their own organizational superiors if they hope to advance or even to retain their present status. Ambitious teacher members within the organization are not likely to risk offending their superiors by advocating policies that might be construed to increase the welfare of their fellow teachers, at the expense of higher officials who make promotional decisions.

Teacher militancy as a driving force in NEA activities was greatly inhibited when its central ideological position and its structure of authority were collaborationist in nature and heavily balanced in favor of a minority of its membership—the school administrators.

Until recently the end result has been that, as an organ for improving the status and working conditions of teachers, who are the overwhelming majority of its membership, the NEA has been mediocre. Its strength was in its numerous activities on behalf of specialists in the field, such as educational researchers; in its ability to impress state and federal legislators with its sheer numbers and thus obtain certain broad benefits, such as tenure; and especially in its ancillary services for members, such as relatively inexpensive hospitalization and automobile insurance and useful employment agency services.

However, in the early 1960s, the NEA began to change. It is generally agreed that when Albert Shanker's New York City teachers union,

355

the United Federation of Teachers, won exclusive collective bargaining rights with the school board in 1961—thereby substantially upgrading the salaries and working conditions of that city's 44,000 teachers—the NEA began to reconsider its position for the first time in its long history. The NEA awakened from its complacency, when suddenly faced with real threats of membership loss to the more aggressive American Federation of Teachers, a labor union affiliated both with Shanker's UFT and with the huge AFL–CIO. The NEA leaders quickly responded in their 1962 annual convention in Denver by asserting that from thenceforth domination of the organization by nonteaching school people should cease, and the basic occupational needs of its largest segment of membership should have first priority. From that point on, teachers began to be elected regularly to the organization's major offices. In 1974, the NEA elected its first black president, a teacher from Des Moines, Iowa.[13]

The organization rather dramatically took on an unfamiliar militancy on behalf of teachers. During the remainder of the 1960s, it advocated and supported use of sanctions against districts believed to be especially unfair to teachers. These sanctions "blacklisted" districts so that no prospective teacher would seek employment there. For a time the NEA thought that the sanction was the ultimate weapon in the struggle between teachers and school managers. On grounds that it was unprofessional, the NEA refused to consider the more extreme tactic of the strike during most of the 1960s. Its chief rival, the AFT, supported the strike. The NEA accepted the notion of professional negotiations between organized teachers and school boards; this was a milder, more collaborative form of discussion of mutual concerns than collective bargaining, the traditional union approach to labor–management problems.

By the 1970s, the NEA and with its comparatively mild policy became very concerned about the inroads upon its membership that its once weak rival, the AFT, was making through use of much stronger tactics of striking, threatening to strike, or withholding contracts en masse. So the NEA began to modify its position on teacher strikes being illegal (which, in most states, they still are), immoral, and unprofessional.

The NEA's new stance is generally to support local teachers' groups that decide to strike or otherwise withhold services, as well as to espouse state and national legislation legalizing collective bargaining for all public employees. To many school administrators, the NEA has become almost as militant as the AFT. School managers are now being urged to quit the organization and to band together in groups that better represent their own special interests and privileges, such as the American Association of School Administrators, which broke away from the NEA umbrella in 1973.

The NEA has changed a great deal in terms of its ideological posture. It was once a mild, collaborationist organization drawing from all elements of the educational occupation and believing that everyone in the field—from the classroom teacher to the superintendent of schools—shares identical concerns that should be resolved cooperatively and professionally. The NEA seems to have become a fairly vocal and concerned *teacher's* organization and is gradually, and perhaps somewhat reluctantly, changing.

The AFT
and the "Confrontationist" Ideal

The American Federation of Teachers originated as a labor union, not a professional association as the NEA did. It claims to represent white-collar, professional workers in their confrontations with school management. Formed between 1916 and 1919, its stated objectives are:

1. To bring associations of teachers into relations of mutual assistance and cooperation.

2. To obtain for them all the rights to which they are entitled.

3. To raise the standards of the teaching profession by securing the conditions essential to the best professional service.

4. To promote such a democratization of the schools as will enable them better to equip their pupils to take places in the industrial, social, and political life of the community.

5. To promote the welfare of the childhood of the nation by providing progressively better educational opportunity for all.[14]

The membership of the AFT was small compared with the NEA until after World War II when increasing numbers of men with families to support began to enter the ranks of American elementary and secondary teachers. Shanker's successful efforts in 1961 and 1962 to organize the UFT in New York City spurred similar efforts in other large metropolitan areas around the country, including Cleveland, Detroit, Pittsburgh, Chicago, Philadelphia, Boston, St. Louis, San Francisco, and Los Angeles.

AFT membership has traditionally been the largest in cities; as more and more city teachers joined the AFT in order to gain broad labor movement support for their efforts, the membership of the organization and its coffers swelled. By 1974, there were over 400,000 members,[15] compared with some 140,000 in 1968, only six years earlier.[16] The 1975 membership figure is claimed to have been 453,000, a 9 percent increase over the 1974 figure.[17] According to Albert Shanker, now president of the AFT, its next major strategy will be to capture the membership of at least 300,000 more unaffiliated teachers by delivering on promises for better salaries and working conditions which it claims the NEA has not succeeded in securing.[18]

According to AFT leaders, only a highly militant organization of teachers, which excludes administrators above the school principal, can secure benefits for the vast majority of teachers. They believe that management cannot operate in the interests of teachers. The AFT claims that management is too distant from the actual educational scene, and that their major concern is financing and running school bureaucracies.

The AFT believes that there is no alternative but to admit that labor (teachers) and management (administrators and school board members) are structurally and ideologically opposed to each other. However undignified and unpleasant this initially may seem, their relationship must be one founded on "confrontationist" behavior.

> All administrators and supervisors in the school system belong on the management team and should be excluded by school board policy from being in the same unit with teachers. Any person who has the authority to supervise, evaluate, or recommend hiring or firing, from the department chairman to the superintendent of schools, is an extension of the school board's management arm, and as such they are executives of the school board, whose primary functions are to implement and enforce the school board dictum. Anything else would be unthinkable.[19]

The belief in the necessity for confrontation between teachers and administrators is echoed by Shanker:

Power is never given to anyone. Power is taken, and it is taken from some-one. Teachers, as one of society's powerless groups, are now starting to take power from supervisors and school boards. This is causing and will continue to cause a realignment of power relationships.[20]

Whether the AFT, with its ethos of confrontation between labor and management, will continue to be successful in its drive to become the chief body representing American teachers remains to be seen. The movement to unionize teachers has had over a decade of phenomenal growth, especially in urban areas and recently in some small communities, based largely upon its ability to deliver on its promises to angry, frustrated, underpaid teachers by means of out-and-out battle with management forces. In 1972 and 1973, a period of spiraling inflation, the average salary of teachers in California—which is one of the higher paying states—was $12,198, while that of elementary school principals was $19,507 and high school principals, $22,238.[21] Nationwide, the comparable figures were $10,254, $15,908, and $16,777 respectively.[22]

Will the NEA and AFT Merge?

For a brief period in the early part of the 1970s, there was serious talk of an impending merger of the NEA and the AFT. The AFT was especially optimistic and began to distribute materials to its members urging them to support such a merger. Myron Lieberman, a leading authority on teacher organizations and exponent of teacher power, wrote an article predicting the "inevitable" merger of the two rival groups sometime during the decade.[23]

The arguments in favor of merger were basically simple: both organizations were advocating essentially the same thing—increased teacher input into the educational decision-making process toward the related ends of improved professional status and working conditions more congenial to learning. Both organizations had become supportive of strong teacher militancy, despite minor philosophical differences over how far they should go in expressing their militant feelings. Whatever differences between the two organizations remained could be resolved once they were restructured into one body. Each group would gain strength from the other; the AFT would gain members by affiliating with the larger NEA, while the NEA would benefit from the availability of some of the more assertive teachers who belonged to the AFT.

But important ideological differences and political considerations still separate the two organizations, especially in regard to affiliation with the AFL–CIO, which the NEA feels is untenable. Talks of merger began to break down in 1973. In 1975, delegates to the annual convention of the

New York State United Teachers (an AFT affiliate) voted to sever ties with the NEA because of claims that the NEA had been directing a deliberate campaign of harassment against the NYSUT. It now appears that with the exception of one maverick state teachers' organization—Florida —the two teacher groups have not found their aims and methods compatible.

To predict which organization will be the major one in the future is not easy. The AFT made its noteworthy gains when frustration of teachers was at an all-time high and when teachers were in great demand by employers and in comparatively short supply as a result of rapidly increasing numbers of school-aged children born during the post–World War II baby boom. By 1972, the twenty-five-year escalation in demand for school teachers had peaked and begun to slow down. Since then, the nation has been in a severe "educational depression" which will probably continue until at least 1980 and possibly longer. Some feel that the number of college students entering the teaching profession will dwindle in intelligent response to the lack of employment opportunities. Apparently this had not happened as late as 1974, according to a Gallup poll of college students.[24] Although the number of students planning to be teachers has declined, large numbers continue to look forward to obtaining teaching jobs during a period of great oversupply. This irony deserves analysis.

Teachers now in practice and those seeking to enter the field will be in a far worse bargaining position vis à vis employers than they were when there were not enough teachers to fill available positions. In 1958, the average young teacher could almost pick and choose districts in which to work, particularly if their subject area was math or science or if they were males seeking employment in elementary schools. Today teachers, especially women teachers, face a tight job market. Those who do succeed in obtaining a position try to hold onto it, instead of changing jobs to broaden their experience during their first few years of occupational life.

From the perspective of job security, it would appear that teachers are likely to be cautious about joining an employee organization such as the AFT that is not viewed with favor by school managers. The fact that the NEA added 213,000 members to its rolls in 1974, a year of severe "educational depression," in part substantiates this idea.[25] On the other hand, simply because teachers today are holding onto their jobs longer, more of them than ever are becoming tenured and being assured of job security.

Coupled with this, teachers are facing unprecedented challenges to their integrity and their utility by parents and taxpayers, as well as by administrators and school boards anxious to demonstrate to the public and its legislative representatives that schools can successfully teach youngsters to read, write, and solve mathematical problems. Some boards

360

have already tried to abolish tenure or reduce its operational effectiveness. The emphasis on the 3 Rs at the expense of other areas of the curriculum, such as science, social studies, and art is probably greater than it has been in the past fifty years in the U.S.* Progressive education appears to be dormant for the moment, particularly in inner-city schools, which may need the benefits of John Dewey's ideas the most.

Given such a climate in which to work, the unionization of teachers may make significant advances, and Shanker may be right in predicting at least 750,000 members for the AFT in the near future. If teachers in the public elementary and secondary schools of this society react to the frustrations of their profession by working for collective-bargaining laws on both state and national levels, we may see a significant alteration in the balance of power between teacher organizations. This alteration would come at the time when teacher morale in this society is at a very low level. Such a change in the organizational affiliations of the nation's teachers could have a very profound impact upon both the status and working conditions of teachers, as well as upon the meaning and purpose of the formal educational enterprise.

Collective Bargaining in Education

In the meantime, both organizations are claiming credit for the relatively new and growing state-by-state passage of collective bargaining laws on behalf of public employees, including teachers. Collective bargaining has long been practiced in private industry, supported by federal legislation such as the Wagner Act (1935) and the Taft–Hartley Act (1947).

Once held to be an illegal conspiracy by employees against their employers and punishable by fines and even imprisonment, recent labor legislation pertaining to teachers promises to have a revolutionary impact upon the relations between teachers, school boards, and administrators who in the past could do little more than negotiate with each other for their respective objectives on an informal or quasi-official basis.

Collective bargaining is predicated upon the assumption that teachers and boards of education, and administrators (i.e., management) have many incompatible interests which must be reconciled by establishing

---

* One recent study shows that the average elementary school teacher spends about 75 minutes a day teaching reading, 18 minutes teaching mathematics, and only 1 or 2 minutes teaching art, science, social studies, and other "non-essentials." The rest of his or her time is spent keeping records and controlling students' behavior.[26]

an essentially adversary relationship. Collective bargaining can be viewed as a process wherein teacher and management representatives are required by law to sit down at the bargaining table together and hammer out their explicit differences until they come to some agreement with binding power.

> Employers are required to negotiate on certain matters. This means that they cannot make decisions about specified matters without achieving the agreement of the representative of the employees prior to announcing the decision. And it implies that the representative of the employees may block the decision until it is ready to give its assent.
>
> Employees are authorized to propose changes in the work relationship. Employers must listen to these proposals and, at the very least, must respond with a thorough explanation of why they cannot reasonably comply with the demand.
>
> Collective representation is mandated. Employees are not authorized to deal directly with their employer on bargainable items. The collective-bargaining process is based upon an agreement developed between the employer and the representative of the employees. Thus, wages, hours, and conditions of employment are determined for employees by agreement between unions and employers and not directly by employees themselves.
>
> All agreements resulting from negotiations must be expressed in writing so that a specified basis for the employment relationship is recorded and communicated in a similar form to all who are affected by it.[27]

What kinds of matters can be negotiated by such a process? Since the board of education, as the employer, is a creature of the state, it can bargain only over areas of policy formation authorized by the state, some of which are mandated in the law requiring CB, and some of which are optional. There are some items which are not open to negotiation since state legislation has already determined what must be done (e.g., provision of tenure).

In general, the "board must bargain to establish wages, hours, and terms and conditions of employment," such as class size.[28] Other items, that is, items that can be subsumed under the nebulous "terms and conditions of employment," which are believed by teacher organizations to be negotiable under collective bargaining laws, pertain to such matters as curriculum and instructional materials; inservice education; evaluation of teachers; modes of discipline (within legally defined limits); grievance procedures; and health and safety practices.

The above list only indicates the broad variety of items that are negotiable under collective bargaining laws. According to one authority, "teacher organizations in each state will have to probe the boundaries of the law as it applies. Militant bargaining and test cases on a number of points will be required to determine the range of possible bargainable issues."[29]

One thing is fairly certain: The advent of public school collective bargaining in the United States will usher in an era of vastly increased organizational affiliativeness on the parts of school teachers, with attendant implications for the future of the NEA and the AFT.

Should You Join a Teachers' Organization?

Power and influence in American society result from working with others on behalf of mutually shared interests and objectives. Whichever of the two organizations discussed in this chapter (or others) you decide to join upon entering the occupation of teaching, it behooves you to give serious thought to joining and participating in acquiring a modicum of authority. Although there is merit in the argument that by remaining independent of political organizations in education—which in fact do make one-sided demands on their members—teachers may retain a sense of personal autonomy over their occupational lives, the question is "at what price and at whose expense?" The most effective way to serve both your own best interests and those of your students is probably by sharing in the broader, long-term endeavor to humanize and democratize the educational institution in American society.

You are part of the best-educated generation of teachers ever to enter the occupation. Your preparation in an institution of higher learning has trained you to be relatively critical; it has not trained you to be a passive jobholder carrying out orders handed down from above. There is little doubt that you must—if you are to become an effective teacher of the young in a social order undergoing basic change—participate actively in deciding and developing the educational program you must employ. There is even less doubt that you must earn a salary commensurate with reasonable living standards. Both ends are legitimate, and whether you are a man or a woman you should not be misled into believing that it is wrong for salaried professionals to want to shape occupational policy and to earn a decent living.

The chief way to work for enhancement of teachers' and learners' lives is to join with fellow teachers in a union such as the AFT or an association such as the NEA. Which organization suits your needs is a matter for your own conscience and circumstances to determine. You will undoubtedly want to begin assessing their relative merits at this time, and gathering additional data to help you make a decision. At present, each organization is worthy of your earnest consideration as a genuinely professional organization.

Summary

American teachers have never been permitted to exercise the same civil rights as most other citizens of this society. But they are speedily catching up in this regard, as well as in terms of their salaries and their working conditions.

Two movements are largely responsible for the recent dramatic advances in the status of the teaching occupation and the privileges of its incumbents. They are the struggle to loosen up the legal constraints upon school teachers through the courts and the teacher power movement, which currently pits the unionization ideals of the traditionally confrontationist American Federation of Teachers against the long powerful National Education Association, which until recently espoused collaboration among all members of the education profession, from teachers to superintendents of schools.

Whether these two important organizations will eventually merge—which would immensely improve the collective-bargaining position of American teachers—is a moot question. The answer must await future ideological and political developments affecting these organizations' leadership and membership. It is even possible that a third organization will emerge to challenge existing arrangements. It is clear that teachers in our society wish to significantly increase their chances to become a respected and responsible human service group in a changing era, demanding substantial restructuring of many institutions.

Suggested Activity

Ask your instructor to invite the presidents of the local affiliates of the NEA and the AFT to debate the merits of their respective organizations.

If this is not feasible, perhaps you can interview each president and tape your conversations with them; of course you must ask their permission to tape the interview and to play it during class. It is advisable to be prepared with about ten specific questions to ask each president.

References and Notes

1. Louis Fischer and David Schimmel, *The Civil Rights of Teachers* (New York: Harper & Row, 1973), p. xi.

2. *Ibid*, p. 160.

3. *Ibid.*, p. 147.

4. *Ibid.*, p. 149.

5. *Ibid.*, pp. 59, 60.

6. Eric F. Rhodes and Richard G. Neal,

The Control of Teacher Militancy, 2nd ed. (Washington, D.C.: Educational Service Bureau, 1971), pp. 2–4.

7. Lloyd Ashby, James McGinnis, and Thomas Persing, *Common Sense in Negotiations in Public Education* (Danville, Ill.: The Interstate Printers and Publishers, 1972), pp. 117–20.

8. *See,* for instance, Theodore H. Lang, "Teacher Tenure as a Management Problem," *Phi Delta Kappan* 56 (March 1975): 459–62.

9. W. Vance Grant and C. George Lind, U.S. Department of Health, Education, and Welfare, Office of Education, *Digest of Educational Statistics* (Washington, D.C.: U.S. Government Printing Office, 1973), p. 11.

10. Harmon Zeigler, *The Political Life of American Teachers* (Englewood Cliffs, N.J.: Prentice-Hall, 1967), p. 30.

11. Ronald C. Corwin, *Militant Professionalism: A Study of Organizational Conflict in High Schools* (New York: Appleton-Century-Crofts, 1970), p. 176.

12. Myron Lieberman, *The Future of Public Education* (Chicago: University of Chicago Press, 1960), p. 192.

13. Theodore Schuchat, "With Education in Washington," *The Educational Digest* 40 (October 1974): 66.

14. Michael H. Moskow and Robert E. Doherty, "United States," in Albert A. Blum, ed., *Teacher Unions and Associations: A Comparative Study* (Urbana: University of Illinois Press, 1969), p. 301.

15. "Newsnotes," *Phi Delta Kappan* 56 (October 1974): 163.

16. Moskow and Doherty, "United States," p. 301.

17. Reported in the *American Teacher* 59 (June 1975): 3.

18. Schuchat, "With Education in Washington," p. 66.

19. Rhodes and Neal, *Control of Militancy,* p. 15.

20. Quoted in Alan Rosenthal, *Pedagogues and Power: Teacher Groups in School Politics* (Syracuse, N.Y.: Syracuse University Press, 1969), p. 20.

21. *Teachers' Salaries and Salary Schedules 1972–1973,* C.A.R.E. Document Number 11 (Burlingame: California Agency for Research in Education, California Teachers Association, 1973), p. viii; and *Salaries and Salary Schedules for Administrators and Special Services for Certificated Personnel 1972–1973,* C.A.R.E. Document No. 13 (Burlingame: C.A.R.E., C.T.A., 1973), p. ix.

22. *Standard Education Almanac,* 7th ed., 1974–1975 (Chicago: Marquis Academic Media, 1975), p. 602.

23. Myron Lieberman, "NEA–AFT Merger: Breakthrough in New York," *Phi Delta Kappan* 53 (June 1972): 625.

24. "Newsnotes," p. 161.

25. Philip W. Semas, "NEA–AFT Merger?" *The Chronicle of Higher Education* 10 (July 21, 1975): 4.

26. Eaton H. Conant, "What Do Teachers Do All Day?" *Saturday Review/World* (June 1974): 55.

27. Robert L. Walter, *The Teacher and Collective Bargaining* (Lincoln, Neb.: Professional Educators Publications, 1975), p. 11.

28. *Ibid.,* p. 37.

29. *Ibid.,* p. 38.

14

The Retreat from Traditional Education

Schooling has become big business in modern American society. It has been largely taken out of the hands of the local lay public, since they have neither the time nor skills to carefully watch over this institution. In the past several years, however, more people have become involved in control of education, especially inner-city blacks and members of the middle- and upper-middle classes of society. While members of the two groups ordinarily have little in common in terms of ethnicity, income, or formal educational background, they do share the conviction that schools belong—or ought to belong—to the people who attend them and their parents, rather than to government officials, bureaucrats, and educational functionaries.

In order to regain client control over the educational process and product, these two groups have been willing to retreat from traditional patterns of authority developed in the years since the end of World War II. These contemporary retreatist movements in education are termed the "community control movement" and the "free school movement."

The Community Control Movement
and the Poor in America

Most poor people in the United States have not received a formal education equal to that offered to more affluent members of this society. This failure to benefit from universal public education still exists, despite more than ten years of heavy federal and state support of "compensatory education" programs for the so-called culturally disadvantaged—programs sponsored and implemented mainly by middle-class Americans.

The liberal ideal of school integration, legally sanctioned since the 1954 Brown decision, is still far from being fully achieved, despite pressures upon local districts by the Department of Health, Education, and Welfare. Although most surveys continue to depict the black community as favoring school integration and although the NAACP supports it, the strong resistance of whites to actual desegregation efforts through busing understandably frustrates black people who have been placing their faith in their liberal allies.[1]

Growing numbers of black and other minority parents have become disenchanted with attempts to compensate educationally for their alleged cultural deficits, as well as to integrate them into a mainstream whose members move from the central city to suburbia as soon as serious talk of desegregating schools is brought up (a behavioral syndrome commonly known as white flight, or "tipping"). The failure of the United States Supreme Court to rule in favor of consolidating Detroit's urban and suburban school districts in *Milliken* v. *Bradley* (1974) may have been the "last straw" for many who had placed their hopes in school integration by means of busing. Abetted by a new spirit of ethnic pride, some poor people living in crowded urban ghettoes have been demanding that the neighborhood schools attended by their children be controlled by neighborhood residents, and that their children be taught by fellow minority educators, hired by the school system with prior consultation and approval of parents. These demands are echoed in these words:

It is the right (their exclusive right) and the duty of parents to educate their children. Neither the church nor the state has the right to take from the home the precious right to educate its young ... No group of "educators," no union, or Board of Education has the inherent right to educate children. Only parents have this right. Parents may confer upon educators the privilege of educating their children, but never the right to do so ... Parents may make use of the state (or the church) as the means of educating their children, but the right to educate belongs exclusively to parents. This is their right irrespective of station in life, or how much education they may have.[2]

Thus wrote the chief representative of the Brooklyn, New York, Oceanhill–Brownsville community in 1970, following the community's effort to take control of the newly **decentralized** school governing board. The Oceanhill–Brownsville affair has been widely publicized because it represented one of the first major efforts by minority parents to take over the schools of their neighborhood and because of the hostilities that ensued between members of the New York City United Federation of Teachers and the neighborhood community members. Conflict occurred over the question of whether or not the elected representatives of local parents have the right to decide who is to teach in the neighborhood schools. In the Oceanhill–Brownsville case, the board of education, superintendent, and the teachers' union fought to prevent a complete takeover by neighborhood parents and their governing board. They managed to do so, after violence, several arrests, much name calling, and a couple of teacher strikes. Shortly afterward, the New York state legislature ordered that a permanent decentralization plan be formulated. In 1969 the Decentralization Act was passed with the following provisions:

1. Thirty to thirty-three local school districts with elected boards, each with its own superintendent and at least 20,000 students
2. An elected central board consisting of seven members, five from each borough and two appointed by the mayor
3. Local school boards may control the curriculum, within the framework of state regulations
4. Local school boards may select textbooks from a list approved by the central board and superintendent
5. Local boards can contract for maintenance and repair up to $250,000 per year
6. High schools continue under control of the central board[3]

Following the New York City modifications in its school system's governing structure, several other major cities decentralized their school

districts to some extent, including Los Angeles, Chicago, Detroit, and Philadelphia.⁴ The trend toward decentralization of governing units in the field of local schooling is apparently here to stay, particularly in large cities with unwieldy districts. Decentralization, however, may not be radical enough surgery for residents of all the subdistricts affected. Decentralization may reduce the size of administrative units, thereby making schools somewhat more responsive to the people in a district, but unless the decentralization is accompanied by specific moves to gather greater input from community members, it remains essentially an administrative strategy—not a means for upgrading and humanizing school systems by bringing them closer to the people.

As an alternative to traditional forms of control, the community control movement seeks to do more than alter geographical boundaries of school districts. It also seeks to bring the parents of school children and their schools much closer together than they have been in the past. This is achieved by placing parents or their representatives in effective positions of power to ensure that personnel hired in the district will be sympathetic with the community's aspirations and that the school curriculum will be what the parents want.

However, there are arguments that can be raised against this seemingly reasonable and humane idea of local community control. For example, it can be argued that American society and education have become too complicated to trust the control of education to lay people, particularly to those with relatively little formal education. This argument in turn can be attacked on several grounds, although the validity of the grounds used may be questionable at times. For instance, it can be asserted that low levels of formal education do not necessarily preclude possession of high intelligence. Or one may respond to the argument about socioeducational complication by saying that it is precisely such conditions that call for the special insights of those who know the subtle nuances of change affecting their own people. Outsiders can never hope to truly understand the real learning needs of ethnic youngsters. Robert J. Taggart, however, concludes that the real reason behind much failure of American educators to reform schools is the widespread public mistrust of educators in this country, as compared to Britain. This is demonstrated by the accountability movement now in vogue and by community control efforts:

> Community control is a direct challenge to whatever autonomy is possible to teachers and principals. In both [accountability and community control], educators are to deliver clearly identified competencies, but in neither are educators given the time or freedom for the experimentation that is necessary for reform.⁵

Another argument used against the community-control movement is that it is regressive: In a pluralistic society, only a multicultural education in open, integrated settings can effectively prepare youngsters for their future encounters with people who may look, think, and behave differently from that to which they are accustomed.[6] Leonard Fein attacks this liberal argument by claiming instead that people have the right to choose their friends, associates, and teachers, instead of falling prey to the logic of social scientists who, according to Fein, tend to think that everyone lives rationally.[7]

Another argument against community control rests on the premise that a sense of community is rare in the U. S. today; if anything, our communities are disintegrating and not even remaining viable. But the community-control-of-schools advocates retort that inner-city ethnic communities are still intact. Owing to the struggle of minorities to survive, coupled with their new-found group pride, the inner-city community is actually thriving culturally, they argue.

According to Fein, the community-control movement of the urban poor involves deep-seated values. Thus, the controversy over this movement cannot be simplistically explained by ideas such as "vested interest in preserving educational jobs by whites" or the "capability of poor people to control their own educational destinies." Fein says that community control is a worthy end, because it reflects the very complexity of our changing society better than present modes of control:

> What is required, then, is a school system which, in its own idiom, reflects the complexity of the American arrangement, rather than one which imposes a specific version of the "right" social ordering on its participants. And that, in turn, means a school system which mirrors the tensions of this arrangement.[8]

Although such a value-based argument is quite persuasive, it is not likely to convince strong opponents of the community control idea, particularly advocates of school integration who sincerely believe that segregated schools are inferior. The opponents of community control argue that this society demands the ability to get along well with all people, if it is to survive as a society and not become a motley aggregate of diverse and alienated ethnic enclaves.

Thus, the problem is immensely complex. Hard data are needed to substantiate claims by both sides in the debate before we can say with assurance how valid the ideal of community control is. Before this happens, the politics of education may intrude and obviate the most sophisticated of sociological, psychological, and philosophical arguments that are extended to support or disclaim the notion of community control.

Some useful guidelines for thinking about the problem have been offered recently by Larry Cuban. He finds that "reformers cluster around the particular outcomes that they predict would result from increased participation, as they define it."[9] The outcomes predicted "can be divided into four groups: ideological, social and individual therapy, political, and educational."[10] Each outcome predicted by reformers is open to serious question. For instance, the ideological argument, which presupposes that community control is in the best tradition of participatory democracy, ignores the fact that there has traditionally been a low level of public participation in American institutional life. Moreover, "people turn out mostly to protest, not just to exercise power or feel democratic. If they have confidence in their leaders or have no cause for protest, evidence indicates that participation remains minimal."[11]

With regard to the notion that community participation helps to relieve the personal and social sense of isolation felt by many ethnic poor today, Cuban notes that (1) "failure to gain tangible outcomes from the promise of participation could harvest a deeper, more infuriating anger, or worse, paralyzing apathy"[12] (recent experiences with urban renewal and model cities programs indicate that this is true); (2) reversing the pattern of traditional low citizen participation in institutional life would be extremely difficult; and (3) reversing the trend in this society of making schooling the province of specialists in education would be unrealistic.[13]

The third outcome of community control, according to reformers, is that it would result in defusing volatile demands from militants by showing that the school is capable of being responsive to the people. Cuban agrees, but argues that defusing political conflict and coopting people will involve more time, energy, and political maneuvering than dealing with the goals of schooling will. If schooling is considered too politicized today by some, community control would politicize education even further. Responding to community demands is also likely to lead to "goal displacement," that is, to a situation in which "more emphasis is placed upon maintaining the support of participants than striving to achieve the goals of effective schooling," as has been the case in New York City in the past few years.[14]

Thus, Cuban finds the possible outcomes of community control to be very uncertain. He joins Fein in urging that we give more thought to our educational values—to the ends to be hoped for and expected of schooling. But instead of concluding with Fein that community control best resolves the value tensions of our pluralistic society, Cuban says that in a confused society in the process of transforming, it would be best to be concerned with examining and clarifying the "values that underlie alternative policies, not coating the issue in layers of statistics, sophistry, or rhetoric."[15]

Because the community-control movement involves primarily public schools and taxpayers' money, it would appear that the process of examining and clarifying values surrounding it will not quickly abate. There is not likely to be a quick and easy solution to this basic educational issue. The federal government itself is ambivalent. On principle, it supports community control by appropriating special monies for neighborhood schools, but it also is trying to desegregate schools. If school districts are decentralized and local parent controls are established, the existing demography in our society would mean that segregation of races and cultures would continue, and the affluent would continue to leave the city to the poor.

Alternative Schools

Open Education.   Stephens defines open education "as an approach to education that is open to change, to new ideas, to scheduling, to use of space, to honest expression of feeling between teacher and pupil and between pupil and pupil, and open to children's participation in significant decision-making in the classroom."[16] A great many educators, including advocates of free schools, would give at least lip service to such an idea today.

Stephens says there are differences between the recent open education movement in this country and the movement in British primary schools and the earlier Progressive Education movement influenced by John Dewey's philosophy of Instrumentalism, both of which have contributed to the open-education philosophy. She says that open education departs from Progressivism "in the more active role of the teacher, greater emphasis on planned environments, clarification of the limits of the child's freedom and greater concern about the curriculum."[17] She also contrasts open education, which is an **in-system development** in the United States, with the free school movement, which exists largely outside the mainstream of public education. She maintains that:

> ... open educators reject many of the approaches of free schools—the generally laissez-faire attitude toward curriculum, unlimited choices for children, the secondary role of teachers, and absence of attention to cognitive skills. . .[18]

Alternative Education in
Public Schools

Smith discusses several types of alternative public schools now becoming available to American youngsters and their parents:[19]

   • *Open schools.*   Conventional or nonconventional learning activities are individualized and organized around interest centers within a classroom or building.

• *Schools-without-Walls.* Began with Philadelphia's Parkway Program in 1969, which permitted a variety of learning activities to be carried on throughout a community, usually at the high school level, and utilized many of the community's cultural and economic resources.

• *Learning Center Schools.* Institutions with learning centers concentrate learning resources in one location available to all of a community's students (e.g., **magnet schools,** "educational parks," career education centers, vocational–technical high schools, etc.).

• *Continuation Schools.* Special schools for regular school dropouts, pregnant teenagers, adults wanting a high school diploma, and other students whose formal education in conventional schools has been interrupted.

• *Multicultural Schools.* Schools (which can be magnet schools, educational parks, etc.) concentrating heavily on the positive aspect of cultural pluralism and on developing ethnic or racial awareness and harmonization. Multicultural schools usually serve a broad spectrum of subcultural groups in a community.

• *Schools-within-Schools.* Any of a variety of types of alternative schools or programs (ranging from highly traditional to extremely unconventional) that are located on the grounds or within the walls of another more conventional public school. Students are involved in such programs by choice.

The above list of recent public school alternatives omits the separate free school, which is normally privately financed and controlled. Nonetheless, Smith and others have observed that a few communities have developed free schools as alternatives *within* their public education systems; for instance, the Murray Road Annex in Newtonville, Massachusetts, in which one hundred fifteen students and eight faculty members and other adults plan their own programs together according to their own interests and needs, and the West Philadelphia Community Free School, a relatively large public high school located in several renovated homes. Students take both basic courses and electives in the Philadelphia community. The program is nongraded and highly individualized.[20]

Deschooling Society.   By far the most radical educational alternative proposed to date has been that of a completely "deschooled society." Ivan Illich[21] is the leader of this movement, along with Everett Reimer.[22] The deschoolers believe that the very notion of schooling has become obsolete. According to them, schools all over the world are presently organized merely to reproduce the established order of things, an order they believe is oppressive to most of the world's people. This is true especially with regard to the social class structure in capitalist or socialist societies. According to Illich:

> This crisis is epochal. We are witnessing the end of the age of schooling. School has lost the power which reigned supreme during the first half of this century, to blind its participants to the divergence between the egalitarian myth its rhetoric serves and the rationalization of a stratified society its certificates produce. The loss of legitimacy of the schooling process as a means of determining competence, as a measure of social value, and as an agent of equality threatens all political systems that rely on schools as the means of reproducing themselves.[23]

Even schools typically considered most radical, such as free schools, inadequately prepare children to live equitably in the modern world, according to Illich. They are superficially reformist in nature and scope, at best, they are not revolutionary:

> Free schools are practical alternatives; they can often be run more cheaply than ordinary schools....
> Free schools, which lead to further free schools in an unbroken chain of attendance, produce the mirage of freedom. Attendance as the result of seduction inculcates the need for specialized treatment more persuasively than the reluctant attendance enforced by truant officers. Free school graduates are easily rendered impotent for life in a society that bears little resemblance to the protected gardens in which they have been cultivated.[24]

Illich and the deschoolers would abolish schools and professional school teachers altogether. Using advanced computer technology humanely, they would replace schools with what they call "learning webs," "peer-matching," and other innovations that place "natural" teachers from the "organic" community in the willing company of learners of every age desiring to acquire the skills and understandings possessed by the former. Since access to elitist educational sources (i.e., schools) would supposedly no longer be available under this plan, all people at every age would have a truly equal opportunity to utilize the revitalized educational institution to their advantage.

The ideas of the deschoolers have been received with the most enthusiasm by a very small and elite element of the educational intellectual community, not by school administrators, teachers, teachers of teachers, or the general public. However, some of their ideas, such as learning webs, have been tried out with moderate success on an extracurricular basis in cities such as Chicago.

Many of these visionary ideas could prove to be a powerful impetus to educational reform by stimulating educators to think outside of their intellectual systems. Although deschooling is a radical idea, it may ultimately help improve schooling as an institutional reality.

The Independent Free School and Radical Educational Reform

Another potentially significant form of retreat from traditional patterns of control and authority is the free school movement, which until recently had grown rapidly since its inception in the late 1960s. Free schools are not the same as a variety of other comparable educational alternatives that have arisen in recent years and that are sometimes confused with free schools. In the long run, the free school movement will probably have the most impact upon the public school system in the United States. To understand why, it is necessary to describe this modern educational rebellion in greater detail.

What is meant by the "free school movement"? As differentiated from publicly controlled and operated forms of alternative education, free schools have been founded by the efforts of more or less alienated young men and women to enlist more or less alienated youngsters and their parents in grassroots efforts to create their own schools outside of the public sector. The free school movement is a **separatist** movement. The people involved in it want to build their own independent educational agencies. They want to escape from the bureaucratic paraphernalia that they believe make public schools untenable, rigid, formalistic, and oppressive to youngsters. They want to abolish grades, adult-imposed curricula, teacher-centered instruction, and administrator-dominated institutions. They want the children and youth to freely determine what they want to learn and the means by which they shall learn. Their conception of the role of the free school teacher is of a resource person and a friend to the learner.

This ideal is based largely, although not entirely,* upon A.S. Neill's Summerhill school in England, a country boarding school established in the 1920s. Summerhill's premise is that only the youngster can determine what and how he or she should learn—or whether he or she should learn anything at all. Some of Neill's students never made an effort to learn to read until they were about to leave Summerhill. According to Neill, these students learned within a few months what it normally takes elementary school-aged youngsters several years to acquire.[25]

Transplanted to the United States, several Summerhillean free schools have been established in rural areas. As Herb Snitzer's Lewis–Wadhams school in rural upstate New York demonstrates, the ideal is not always perfectly achieved.[26] There are variations in free schools according to location, creator, and students. Snitzer went to England to learn about free education from Neill himself, and later developed a boarding school for well-to-do children on his farm. As he describes his endeavor, Lewis–Wadhams is relatively successful in attracting paying students because it is a secure haven for many children and adolescents who have not been very happy with their former public or private schools. At Lewis–Wadhams, students live in pleasant surroundings, engage in a wide variety of outdoor recreational activities if they wish, have opportunities to talk their personal problems over with intelligent and caring adults, develop their own "courses," select their teachers, and generally exist in a rather congenial camp-like atmosphere.

But not all free schools are like Snitzer's. About 91 percent are close to being "shoestring" daytime operations in medium- and large-sized cities.[27] George Dennison's small (twenty-three students, three teachers) First Street School on New York's Lower East Side catered to poor black, white, and Puerto Rican children in almost equal proportions.[28] Depending heavily upon Dennison's interpretation of John Dewey's educational philosophy, the school was apparently able to liberate the spirits of these disadvantaged youngsters as effectively as did Snitzer's upper-middle class paradise in the country.

Free schools are usually small operations with tuition charges† and staffed by three to four lowly paid teachers, including a leader (not

---

* The philosophical and empirical sources of free schools vary. Existential and Instrumental philosophies and their educational applications developed by writers such as A. S. Neill, Carl Rogers, John Dewey, Herbert Kohl, George Dennison, Jonathan Kozol, and others have been influential in the thinking of different free school organizers.

† Thus, the term "free" school obviously does not refer to admission practices.

an administrator), who work with fifteen to forty students. Staff members normally have to share a variety of housekeeping and other non-instructional tasks besides teaching. In one free high school with which the author was personally acquainted, some of the teachers were credentialled to work in public elementary or high schools, while others had absolutely no background in formal education prior to becoming involved with the free school.

Lack of previous educational training or experience has been one of the problems facing the early inaugurators of free schools. Many students or their parents discovered after a short time that the ability of the faculty to accomplish what they idealistically had promised was less than had been expected. So after a year or two parents often withdrew their children in frustration and many free schools disbanded. In some cases where free school faculty and students engaged in activities that were highly offensive to neighboring homeowners or shopkeepers, their inability to produce educational results was exacerbated by community–school or intra-school frictions, which resulted in the school's failure. A combination of factors have worked against the acceptance of free schools; in a few instances, these have included strong idealism, unsupported by adequate formal educational experience; drug use by some students and faculty (even though not officially condoned by the faculty); efforts by hostile neighbors and the FBI to intimidate students and faculty for their radical political beliefs; and eventual disorganization and demoralization of the participants.[29]

Having learned from the bitter experience of some of the early movement leaders—who often possessed more charisma than caution and skill in teaching—those in charge of many of the modern free schools that have survived or that are just being established are careful to hire faculty members with some teacher education and experience in public education. They are willing to compromise with community values and expectations to a degree, in order to avoid antagonizing the community.

In the San Francisco area there has been an effort to develop an accreditation program for alternative schools. Accreditation could greatly enhance the alternative schools' ability to operate harmoniously and without undue community interference, as well as increase the chances of graduates being accepted by colleges and universities. Actually, college acceptance is not a serious problem for students in alternative schools since many public and private institutions of higher learning will accept them on the basis of entrance test scores.

The proposal for a Pacific Regional Association of Alternative Schools lists the following as membership prerequisites:

A. A statement of philosophy and purpose
B. Compliance with the following criteria of responsiveness:
    1. Curriculum of school is based on student needs

2. Students have major role in directing and determining what and how they shall learn along with experienced faculty and other adults

3. A competent faculty shall be available to implement such a program—credentialed or not

4. Evidence of willingness to adapt curriculum to minimum legal demands of the state in which school is located[30]

In addition, P.R.A.A.S.-affiliated schools would also be expected to comply with a non-racial, non-sexist policy; they should also involve parents a great deal and offer scholarships to low-income minority children.[31]

Serious discussion of accreditation for alternative schools indicates that some of these schools are still having a difficult time gaining accreditation from the more traditional agencies that are responsible for accrediting public and private schools. The growing numbers of alternative schools seem to indicate that the movement is not temporary or faddish, and so it may gain legitimacy by accreditation soon.

If the free school separatists can unite with community-control retreatists and others who seek significant alternatives in education to obtain passage of federal legislation providing for use of educational vouchers by parents, their position in their communities and in society at large will be greatly strengthened. The voucher system has been proposed by Christopher Jencks and other educators who believe that public schools have failed to offer all youngsters equality of opportunity. It is being tested by the federal government in Alum Rock (San Jose), California. The voucher system proposal would not use property or other state and local taxes for *direct* support of public schools. The voucher system would allow parents to *choose* the type of school to which they send their children by giving a lump sum of money in the form of a voucher for each of their school-aged children. The amount would be roughly equivalent to that currently being spent on children for schooling from the public treasury. The parents then could send their children to the school of their choice—either public or private. Of course, provisions would have to be built into the law preventing schools involved from discriminating against children by refusing to admit on the basis of race, class, or ethnicity.

Under the voucher system, free schools could theoretically compete much more strongly with public schools, because they would no longer be forced to charge high tuition fees that only upper-income parents usually can afford. This would permit free schools to hire the most qualified teachers of their choice and to enrich the learning environment, which is too often seriously impoverished in alternative schools despite the best intentions of unusually enthusiastic and dedicated faculty, parents, and students. Vouchers, however, have been strenuously resisted by many public school people, including teachers and their representative organizations. They have their own vested interests in the public school monopoly in formal education, which might be threatened if private schools were to develop a competitive edge. It is this topic of competitiveness to which we now turn.

Implications of the Free School
Movement for Public Education

Until the onset of a major recession in the 1970s, free schools had been growing by leaps and bounds; their growth started around 1968 when there were only about thirty free schools in the United States.[32] They still represent only a small fraction of the total sources of schooling available to youngsters in this society, due to their comparatively large tuition charges at a time of economic crisis, their high failure rate, their lack of capital funding, their small enrollment policies, and the fact that most parents are conservative about education, even when they are highly progressive politically, economically, and in their personal lifestyles.

At present, most free schools are attended by both academically successful and unsuccessful children of upper-middle class, college educated parents who are unusually liberal in their overall orientations to their environment. Free schools also enroll children of the lower-middle class, who have attended public schools, met with failure, and were sent to a free school as the final recourse. Jonathan Kozol has urged the widespread creation of free schools for the underprivileged poor who, he claims, have the most to gain from radical educational reforms.[33]

Public school officials actually have little reason to feel threatened by the developing free school movement as yet. In fact, they have already coopted the notion of educational alternatives into their own schools, as we said earlier. To date, the cooptation of public alternative educational forms has not been very extensive nor as highly innovative as some would like.

Added to the relative insignificance of educational reform efforts by boards of education and public school people is the oversupply of individuals trying to enter the field of education when the birthrate is declining. Some of them will not be able to readily secure public school positions, although they are young, enthusiastic, intelligent members of the "new breed" of prospective teachers described in Chapter 1.

Insofar as the free school movement continues to grow and eventually to thrive outside of conventional school boundaries, it will almost inevitably draw clients away from the troubled public school system, especially if it can avoid projecting an image of exclusivity. This, in turn, is likely to force school officials to take a closer look at their own institution in the near future to see what is wrong and how problems can be corrected. Successful private free schools can compete with public schools for institutional dominance—for students, money, programs, and personnel.[34] If the movement grows—and installation of new, more liberalized financing systems such as the voucher could greatly facilitate such growth—public school people, already worried about losses of revenue from a highly critical public, are likely to become seriously concerned with its competition for dominance.

Taking into account the inhibiting influence of a temporary period of recession, there is every likelihood that the free school movement, as one significant alternative form of universal education operating from outside of traditional school boundaries, will grow and thrive. As the public schools are now organized and operated, they seem unable to garner sufficient creative energy to respond fully to the demands of the American people. Free schools are established in the first place in order to cater to particular demands. Their very intent is to be highly responsive to the client. They possess built-in mechanisms of what earlier we called ultra-stability from the start. Their purpose is to meet the varied and changing learning needs of any and all individuals and groups in a society.

In the years to come many young, dynamic teachers, who are unable to obtain positions in conventional schools, will perhaps be available to offer their services at reduced rates to such interesting enterprises, for a few years after leaving college.

The free school movement should not be taken lightly, as many educators of both traditional and radical outlooks have done during the early and difficult phase of its development.[35] With the help of the shared experience of its widespread network of followers, the movement is likely to overcome its initial problems of recruiting competent personnel, being accepted by the community, and working out its organizational and fiscal difficulties. It may be argued that such an optimistic prospect is to be welcomed, rather than discouraged, by educators interested in working in the public schools as well as those contemplating careers elsewhere. It may be claimed that anything that helps to invigorate public education and to maintain its responsiveness is worthy of support.

Should You Participate in the Retreat from the Educational Mainstream?

The suggestion was made in the previous section that the free school movement may deserve to be supported in principle by all educators, whether they work in public school systems or not, and whether they are members of the AFT, the NEA, or the American Association of School

Administrators or not. To support the free school movement is somewhat comparable to supporting two-party or multi-party politics. Advocacy of a one-party system runs counter to the democratic ideals of this society and to the realities of the social change process, a process highly dependent upon goading complacent powers by creatively dissenting.

But should *you* become personally involved in the retreatist movement, either by opening or working in a free school or by teaching in a public school operating under the auspices of community-control activists? It is one thing to support educational reforms from afar because they seem to be worthwhile efforts, and yet another to become directly involved with reform activities.

If you agree philosophically with those who urge community control at the possible expense of school desegregation, and you are a member of a minority group who wishes to help to improve the status of your group, you may perhaps consider joining the community control movement. Some people are emotionally tied to the community control movement, although they may agree intellectually with the arguments for integration.

On the other hand, if you are not a minority-group member, you may or may not be welcome in a decentralized public school under tight community control, no matter how sympathetic you may be with the idea. As a perceived representative of the dominant group in American society, you will need to ask yourself candidly whether you would be successful and happy working in an environment in which majority-group members are sometimes viewed as oppressors. Although it may be possible for some caring and intelligent dominant-group teachers to be accepted and successful in working with minority children and their parents in decentralized districts, it is not possible for everyone to do so. It may become even more difficult in the future, unless the problem of racism is solved.

Thus, a prospective teacher who wants to work with the poor, and is highly secure as a human being, and is well prepared, perhaps should consider working in a community school, regardless of his or her ethnicity. On the other hand, if you have any doubts about your personal and professional strength, the emotional and social risks of assuming such a difficult teaching position would be very great.

You should not consider participating actively in the free school movement simply because you may have been told it offers opportunities for young teachers who cannot obtain jobs in the public schools. Many college students visit local free schools and come back to their education classes filled with amazement at the easygoing atmosphere, the spontaneous relations between youngsters and adults, and the apparent ease with which students learn in an environment that allows for a high degree of self-motivated and self-disciplined explorations by learners.

Yet not all of these observers are well-advised to actually become free school faculty members. It takes a certain kind of person to do the work with zeal and contentment. The teacher needs to be highly democratic in temperament, a quality not possessed by everyone.[36] The failure of many free school teachers to exhibit this type of temperament has apparently been partly responsible for the ultimate demise of a number of free schools. Free school teachers often start out with great enthusiasm, but quickly enter a cycle of regression from early optimism to hostility, defensiveness, discouragement, and fatigue.[37]

You should also possess a coherent philosophy of education that is consonant with the free school ideal, whether this philosophy is Instrumentalist in overall orientation or Existentialist; not everyone who admires the movement from a distance really holds such a philosophy. Many people talk glibly about the virtues of student freedom to learn, but when actually confronted with the opportunity to free their children in their own classes, they quickly revert to adult-centered, highly structured modes of behavior. To be a free school teacher, you must genuinely believe in the movement's philosophy of freedom in order to put it to work with youngsters.

A free school teacher also needs sizable resources of energy and the willingness to expend this energy for little pay; the hours are usually long and financial rewards small. And, in light of current economic realities and the high failure rate of even well-run free schools, strong risk-taking capabilities are needed by individuals who want to work in free schools.

Most communities have a number of parents and their children who, for one reason or another, feel they are not being served adequately by available educational facilities. Perhaps you can gather some of your friends and together start your own free school. It is conceivable that you can succeed in starting a community free school with the help of such parents and their children. You should keep your fees moderate, find a free or inexpensive building in which to house your school, and perhaps apply for grant monies now available from the federal government for innovative educational projects. You could seek the volunteer help of local resource people knowledgeable about some subject your students want to study, such as psychology, education, the legal system, language arts, photography, feminism, sculpture, conversational Spanish, auto mechanics, drama, or American Indian History.

On the other hand, if you do not wish to retreat very far from traditional educational forms, but desire to participate in what may be becoming a significant in-system educational reform movement, alternative public education of one sort or another may be of interest to you and worth exploring further.[38]

This is an exciting time of unprecedented opportunity in the field of education for those who are able to broaden their vision to see beyond the traditional classroom concept, and for those who have a genuine desire to explore new avenues now in process of being realized for the contemporary generation of learners.

Summary

Failure of the traditional American public school system to adequately meet the real educational needs of both poor and middle-class youngsters in recent years has led to two separate reactions to the prevailing pattern of school authority.

The community control–decentralization movement of the inner-city poor stands in sharp contrast to the independent free school movement of upper-middle-class suburbia. The first is an in-system effort to make existing public schools and credentialled educators more accountable to the people who send their children to them. The second is an effort to separate from the public schools altogether in order to offer young people a chance to learn whatever they want to learn by a variety of means; the conviction of this movement is that it is the best way to ensure a personally rewarding education.

Both movements have had their detractors and problems of survival Although it is still too soon to tell what the future portends for them, it is possible that each will leave its mark upon the educational institution. There is room for serious, intelligent teachers in each of these retreatist movements, or, perhaps, in public school alternative education, at a time of unprecedented disequilibrium in the educational system.

Related Concepts

decentralization   The dividing of a school district into several smaller subdistricts, each with its own administrative leadership and policies

in-system developments   Having to do with activities internal to a social organization

magnet school   A school possessing unusually valuable resources for learning, compared with other schools in a district. In recent years, magnet schools have been developed in order to attract students of diverse racial and ethnic groups in many communities undergoing desegregation.

separatism   Outside of conventional arrangements. Separatists in education desire to disaffiliate from the prevailing school system and to independently start their own schools on a private basis.

Suggested Activity

Arrange a visit to a local free school and to an inner-city school with strong community control. Be prepared to help out on the day of your visitation. After the experience, report to your class on what you have learned and how you felt about each kind of educational arrangement.

References and Notes

1. For a thorough exposition of this point of view, see Leonard J. Fein, *The Ecology of the Public Schools: An Inquiry into Community Control* (Indianapolis: Bobbs-Merrill, 1971).

2. Reverend C. Herbert Oliver, "Community Control of Schools," in Sheldon Marcus and Harry N. Rivlin, eds., *Conflicts in Urban Education* (New York: Basic Books, 1970), pp. 115, 116.

3. Allen C. Ornstein, *Urban Education: Student Unrest, Teacher Behavior, and Black Power* (Columbus, Ohio: Charles E. Merrill, 1972), pp. 151, 152.

4. *Ibid.*, pp. 153–61.

5. Robert J. Taggart, "Open Education Without Professional Autonomy?" *The Education Digest* 40 (September 1974): 5.

6. Jane Mercer, with Marietta Coleman and Jack Harloe, *Racial/Ethnic Segregation and Desegregation in American Public Education*, United States Office of Education OEC-9-72-0137. Under the provisions of Title IV, Section 403, of Public Law 88-352, The Civil Rights Act of 1964 (Riverside: University of California, 1973). Mimeographed.

7. Fein, *Ecology of Schools*, p. 36.

8. *Ibid.*, p. 159.

9. Larry Cuban, "Community Participation and Urban School Reform," *Changing Education* 6 (Summer 1974): 24.

10. *Ibid.*

11. *Ibid.*

12. *Ibid.*, p. 26.

13. *Ibid.*

14. *Ibid.* see also Martin Schiff, "The Educational Failure of Community Control in Inner-City New York," *Phi Delta Kappan* 57 (February 1976): 375–78.

15. *Ibid.*

16. Lillian S. Stephens, *The Teacher's Guide to Open Education* (New York: Holt, Rinehart and Winston, 1974), p. 27.

17. *Ibid.*, p. 29.

18. *Ibid.*, pp. 31, 32.

19. Vernon H. Smith, *Alternative Schools: The Development of Options in*

Public Education (Lincoln, Neb.: Professional Educators Publications, 1974), pp. 16, 17.

20. *Ibid.,* pp. 35, 36.

21. Ivan Illich, *Deschooling Society* (New York: Harper & Row, 1971).

22. Everett Reimer, *School Is Dead: Alternatives in Education* (Garden City, N.Y.: Doubleday and Co., 1972).

23. Ivan Illich, "After Deschooling, What?" in Alan Gartner, Colin Greer, and Frank Riessman, eds., *After Deschooling, What?* (New York: Social Policy, 1973), pp. 5, 6.

24. *Ibid.,* pp. 14, 15.

25. A. S. Neill, *Summerhill: A Radical Approach to Child Rearing* (New York: Hart Publishing Company, 1960).

26. *See* Herb Snitzer in collaboration with Doris Ransohoff, *Today is for Children: Numbers Can Wait* (New York: The Macmillan Company, 1972).

27. Allen Graubard, *Free the Children: Radical Reform and the Free School Movement* (New York: Pantheon Books, 1972), p. 41.

28. George Dennison, *The Lives of Children: The Story of the First Street School* (New York: Random House, 1969), p. 3.

29. Steve Bhaerman and Joel Denker, *No Particular Place to Go: The Making of a Free School* (New York: Simon and Schuster, 1972).

30. *Prisma* (November 1974): 11. Published by Orpheus Publications, Bay Area Center for Alternative Education, San Francisco.

31. *Ibid.*

32. Graubard, *Free the Children,* pp. 40, 41.

33. Jonathan Kozol, *Free Schools* (Boston; Houghton Mifflin Company, 1972).

34. According to Leonard Solo of the Alternative Public School, Cambridge, Massachusetts, "statistics indicate that of 3,500 private alternative schools founded since 1964, about 20 percent have failed . . . any impression that all alternative schools are short-lived is without foundation." (Leonard Solo, "Alternative Views of Alternative School Failures," *Educational Researcher* 4 [July–August 1975]: 2.)

35. Detractors of the radical perspective include Marxists who feel that the movement can ultimately succeed only if it creates "not a temporary and privileged oasis of freedom, but an understanding of oppression and how to fight it in capitalist society . . . Yet a politically radical free-school movement could well provide a seed bed for revolutionaries. . . ." (*See* Samuel Bowles and Herbert Gintis, *Schooling in Capitalist America: Educational Reform and the Contradictions of Economic Life* [New York: Basic Books, 1976], p. 255.)

36. An interesting critical analysis of the problem of control in traditional and free school situations is offered by James H. Crouse and Paul T. McFarlane, "Monopoly, Myth, and Convivial Access to the Tools of Learning," *Phi Delta Kappan* 56 (May 1975): 591–95.

37. Chris Argris, "Alternative Schools: A Behavioral Analysis," *Teachers College Record* 75 (May 1974): 429–52.

38. *See* Mario D. Fantini, *Public Schools of Choice: A Plan for the Reform of American Education* (New York: Simon and Schuster, 1973).

The Nature of School Organization

15

The School as a Distinctive
Social System

Schools are social systems with unique functions to perform for society. In considering their organization, it is useful to apply a model developed by social psychologist Erving Goffman. Goffman's well-known concept of "total institutions" was originally applied to analysis of the organization and operation of mental asylums,[1] and later to the military. The concept can also help us to envision the workings of elementary and secondary schools.[2]

A "total institution" is one that strives to completely strip away the trappings of the external world from the entering member and to replace them with institutional trappings in order to facilitate the institution's governing of its members.[3] In the case of a hospital, the stripping process is literal. When new patients are admitted, they are often immediately taken in wheelchairs to their rooms, requested to leave their valuables in the safekeeping of others, and instructed to undress and change into unflattering gowns, or "hospital uniforms." This initial deculturization process is followed by reculturization to their new social milieu. Visitors are generally allowed only at specific hours so as not to interfere with hospital routine, meal times are different from the hours to which most people are accustomed, and patients are more or less constantly subjected to the unquestionable and sometimes mysterious orders of nurses, physicians, orderlies, and other personnel. Long-term patients, like inmates anywhere, tend to develop an underground life of their own in order to escape temporarily from official demands.

A similar pattern is followed by the military. The initial deculturalization of new inductees is symbolized by the shearing of the recruit's hair and the admonition to unhesitatingly obey all orders given by one's superiors.

Considering the above examples of how total institutions operate to deculturize new members and to reculturize them to the formal requirements of their new social systems, by what logic, if any, may we consider schools as total institutions? Hospitals, the military, and prisons are institutions that take charge of the lives of their members twenty-four hours a day, whereas elementary and secondary schools in American society are institutions in which most children spend only about a fourth or a third of their total day; the remainder of their time is spent at home with their parents and siblings and on the streets with their peers. In comparison with hospitals, prisons, the military, and boarding schools, most public schools in American society are not total institutions, especially in the eyes of those who feel least intimidated by their academic requirements, the dominant middle classes.[4] But it may be fair to consider schools as "semi-total institutions." Although most children attend school only five to seven hours a day, during the limited period of their stay, children are treated in many ways like patients or inmates of total institutions.

The most graphic, and often poignant, example of entering such an institution is the five-year-old's separation from his or her mother on the first day of school. For many parents, this day marks the end of their exclusive familial dominion over the lives of their children and the beginning of a sharing of control with the agents of an essentially foreign institution. From the time children are registered for school at age five or six, until the time they drop out or graduate at age sixteen or eighteen, they are members of this semi-total institution, members of a little society with its own separate culture.

Children are inducted into the special society and culture of schooling by a variety of mechanisms that are common to most schools in the greater society, as well as unique to their own elementary or secondary school. They are quickly taught to raise their hands before speaking in class, to ask their teacher for permission to go to the bathroom, to be prompt, and to achieve in the "school game" by scoring high grades and belonging to clubs, playing sports, and planning for further education upon leaving the public school system. They are taught to obey their teachers at all times and not to talk back, or fight, or play, or swear. In short, they are taught the universal culture of the American school—a middle-class culture for which some students may not have been prepared by their earlier family experiences.

School children also learn the special traditions, folkways, and mores of their particular school. Its subcultural patterns include its degree of emphasis upon the acquisition of "basic skills" as opposed to "life adjustment" competencies, its football cheers, its nicknames for teachers, its dress code, and its customary ways of dealing with troublemakers.

Formal Aspects of the Social System of Schooling

Like most other complex institutions, modern schools develop an official structure, personnel and client roles, and programs of operation.

Is the School a Bureaucracy?

Many writers on education (particularly critics, who use the term pejoratively) refer loosely to the American school as a bureaucracy.

A bureaucracy can be defined as involving:

> a clear-cut division of integrated activities which are regarded as duties inherent in the office. A system of differentiated controls and sanctions is stated in the regulations. The assignment of roles occurs on the basis of technical qualifications which are ascertained through formalized, impersonal procedures (e.g., examinations). Within the structure of hierarchically arranged authority, the activities of "trained and salaried experts" are governed by general, abstract, clearly defined rules which preclude the necessity for the issuance of specific instructions for each specific case.[5]

Most schools are organized hierarchically from the board of education and the central administration down through the ranks of middle-level managers (principals) and instructional specialists (curriculum directors and supervisors) to the teachers and pupils. Schools have many written regulations and rules for all parties. They are operated by personnel assigned on the basis of their technical qualifications, which are ascertained by evidence such as teaching or administrative credentials. Some scholars, however, have rejected the bureaucratic conception of schools, at least in part. Robert Dreeban puts it:

> ... despite the pyramidal structure of school systems, the hierarchy extending down to the level of pupils, and the importance of rules in some aspects of school system operation, these systems depart in many critical ways from the classical model of bureaucracies, and it is these departures that relate closely to the peculiarities of the teacher's work. Perhaps the

distinguishing characteristic of school systems is the vague connection between policy formation at both the high and middle levels of the hierarchy and its implementation at the level where instruction takes place —the classroom (where teachers respond not so much to orders from above as to events occurring daily and hourly involving their interrelations with students not necessarily perfectly adapted to the demands of the semi-total institution).

Schools and school systems do, however, have many of the trappings of bureaucracy: regulations that do not mean anything, a steady flow of trivial memoranda, forms to fill out and file, and so on through a long list of inane rituals. These phenomena are partly, and more importantly, attempts by those occupying managerial and supervisory positions to exert some degree of control over unpredictable exigencies and over people who may be inexperienced or inept, yet insulated by the privacy and dispersion of classrooms.[6]

Can we accept Dreeban's semi-bureaucratic conception of schools? Schools today are largely bureaucratic in intent, even if those who operate schools often fail to realize their intentions completely. Many upper-echelon control groups who manage school systems would like to make their operation as highly formalized as possible—in the classical bureaucratic sense. Fortunately or unfortunately, they rarely can go as far as they would like because teaching does not lend itself to strict regulation and regimentation. This natural limitation upon the power of control groups clearly supports Dreeban's argument that schools are less fully bureaucratized than many writers realize. However, teachers and students would not necessarily completely remove the bureaucratic characteristics schools already possess if they could, since bureaucracies are not always wholly bad.

A major study comparing large and relatively highly bureaucratized school systems with smaller, less bureaucratized systems in the St. Louis metropolitan area found that most teachers in highly bureaucratized systems feel more autonomous than do teachers in less formalized systems. This is because "bureaucracy provides the teacher with an understandable and predictable ethos in which to pursue his profession. This predictability, far from reducing a sense of power, sets a higher level of sense of power than is found in the less bureaucratized school organization."[7] It would appear, then, that bureaucracies are not inherently stifling and dehumanizing. Melvin L. Kohn also corroborates this idea. In a study of 3,101 men, he concluded that men who work in bureaucratic organizations tend to be more intellectually flexible, more open to new experience, and more self-directed than are men who work in non-bureaucratic organizations. This is partly due to their being more highly educated on the average and partly because bureaucracies offer employees greater job protection, somewhat higher income, and much more complex work, than do non-bureaucratic organizations.

The power of nonbureaucratic organizations over their employees is more complete and may be more capricious. Thus, the alternative circumscribed authority is likely to be, not less authority, but personal, potentially arbitrary authority.[8]

Kohn's study helps debunk the widely held myth that bureaucracies are inherently inferior to non-bureaucracies. But it does not examine the extent to which both bureaucracies and non-bureaucracies adapt to their external environments. There is little evidence that small businesses or religious organizations are more open to change than schools are. On the other hand, scientific and artistic institutions, despite their differences in orientation, appear to be structured for change.

Nor does Kohn's study tell us much about the special semi-bureaucracy of the school. Are people who aspire and are selected to work in schools less flexible on the whole than workers in other bureaucracies, for example? If so, then this characteristic alone could help account for the fact that American schools have not been as highly responsive to the requirements of life in an emergent Post–Industrial society as they should be.

It behooves us now to take a closer look at the people who work in the modern school. Our fundamental concern is for the relationship between what the school is capable of doing for society and the changing educational needs of the people who comprise the society.

The Staff of the Modern School

The official **role system** of teaching encompasses all formal positions that influence the teacher's work. Role expectations are written or unwritten. The role system of teaching is hierarchical; it does not take into consideration the reciprocal expectations held by teachers for those above them in the system. Such reciprocal expectations develop on an unofficial basis in highly or lowly bureaucratized schools.* The positions associated with the role system of teaching are shown in Figure 15–1.

Teachers

According to a recent NEA study, the typical elementary teacher in the United States in 1970 was a woman whose father was a blue-collar

---

* The rapid rise in militant teacher organizations may be changing this one-way model.

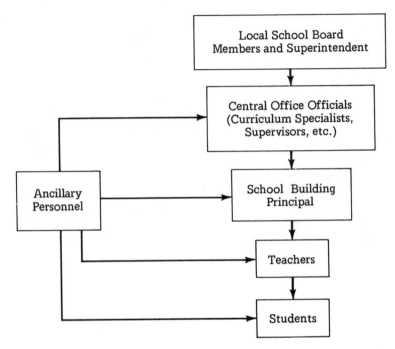

FIGURE 15–1. *Highly Simplified Role System of Local Educational Positions*

worker or a farmer or, increasingly, a middle-class businessman or professional.[9] She was thirty-seven years of age, married, possessed a bachelor's
degree and eight years of teaching experience, five of which had been
spent in her present school system. She was normally under a male
principal, had twenty-seven pupils and a duty-free lunch period of forty
minutes. She attended about seventeen faculty meetings a year, devoted
eight hours in addition to classroom work to nonpaid school-related
duties, and worked an average of 45.8 hours a week. She earned $9,092
annually. Although she was a PTA and NEA member, she did not belong
to any other professional local, state, or national educational associations. She said she became a teacher in order to work with young people
and would choose teaching again in the same school system if she could
choose again.

The typical secondary teacher was a man whose father was a blue-
collar worker or farmer. He was thirty-three years old, married, held a
bachelor's or perhaps a higher degree, and had seven years teaching
experience. He worked with 134 pupils a day, averaging 26 per class.
Unlike his counterpart in the elementary schools, he had five preparation
periods a week. He had a half-hour, duty-free lunch period and attended

fourteen faculty meetings a year. Like the elementary school teacher, he spent eight hours a week without pay on school-related duties other than instruction, and worked approximately 48.1 hours per week. His average annual salary was $9,449. He belonged to two or more local and state educational associations, including the PTA and a subject-matter or professional special-interest organization. He also says that he became a teacher in order to work with young people, but he also cites a special interest in a particular subject. He was less likely to choose teaching again than his female colleagues at the secondary level. (See Chapter 13 for a discussion of sex-related differences in occupational satisfaction associated with teacher militancy.)

The most significant member of the average teacher's role set is the school principal, especially at the elementary school level.[10] In the formal organization of the school, he (in 1974 only 13.5 percent of U.S. principals were women, of whom 95 percent were elementary school principals)[11] is the position incumbent to whom teachers most often refer mentally and emotionally when considering a proposed course of action. If teachers are considering, for example, a particular method of instruction or a particular way of disciplining a student, their minds usually flash to the image they hold of the principal, and they hypothesize how

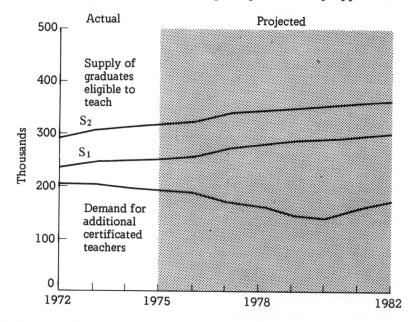

FIGURE 15–2. *Supply and Demand of Classroom Teachers (Education Division, Department of Health, Education, and Welfare, The Condition of Education [Washington, D.C.: U.S. Government Printing Office, 1976], p. 248)*

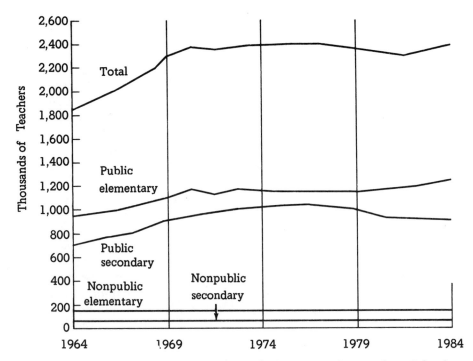

FIGURE 15–3.   *Classroom Teachers in Elementary and Secondary Schools: 1964–1984 (Education Division, Department of Health, Education, and Welfare, Projections of Education Statistics to 1984–85 [Washington, D.C.: U.S. Government Printing Office, 1976], p. 5.)*

he will regard their prospective behavior. More than any other reference figures associated with schooling—including superintendents, school psychologists, parents, or students—teachers tend to refer their occupational actions to their principals. He or she is the most significant other in the determination of which roles teachers play and how they enact their roles. Although the tendency to orient and act in terms of the expectations of the building principal may be lessening with the rising emphasis on teacher power, it does continue to predominate.

The tendency has obvious implications for a variety of problematic concerns, including the entire matter of teacher professionalization and the alteration of schooling systems. If teachers are most deeply influenced by their perceptions of how their principals will react to their behavior, then the kinds of significant modifications in their occupational behavior currently being urged by educational reformers must depend heavily upon concomitant modifications in teachers' traditional personal and occupational role images vis à vis the school principal, as well as upon modifications in teachers' long-standing expectations for their roles.

Exhortation of teachers to be more creative—extremely common today—in and of itself will do little to help upgrade the profession; the problem is primarily one of organizational (systemic) overhaul, in which the mutual relations of two key groups of institutional role incumbents—teachers and principals—are central to the entire enterprise and its development.

The Building Principal

The principal is also tied to a pattern of expectations for his (or her) own role, which makes it extremely unlikely that he can officially encourage his teachers to behave in ways other than those approved by administrative superordinates. As we noted in Chapter 13, the principal may acquire his office by demonstrating exceptional loyalty to his superiors; he is not likely to deviate from his perception of their expectations if he wishes to retain his position in the school system hierarchy.

Unofficially, of course, the principal can behave in ways that deviate from the system norms, and within these norms, he can indulge personal preferences for methods and styles of behavior in his own school. For instance, within normative system limits, the principal can allow teachers to experiment with instructional methods, especially if such experiments are considered relatively unimportant to school officials and parents. The principal is a "balancing agent," juggling the demands of school officials and those of parents and other community groups; like most school administrators, he is a "politician," as well as a building manager.[12] But if a teacher wants to teach reading or math or perhaps social studies or English in ways radically different from those approved by the principal or his superiors, he is unlikely to give his stamp of approval to the teacher. If an elementary school teacher does not hold a daily flag salute, the principal who learns of the omission from parents or students may suspect the teacher's loyalty to the society and school system and censure the teacher. If a teacher wears a miniskirt to school, and the principal does not consider this to be proper garb for representatives of the school in the community, he may take steps to prevent future breaches of the dress code.

Thus, the school principal, like the teacher, is bound by norms and role expectations of the wider social system of which he is considered an integral part. And, "the principal's view of the system—what it will or will not tolerate—was a decisive factor [in what teachers did]. . . . A number of principals were sincere in saying that they personally had no objections [to teachers breaking with traditional school system norms in their classrooms], but that they could not agree to the procedure because it was counter to rules and regulations, i.e., the system and its traditions."[13]

Specialists

Generally above the building principal in official rank, curriculum directors, subject-matter supervisors, consultants, and other specialists are
increasingly being viewed by teachers as extraneous. Officially, they are
employed to facilitate the work of the classroom teacher by offering the
latest in knowledge and skills in a given curricular area. But growing
numbers of teachers with full college degrees and teaching credentials
feel that they know their subject specialties as well as an outside expert
and, further, know best how to apply this knowledge when working with
their own students. As a result, central office specialists are increasingly
either being politely or coolly received by experienced teachers, and
quickly forgotten when they have left. Some specialists do develop unusual rapport with teachers and offer practical ideas.

On the other hand, new teachers often feel the need for help in the
classroom because they acquire only the rudiments of teaching before
obtaining full-time employment. The predicament of the beginning
teacher may not be a failing of teacher-preparation institutions, but rather

a result of state laws and general norms for teacher training that are still not as rigorous as for the training of other professionals.[14] New teachers are typically expected to perform the same kinds of tasks with much the same results as older, more experienced teachers.[15] Hence, they rely more upon help from central office specialists and their colleagues. The nature of the supervision received by the beginning teacher too often seems inadequate, and causes them to reject whatever help such experts might have to give.

For instance, a common practice is for a supervisor to announce that he or she will be visiting a new teacher in the near future to observe the teacher's work in the classroom. This obviously is a stressful condition in which to be teaching. After the formal observation, the new teacher and supervisor often have a conference in which the teacher is presented with an official evaluation that is recorded in his or her personnel file. Whether or not the novice is also given any real help is dependent upon who is supervising. Pre-announced visits two-to-four times a year in the beginning of a teacher's career are usually prepared for carefully by the novice, so these visits do not give the supervisor a reliable impression of the teacher's day-to-day performance. For these and related reasons, the supervisor rarely receives an accurate impression of the teacher's strengths and weaknesses. And, because of the widespread norm barring administrators and supervisors from entering a classroom unannounced most supervisors, who hold **boundary positions** in school systems, avoid coming into a teacher's classroom without announcing the impending visit well in advance.

If the rigid, formal, evaluation procedures by supervisors were abolished or at least substantially modified, all teachers would feel more comfortable admitting that they sometimes need help in their work. Instead of resenting specialists, who often possess unusually advanced skills and knowledge, teachers might welcome them into their classrooms. It is doubtful, however, that the evaluation system will be abolished until American teachers successfully demonstrate a higher degree of professionalism. Professionals do not need supervision and will not allow it, although they may occasionally request help from peers.

Ancillary Personnel

A number of other participants in the role system of teaching will be mentioned briefly. The school psychologist usually spends most of his or her time giving tests to groups of students. Occasionally he or she may find time to work on a one-to-one basis with troubled youngsters. School systems also occasionally hire social workers to help improve communication between school and home and to investigate the situations of youngsters believed to be in exceptional difficulty at home. However, more often the school nurse takes on these roles since school social workers have not been widely employed in schools as yet.

There are increasing numbers of teacher's aides, or paraprofessionals available to help teachers, particularly in inner-city schools. Often they are mothers of youngsters attending a school. Their job is to handle some of the clerical work and to interact directly with youngsters on an individual or small-group tutorial basis. Some aides also make home calls, in lieu of the school social worker, nurse, or teacher. Many teachers are accustomed to having an aide in their classrooms, although a few insecure teachers claim that paraprofessionals are often hired to provide a regular teaching service at cheap wages. The employment of paraprofessionals in modern schools may be a permanent innovation of the last ten to fifteen years, which may eventually be common throughout the United States.

In almost all schools there are also several secretaries. Teachers send "difficult" students to them in order to calm the classroom. Secretaries meet parents and the public before the principal does, and screen visitors to the school. They may become listening posts for anxious teachers and students, or the confidante of the principal. The school secretary often has an important position in the unofficial role system of the school although her official office may be viewed as insignificant.

In an unofficial way, the school custodian may be an important person. If he thinks highly of a teacher, for example, he may be able to secure materials for the teacher's use in project work with students, or he may actually construct special classroom equipment for the teacher. If a teacher annoys the custodian by leaving his or her classroom in disorder at the end of the day, he may refuse to be cooperative; in extreme cases, he may even complain about the teacher to the principal.

These are some of the important personnel in the school community, viewed primarily from an official stance. Some of the ancillary members of the teacher's role set, in their informal, unofficial, capacities, may have an important impact upon a teacher's ultimate success or failure.

Students

In the formal organization of schooling, students are the clients toward whom all energies are directed. (Parents are often considered clients, as well.) As indicated earlier, the school is officially established to serve the educational needs of all youngsters growing up in the society, whatever their social origins or apparent intellectual, social, or emotional capacities. With the possible exception of students in progressive or alternative schools, youngsters who attend public schools are the recipients of services ordered by adults, presumably on their behalf.

Realizing who butters his or her bread (school board members, principals, and parents), the teacher is usually less attentive to the role expectations of students than to more powerful adults in the school milieu.[16] It is unfortunate that teachers are often required by the system in which they work to put the expectations of people other than their students first and foremost. According to substantial research on role perceptions and errors in perception, most teachers need not fear the disapproval of their efforts by principals and parents as much as they reportedly do.[17]

Teachers who wish to succeed in the prevailing public school system, however, should realize that at least part of their success will depend on their ability to subtly balance the expectations of their students with those of influential adults in the system. Failure to do this may result in early termination or other difficulties.

Teaching is a field that demands patience and diplomacy, as well as personal integrity. Teachers need training in the politics of the role, which they rarely receive in schools of education. Lack of such training has in recent years caused many new teachers to criticize their preparatory institutions after they have acquired full-time jobs in which the demands of their significant others appear to run contrary to what they were taught to expect.[18] Teachers-to-be need formal preparation concerned with the politics of their teaching role, just as much as they need culture therapy, sensitivity training, methods courses, and student teaching concerned with making them empathetic and skillful technicians in the classroom.

For students to be well served by the school in a period of great change in the society and culture at large, their teachers need to be able to respond to student needs and expectations as much as—if not a great deal more than—to the expectations of adults. In order to do this, teachers need to become experts in human relations with both children and adults.

In sum, the central clients of schools are the students, but schools have been organized to serve adults instead. In a rapidly changing society, the expectations of adults for the education of children may run contrary to their actual needs. It is difficult for most adults to visualize the vast ramifications of this phenomenon or to comprehend its implications for the future. In order for public school teachers to adequately serve their primary clients they must learn to deal authentically—that is, diplomatically, politically, self-confidently, and caringly—with adults as well as with children.

The Curriculum of the
Contemporary School

There is no universal curriculum or formal school program offered throughout the United States, although there are striking similarities between programs nationwide. One major area of difference can be found in suburban and inner-city schools. Most schools for affluent mainstream youngsters offer students a far better curriculum than do most schools in the inner-city, which are frequently forced to devote all curriculum plans to teaching "basic skills" and little else.

According to writers on the topic, four factors shape curriculum priorities: the demands of society; the characteristics of students; the organized scholarly disciplines; and a philosophy of education.[19] Criteria for selecting curricular content include the following:

• Is the content appropriate to the interests and abilities of the learners toward whom it is to be directed?
• Does it reflect the present state of knowledge?
• Does it enable the student to understand, appreciate, and think critically about his cultural heritage?
• Does it contribute to the student's ability to assume citizenship responsibilities?
• Does it enable him to understand himself and his relations to others?
• Can it help the student to choose a way of life wisely and to live intelligently?
• Does the content enable the student to develop general abilities and skills needed for effective living in the immediate future?[20]

The variety of patterns by means of which formal curriculums are organized include, among others:

• The familiar "straight subject" curriculum
• The "structure of the disciplines" approach advocated by Jerome Bruner and others during the 1960s, wherein students were to "become" scientists, historians, mathematicians, etc., by actively becoming involved in the investigative processes employed by scholars
• The "broad fields" curriculum, which draws subject matter from two or more fields in an effort to make learning interdisciplinary
• The "life functions–social process" curriculum, which breaks completely from disciplines in an attempt to help students learn about

desirable and worthy tasks, such as making a home, expressing religious feelings, becoming involved in community action projects, etc.
  • The "activity," or "experience" curriculum, especially praised by the educational progressivists as a means by which young children learn from "units of experience" what they "intrinsically" want to learn
  • The "core" curriculum, involving blocked time in an endeavor to help youngsters study social problems, the arts, literature, and other concerns amenable to an interdisciplinary approach[21]

Despite the wide variety of theoretical approaches to curriculum available to students of education, most school systems and classrooms today continue to operate with a traditional, subject-centered curriculum.

In most elementary schools teachers are expected to teach reading, mathematics, science and health, history and geography (or social studies), physical education, art and music. This list of subjects was also a typical curriculum at the turn of the century. Although the subject-matter orientation to curriculum remains the same as in the past, some of the concepts and data taught and technologies employed to teach them may have changed considerably.

A typical junior or senior high school curriculum includes such subjects as world history, American history, American government, algebra, American literature, chemistry, and French. Sometimes psychology, sociology, philosophy, or some other social science or humanity is added to the conventional list of subjects. And, some senior high schools have "career education" courses to help young people prepare more realistically for the world of work by actually seeing businesses in operation and working in them.

Reading and math are still the most important subjects in elementary and secondary schools today. In California, often a bellweather for the rest of the nation in educational matters, concern for the apparent functional illiteracy of high school graduates had become so widespread that in 1970 a new teacher credentialling law, known as the Ryan Act, required all prospective secondary and elementary school teachers to pass a course in the teaching of reading before being eligible to receive a teaching credential.

Marshall McLuhan and his theories of media use may hold some repute among scholars; professors of education may still admire William H. Kilpatrick's unit–project–experience curriculum based on Dewey's ideas of Progressive Education; sex and family life education may be taught in a number of schools; and perhaps we should be developing a curriculum to help children survive the Post-Industrial age by offering studies of leisure and work, art and self-actualization, experimental family styles, women and men, racial and ethnic relations, and other contemporary problems of living. But most educators still concentrate on the traditional basic skills of print literacy and numerical ability. The vast majority of elementary and secondary schools in American society continue to apply curricula developed in the nineteenth-century Industrial Age as the age of Post-Industrialism evolves in the 1970s. As one partially disillusioned writer presents the matter:

> The culture of the schools needs to be changed so that the students who go through them can look back upon their experiences and feel they are prepared to live lives full of meaning. We should challenge almost everything that goes on in schools.[22]

This appears to be true with regard to curriculum, as well as most other formal aspects of school society and culture. But, according to at least one group of researchers, this may be more easily said than done:

> Both educators and parents . . . are often profoundly disquieted by innovative curricula and procedures. After all, people know the effects of traditional schooling from personal experience, but few can predict the effects of new approaches on their children.[23]

Informal Aspects of the Social System of Schooling

Not only are modern schools highly organized on a formal basis, but over time they also develop systems of human interaction and programs of learning on an unofficial basis in order to meet the everyday human needs of the various people who work in schools and who attend them.

Cultural Variation and the Schools

The American school, like most other institutions, is a center of vibrant collective living. Even if efforts are continually made to control the informal culture within the school by segregating the sexes, by suppressing spontaneous expressions of emotion not directly related to lessons, or by sanctioning casual dress or language patterns, the cultural life continues without official sanction.

> Teachers have always known that it was not necessary for the students of strange customs to cross the seas to find material. Folklore and myth, tradition, taboo, magic rites, ceremonials of all sorts, collective representations, participation mystique, all abound in the front yard of every

school, and occasionally they creep upstairs and are incorporated into the more formal portions of school life.

There are, in the school, complex rituals of personal relationships, a set of folkways, mores, and irrational sanctions, a moral code based upon them. There are games which are sublimated wars, teams, and an elaborate set of ceremonies concerning them. There are traditions, and traditionalists waging their world-old battle against innovators. There are laws, and there is the problem of enforcing them ... There are specialized societies with a rigid structure and a limited membership ... There are customs regulating the relations of the sexes. All these things make up a world that is different from the world of adults.[24]

There is an infinite variety of cultural styles in schools in American society, which are dependent upon factors such as the school's location and leadership in the school. Brembeck, for example, sees schools from a crosscultural perspective, as mirrors of diverse cultural styles in a community. He lists several broad types, which are discussed in the following paragraph.[25]

Town Schools. Reflecting the small town of the past, this ideal type strives to hold its students to values of the present, according to Brembeck. It has a fairly professional staff and maintains relatively personal relations among its staff and between school and community. The town school usually has a heterogeneous student body to serve, so it offers some degree of diversity in curriculum and teaching style, within an overall set of homogeneous local traditions. Its personnel tend to be ambivalent about change and innovation. It operates primarily from a present-time frame of reference, which is directed more on behalf of its students' needs to cope pragmatically with life outside school than to traditional academic concerns.

Village Schools. In these schools, the child is held close to rural tradition, if possible. Although the school of nineteenth-century rural America has almost disappeared, some residues remain, especially on the fringes of cities and suburbs. (These fringe villages often are scenes of conflict between the old and the new as urbanites begin to move in.) The village school was the original community school, which emphasized the pragmatic in its curriculum, such as homemaking and 4H clubs. Because they were small and provincial, they were more organic. They tried to conserve local and regional traditions.

In developing nations, village schools may be a major part of a nation's modernization program. In other contexts, they are often highly resistant to efforts to change their ways. In the United States, many rural schools in transition now face difficulties similar to those of schools located in the slums of large cities, such as student alienation and lack of academic incentives.

Urban Schools.   Brembeck says that in this type of modern school, children are taught to renounce their past and to acquire a new way of life suitable to their new society. Urban schools may have a cosmopolitan orientation, if not located in the slums. But most of today's urban schools are ghetto schools because of the exodus of the middle-classes to suburbia.

In the past, the personnel of urban schools were often highly motivated, proud, and skilled. More recently, new and inexperienced teachers, who often go to the inner-city for their first experience, have encountered such difficulties in working with poor minority children that they have often left as soon as they found other employment. It was natural that problems would arise between resentful ghetto parents and children and their teachers. These problems have included bigotry and fear, as well as cultural misunderstandings. Various attempts are currently being made to remedy the problems of inner-city schools, including development of compensatory education programs, school desegregation, and school decentralization and community control. So far, few of these efforts have reaped positive educational benefits. Recently some of the "new breed" of teachers have begun to ask for assignment to urban ghetto schools in hopes of finding real meaning in their careers by working with the people who most need a quality education.

Suburban Schools.   In this epitome of the American school ideal, the child is oriented toward the future as a means of acquiring or retaining

mainstream socioeconomic status. Suburban schools in the United States usually have a relatively homogeneous client system to serve. Suburban parents are typically very interested in and protective of the schools that they may have helped directly to build. They may support powerful pressure groups on the local level that either help or hinder the school's efforts. Usually the middle-class suburban school has a strong academic orientation, due to the parents' stress on a college education. Wealthy suburban schools may sometimes offer ideal opportunities for teachers and other school personnel to be innovative with instructional technology.

One of the problems of segregated suburban schools, despite their enrichment offerings to students, is that youngsters are isolated from the cultural and social diversity of the larger society. Because most children will probably live in a more or less cosmopolitan area when they grow up, they need to be prepared for the numerous implications of cultural diversity by schools and their teachers; they cannot be protected artificially. Furthermore, the world has grown smaller, and the educational needs of today's children everywhere no longer can be met by teachers with outlooks confined to a village, small town, suburb, or inner-city. The professional teacher must have a national and world vision in this day and age.

School Climate

Continuing the contrasting of different school cultures, Brembeck also presents an interesting model of school climate, a rather nebulous quality of the informal culture of schooling. It connotes the atmosphere peculiar to a school.

To a large extent, school climate is set by the building principal, according to Brembeck and many other educational scholars. Brembeck lists five characteristic types of school climate, ranging from an "open" climate on one end of the continuum to a "closed" climate at the other end. An "open" climate is achieved by the capable and warm leadership qualities of the principal, which help to produce an optimum esprit de corps among the staff that frees them for positive team efforts on behalf of their clients.[26] The "closed" climate results from authoritarian conduct by the principal, which creates low morale and poor teaching and learning.

In between these two extremes, but more toward the "open" end, is the "autonomous" climate; it is a business-like environment in which teachers are largely free to do as they please and to do it well. Morale is fairly high and professionalism is encouraged. There is also a "controlled" climate, in which the principal is a tough, fair, impersonal taskmaster; here, the staff morale is moderately high, and a fair degree of success is felt by teachers and students in their efforts. In the "familiar" climate, the principal strives to be a friend to teachers and students, but is weak and ineffectual as a task leader. In a "familiar" climate, although everyone appears contented and school members are free to explore each other's personalities, little of educational value is accomplished by the students. Next to the closed end of the continuum, Brembeck places the "paternal" climate. Here, the principal's need for authority is great, and if teachers come to him for help in a way that reinforces his father image, he is apt to be pleasant and accommodating. Unfortunately, everyone becomes so habituated to depending upon their authoritarian "father" for guidance that they do not express much personal initiative, become demoralized, and often fail to reach their students.

It seems that there is a progression of "good" school climates through "mediocre" to "bad" in this model. But it may be more worthwhile to use Brembeck's formulation without overemphasizing its apparent normative connotations. Most educators would probably agree that the "closed," "paternal," and even "familiar" climates are not acceptable for the operation of humane and effective schools in a democracy. But "closed" and "paternal" climates are relatively widespread in our society. A serious case can be made for reserving our judgment about the merits of "open," "autonomous," and "controlled" climates until more research is done using such a model as the source of hypotheses. It is conceivable that some teachers would be most happy and productive in an "open" climate. Others, who are more professionally inclined and prepared, might do best in an "autonomous" environment. Until teacher-preparation institutions are reformed in order to develop more autonomous and open teachers, it might be best to not consider all "controlled" climates negatively.

In sum, there appears to be no one type of school culture that is inherently the best one for all teachers. It is probably as unwise to place all novice teachers in an urban school as it is to place all of them in a wealthy suburban school. It also seems unwise for teachers to cling to a prestige–reward system that encourages horizontal mobility from the inner-city to the suburbs after gaining experience and seniority in a system. Some teachers will undoubtedly be happier and do a better job throughout their careers in Watts or Harlem while others may be needed in Beverly Hills or Shaker Heights. The same is true of school climate; no one kind of climate and the leadership behind it is suitable for every teacher, any more than one type of curriculum is suitable for every child.

If all children are to be reached, instructional personnel should be allocated on the basis of where they are apt to be happiest and most successful with children. All teachers should receive a decent salary wherever they work, be treated as emerging professionals, and in other ways encouraged for honest, sincere efforts in variable school cultures.

The Informal Personnel and
Client Structure

Another important element of the unofficial organization of school social life is the way in which its various human participants pattern their daily behavior, beyond that dictated by official pronouncements, written guidelines, and community demands. Prichard and Buxton also list a number of informal roles commonly developed among staff and faculty members. They include:

- The "Detective," who knows everyone's secrets and problems
- The "Matchmaker," who is constantly arranging romances
- The "Ego-Supporter," who always tells everyone how great they're doing
- The "Mediator," who steps in to resolve all frictions between personnel
- The "Medical Practitioner," who has advice to offer on every little or large physical problem
- The "Bitcher," who complains constantly about everything
- The "Friend," who eases tensions by supportive interactions
- The "Romeo," who is continually "on the make"
- The "Tattletale," who cannot be trusted because everything said is repeated to the administration
- The "Moral Crusader," who always has a cause for everyone to join.[28]

Similar informal roles operate within the student body of most elementary and especially secondary schools.

The latent functions of informal primary relations may be as important for the school system and society as the more formalized official aspects of school operation.[29] Studies of workers in industry have clearly demonstrated that worker morale and productivity are often influenced by subtle processes of personal interaction between the workers.[30] In the school, teacher and student morale and learning are also affected by the informal role relationships that evolve from daily living in the small society of the school.

For example, cliques may arise over time among the teachers based upon their unofficial positions in the school organization. Older and experienced teachers with no more formally designated authority may "lead" a clique that votes in unanimity on important issues at faculty meetings. The top-ranking members of such a clique may be seen frequently in the principal's office discussing how to proceed on matters of schoolwide concern, including those pertaining to the retention or dismissal of untenured teachers or assignments to difficult classes. Unwill-

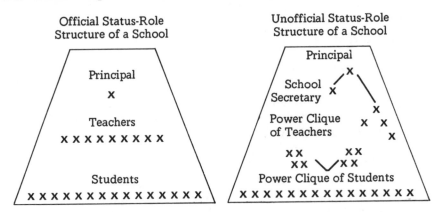

FIGURE 15–4.   *Two Types of Status-Role Structure in a School*

ingness to consider the advice of such teachers may be detrimental to the career of a principal. The informal influence of the teacher clique is real and can be used on a widespread basis to resist his mandates. Conversely, the influence of such opinion leaders on the instructional staff may be as valuable to an innovative principal as the influence of opinion leaders on students in the classroom is to knowledgeable teachers.

Howard Becker has illustrated this effect on teachers and principals in his discussion of Chicago schools and their relations with parents.[31] According to Becker, there is a norm prevailing among school people that requires principals to almost invariably side with teachers in conflicts between teachers and parents. If a principal breaks this normative code by taking a parent's side in a given case and censuring one of his teachers, life may be made very difficult for him by powerful clique groups of unofficially organized teachers who do not want a precedent set that might eventually break down their customary defenses against criticisms or pressures from parents.

The teacher who is young or new to a school and who ostentatiously goes beyond the customary call of duty in his or her desire to be successful may be informally censured by more senior teachers who feel that the new teacher's zeal may cause the principal to suspect that his other teachers are not exerting enough effort. Of course, the same sort of pattern prevails among students. It is not uncommon for an academically successful student to be accused of currying favor with the teacher.

The best efforts of schools often go awry not necessarily because these efforts are poorly planned and executed by the officials who devise them, but because of the informal customs and traditions developed by influential faculty members and students, who are committed to preserving the informal culture.

To successfully change existing informal practices requires agents

of change, such as innovative principals, creative teachers, and curriculum experts to devise mechanisms to destructure informal patterns of
human relations in the school sociocultural system and to restructure
these informal patterns along more accommodating lines.

The Invisible Curriculum

Just as there are unofficial status-role relationships in schools that parallel officially designated relations, an invisible curriculum competes with
or supplements the formal school program. Michael Apple has defined
this concept as follows:

> A good deal of the focus [of critics of the schools] has been on what
> Jackson (1968) has so felicitously labeled the "hidden curriculum"—that
> is, on the norms and values that are implicitly, but effectively, taught in
> schools and that are not usually talked about in teachers' statements of
> ends or goals.[32]

Included among the important components of the invisible curriculum are respect for traditional sex-role differences, for the sacredness
of time, for the value of competitiveness, and for the propriety of the
social-class structure prevailing in American society. In school, American
youngsters also are unofficially taught:

> ... more or less unquestioning respect for authority, willingness to ac-
> cept authority's definitions of work and play, dependence for approval on
> authority more than on peers, willingness to perform relatively meaning-
> less work with great regularity, and high valuation of money and
> grades...[33]

The invisible curriculum refers primarily to values and norms taught
implicitly. Because of the discrepancy between explicitly taught norms
and values and implicitly taught ones, many schools alienate students
who recognize contradictions presented to them.

Is there an alternative for American schools, other than to teach two
contradicting curriculums at a time when norms and values in society at
large are undergoing profound transformation? Students can be openly
taught to choose from among all the diverse norms and values that exist
today. If schools are to become truly meaningful educational agencies,
they must recognize that too often they are imposing two programs upon
youngsters, both of which are open to serious question and only one of
which is frankly acknowledged.

Because of its subtle nature, the hidden curriculum cannot be
abolished or legislated out of existence. However, by recognizing its
existence and admitting that much that is taught in schools unofficially
may be subtle propaganda, the schools will at least examine the un-

spoken assumptions upon which they base their unofficial programs. They will thereby be more cautious of what they impose on the young people of a pluralistic society undergoing tranformation. (A further step beyond self-examination is the teaching of alternative values and value clarification procedures, discussed in Chapter 10.)

Thus, the invisible curriculum, like the informal status-role structure operating behind the scenes in present-day schools, has enormous influence on students, whether for their benefit or for their detriment.

What Primarily Directs the School— Bureaucracy or the Informal School Culture?

Although official policies and programs of instruction are certainly essential to the educational process, the subtle day-to-day events that comprise meaningful life in the informal school subculture are perhaps equally important.

If you want to gain deeper insight into the patterns of this cultural life, Willard Waller's *The Sociology of Teaching* and Philip Jackson's *Life in Classrooms,* as well as some of the recent descriptions of school cultures by former urban teachers, will provide more material to gain such insight.[34] Beyond reading reports and descriptions of the school's cultural life, when you enter a school to observe or to student teach or to begin your career, it may be useful to consider the proposition that every school system and school develops its own highly unique set of mores and folkways to which "tourists" and "residents" alike are expected to adhere. To break boldly with ingrained cultural conventions, even with the best of intentions, may be considered a sign of disrespect that risks ostracism. Over-conformity to custom by cautious teachers, however, may at times prevent their students from receiving the best education.[35] There may be times when it is best and morally correct to be a nonconformist.

The politics of teaching involves learning to use personal courage intelligently and patiently in a world of imperfect people; it means avoiding arrogant behavior as well as irresponsible passivity. Properly understood and practiced, the politics of teaching may be the quintessence of humane self-actualization by teachers in schools. It requires an understanding of the formal and informal aspects of the American system of education, as well as a deep understanding of one's personal capabilities and limitations in relation to the ends one wishes to achieve with other people. Can you think of some other, more specific ingredients required for an effective "politics of teaching"?

Summary

Schools are small societies, and most are semi-total institutions. Officially, they tend to be bureaucratically organized, at least in part; unofficially, they develop over time a subculture of their own.

American schools are organized formally around a more or less universal status-role structure involving primarily teachers, administrators, educational specialists, supervisors and students. The principal is the chief source of teacher concern and influence in this role system. In the daily cultural life of the school, there almost always develops a separate informal role system centering largely on the expectations of leading members of teacher and student cliques.

Although many theories exist about what the curriculum of the school should be and how it should be developed and implemented, the typical elementary and secondary curriculum in the United States today remains "Essentialistic"—that is, it is a blend of subjects, skills, and knowledge believed to be essential to all people everywhere, such as reading, mathematics, history, and the physical sciences. Alongside this formal curriculum operates an "invisible" curriculum of implicit norms and values that often contradict and conflict with the norms and values officially listed by school people in public statements of purpose and in curriculum guides.

Both bureaucracy and the informal culture apparently play important parts in directing what happens in school. The informal culture may have an especially great impact on what goes on in schools and what results from their operation. Teachers who desire to behave authentically in the best interests of their students may often need (among other traits) to be experts in the "politics of teaching"—to know themselves and their behavioral capacities and limitations in relation to the expectations of others in the social system of schooling.

Related Concepts

boundary position   A position, status, or office that is marginal to (on the boundaries of) one or more different positions in one or more social systems. For example, the university supervisor of student teaching is frequently marginal to both the public school system and its teachers and the rest of the faculty in his university; he is on the boundaries of two central positions in two interrelated social organizations. Boundary positions are often quite tenuous, and their incumbents are subject to unusual amounts of role strain.

role system   The most general concept for describing status-role relationships at an interpersonal level. Technically, a "role system is a set of functionally specific, interrelated behaviors generated by interdependent tasks (in a social organization)."[36] The role system of teaching includes members of teachers' immediate role set and all other positions that influence or are influenced by teachers, such as board of education members, superintendents, professors of education, and teacher-organization leaders.

Suggested Activity

As you do fieldwork in a particular school, develop a list of informal practices and character types that appear to give that school a unique flavor, or personality. For instance, observe patterns of dress and speech, treatment of beginning teachers by more senior ones, expressed teacher attitudes toward parents, kinds of bulletin board displays, and individual idiosyncrasies on the parts of faculty members. This will require a fairly sustained series of observations in diverse contexts within the school, but in the end it should lead to a more or less accurate profile of the informal aspects of the school's life and culture.

You could also repeat this activity in another school, and then make some perhaps enlightening comparisons.

References and Notes

1. Erving Goffman, *Asylums* (Garden City, N.Y.: Doubleday, Anchor Books, 1961).

2. Jack L. Nelson and Frank P. Besag, *Sociological Perspectives in Education: Models for Analysis* (New York: Pitman Publishing Corp., 1970), pp. 59–73.

3. Goffman, *Asylums*.

4. Nelson and Besag, *Sociological Perspectives*, p. 73.

5. Robert K. Merton, "Bureaucratic Structure and Personality," in Merton, et al., eds., *Reader in Bureaucracy* (Glencoe, Ill.: The Free Press, 1952), p. 362.

6. Robert Dreeban, *The Nature of Teaching: Schools and the Work of Teachers* (Glenview, Ill.: Scott, Foresman and Co., 1970), pp. 47, 48.

7. Gerald H. Moeller, "Bureaucracy and Teachers' Sense of Power," in Sam D. Sieber and David E. Wilder, eds., *The School in Society: Studies in the Sociology of Education* (New York: The Free Press, 1973), p. 211.

8. Melvin L. Kohn, "Bureaucratic Man: A Portrait and an Interpretation," *American Sociological Review* 36 (June 1971): 473.

9. Research Report 1972–73. Elizabeth Moffatt, *Status of the American Public School Teacher, 1970–71* (Washington, D.C.: Research Division, National Education Association, 1972), pp. 58, 90 (ERIC EA 004 437).

10. There are too many studies supporting this claim to cite a single one. However, one of the most interesting discussions of this position in relation to teachers is Seymour B. Sarason, *The Culture of the School and the Problem of Change* (Boston: Allyn and Bacon, 1971), pp. 111–50.

11. Andrew Fishel and Janice Pottker, "Women in Educational Governance: A Statistical Portrait," *Educational Researcher* 3 (July/August 1974): 5.

12. George Spindler, "The Role of the School Administrator," in George Spindler, ed., *Education and Culture: Anthropological Approaches* (New York: Holt, Rinehart, and Winston, 1963), p. 238.

13. Sarason, *The Culture of the School*, p. 139.

14. *See* Wilbert Moore, *The Professions: Rules and Roles* (New York: Russell Sage Foundation, 1970).

15. An excellent discussion of the expectations held for beginning teachers and some of their major problems is found in Elizabeth M. Eddy, *Becoming a Teacher: The Passage to Professional Status* (New York: Columbia Teachers College Press, 1969).

16. Carl W. Backman and Paul F. Secord, *A Social Psychological View of Education* (New York: Harcourt, Brace and World, 1969), pp. 119, 120.

17. *See,* for example, Bruce Biddle, Howard Rosencranz, Edward Tomich, and J. Pascal Twyman, "Shared Inaccuracies in the Role of Teacher," in Bruce Biddle and Edwin J. Thomas, eds., *Role Theory: Concepts and Research* (New York: John Wiley & Sons, 1966), pp. 302–10; and John M. Foskett, *Role Consensus: The Case of the Elementary School Teacher* (Eugene: The Center for the Advanced Study of Educational Administration, University of Oregon, 1969), pp. 115–17.

18. Lawrence Drabick, "Perceivers of the Teacher Role: The Teacher Educator," *Journal of Teacher Education* 18 (Spring 1967): 55, 56.

19. John Martin Rich, *Challenge and Response: Education in American Culture* (New York: John Wiley & Sons, 1974), p. 242.

20. *Ibid.,* p. 247.

21. *Ibid.,* pp. 254–59.

22. Harvey Laudin, *Victims of Culture* (Columbus, Ohio: Charles E. Merrill Publishing Company, 1973), p. 57.

23. P. Carpenter-Huffman, G.R. Hall, and G.C. Sumner, *Change in Education: Insights from Performance Contracting* (Cambridge, Mass.: Ballinger Publishing Company, 1974), p. 8.

24. Willard Waller, *The Sociology of Teaching* (New York: John Wiley & Sons, 1932), p. 103.

25. Cole Brembeck, *Social Foundations of Education: Environmental Influences in Teaching and Learning,* 2nd ed. (New York: John Wiley & Sons, 1971), pp. 313–41.

26. *Ibid.,* pp. 429–37.

27. Keith W. Prichard and Thomas H. Buxton, *Concepts and Theories in Soci-*

ology of Education (Lincoln, Nebraska: Professional Educators Publications, 1973), p. 127.

28. Ibid., p. 128.

29. Jules Henry, "Spontaneity, Initiative, and Creativity in Suburban Classrooms," in Education and Culture, pp. 215–33; Philip W. Jackson, Life in Classrooms (New York: Holt, Rinehart, and Winston, 1968).

30. This phenomenon has been beautifully treated in a biographical manner by Studs Terkel, Working: People Talk About What They Do All Day and How They Feel About What They Do (New York: Pantheon Books, 1973).

31. Howard S. Becker, "Schools and Systems of Stratification," in A.H. Halsey, Jean Floud, and C. Arnold, eds., Education, Economy, and Society: A Reader in the Sociology of Education (New York: The Free Press, 1961), pp. 101, 102.

32. Michael W. Apple, "The Hidden Curriculum and the Nature of Conflict," Interchange 2/4 (1971): 27.

33. Miriam Wasserman, ed., Demystifying School: Writings and Experiences (New York: Praeger Publishers, 1974), p. 34.

34. An example of such descriptions is James Herndon's The Way It Spozed to Be (New York: Simon and Schuster, 1968).

35. Backman and Secord, Social Psychology, p. 133.

36. Daniel Katz and Robert L. Kahn, The Social Psychology of Organizations (New York: John Wiley & Sons, 1966), p. 455.

16

Teacher Leadership in the Classroom Community

School classrooms, which are at the heart of the educational enterprise, are societies in their own right. At the beginning of the school year, a classroom is an unorganized aggregate, but it gradually evolves into an organized social system. This occurs whether or not the teacher consciously tries to shape the society within the classroom. Teachers should be aware of the dynamics of instructional groups[1] and be able to apply principles of human relations to the formation of a classroom social system that promotes optimal, enjoyable learning. In the final analysis, this entails harmonizing teacher and student roles and personalities.

The theoretical structure of human behavior in social systems is illustrated in Figure 16–1. Until recently, most teachers have emphasized the "nomothetic dimension" (that directed by public expectation) of classroom social life, thus exaggerating their students' and their own role behavior, while suppressing the expression of unique personalities. Classrooms that stress only institutional expectations of behavior are to a greater or lesser degree dominated by the teacher. The teacher's central attitude in such classrooms is distilled in the statement: "This is what we are going to do today."

A minority of teachers, especially since the movement to "humanize" American education, exaggerate the "idiographic dimension" of classroom social interaction. Their intent is to allow maximum flowering of their students' and their own individual personalities at the expense of role-related institutional expectations. These teachers attempt to operate student-dominated classrooms in which the underlying attitude is summed up in the question: "What do you kids want to do today?"

417

Nomothetic Dimension

Idiographic Dimension

FIGURE 16–1.   *A General Model of Human Behavior in a Social Organization (From Jacob W. Getzels and Herbert A. Thelen, "The Classroom Group as a Unique Social System," in The Dynamics of Instructional Groups, the Fifty-ninth Yearbook of the National Society for the Study of Education [Chicago: University of Chicago Press, 1960]. Reprinted with permission of the National Society for the Study of Education.)*

A third alternative, however, is to harmonize the public and the personal dimensions of life in school classrooms in such a way that institutional role expectations and idiosyncratic personality needs and temperaments merge in a transaction between individual and society. Later in this chapter, we will consider some ways in which such "transactional classrooms" can be developed.[2]

Conventional Classroom Systems

Most classroom systems in American society are teacher dominated; that is, the teacher uses the delegated authority of his or her institutional position to accomplish his or her ends with students. Students are also viewed primarily as position incumbents, not as unique persons with private needs. The teacher's power to influence students in the "nomothetic classroom" derives from his or her role position, not from personal charisma. Students are expected to know their own positions and accompanying privileges and obligations, which are always reciprocal to the teacher's expectations and ultimately to those of the community and society. The following are two *extreme* examples of conventional classrooms.

Mrs. R.   An experienced teacher, Mrs. R teaches kindergarten in a middle-class urban school in the West. When an observer enters her room, he first notices the great docility of her pupils, who are sitting at tables cutting and pasting letters, walking obediently to their learning stations, or sitting on the floor listening to their teacher read them a story.

Mrs. R never raises her voice to reprimand the children. Over the years, she has become accomplished at subtly exercising her institutionalized authority as a teacher. She does this primarily in two ways: (1) by manipulating the sentiments of the parents of her pupils on behalf of the school's aims as a socializing agency, and (2) by carefully planning classroom activities to accomplish mutually agreed-upon ends. As a result of her great skill and willingness to work very hard, Mrs. R's young pupils are obedient toward her. There are few discipline problems in her class because students know that if they misbehave, they will incur the combined displeasure of their parents, their peers, the school principal, and Mrs. R.

Students speak to Mrs. R or to their peers in the classroom only if expressly asked to speak. They are said to be progressing rapidly in Mrs. R's room and their middle-class parents are pleased. As a result of the positive feedback she has received over the years, Mrs. R has great confidence in her teaching ability. Some might accuse her of creating passive, docile conformists, but such criticism would not be well taken by the school or by the larger community.

In short, Mrs. R runs a tight ship with consummate skill. She is a successful teacher of a conventional American classroom. But when school lets out for the day, Mrs. R's pupils may abandon the norms and role expectations imposed on them from above at school. These "docile" youngsters may run and jump with glee at having been released from the near total institutional confinement of their kindergarten classroom.

Mr. D. Mr. D teaches sixth grade at an almost all black inner-city neighborhood school in the Midwest. He is in his mid-twenties and has held his present position for four years. It is doubtful that Mr. D will teach much longer unless he receives an in-system transfer to a less difficult school. Mr. D has been attacked by several of his students. Observation in Mr. D's classroom suggests that he lacks the kinds of manipulative skills possessed by Mrs. R. In a lower-class minority school today, lack of such skills can be disastrous if the teacher wishes to have a conventional classroom based on a nomothetic, role-dominated authority.

Mr. D does not go out of his way to know the parents of his students, and he does not carefully plan his daily and weekly activities, as does Mrs. R. He assumes that it is the student's responsibility to accept anything and everything he offers them because he is the teacher. He offers them English grammar, spelling taught from a workbook, history of the Puritan colonists, and geography—all taught directly from textbooks, which few of his students are able to read. When students consistently fail to pass daily and weekly quizzes and tests on textbook material, he screams at them in frustration and tells them they are lazy and stupid. He also punishes his class for not obeying his orders instantly by keeping them after school. As a result of the tremendous hostility he continually provokes, a serious incident involving one or more of his more volatile students is precipitated every few weeks. In order to retain his position, he refrains from reporting these incidents to his superiors. Mr. D has no resources to deal competently and humanely with his students in a particularly difficult situation.

The two elementary school situations depicted above are extremes, but elements of their classroom climates are real. At the junior and senior high school levels, such extreme differences in operating conventional, teacher-centered, role-dominated classrooms also exist. Students who have not dropped out of school are older and they have generally come to accept the deadliness of such classrooms as part of the school game. They tolerate impersonal teachers because they feel they have no other choice if they want to graduate from school and enter college or find a job. If asked whether or not many of their former teachers influenced them deeply, they will usually reply in the negative. The few teachers whom they do remember did not operate conventional, role-dominated classrooms or, if they did, they forgot their roles long enough to display a modicum of humanity toward their students. It seems "safer" for most teachers to operate according to the book—rather than to become involved with the personalities of their students. Students have also learned that it is best to do as they are told in school, since there are few, if any, alternative routes to adulthood.

Actually, most of the teachers who are forgotten by students do not represent extremes of personality or teaching style; they usually are the great majority of reasonably well prepared, motivated, and caring teachers. If this is the case, then it is probably not the teachers who are to blame for the failure of many students today; it is the conventional classroom *system* that is at fault. The nomothetic, or role-dominated, social system is quite inflexible and does not allow for much emotional expression by either teachers or their students.

The Idiographic Alternative to the Conventional Classroom

Unfortunately, extremes in human organizations usually breed opposite extremes.[3] The conventional teacher-dominated classroom system of most American schools has provoked much criticism by psychologists and educators in the past several years. The new "humanists"—people as diverse in training and work background as Carl Rogers and Herbert Kohl[4]—have urged that classrooms become centers of student-centered learning. Many argue that the traditional emphasis on adult and student roles should be replaced by an emphasis on adult and student *feelings*. The extremes of this humanistic trend are found in the free school movement, while alternative schools, open classrooms, and other innovations in educational values are being developed within a number of public school systems in order to humanize the classroom.

Whatever the specific structure instituted, the emphasis in a student-centered classroom is on children and their unique social and emotional needs. Perhaps the debatable issue is over just how far society can go in striving to meet the expressed needs of individuals, without sacrificing the needs of the group or creating antisocial behavior. The problem of social interaction and purpose in classrooms may be a problem of defining the nature and purpose of a society undergoing fundamental change. In its rhetoric at least, our society seems to be enamored of a new version of unfettered freedom and individualism.

Proponents of the new humanism in education urge that "phoney role playing" be abandoned so that more authentic learning will occur. They believe that authentic learning is an intensely personal and private process, as opposed to a more interpersonal one. Rogers admits his indebtedness to John Dewey and the Instrumentalists, who, however, were interactionists—not extreme personalists. The following principles and hypotheses about "idiographic," or "student-centered" teaching are Rogers's:

• We cannot teach another person directly; we can only facilitate his learning.
• A person learns significantly only those things which he perceives as being involved in the maintenance of, or enhancement of, the structure of self.
• Experience which, if assimilated, would involve a change in the organization of self tends to be resisted through denial or distortion of symbolization.
• The structure and organization of self appears to become more rigid under threat; to relax its boundaries when completely free of threat. Experience which is perceived as inconsistent with the self can only be assimilated if the current organization of self is relaxed and expanded to include it.
• The educational situation which most effectively promotes significant learning is one in which (1) threat to the self of the learner is reduced to a minimum, and (2) differentiated perception of the field of experience is facilitated.[5]

When applied to teaching and learning, these principles do not necessarily preclude the development of groups. The individual is permitted to be free to learn within a permissive group structure.[6]

However, a number of less interpersonally oriented Existential humanists have ignored the group aspects of classroom learning in their zeal to counteract the excesses of extreme institutional domination of the learning process. Their conceptions of student-oriented teaching may be termed "radically idiographic." In a radically idiographic classroom, students are considered to be so unique in temperament and need that any imposition of a group structure is interpreted as a threat to their personhood. The ideal of the radical "humanists" is to avoid classes altogether; they would prefer to conduct tutorials, or independent studies in which the student would be unburdened by pressures to conform to the norms and role expectations of peers or teachers.

However, since tutorials and independent studies are not feasible for most teachers and students in our nation's understaffed elementary and secondary schools (in spite of the current oversupply of teachers, most experts agree that our schools are understaffed), the best accommodation to this theory of classroom structure would be to make the existing classroom system as highly charged with life and love as can be tolerated by all concerned, including parents and school officials. In our achievement-oriented culture, the toleration level of significant others such as parents and school officials is normally far less than that of the Existential, humanistic teacher. Such a teacher has little likelihood of surviving his or her first year on the job.[7] Even if the students responded to radically humanistic teaching, and if parents and school officials supported such teaching, it is improbable that the idiographically oriented teacher could retain the same values which he or she started out with at the beginning of the semester. If not carefully guided, both students and teacher would quickly find it more gratifying to revert to some of the norms and roles to which they had grown accustomed in their formative years.

The only way in which a classroom system oriented to extreme Existential and humanistic ideas could be realized would be if everyone involved were reared from birth without interpersonal involvement of any kind—which of course is impossible. Even if this were possible, rules and roles for the group would inevitably evolve in order to make life more tolerable. In short, the completely idiographic alternative to the conventional nomothetic classroom system is probably an unrealizable ideal. About the most that school teachers who have been seduced by such a vision can do to make their educational efforts with students less routine and more personally meaningful is to strive continually to inject as much of their personalities into their teaching as is feasible. Of course, there are restrictions upon the inclusion of feelings in classrooms, and there are limits upon the average teacher's time.[8]

Teachers who desire to make their classrooms more interesting, exciting, and pleasurable places in which to live and work can also allow their students to express themselves more freely than has been the custom in the formal educational institutions of America. Within the very real and significant limitations of their institutionalized roles and those of their students, teachers can improve their classroom climates and thereby better approximate the ideal proposed by Carl Rogers.

Recent Pressures on Alternative Classroom Systems

Unless and until truly significant changes in the values of Americans begin to exert an impact on policies of schools—an impact only hinted at to date by the teacher-power and free-school movements—classroom teachers will be pressured to expend less time and energy allowing personality factors to emerge as they work with children.[9]

Practicing teachers are becoming anxious about the demands being imposed upon them by communities and administrative superordinates. Many say that they are being told to cut back even further from innovative instruction methods and orientations so harshly criticized by the Essentialists in the 1950s and 1960s.[10] Teachers are being asked to concentrate more upon writing **behavioral objectives** and raising achievement-test scores in the "basic skills." Reading, math, history, and geography once again appear to dominate the curriculum. The humanizing components of the program, usually considered to be social studies, the arts, music, and literature, are receiving less attention.

Many of the numerous innovations that were created and optimistically tried in the 1960s are being rejected in the 1970s.[11] Teachers are again being encouraged to impart only the fundamentals of knowlege, at the expense of the personal and cultural elements of education. Such a climate in the field of education does not bode well for a highly idiographic classroom system. Perhaps other institutional and extra-institutional forces will produce as yet unforeseen major changes in American education.

Until these forces come into play, it is important that prospective teachers in public schools (where most jobs in education exist and will continue to exist) become aware of and skilled at developing "transactional" classroom systems. These classrooms respect both the unique individual and institutional norms and roles. Perhaps future empirical research on the development and operation of private free schools that use moderate—not extreme—idiographic modes of interacting may demonstrate the efficacy of such modes in less fully institutionalized settings. Some research results are already available to partly confirm this speculation. In a comparison of "successful" and "unsuccessful" alternative secondary schools, Deal found that:

> Those schools that "made it" did so because they were able to find an organizational middle ground by maintaining a highly individualized or pluralistic structure but one that was also well integrated and formalized ... They had compromised somewhat their original participatory, democratic, "hang loose" approach to organization but were able to maintain the integrity of the other elements in their alternative approach to instruction.[12]

The Transactional Classroom System

The best hope for effectiveness and self-fulfillment for most teachers is likely to come from having learned to successfully develop transactional styles of working with youngsters.

> ... the transactional mode is not just a compromise. Instead, the aim throughout is to acquire a thorough awareness of the limits and resources of both individual and institution within which the teaching-learning process may occur ... and to make an intelligent application of the two as a particular problem may demand ... Institutional roles are developed

424

independently of the role-incumbents, but they are adapted to the personalities of the actual individual incumbents. Expectations are defined as sharply as they can be but not so sharply that they prohibit appropriate behavior in terms of need-depositions ... The standard of behavior is both individual integration and institutional adjustment ... the processes in the classroom may be seen as a dynamic transaction between roles and personality.[13]

Gorman calls such a style "group-centered" teaching, because the intent is to transform the participants from a motley aggregate at the beginning of the year to a learning group as time goes on. This is accomplished by employing principles of group dynamics in a creative manner so that lines of affective communication open up each member to each other member.[14] Gorman lists the following distinctions between conventional and group-centered teaching:

(Nomothetic Mode)	*(Transactional Mode)*
1. Teacher domination	1. Teacher as special member of group
2. Teacher as sole leader	2. Group-centered shared leadership
3. Extrinsic control in hands of teacher	3. Intrinsic control in hands of individuals, including teacher
4. Active membership of teacher plus two or three verbal students	4. Active membership of total group
5. Stress on subject with exclusion of personal social needs	5. Stress on *both* cognitive *and* affective elements
6. Heavy dependency on teacher as planner, initiator, and evaluator	6. Student self-direction and independence
7. Formal recitation by small percentage of students	7. Spontaneous participation by all
8. Selective inattention by students	8. Careful listening with feedback checks
9. An aggregate of noncohesive individuals	9. A cohesive group of interacting individuals
10. Student learning with the intent of passing tests and obtaining grades	10. Student learning to satisfy needs to know and to grow
11. Guarded, hidden feelings	11. A norm of openness and spontaneous expression of feelings
12. Unchecked assumptions	12. Positive feelings that the assumptions should be checked

13. Neutral feelings toward the meaninglessness of the learning experience	13. Positive feelings that the experience has personal meanings and values
14. Vague student anxiety	14. Personal security
15. Preoccupation with self and projection of "good" self-image	15. Sensitivity to verbally and nonverbally expressed needs of others
16. Student fear of speaking in a group situation	16. Confidence in expressing feelings, knowledge, and direction
17. View of teacher as nonhuman object	17. View of teacher as human being with feelings similar to those of students[15]

Do students learn anything other than effective human relations techniques in a transactional, or group-centered, classroom? According to the experience of therapists and teachers who have developed approximations of such open classrooms, students do learn more than they do in conventional classrooms. In Gorman's words:

> Teachers are beginning slowly to understand that any group setting is packed with human relations needs that have to be met before people can get on with the learning of subject matter. Large numbers of students find the traditional classroom actively harmful to their self-images day after day. Many withdraw physically and become dropout statistics; much larger numbers stay physically while withdrawing psychologically. Still others do not withdraw, but learn to play the highly sophisticated game of teacher and students much in the same way that they role-played cops and robbers at earlier ages. Their real world of personal meaning, where they can authentically play themselves, usually exists outside the classroom ... Teachers should be—and are to some extent—scholars in their subject disciplines. But teaching is not accomplished by the teachers demonstrating to their students how learned they, the teachers, are. Teaching is accomplished only when learners learn, retain what they learn, and develop both the urge to use their learning in later situations and some methodology for putting learnings to work...
>
> Humanistic teaching and affect education does not call for the abandonment of present curriculum content—except for some of the "crap" we have come to value—but rather asks us to reexamine it in terms of its relevance. And, just as important as this, we must come to view methodology more on equal terms with content...[16]

The transactional classroom depends for its success upon the sensitive application of widely accepted principles of human relations toward the goal of meaningful student involvement and student learning. Although it is not a panacea for all the problems presently facing formal education, the transactional mode may be a valuable aid to the restoration of meaning in a human endeavor that seems to have forgotten what Socrates knew: Teaching and learning involve a profound **dialogic relationship.**

How Can You Create a Transactional Classroom?

Socrates was a gifted teacher. In almost every school, there are one or two teachers who are especially respected by students, parents, fellow teachers, and administrators of every philosophical persuasion. They are considered outstanding because of their ability to make a powerful impact upon their students. These gifted teachers often give the impression of knowing almost instinctively what to do and when to do it. They usually have had the same sort of professional preparation as have their colleagues, but they seem to possess something extra that translates into a vital and motivating relationship with their students.

Although we do not know whether such rare teachers are "born" rather than "made," we do know that their classrooms are usually transactional in nature. Students and teacher seem to be exceptionally involved with each other, and everyone is eager to accomplish the academic tasks expected of him or her. Roles and personalities are subtly harmonized so that the two major problems of all classroom groups— group productivity and group cohesiveness—are resolved to a far greater degree than they are in ordinary classrooms.[17] The great majority of prospective teachers can learn to create effective transactional classrooms.

Among other foundational writers in education, Gorman has developed an **analytic model** and a **concrete model,** designed to help teachers learn to create a transactional classroom. Some of his basic ideas are discussed in the following paragraphs. For more specialized help in becoming a transactional teacher, you will need to integrate these foundational ideas with your work in methods courses and in workshops.

A key assumption underlying transactional teaching is that the classroom is neither autocratic nor anarchic; it is a democracy with rules developed by the participants, including the teacher who is a special member of the group.[18] At the outset, the teacher meets his or her students, not as a formed group, but as an aggregate of disparate individuals with varying backgrounds of knowledge, skills, values, self-concepts, expectations, and social and academic needs. This mass of individuals has certain assumptions concerning what schools and teachers do, and how they are supposed to behave in class. From this initial point, the job of the teacher is to work with the aggregate in ways that facilitate effective communication.

Eventually, the transactional teacher will create a cohesive and productive group wherein each student member feels a sense of belonging. This is done by encouraging verbal and nonverbal interaction between teacher and students and between student peers. This process is not separated from daily academic work but is an integral component of study and demands that the teacher treat each student with respect for his or her feelings and expectations. The student is not considered an object to be molded according to a preformed pattern. As time goes on, and the students and teacher share ideas and feelings, efforts are made by both to reinforce or to change the original aggregate structure by suggesting and discussing rules ("norm inputs," in Gorman's terms) relating to control and direction of classroom activities. After a couple of weeks, the teacher gets a "feel" for the class, which he or she shares with the class. In turn, the class is urged to react to the teacher's feelings, either orally or by formal or informal written reactions.

As the mass begins to become a group, the teacher and students consider their feelings about the effectiveness of the interaction process in the class and their general satisfaction with it. Shared feelings and suggestions are accepted and responded to with continued openness to written and oral feedback from students. Negative as well as positive feelings are permitted, and alternatives to disliked behaviors are sought. These suggestions and alternatives are experimented with in an effort to get to know each other better, to test limits of control, to reinforce acceptable norms, and to change disagreeable ones.

After a month or so, the teacher begins to feel satisfied about the developing group. Students work through their individual and interpersonal problems and begin to trust the teacher. Most students become more self-directed, although a few remain overly dependent on the teacher as an authority figure. But in general, new norms are accepted for working together and expressing feelings openly, and a special group climate emerges.

In the last stage of group development, which Gorman terms "behavior change," teacher and students know what each expects of the other and why, so that the style of the class no longer is the teacher's alone. It is a composite outgrowth of the teacher's ideas and those of his or her students. By this time, Gorman says "You are learning to be democratic without being overly permissive and without going too fast for the students who are so used to being told what to do all the time."[19] Furthermore:

> Participant background has changed, and the Aggregate-Group structure is far along the way toward group status. Problems have by no means disappeared, but there is widespread support for the open expression of feelings, and the class has had some good experiences in resolving

problems. Cognitive knowledge, as measured by a variety of measurement devices prepared by students as well as teacher, is very good. It could be better, but motivation is high and students are doing a good job of learning how to learn. Affective knowledge, also measured by teacher and students, is growing and becoming increasingly effective in classroom use.[20]

Gorman's version of transactional, or group-centered classroom system development is outlined in Figure 16–2.

The transactional classroom model in Figure 16–2 specifies some of the salient actions intelligent and humanistic teachers can make to lead children from conventional, teacher-dominated group forms to more democratic student–teacher learning groups. A primary requirement of the model is a willingness to allow feelings to be expressed and shared along with cognitions. The transactional teacher believes that to happily and successfully learn in school classrooms requires a strong sense of belongingness on the part of the student. Anxieties and feelings of alienation are avoided by instilling a sense of belonging in each student. In the transactional classroom, everyone—whatever their cultural or individual idiosyncracy—is made to feel that he or she belongs fully to the group. All students thereby gain from the contributions of other members and contribute freely to others. The transactional classroom might be viewed as the formal educational equivalent of a socially and morally integrated community.

You can build your own transactional classroom in almost any type of school culture. Although there are other factors to consider, your success will probably depend heavily upon your personal philosophy of education and teaching, the kinds of experiences you had as a child, and your experiences in college and in your teacher-education program. Most of all, your willingness to experiment in your own classroom with the transactional model of teaching will determine the degree of your success. Some of the most highly regarded educators in history have employed the transactional mode of teaching with their own pupils. Socrates did this intuitively, and today many of the finest elementary and secondary teachers do so self-consciously.

Summary

Like schools themselves, classrooms are small societies with their own cultural values, norms, role expectations, and personality configurations. Most classrooms are "nomothetic," or teacher-dominated. This type of classroom has been criticized by some educators who urge the abolition

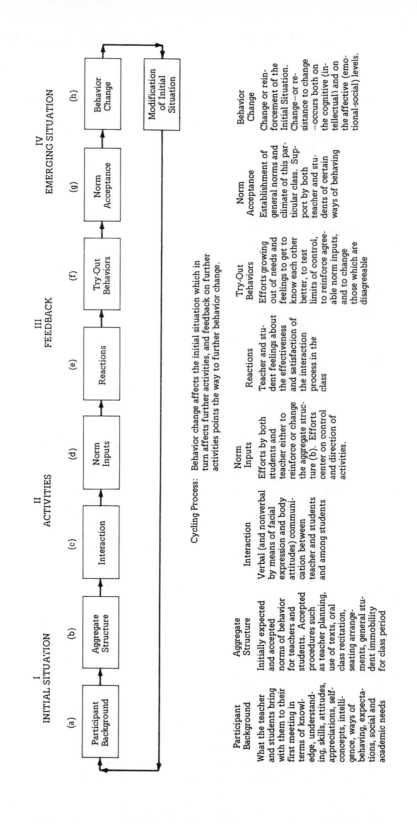

FIGURE 16–2. *A Framework for Developing a Transactional Classroom (From Alfred H. Gorman, Teachers and Learners: The Interactive Process of Education, 2nd ed. [Boston: Allyn and Bacon, 1974], pp. 40–41. Reprinted by permission.]*

of strictly defined classroom roles and their replacement with respect for the unique personality of the student.

However, recent pressures on schools from educational Essentialists portend an unfavorable outlook for extremely idiographically-oriented teachers and classrooms. More and more social psychologists also reject extreme dichotomization of roles and personality. In considering approaches to building a viable classroom system, then, it is probably best to think in terms of a transaction between the personal needs of the individuals comprising the schooling enterprise and their diverse positions and role expectations.

The transactional classroom is constructed on several principles of group dynamics. Its basic premise is that the development of a sense of belonging will ensure a cohesive classroom community in which individuality can be safely expressed. Teachers of a variety of philosophic persuasions and backgrounds and of diverse talents can learn to construct such emotionally secure, democratic, and productive classrooms.

Related Concepts

analytic model   "A constructed simplification of some part of reality that retains only those features regarded as essential for relating similar processes whenever and wherever they occur."[21] Useful for analyzing complex phenomena of a general nature.

concrete model   "Based on an analytic model, but uses more of the content of actual cases."[22] Used to help resolve actual problems confronting individuals or groups.

behavioral objective   Most simply understood as a lesson objective, in which the methods of evaluating the results of teaching are built into the written objective; for example, "Students will demonstrate proficiency in writing behavioral objectives by composing three, one each in the cognitive, psychomotor, and affective domains."

dialogic relationship   A relationship between two or more people (such as teachers and students) in which free-flowing communication exists, and the openness of this communication is conducive to optimal learning of a personal and social nature.

Suggested Activity

Think of the three best teachers you have had in elementary and secondary school; that is, the three teachers you remember most not only because the classes were enjoyable, but because you also learned a great deal. In light of the Gorman and other models presented in this chapter, try to explain what it was about these three teachers and their classes that made them so memorable.

Share your conclusions with the other students in your education class, and try to ascertain whether there are some common principles of excellent teaching that the entire group can agree upon and list.

References and Notes

1. See *The Dynamics of Instructional Groups,* The Fifty-ninth Yearbook of the National Society for the Study of Education, Part II, Nelson B. Henry, ed. (Chicago: University of Chicago Press, 1960).

2. Jacob W. Getzels and Herbert A. Thelen, "The Classroom Group as a Unique Social System," in *The Dynamics of Instructional Groups,* pp. 77–82.

3. The products bred from such organizational extremes may be termed "anti systems." See S.N. Eisenstadt, "Processes of Change and Institutionalization of the Political Systems of Centralized Empires," in George K. Zollschan and Walter Hirsch, eds., *Explorations in Social Change* (Boston: Houghton Mifflin Company, 1964), pp. 319–44.

4. See, for instance, one of Carl Rogers' major early works, *Client-Centered Therapy* (Cambridge, Mass: The Riverside Press, 1951), and Herbert Kohl, *The Open Classroom: A Practical Guide to a New Way of Teaching* (New York: Random House, 1969).

5. Rogers, *Client-Centered Therapy,* pp. 389–91.

6. *Ibid.,* p. 427.

7. There was a spate of popular autobiographical descriptions of teaching, published in the late 1960s. Several of the writers claim that as a result of their efforts to humanize their classrooms, they were either fired or otherwise induced to quit after a year or two. See, for instance, Sunny Decker, *An Empty Spoon* (New York: Harper & Row, 1969); James Herndon, *The Way It Spozed To Be* (New York: Simon and Schuster, 1968); Jonathan Kozol, *Death at an Early Age: The Destruction of the Hearts and Minds of Negro Children in the Boston Public Schools* (Boston: Houghton Mifflin, 1967).

8. Time is a commodity of which most teachers have far too little. An excellent study of time and other factors affecting the work of teachers in their classrooms, is Philip W. Jackson, *Life in Classrooms* (New York: Holt, Rinehart and Winston, 1968).

9. For comprehensive treatment of educational objectives at the policy level and in terms of curriculum and instruction, see Benjamin S. Bloom, et al. *Taxonomy of Educational Objectives, The Classification of Educational Goals* (New York: Longmans, Green, 1956–64); and Richard L. Derr, *A Taxonomy of Social Purposes of Public Schools* (New York: David McKay Company, 1973).

10. Arthur Bestor, *Educational Wastelands: The Retreat from Learning in our*

Public Schools (Urbana: University of Illinois Press, 1953); James D. Koerner, *The Miseducation of American Teachers* (Boston: Houghton Mifflin, 1963); Hyman Rickover, *American Education, A National Failure: The Problem of Our Schools and What We Can Learn from England* (New York: Dutton, 1963).

11. For a balanced discussion of the failure of educational innovations in recent years, *see* P. Carpenter-Huffman, G.R. Hall, and G.C. Sumner, *Change in Education: Insights from Performance Contracting* (Cambridge, Mass.: Ballinger Publishing Company, 1974).

12. Terrence E. Deal, "An Organizational Explanation of the Failure of Alternative Secondary Schools," *Educational Researcher* 4 (April 1975): 15, 16.

13. Getzels and Thelen, "Classroom Group as Social System," pp. 78, 79.

14. Alfred H. Gorman, *Teachers and Learners: The Interactive Process of Education*, 2nd ed. (Boston: Allyn and Bacon, 1974).

15. *Ibid.*, pp. 50, 51.

16. *Ibid.*, pp. 12, 19.

17. Gale E. Jensen, "The Social Structure of the Classroom Group: An Observational Framework," *Journal of Educational Psychology* 46 (May 1955): 362–74.

18. The terms originally employed to describe group leadership styles in the classic research of Kurt Lewin and his colleagues (Lippitt and White) were "authoritarian," "laissez faire," and "democratic." *See* Kurt Lewin, "Studies in Group Decision," and Ralph White and Ronald Lippitt, "Leader Behavior and Member Reaction in Three Social Climates," in Dorwin Cartwright and Alvin Zander, eds., *Group Dynamics: Research and Theory* (New York: Harper & Row, Publishers, 1953).

19. Gorman, *Teachers and Learners*, p. 49.

20. *Ibid.*

21. Robert Chin, "The Utility of System Models and Developmental Models for Practitioners," in Warren G. Bennis, Kenneth D. Benne, and Robert Chin, eds., *The Planning of Change*, 2nd ed. (New York: Holt, Rinehart, and Winston, 1969), p. 298.

22. *Ibid.*

17

The Organization of Schools for Innovation and Change

Formal education at all levels has become a top priority in the United States since the end of World War II. This is partly a reflection of the changing requirements for occupational success and personal happiness in modern society and partly a function of demographic pressures. The scope of the schooling enterprise has been expanded to better serve millions of Americans who have not received the educational benefits that the majority has enjoyed.

Ours has become a heavily "schooled society."[1] There appears to be no sign that this cultural pattern will decrease substantially in the near future, although conventional forms of schooling may become greatly modified and in some instances replaced by newer forms. To adequately serve the changing needs and demands of a heterogeneous population, formal educational institutions must adapt, extend, and perhaps abolish some of their traditional functions. Schools also need to rapidly update their internal operations in the areas of curriculum, teaching roles, use of instructional media, and the like. Contemporary school people have already made strenuous efforts to modify some of the school's internal operations. However, most are reluctant to alter its basic functions to meet the demands for fundamentally different kinds of learning suitable to a new age.

The Educational Revolution

The amount of change in the importance of formal education and in related efforts to increase the efficiency and effectiveness of school operations has been so great that the term "educational revolution" is sometimes applied to this phenomenon. Examples of the many kinds of innovations created and diffused during this educational revolution include the "teaching machine" and "programmed learning," which systematically increase the rate and extent of acquiring basic skills and knowledge on a more or less individualized basis; the development of types of educational "hardware," such as computers, videotape players, pupil-operated film projectors, and other mechanical and electronic instruments for facilitating learning; the development of multiracial readers, self-scoring workbooks, and similar printed materials; "differentiated staffing"; "team teaching"; "open spacing"; and "year-round schools," which extend the impact on student learning of instructional personnel and environmental resources.

Other recent innovations include "performance contracting," whereby private companies are hired by school systems to teach fundamental skills, such as reading, and are paid according to results determined by pre- and post-standardized achievement testing; "new math," "new social studies," and "new science," which are all intended to broaden and deepen learning of complex disciplines at earlier ages by involving students directly in the processes that advanced scholars employ to acquire knowledge. Curricular innovations such as "ethnic studies" are intended to increase awareness of the subcultural identities of blacks, women, and other minorities in our pluralistic society. "Performance-based teacher education" is designed to make prospective teachers more accountable for what they acquire in schools of education by insisting that they demonstrate behavioral proficiency. The Teacher Corps is a federally sponsored effort to prepare dedicated teachers for careers in depressed rural areas or inner-city ghettos. "Community control," the "voucher system," and other public and nonpublic school alternatives to traditional educational authority are being discussed or implemented. Busing and related means are being used to mix youngsters of different ethnic and socioeconomic backgrounds in schools in order to achieve greater equality of educational opportunity and to reduce the social distance between traditionally segregated groups.

Not all of these innovations have been successful. For example, busing to integrate schools has met with severe resistance from irate dominant-group parents, in spite of federal requirements that schools desegregate. Reasons why some innovations are more rapidly and fully diffused throughout schools and school systems than others will be discussed shortly. For the moment, we simply want to consider some of the kinds of changes that have been and are being attempted, successfully and unsuccessfully, by school people in an effort to make formal education more adaptive to the times in which we live.

In a period when the institution's importance has reached an all-time high in terms of sheer numbers to be educated, the totality of these efforts and the scope of demand for refined and increased services calls for an "educational reformation," if not yet an educational revolution.

Romance and Reality in Education:
Significant Change and the Limits of the
School's Capacity to Serve Society

Table 17–1 lists a variety of changes in education that **futurists** predict will occur in the next several years. Many of these changes are rather significant departures from the closed teaching systems of the past and present. Of course, it is not an absolute certainty that they will actually come about. Significant changes in the field of education usually involve changing human values relating to the teaching and learning process, especially values relating to the ultimate purposes of that process. In the area of student–teacher relations in Table 17–1, one of the trends listed is greater exposure to and respect for feelings; this represents a major value change entailing an **"I–Thou" relationship** between student and teacher.

Most people would probably agree that this kind of change in education seems to be warranted in a depersonalized mass society. But because such a change in educational values is so dependent upon concomitant changes in the core values that Americans have about the proper attitudes and behaviors of adults toward children, such change is not readily achieved.

Superficial, Not Significant Changes

Changes in the central values of any people take place much more slowly than changes in the technologies that they employ primarily to sustain existing values. There is often a degree of cultural lag separating the material aspects of a culture (its techniques for accomplishing its ends) and the nonmaterial aspects (the ends themselves). This has been true of American culture to date, and seems likely to remain true for a while, even though our central values are now also in transition, according to students of social change.[2]

Everett Rogers and Floyd Shoemaker's important work on social innovation and its diffusion throughout social systems is useful. They list five attributes of innovations as critical for successful and lasting diffusion:

- Relative advantage of a new idea, compared to existing ideas
- Compatibility of the new idea with prior arrangements in the system it is intended to alter
- Its complexity; innovations simple to understand or use are more likely to be accepted and readily diffused than complex ones
- Its "trialability," or ease of testing and investing in on a small scale
- And its "observability," or "communicability"; the easier it is to infer its results, the greater the likelihood of an innovation's being accepted.[3]

Compatibility is especially relevant to our discussion of significant changes in education. For,

> Most changes of any significance have repercussions that transcend the immediate spheres of the change. The greater these effects are and the more adjustments that they require, the more difficult it is to persuade people to undertake the initial change. In particular, an innovation that strikes at the basic values or traditional codes of behavior has a substantial barrier to overcome if it is to be accepted. . .[4]

Powerful valuational innovations, such as a fundamental alteration of child–adult attitudes and behaviors, often require a social movement involving conflict between people in favor of the change and people opposed to it. However, technological innovation, which is the type of innovation usually associated with formal education, frequently needs only demonstrate to authorized system decision makers the advantages of a particular technical innovation. No innovation or proposed change in the status quo is easy to diffuse, even if it is compatible with existing values. Many teachers, for example, ignore supposedly workable innovations handed down to them as dicta from above.[5]

The kinds of innovations that have survived in American education have been mainly technological, not valuational. Better ways to accomplish current valued goals through the organization of the school, its curriculum, its instructional media, and the roles of teachers have been widely accepted. Changes such as school integration, humanizing the classroom, building in radical alternatives to the prevailing subject-centered Essentialist curriculum, and equalizing the status of teachers with that of administrators have met with severe resistance from vested interests who wish to retain existing priorities. The innovations that are the most difficult to diffuse are the kinds of changes that many broad-visioned people believe are most pertinent to the emergent Post-Industrial age.

The most difficult to diffuse of all innovations in education—some version of the philosophy of Social Reconstruction—is the most signifi-

Table 17–1. From Yesterday to Tomorrow: The Basic Long-Term Multifold Trend in Education

CLOSED TEACHING SYSTEMS	OPEN LEARNING SYSTEMS
ALTERNATE TITLES	
Teacher and/or institution centered	Student and/or child centered
Tight system: Rational mechanics; Cause-effect paradigm	Loose system
Control-centered	Learning-centered; Inquiry approach; Developmental; Discovery education
SOCIETAL CONTEXT	
Agricultural; Industrial	Postindustrial; Knowledge-based, Service society
Autocratic; Plutocratic; Gerontocratic	Democratic; Meritocratic; Self-renewing
Static and simple	Dynamic and complex
BELIEFS ABOUT LEARNING	
Teaching results in learning	Good teaching aids learning, bad teaching inhibits it
Learning requires discipline, work, drill, memorization, pain control	Learning is enjoyable, follows from pursuit of interests
Teacher as source of knowledge, student as passive absorber	Learning from many sources, including peers; student as active participant
Capability confined to a few; the genius, the gifted	Extensive latent potential in all
ADMINISTRATION	
Input oriented	Input-Service-Benefit oriented, PPBS
Hierarchical leadership	Pluralistic, participatory
CURRICULUM	
Narrow, fixed, retrospective	Broad, changing present and future-oriented
Classics, Principles, Truth, facts, deduction, Maxims	Methods, principles, induction, creativity, intuition, randomness
Determined by teacher and/or extra-classroom authority	Determined by teacher and/or student
Programmatic, sequential; Lesson plans strictly followed	Interchangeable programettes, Modular learning: Lesson plan as guide to options
Group study prescribed for all students	Independent study designed to fit individual needs and interests
Western culture as superior to primitive, heathens, Noble Savages, and the underdeveloped; Us–Them: emphasis on differences	Humanistic, pan-cultural; Us: emphasis on similarities
STUDENT–TEACHER RELATIONS	
Students are a collectivity	Compensatory education for exceptional children, the physically and linguistically handicapped, the underprivileged
Teacher as Authority, student as follower; control as instrumental technique	Professional as Learning Facilitator or Senior Learner; student as junior colleague
Feeling Withheld; I–It	Feelings exposed and respected, student evaluation of teachers; I–Thou
Single Teacher	Multi-adult exposure, team teaching, guests, differentiated staffing

438

Table 17–1. *Continued*

CLOSED TEACHING SYSTEMS	OPEN LEARNING SYSTEMS
STUDENT CONDUCT	
Compulsory attendance: no choice of institution	Optional participation: alternatives offered
Physical punishment for "Misbehavior"	Counseling for personal difficulties
No student recourse for injustice	Ombudsman, legal measures
Dropping out is fault of student; shaming for ignorance	Many possible sources of failure: environmental, institutional and individual
Established rules and routines	Democratic development of rules and routines as necessary
FEEDBACK	
Formal, mechanistic, "Right" answers	Multi-faceted, formal and informal, open-ended
Strong reliance on quantitative measures	Use of quantitative measures as necessary
REWARDS	
Grades, fixed proportion of failures, class rankings, honors, medals, degrees	Pass-fail, non-grading
Recognition through competition in a few areas of excellence	Deemphasis of competition, promotion of diversity and many areas of excellence; a taste of success for all
Learning has vocational and social utility	Rewards of learning are inherent
GOALS	
Socialization, training, moral education, passing on civilization, knowing; education of intellect only	Development of whole individual, investigation of cultural heritage, questioning
Getting an Education, being educated, terminal education	Learning how to learn, lifelong learning, education as a beginning
EXTRA-CLASSROOM ENVIRONMENT	
Restrictive, "In Loco Parentis"	Permissive, largely peer controlled
Physical and intellectual separation from world	Interlinkage of school and life, "School Without Walls"
SPACE	
"Grid" architecture, stationary furniture	Omnidirectional space and flexible furnishings, choice of environments
Arbitrarily assigned seats	Student freedom to choose seats
Teaching in classrooms	Learning in classrooms, learning resource center, home, dormitory, community, world
Specially designated learning institutions, outside learning ignored	Recognition and encouragement of formal and informal learning opportunities throughout society, equivalent credit for outside learning
TIME	
Collective pace	Individual pace
Ordered structure of class hours and course credits	Flexible scheduling
Uninterrupted schooling, followed by uninterrupted work	Learning and work interspersed throughout lifetime; learning a living

From Michael Marien, "The Basic Long-Term Multifold Trend in Education," *The Futurist* 4 (December 1970): 222–23. Reprinted with permission of *The Futurist,* published by the World Future Society, P.O. Box 30369 (Bethesda), Washington, D.C. 20014.

cant as well, according to its proponents. This philosophy of education recommends that formal education institutions take the lead in altering modern Western civilization at its very core. However, as Levin argues:

> ... significant changes in education [Social Reconstructionism] occur only as a consequence of changes in the overall social economic, and political relations that characterize a polity; no set of educational reforms will succeed if they violate the major tenets of our social, economic, and political system. In any stable (nonrevolutionary) society the educational system will always be a major vehicle for transmitting the culture and preserving the status quo, academic debates and utopian visions notwithstanding.[6]

Social Reconstruction led by schools actually is a revolutionary idea, not a reformist one. It is probably an unrealistic ideal because it goes to extremes in advocating the radical overhauling of extant core values held by powerful vested interests in society, both in the schools and outside of them. But meaningful reforms, such as new ways of financing public education, can be realized if they fall within stable or changing value boundaries. Thus, some significant change in education is possible through the processes discussed by students of technological innovation.[7] These processes are not critically dependent upon the element of conflict between influential status-quo interests and interests of change.

Inherent Limits of Change

Most organizations, including schools, have built-in limitations to their capacity for change. Limitations on the capacity for change are inherent in most organizations for the following reasons: There is a sense of advantage in the status quo; a desire by organization managers to protect "quality"; fear of the psychic costs of change; the programmed conservatism of most organization members; and lack of expendable resources.[8] Even if an organization is able to overcome these kinds of obstacles, it may not go far enough to achieve meaningful and long-lasting change:

> After an organization has been changed even a little, it begins to freeze into its new pattern almost at once; it does not remain loosely structured and flexible. All the tendencies that inhibited change in its prior configuration promptly make themselves felt in the new one. Furthermore, a set of forces limiting the extent and speed of change begins to take effect.[9]

Administrative reaction to serious proposals for organizational reform can be devastating to the organization member proposing change, thus discouraging many would-be innovators from even approaching **opinion leaders** with novel ideas for improving their organizations. O'Day concludes that the reaction of organization authority figures to reform initiatives of subordinates is normally a series of "intimidation rituals," including nullification of the proposal; isolation of the reformer from his or her fellows; defamation of his or her character and motives; and finally, expulsion from the organization if he or she refuses to cease reform efforts.[10]

However, O'Day, among other students of socio-organizational change, makes an important observation about reformist efforts that suggest that reformers can play an important role in changing an organization:

> The serious reformer should be prepared to take advantage of organiza-
> tional crisis . . . For it is in a time of crisis that an organization is open to
> solutions to the basic problem of survival. Organizational members will
> be eager to adopt new structures that promise to relieve the uncertainty
> and anxiety generated by a crisis . . . Such an organization might not be
> capable of successfully administering the intimidation rituals.[11]

Thus, the timing of meaningful proposals for change is also an important determinant of their success or failure.

Taken together, these and other variables shed some light on the question of why significant (as differentiated from technological) changes in the field of education have been so slow to develop, despite the pleas of many professionals and lay people for such changes. To the extent that proposed changes require radical revision of prevailing core values in school and society (as Social Reconstructionism in its pure form does), they may properly be called romantic and utopian. Even moderate, although value-laden, innovations such as school integration are likely to meet with strong resistance from vested interests in the social order at large as well as with barriers intrinsic to organizational life in general.

Innovations in educational technology are the kinds of changes generally suggested as indicative of the educational revolution now in process in the United States. If school people are able and willing to learn about the conditions under which successful and significant innovations have been and are being diffused throughout social systems, they can hope for desirable reforms in the formal education institution, if not for an overhauling of the system.

The school's capacity for meaningful change is frankly limited; but the limits are probably far greater than some educators have recently been led to believe by disillusioned observers who reason that because of past failures of the American school then, ispo facto, it will never succeed.[12] Perhaps the reply to such defeatism is to actually get out and do it, albeit with extreme caution.[13]

Some Principles about Social Change
Applicable to Contemporary Schools

In order to bring many of the ideas about the phenomenon of sociocultural change to bear on contemporary educational problems, a few selected principles derived from several important models will be presented. (In Chapter 2 these were summarized under the labels "Consensus," "Dissensus," and "Variable" models of change.[14]) The following list is by no means exhaustive, and some technical language has been omitted for the sake of clarity. This discussion serves to introduce the complex and important matters of innovation and change in the formal education institution.[15]

Sociocultural Change is Ultimately Derived from the Prevailing Structure of a Social Organization. It is largely limited by basic values and norms held by influential members of the system, such as upper-echelon school officials.

Persons in Organizational Positions Carry Out Sociocultural Change. Teachers play culturally patterned roles. Deviant role playing, such as a new teacher working with students in unconventional ways, have important implications for basic change under conditions of crisis.

Change Is Often Intrusive. In a closed system, such as a school in a rural community, change is often unwelcomed. But once the system's boundaries have been successfully intruded upon (by more cosmopolitan city dwellers, for example), a system is open to further changes from both outside and inside its boundaries. An "invasion" of city people to a rural school system that threatens traditional disciplinary practices usually leads to increasing student and teacher dissatisfaction with discipline practices as well as with other conventional practices.

Following Initial Intrusion, the Primary Sources of Change Are Internal Structural Tensions. For example, changed disciplinary practices that are forced on a school system from outside often provoke anxieties in senior faculty members, which in turn may drive them to quit; this would offer opportunities to newcomers with different ideas about discipline. Senior teachers might become less distant in their interactions with students and more willing to accept student ideas.

Efforts to Reduce Tensions with Innovative Methods Usually Have Unin-

tended Side Effects.   For instance, if the creation of teaching teams to increase learning results comes under attack from the community, greater loyalty among teachers and more united opposition to arbitrary demands from non-teachers may result. Or the situation may produce unusual student behavior problems which in turn may force teachers and administrators to retract their expectations for proper student behavior. Tension-reducing innovations may fail or succeed, bring temporary or permanent change, be smallscale or largescale, reformist or revolutionary, depending upon unique system conditions.

There are three basic conditions under which pattern maintenance, or integrative, structures (i.e., most elementary and secondary schools) may alter their functions to become more adaptable and responsive to changing times:

• *Successful competition for dominance with other structures.* Schools are now competing with the family and the church for the right to teach sex education, for example.

• *Gradual accretion.*   Over long periods of time, the American school has been releasing its selecting-and-sorting function to institutions of higher education and has been taking on human guidance and counseling functions of a non-vocational character for students and, increasingly, for parents.

• *Development of a rational society.*   Despite appalling instances of irrationality in modern society, by and large our world today is operated on the basis of reason far more than it was 2,000 or even 200 years ago. Schools increasingly reflect this trend in many areas; for instance, greater interest is shown in understanding the child instead of automatically censoring him or her for misbehavior.

The Direction of Change Is Structurally Determined and Largely Limited by the Core Values of the System's Members.   The kinds of changes in which American schools may participate will ultimately depend not only upon the school's unique, established organizational structure and accepted reason for existing (which of course may be modified over time), but also upon evolutionary trends in interrelated institutions (such as the family) and in values.

Vested Interests Set Goals for Change and Filter Innovations.   The following are corollaries to this idea:

• Success of technological innovations is related primarily to criteria of efficiency. Performance contracting, for example, has failed to demonstrate clear evidence of more efficient teaching of reading and other skills, so it is being rapidly abandoned. However, it was eagerly accepted by school officials across the U.S. between 1969 and 1973.[16]

  • Success of valuational innovations is related primarily to criteria of core value safety. Efforts to include religious instruction in public schools, for example, have been strenuously resisted by judges, school officials, public-interest groups, and other guardians of society's values, largely because of fear that such instruction would violate written and implicit historic precedents representing the value of separation of church and state.

  • Social conflict or social apathy and its consequences may arise out of the inability of vested interests to agree to accept significant innovations, primarily in the realm of values. The community control movement, for example, has experienced much dissension between minority-group parents and school officials who have been unable to come to terms on the issue of who is to ultimately control the public schools.

The Valuational Innovator's Place Is Usually Marginal in a Social Organization. His or her role as an **agent of change** is to seek new goals for the organization. For example, a university supervisor of student teachers who tries to create and implement a novel way of training future teachers so that they will be constructively critical rather than habituated to passively accept whatever they are told by superordinates, is a valuational innovator. Such "men of broad vision"[17] may be coopted from their marginal status temporarily by organization elites for purposes of helping to solve system problems during periods of relative crisis; for example, the innovative inner-city university supervisor may be invited to act as a consultant for teacher–pupil relations when loss of pupil control by teachers is extremely widespread in a school.

The Technological Innovator's Place Is Normally Within System Structures. His or her role is primarily to seek new means to ends already determined; for example, the downtown curriculum specialist who attempts to devise new methods of teaching reading to potential high school dropouts.

The opinion leader's place is usually as a leader within an organization. His or her role in the process of change is to facilitate the diffusion of innovations made by others, if convinced of their merit. An example of the important screening and diffusing role of the opinion leader is found in urban schools utilizing "resource teachers" for the first time. In such situations, the resource teacher, usually selected from the ranks of his or her fellow teachers, may meet with strong resistance from other teachers when he or she first introduces a novel method of working with students. Hence, he or she may be wise to initially present the idea to the school principal or department head, who usually has a far greater influence over other teachers than does the resource teacher.

The Opportunity to Innovate and Successfully Diffuse Innovations Tends to Increase in Direct Proportion to a Social System's Level of Tension. This is true for both technological and valuational innovations. Other things being equal, *necessity is the mother of invention.* It is usually futile to attempt to change educational practices until existing affairs have deteriorated to a point where most of the concerned parties—teachers, administrators, parents, students—are sufficiently distressed to tolerate, if not welcome, novelties that require a distinct departure from the ways in which they have become accustomed to think and behave. The open classroom system, for instance, is likely to become widespread in the United States only when sufficiently large numbers of students have failed to meet conventional adult academic expectations or have dropped out from public schools to enter the workforce or to attend private alternative schools. This would force parents, school officials, and teachers to risk abandoning obsolete authoritarian classroom operations and the security they represent in order to obtain greater security through unaccustomed practices.

An exception to this proposition is found in *"ultrastable"* organizations—systems that have been intentionally constructed or reconstructed to provide for continuous feedback about results of their operation. Feedback ensures that the organization will adapt before it reaches a high level of tension or stage of crisis.[18] Most school systems are far from ultrastable; if anything, they tend to suffer from severe cultural lag. The sole exception appears to be represented by schools whose official ideology is to allow students themselves to determine what they shall study and how—that is, perhaps some free schools and Progressive schools. In these schools, ultrastability is presumably built into the operation of the enterprise from the beginning, by definition.

*Six General Stages in the Change Process.**

1. A serious problem affects an organization, causing stress and tension; for example, illegal ethnic and racial imbalances in a school district.

---

* I am especially indebted to the following scholars for the material on stages in the change process: Alvin Boskoff, "Functional Analysis as a Source of a Theoretical Repertory and Research Tasks in the Study of Social Change," in George K. Zollschan and Walter Hirsch, eds., *Explorations in Social Change* (Boston: Houghton Mifflin, 1964), pp. 213–43, and Everett M. Rogers, with Floyd Shoemaker, *Communication of Innovations: A Cross-Cultural Approach* (New York: The Free Press, 1971).

2. Problem-solving and tension-reducing innovations in valuational and/or technological realms are made; for example, students are bused, district boundaries are redrawn, and housing barriers are removed. Innovations are made by individuals in any or all of the following types of positions: management functionaries (school policy makers and administrators); technical and expert personnel (curriculum specialists, experienced teachers, supervisors); and marginal position incumbents and "outsiders" (some untenured teachers, student teachers, college supervisors).

3. Innovations are screened and accepted or rejected by vested interests within the institution. In the case of illegal segregation, this filtering phase normally involves the school board out in front before the public and the school superintendent and his aides behind the scenes.

4. Diffusion of accepted innovations occurs throughout the system, resulting in system-wide adoption, non-adoption, or adoption followed by discontinuance. If an open-enrollment system, for example, is adopted as the innovation for a school system in order to relieve the problem of segregated schools, the program would normally be implemented gradually, perhaps starting with senior high school students and each year moving downward through the school population.

5. "Anti-systems" or "anti-institutions" evolve as negative by-products of the institutionalization process.[19] First a few standing alone, than many minority-group members and their allies acting in concert might denigrate open enrollment as being inadequate for the eradication of segregated schools and the fulfillment of the letter of the law. The NAACP, for instance, might eventually initiate lawsuits against the district if it failed to comply with demands for more adequate desegregation policies. At the same time, ad hoc dominant groups might emerge to resist open enrollment on the grounds that it allegedly violates their sense of educational values and promotes unnecessary racial frictions.

6. Repetition of the cycle. If sufficient anti-system pressure is mobilized to seriously challenge the efficacy of an open enrollment policy, the practice might be discontinued after it has been partially diffused.[20] The search for ways out of the difficulties of complying with the legal requirement of balancing schools racially and ethnically begins once again.

Some Thoughts about Change in School Organizations

Loosely applying the several principles of social change listed above to contemporary formal education, we can draw three major conclusions.

Concerning the Main Actors
in the Drama

Within certain normative limits, there appears to be opportunity for much updating of the expanding structure of schooling in America by a variety of persons associated with the institution. These people range from board-of-education members and higher-echelon administrators in positions to screen novel proposals for improvement; to middle-level managers who, in their capacities as school opinion leaders, can often aid creative individuals in obtaining a fair hearing for their innovative ideas; to instructional specialists associated indirectly with the classroom (teachers of teachers, curriculum specialists, and classroom teachers), whose experience and professional knowledge enable them to develop potentially useful novelties in educational technology according to their perceptions of socioeducational conditions.

Of special interest to those concerned with significant change in education is the so-called "marginal man" of broad vision. Marginal men are potential innovators in the realm of human values, who are often products of minority-group backgrounds. They are horizontally or vertically mobile as a result of one or more special circumstances in their personal lives; for example, unrepresentative physical features, unusual educational opportunities or career aspirations, or other factors in their self-development that separate them from the majority of their fellows. Accordingly, they are often uniquely situated in society and especially sensitive to its problems. They also often lack firm roots in any social group. Consequently, they can more clearly see needs which more firmly entrenched people are unable to recognize in their relative security and ethnocentrism. At one time, the marginal person was "the historic wandering Jew."[21] Today he or she is likely to be black or female.

American schools could benefit from the recognition of the marginal person as a source of innovation. Many unusually sensitive and creative individuals have avoided teaching as a career because they surmised that those who were different and intrusive to the established social system of schooling were not welcome in the field. The exceptional talents of marginal people often dissipate or are applied to other careers that are more receptive to such individuals. The important job of working with children has not been attractive to the marginal person. Such people should reassess their career priorities and opportunities. And those who employ and work with teachers should encourage school personnel to reassess their own assumptions about who "fits" the occupation. Creative minority students should especially be sought for employment in schools, not only because Affirmative Action policies require it, but because some of society's richest resources of educational talent are likely to be found in subcultural groups.

Concerning the Symptoms of
Need for Change

Those who desire to improve the working of the schools, whether they are professional educators or others, especially need to understand the importance of recognizing the real tensions and stresses that plague contemporary school systems and that confuse and depress parents, professionals, and students. Inordinate amounts of energy spent on trying to mask growing symptoms of institutional and social difficulty—improving public relations, transferring angry or uncooperative teachers to other schools within a system, or suspending troublesome students arbitrarily —are superficial strategies that avoid real educational problems.

Time and effort would be better spent in searching for the underlying sources of tensions. Then something concrete and adequate could be done to remove the symptoms by first trying to remove the probable causes. This could involve altering the curriculum, offering students more freedom to explore what they want to on their own, giving teachers a greater say in the preparation of educational policies, or more profound alteration of the structure of education and society. It is time to stop talking about the real tensions in modern schools and to begin finding out why they prevail and acting to reduce them by bringing about appropriate changes in the organization and operation of the schooling enterprise.

Concerning Ultrastability

Piecemeal efforts, or efforts made only when a serious problem, conflict of interest, or other crisis is imminent, only prolong basic problems. To avoid this, educators and the public should plan and prepare to act upon plans for ultrastabilizing our schooling system overall. This entails building into the basic structure of schooling systems substantial information-seeking and reacting mechanisms for making and keeping the schools self-renewing. The schools would thus be able to continually respond to environmental demands as they are made or they could even anticipate needed changes. Educators need to consciously develop an effective adaptive institution to take the place of a pattern-maintenance one, in order to begin to keep pace with the rest of society in an age of change. The school is competing with other social agencies for institutional dominance, and is gradually adding new tasks to its repertoire.

The school is in an unprecedented position to use the new intellectual technologies of an increasingly rational society to aid in the performance of its varied functions. We now have the capability of building self-renewing mechanisms into the institution with reasonable assurance of success and with measures available for minimizing unintended side-effects that are bound to emerge when anything new and different is attempted.

INFORMATION FEEDBACK

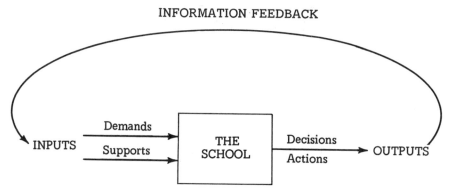

FIGURE 17–1.   *A Simple Flow Model of the School in Relation to Its Environment. The ultrastable or self-renewing school has built-in mechanisms for acknowledging the feedback it receives from the changing environment that supports it and makes new demands upon it.*

How Can You Participate in Bringing about Significant Educational Change?

There are few easy answers to the problem of bringing about significant alterations in established formal educational organizations. This is an extremely complex matter only now beginning to be carefully studied by scholars. An introductory text in the foundations of education is not the place to try to deal comprehensively with it. It does seem appropriate, however, to introduce the problem to you, as a prospective teacher, to consider since you will invariably be affected by it. Some very general speculations about how teachers can cope with some of its challenges are suggested here.

There appear to be two broad dimensions in which modern teachers who remain in the established schooling system can participate (if they choose to) in bringing about significant educational change: (1) as a member of an occupational group and (2) as an individual.

As a Member of an Occupational Group

Prospective teachers presently have at least two large-scale, increasingly powerful, more or less forward-looking organizations to represent their dominant professional concerns. Many of the changes most needed in the field of formal education in the present period of history are likely to be directly or indirectly influenced by organized teacher groups; changes will not occur as the result of goodwill voluntarily proferred by interests representing the status quo. Better salaries, improved programs, and increased opportunities to work affectively with youngsters will be achieved only by teachers themselves. Illusions of institutional solvency and professional harmony among fellow educators of all ranks are fading rapidly as they are openly challenged by the leaders of powerful teacher organizations. Part of the cause of current tensions is the scarcity of jobs in the field of education.

This is not to suggest that every challenge facing teachers and students today can be met successfully through organized confrontation or large-scale educational politics. Rather, it is to suggest that many of the truly significant (i.e., valuational) problems affecting schools and teachers probably can be resolved in no other way at this time in the history of this society. Questions of fundamental educational purpose and policy, school curriculum, and professional roles are too important to too many different groups of people to expect accommodations of these differences to come about through reasoned dialogue.

Once the most crucial dilemmas facing modern education have been dealt with through the democratic process of visible educational politics, through which some basic decisions can be achieved about what the modern school's ends and means shall be, then perhaps we can convincingly talk of collaborative reasoning with fellow educators of all ranks and with lay people in a general public forum. Until such broad political decisions have been reached and formal education has been ultrastabilized, we cannot speak and act as if there already were sufficient unity and consensus among the American people to work out the major difficulties facing our schools.

As a teacher, you possess a legitimate right to participate actively in the larger struggle to win gains for the schools in this era of basic social transformation. The idea that teachers should allow others to make important decisions for them has been fostered by a long history of occupational socialization that equates teachers of children and youth with operatives on an assembly line—an illusion born of the Industrial Revolution in Europe and America, and fed by remnants of earlier European forms of religious authoritarianism. The Industrial era of Western civilization has ended. In a Post-Industrial service society, teachers especially must learn to think and behave as morally responsible decision makers, rather than as slavish implementers of the decisions made for them by others not working on the front lines of educational endeavor. As Donald Arnstine said in his presidential address to the Philosophy of Education Society:

> Of all the groups of people broadly concerned with education, only school teachers have the potential for initiating change. The training and experience that teachers can bring to bear upon the insight gained from daily contact with children makes them far more qualified to initiate

450

changes than those who try it from administrative and legislative offices. Equally important, teachers directly undergo the consequences of change. If an experiment was ill-advised, they will be the first to hear about it and the most concerned to do something about it. This distinguishes teachers from people whose only conception of the value of a proposed change is based on how much they liked the original idea and how much it costs to act on it.[22]

The occupational organizations representing teachers' interests are probably among the best hopes our society has of creating an open, democratic, and universal educational institution for the emerging age. Underlying the active efforts of such organizations is the conscience of the American people with regard to its children, perhaps at its most ethically advanced level.[23] Of course, you can argue that these organizations have worked only imperfectly to bring this conscience to bear on educational problems, or that they might become corrupted once they have begun to achieve substantial success in their efforts to humanize the institution. In either case, it is up to their members to reform them from inside or abandon them for other interest groups that have not become compromised.

At present, however, both the NEA and the AFT appear to be developing into reasonably strong, ethical organizations representing teachers. Whichever of these or other organizations you decide to join upon becoming a member of the profession, you should consider joining and actively participating in some representative group or movement devoted to bringing about meaningful change in the structure of formal education through the political process.

As an Individual Teacher

Notwithstanding the importance of organized efforts by teachers to make schooling more responsive to the times in which we live, there are some things you may do throughout your career as an individual member of a school faculty.

You can try to always exercise critical judgment about matters that are more than merely routine ones for orderly operation of schools; that is, you should be thoughtful and critical about innovative or unusual ideas in your area of professional competence. Pressures to accept educational innovations without critical examination are common in schools; such pressures that are exerted on almost all teachers in the public schools too often have the long-term effect of reducing the eagerness to experiment and try out new ideas found in many beginning teachers. As a teacher, you can refuse to be told "how to" by other well-meaning people, if you believe that teaching is, or should be, a professional endeavor in which the individual practitioner determines how, when, and why to perform various operations. In the final analysis, no one else can properly decide these kinds of things for you. In your area of subject specialization, you may legitimately strive to retain your personal integrity, whether you teach first grade or twelfth grade. In general, then, you can continually make an intelligent effort to obtain and retain whatever professional autonomy you believe teachers should possess in the face of conscious or unconscious attempts by other teachers, administrators, parents, textbook writers, or others to undermine your sense of self-respect.

On the other hand, when you are asked to cooperate with colleagues to try out new ideas for instructing youngsters or for working more effectively with parents, you should give fair consideration to the merits of such requests, rather than turn them down immediately simply because you have become accustomed to other ways of doing things or because you believe in professional autonomy. In the sense that good schools are comprised of many diverse people engaged in a common goal of serving human beings, teaching is largely a team endeavor, not an idiosyncratic one. Between the extremes of absolutely self-determined decision making and the more common extreme of excessive dependence upon decisions made by others, there is room to express personal judgment in a team setting. You may occasionally have to compromise with your peers for the greater good of the whole.

The technical aspects of occupational life involve specialized training by knowledgeable people; in this aspect, consensual modes of thinking are perhaps most useful and appropriate. And, since it is not always readily apparent exactly when a teacher is legitimately obliged to be independent and when he or she should sacrifice some personal value for the team, you must keep yourself highly informed about and active in your profession, as well as willing to tolerate a degree of ambiguity in your daily work. The pleasure in this career resides precisely in its continual and dynamic challenges to think and to test out various behaviors, with other adults, as well as with youngsters.

Table 17–2 is an inventory that measures the flexibility of teachers and administrators and that you can administer to yourself. The first set of questions is directed to school administrators as well as to teachers; the second set contains questions directed separately to teachers, principals, and superintendents.

Summary

American society is currently going through what some term an educational revolution, although educational reform is a more accurate description. Many novel ideas for improving the technology of teaching and schooling in general are being created and tested, some successfully, others unsuccessfully. Novel ideas in the realm of educational values, which are the most significant kind, are not as yet being experimented with on a scale which they should be, since there is always greater difficulty in developing and diffusing such ideas.

A rich literature in the area of social change and the future is beginning to be developed by social scientists, and some of the principles concerning the change process are now available for use by concerned educators.[24]

One of the important ways in which teachers can help to bring about needed changes in formal education is through political involvement in their representative professional organizations. Another way is through intelligent and patient efforts on an individual basis at their own schools, working cooperatively with others, as well as independently on behalf of the youngsters they serve.

Related Concepts

agent of change   Anyone who participates actively in the creation or diffusion of new ideas or technologies, whether as an innovator, an opinion leader, a consultant, or an early consumer of an innovation; a person who facilitates the change process in one way or another

futurists   People interested in studying the future, especially by applying scientific principles to the predictions of its forms. Futurism is attracting more study in a society undergoing massive, constant transformation.

I–Thou relationship   A relationship usually associated with the great

Table 17–2.   An Inventory of Change-Proneness

No, Never	No, Almost Never	Usually Not, Infrequently	Sometimes, Yes and No	Usually Yes, Frequently	Yes Almost Always	Yes, Always
1	2	3	4	5	6	7

Common Questions for Teachers–Principals–Superintendents

1.	1 4 7		Is your general disposition toward new ideas and programs one of open-minded optimism?
2.	1 4 7		Are you willing to try something new—something that will require extra initial effort on your part?

Table 17–2. *Continued*

1 3.	4	7	Are you willing to try something new even if it may fail? (Your answer should not apply to fragmented or poorly planned and structured ideas and programs.)
1 4.	4	7	Does your selection of innovations reflect careful thought about the overall needs and priorities of your situation?
1 5.	4	7	When an educational innovation is considered, do you develop or help develop a strategy or plan of action for bringing about its successful implementation?
1 6.	4	7	Do you feel that you have sufficient freedom to initiate new programs and/or ideas?
1 7.	4	7	Do you exercise persistence and diplomacy in sticking with an innovation you would like to try, believing "Powers that be" can be brought around from what may be an initial coolness?
1 8.	4	7	Are you willing to have your innovation brought under careful scrutiny by your colleagues and others with inherent possibilities of conflicting points of view—personal as well as professional?
1 9.	4	7	Do you make a special effort to read about innovations and changes in your field?
1 10.	4	7	Do you take time to consider and seek to gain greater insight into the processes of educational change?
1 11.	4	7	Do coffee hour or informal conversations include new ideas and developments in curriculum and instruction?
1 12.	4	7	Are you aware (in terms of knowing some details) of the growing importance of research, experimentation, and innovation in American education?

Specific Questions for

Teachers	Principals	Superintendents
1. Do you take the initiative in contacting other schools and/or school systems that are trying an idea or program that is of interest to you?	1. Do you encourage and/or provide leadership in developing a planned sequence (strategy) for change when your school introduces a new idea or program?	1. Does your system have a research and development program (probably more development than basic research) that has sufficient financial support to undertake meaningful projects?
2. Do you bring new ideas and developments to the attention of colleagues as well as appropriate administrative personnel?	2. Do you seek opportunities to provide your staff and your principals with constructive ideas and suggestions relating to curriculum and instruction?	2. Do you seek opportunities to provide your staff and your principals with constructive ideas and suggestions relating to curriculum and instruction?

Table 17–2. *Continued*

3. Are you willing to ask yourself "why" about your teaching methods and the materials used?

4. Do you feel that your principal encourages you to innovate and to try new ideas and programs?

5. Do you feel that the superintendent and the central office encourages you to innovate and to try new ideas and programs?

---

3. Is your image among teachers that of an instructional leader —one interested in and supportive of new ideas?

4. Are you willing to "stick your neck out" (assuming the idea has merit) for a teacher who is interested in trying something new?

5. Are some staff meetings devoted to new developments and programs in curriculum and instruction?

6. Do you have a systematic plan for sharing new ideas and programs with your faculty?

7. Does the professional library in your school contain literature on the process of change?

---

3. Is your image among teachers that of an instructional leader—one interested in and supportive of new ideas?

4. Are you willing to "stick your neck out" (assuming the idea has merit) for a member of your staff?

5. Are some staff meetings devoted to new developments and programs in curriculum and instruction?

6. Do you have a systematic plan for disseminating new ideas and programs to administrators and teachers in your system?

7. Does the central professional library for your system contain literature on the process of change?

8. Does your school system have an individual who is a specialist in innovation and the process of change and who devotes at least a portion of his time to such responsibilities?

9. Has the board of education had an opportunity to learn about educational change, both in terms of directions as well as processes of change?

Richard I. Miller, "Some Observations and Suggestions," in Richard I. Miller, ed., *Perspectives on Educational Change* (New York: Appleton-Century-Crofts, 1967), p. 382–84. Reprinted with permission.

existential philosopher Martin Buber who placed primary emphasis upon the need for personalized, almost sacred relations between fellow human beings. To Buber, the ideal relationship between teacher and student is an "I–Thou" one, not an "I–it" one.

opinion leaders   People with high prestige in social systems whose ideas are usually carefully and respectfully considered by other members of the system. They often learn of new ideas before most other people in their milieu. Opinion leaders are extremely influential in determining whether an innovation will be widely diffused or not.

Suggested Activity

Answer the questions in the inventory of change-proneness on pages 453–455. Then ask yourself what specific kinds of changes you can make to increase your ability to adapt to changing educational conditions.

References and Notes

1.   Ivan Illich, *Deschooling Society* (New York: Harper & Row, 1971).

2.   The theory of cultural lag was first introduced by William Fielding Ogburn in 1922. *See* his *Social Change with Respect to Culture and Original Nature* (New York: Viking Press, 1952). It has since been modified to account for the fact that in modern or modernizing societies non-material parts of culture, including the educational institution, may take the lead in the change process, instead of lagging behind other institutions. *See also* Johannes Ponsioen, *The Analysis of Social Change Reconsidered: A Sociological Study* (The Hague: Mouton and Company, 1962), pp. 47–49.

3.   Everett M. Rogers with F. Floyd Shoemaker, *Communication of Innovations: A Cross-Cultural Approach* (New York: The Free Press, 1971), p. 137.

4.   P. Carpenter-Huffman, G.R. Hall, and G.C. Sumner, *Change in Education: Insights from Performance Contracting* (Cambridge, Mass., Ballinger Publishing Company, 1974), p. 5.

5.   An excellent research-based attempt to correct this situation is provided by Ronald Lippitt and colleagues, "The Teacher as Innovator, Seeker, and Sharer of New Practices," in Richard I. Miller, ed., *Perspectives on Educational Change* (New York: Appleton-Century-Crofts, Division of Meredith Publishing Company, 1967), pp. 307–24.

6.   Henry M. Levin, "Educational Reform and Social Change," *The Journal of Applied Behavioral Science* 10 (July–Aug.–Sept. 1974): 304.

7.   *See* especially Matthew B. Miles, ed., *Innovation in Education* (New York: Co-

lumbia Teachers College Press, Columbia University, 1964).

8.   Herbert Kauffman, *The Limits of Organizational Change* (University: The University of Alabama Press, 1971).

9.   *Ibid.*, p. 68.

10.   Rory O'Day, "Intimidation Rituals: Reactions to Reform," *Journal of Applied Behavioral Science* 10 (July–Aug.–Sept.): 373–80.

11.   *Ibid.*, p. 385.

12.   *See* Christopher Jencks, et al., *Inequality: A Reassessment of the Effect of Family and Schooling in America* (New York: Basic Books, 1972).

13.   *See* Bettina J. Huber, "Some Thoughts on Creating the Future," *Sociological Inquiry* 44 (1974): 29–39.

14.   Two other excellent sources of information about the leading social scientific models of change in use today are Robert Chin, "The Utility of System Models and Developmental Models for Practitioners," in Warren G. Bennis, Kenneth D. Benne, and Robert Chin, eds., *The Planning of Change,* 2nd ed., (New York: Holt, Rinehart and Winston, 1969), pp. 297–312; James E. Crowfoot and Mark A. Chesler, "Contemporary Perspectives on Planned Social Change: A Comparison," *Journal of Applied Behavioral Science* 10 (1974): 278–303.

15.   These principles (twenty-three in a complete listing) were first developed by the author for use in evaluating the educational philosophy of Social Reconstructionism. They have since been refined and elaborated for purposes of evaluating strategies of planned change for the teaching role system in the United States.

16.   Carpenter-Huffman, et al., *Change in Education.*

17.   The term is borrowed from Leon Warshay's "Breadth of Perspective and Social Change," in George K. Zollschan and Walter Hirsch, eds., *Explorations in Social Change* (Boston: Houghton Mifflin, 1964), pp. 319–44.

18.   *See* Mervyn L. Cadwallader, "The Cybernetic Analysis of Change," in Amatai Etzioni and Eva Etzioni, eds., *Social Change: Sources, Patterns, and Consequences* (New York: Basic Books, 1964), p. 160.

19.   The term "anti system" has been borrowed from S.N. Eisenstadt, "Processes of Change and Institutionalization of the Political Systems of Centralized Empires," in *Explorations in Social Change,* pp. 432–50; "anti-institutions" is taken fom Maurice Punch, "The Sociology of the Anti-Institution," *The British Journal of Sociology* 25 (September 1974): 312–25.

20.   Sometimes discontinued innovative practices are resurrected, perhaps with some refinements added. Thus, the following words of hope by two change planners after a major conference dealing with the "failure" of projects Head Start and Follow Through: ". . . on balance, the conferees agreed that the preferred course was not to give up on planned variation in education, but to try harder, recognizing the pitfalls and building on the lessons of Follow Through and Head Start Planned Variation. Most of the participants looked forward to a day when more sensitive measuring instruments, more fully developed models, and more carefully designed field studies would make a major contribution to improving the effectiveness of education." Alice M. Rivlin and P. Michael Timpane, "Planned Variation in Education: An Assessment," in

Alice M. Rivlin and P. Michael Timpane, eds., *Planned Variation in Education: Should We Give Up Or Try Harder?* (Washington, D.C.: The Brookings Institution, 1975), p. 21.

21.   Robert Park, *Race and Culture* (Glencoe, Ill.: The Free Press, 1950).

22.   Donald Arnstine, "The Use of Coercion in Changing the Schools," *Educational Theory* 23 (Fall 1973): 287.

23.   *See* Myron Lieberman, *Education As A Profession* (Englewood Cliffs, N.J.: Prentice-Hall, 1956); and *The Future of Public Education* (Chicago: The University of Chicago Press, 1960).

24.   A very able compilation of recent thinking about futurism in relation to education is Louis Rubin, ed., *The Future of Education: Perspectives on Tomorrow's Schooling* (Boston: Allyn and Bacon, 1975).

18

Toward a Dynamic
Teaching Profession

Throughout this book a number of issues have been raised and discussed: community control, teacher power, free schools, desegregation, philosophies of education, the meaning of work and leisure, school finance, institutionalized sexism, teacher and student rights, religion and the schools, and the overriding issue of bringing about significant alterations in the education of youngsters growing up in a Post-Industrial civilization. In the final analysis, perhaps an even more basic concern is how to prepare teachers to face these issues and to deal constructively with them.

The Conventional Wisdom of Teacher Education

The job of teacher preparation belongs to the institution of teacher education. The conventional wisdom of teacher education maintains that the American formal education system is a more or less finished product, instead of being a changing one. The institution of teacher education in this society has evolved largely out of a normal school tradition intended to rapidly train large numbers of women and other people interested in modest social mobility.

Making Industrial man out of Agricultural man through the process of formal education was perceived as a fairly simple task over one hundred years ago by Horace Mann and other leaders of the public school movement. The teacher of this era offered basic instruction in the essentials of learning. Children were selected and sorted by the educational process into factory owners and managers, professionals, and small entrepreneurs. Few people, including teachers, questioned this system since it seemed to reflect the needs of the Industrial way of life; it became firmly established and entrenched in the American way of life. Although it was flexible enough to accommodate some parts of the continual stream of new knowledge accumulating in the society at large, the American system of universal public education has never been able to completely keep up with all of the tremendous demands made upon it. John Dewey and the Progressivists, however, did try to formulate and institute a pragmatic way to do this between 1920 and 1940.

In order to prepare personnel to work in Industrial society, teacher-education institutions gradually expanded their normal-school beginnings to include preparation of school administrators and ancillary service workers as well as teachers. They eventually became colleges of education, schools of education, or departments of education in four-year colleges and universities. In time, some of them followed the liberal arts tradition, and a few began to offer the doctorate to would-be "teachers of teachers."

Most of the new corps of Ed.D.'s and Ph.D.'s in education worked in schools of education geared to train prospective elementary and secondary school teachers along the same general lines as the founders of the public school movement had envisioned in the nineteenth century. The emphasis was on the inculcation of methods of teaching reading, history, science, or whatever subjects were in demand at a given time and in a given place. Other courses that were gradually added to the teacher-education institution's repertoire were more or less theoretical, such as the Foundations of Education, History of Education, School and Society, Philosophy of Education, and Human Growth and Development. Sandwiched between foundations coursework and the methods of teaching specific subjects are courses such as Elementary School Curriculum, Secondary School Curriculum, and similar broad surveys of typical and experimental school programs. Crowning this professional sequence is student teaching, the capstone experience for most prospective teachers. In this field experience, a student enters a local elementary or secondary school classroom to acquire some minimal practice in the "how-to" aspects of working with youngsters. The assumption here is that there is no substitute for the real thing.

The program of teacher education described above has proved disappointing, not so much because of its arrangement or the kinds of courses provided, as because of the underlying assumption of the program. American formal education never has been a "finished product"; to prepare teachers as if it were is almost to ensure their obsolescence even before they leave the teacher-preparation institution.

Teachers in the Post-Industrial world need to be able to think for themselves, to be open to a myriad of novel demands from their students who are growing up in a new and constantly shifting milieu. As has been said and implied throughout this book, modern teachers need to be responsible for making up their own minds about most matters affecting their work. They should not have major educational decisions made for them by others.

Under the impetus of Progressivism and related student-centered movements and under the leadership of some dedicated and brilliant educational scholars, a number of schools of education have made serious efforts to develop decision-making inclinations and skills in their clientele. However, most have been unable to sustain the effort largely because their influence in the wider academic community has never been great enough to garner needed support. Innovative educators have also been under persistent attack from the society at large, and in recent years state legislators have severely curtailed the more progressive activities of many schools of education.

The challenge for institutions of teacher education is to find ways to offset the restrictions to whatever limited progress they have been making in their efforts to prepare caring, thinking educators. This is a challenge of such major proportions that we will not consider its ramifi-

461

cations here, except to say that it will demand great courage and resource-fulness on the parts of educators who work to develop truly authentic teachers.

Do You Have What It Takes To Be an Authentic Teacher in a Changing Society?

Now is the time to take stock of your talents and true interests and to decide whether or not you have what it takes to be a real teacher. If you think you do have what it takes, then you can begin to put forth the kind of committed effort in your chosen career that is required for success. Here are some of the kinds of questions you might ask yourself and then try to answer frankly:

- Do I have good physical and mental health?
- Am I willing to spend long hours on the job, both at school and at home? Am I willing to work during the summer as year-round schools become more common?
- Can I work with people of all ages, backgrounds, and opinions without sacrificing my personal convictions or stubbornly refusing to compromise?
- Do I like young people and respect them enough to work on their behalf, even when this occasionally produces conflicts of interest that may be emotionally unsettling?
- Do I have an intelligence that I enjoy applying?
- Am I a highly creative person, especially in my interpersonal relations? Am I open to the ideas of other creative people?
- Do I want to perform an important social service without being a servant?
- Am I willing to join and participate in a teacher's organization, even if this means becoming directly involved at times with some militant professionals who may be at odds with my superiors?
- Do I like to read and keep up with recent developments in my specialty as well as in my profession generally?
- Do I enjoy working in a dynamic milieu with opportunities for self-exploration and exploration of means to fulfill the changing learning needs of diverse youngsters?

If so, then the rewards of a career in teaching today can be sub-stantial, both personally and professionally.

Index